PERILOUS
STATECRAFT

Also by Michael A. Ledeen

WEST EUROPEAN COMMUNISM AND AMERICAN FOREIGN
POLICY *(1987)*

GRAVE NEW WORLD *(1985)*

DEBACLE: THE AMERICAN FAILURE IN IRAN (with William Lewis) *(1981)*

ITALY IN CRISIS *(1977)*

INTERVISTA SUL FASCISMO (with Renzo de Felice) *(1975)*

THE FIRST DUCE: D'ANNUNZIO AT FIUME *(1974)*

UNIVERSAL FASCISM: THE THEORY AND PRACTICE OF THE FASCIST
INTERNATIONAL *(1969)*

PERILOUS STATECRAFT

*An Insider's Account
of the Iran-Contra Affair*

Michael A. Ledeen

CHARLES SCRIBNER'S SONS · NEW YORK

Charles Scribner's Sons
Macmillan Publishing Company
866 Third Avenue, New York, NY 10022
Collier Macmillan Canada, Inc.

All photographs appear by arrangement with AP/Wide World Photos.

Library of Congress Cataloging-in-Publication Data
Ledeen, Michael Arthur, 1941–
   Perilous statecraft : an insider's account of the Iran-Contra
affair / by Michael A. Ledeen.
   p.   cm.
   Includes index.
   ISBN 0-684-18994-1
   1. Iran-Contra Affair, 1985–   —Personal narratives. 2. Ledeen,
Michael Arthur, 1941–   . I. Title.
E876.L44   1988
955'.054—dc19   88-19014   CIP

Macmillan books are available at special discounts for bulk purchases for sales promotions, premiums, fund-raising, or educational use. For details, contact:

Special Sales Director
Macmillan Publishing Company
866 Third Avenue
New York, NY 10022

10 9 8 7 6 5 4 3 2 1

Printed in the United States of America

Contents

Contents

Preface

In 1804, Napoleon ordered the assassination of the Duc d'Enghien, and the event was aptly described at the time by Talleyrand, Bonaparte's foreign minister: "It is worse than a crime, it is a mistake."[1]

Talleyrand's words sum up my feelings about the Iran-Contra affair, and the national frenzy of investigation, revelation, and prosecution that ensued. While the investigators, elected representatives, lawyers, and judges who have dealt with the affair have carried out their actions within the context of the criminal code, the persons at the heart of the affair were operating in quite a different world. They were concerned with the national security of the United States, and felt that their actions were in the best interests of the country. I believe that none of them—from officials like North, Poindexter, McFarlane, and Casey to private citizens like Secord and Hakim to foreign intermediaries like Khashoggi and Ghorbanifar—felt he was doing anything improper, let alone illegal. And while courts may eventually decide that illegalities were committed (indeed, as of the date this book went to press, three people had already pled guilty to various charges), Iran-Contra cannot be understood if it is treated as a criminal action. Indeed, I believe that the congressional committees that investigated the affair failed to understand what had happened, because they insisted on "criminalizing" the entire investigation.

The slogan "follow the money" dominated the early phases of the hearings, as journalists and investigators alike assumed that, once all the money had been accounted for, it would be possible to identify the motives of the major players. The unspoken assumption was that once the money trail had been established, there would be evidence

1. Talleyrand seems to have appropriated the phrase from one of his colleagues, M. Boulay de la Meurthe.

of wrongdoing as well. The money *was* accounted for, but the accounting did not explain the behavior of North, Poindexter, Secord, and the others, nor has it provided convincing evidence of illegal acts. In fact, when it was discovered that eight million dollars remained in Hakim's Swiss bank accounts, this raised new questions: Why had the money not gone to the *contras* or to private individuals? For what purpose was it being saved?

The answers to these questions lie within the personalities of the individuals involved in the affair, and in their views of America's proper role in the world. To be sure, there are other, more mundane components to the explanations. Some individuals did want to make a profit. But the profit motive does not explain Iran-Contra, although from time to time it played a role, sometimes an important one.

Because the investigators were looking for evidence of criminal activity, they failed to spend sufficient time on several crucial elements that help in understanding the affair. Some of these are:

- The role of Israel, from the first contacts with Iran to the crucial decision to link the Iran initiative with the secret efforts to keep the *contras* on the battlefield in 1986. The role of Amiram Nir, the adviser to the Israeli prime minister, is of particular importance.
- The psychological crisis of National Security Adviser Robert "Bud" McFarlane in the second half of 1985, a year before he attempted to commit suicide. Out of concern for his well-being, and respect for his contribution to the country, this subject was not explored at all, even though it was clear to most everyone that it must help explain the critical decisions taken in the White House.
- The personality of Lt. Col. Oliver North. Having severely underestimated his intelligence and charisma, the committees were poorly placed to find out what really made him tick.
- The shadowy figure of Manucher Ghorbanifar. He was written off as a pathological liar and con man. But if that was true, how can one explain the fact that he, and only he, was present from beginning to end? Who were his contacts at the highest level of the Iranian regime? What were his real motives?
- The real role of William Casey. Was he the mastermind of the Iran-Contra affair? Or was he the ultimate scapegoat?

All of these questions, and many more, are explored in the pages that follow. Some of the information is new, reported here for the first time. Other information will look different to those who have followed Iran-Contra closely, for I have tried to put it in its proper context. For example, it will not come as a surprise that the CIA decided in 1984 to cut off all support to the maverick *contra* leader Eden Pastora. But it may come as a surprise to learn that one major reason for that decision was the belief that Pastora's closest adviser was a Cuban agent.

I do not believe that it is possible to understand Iran-Contra on the basis of the reports of the various congressional committees, the Tower Commission, or the great mass of newspaper and magazine reportage. Too many crucial facts were either ignored or undiscovered, and too many central questions were never asked. This book is an attempt to correct the record, both on the major events and personalities in the Iran-Contra affair, and on the issues that motivated the leading figures. If I have succeeded, the events and the people will make sense. One will be able to understand why they did what they did, whatever one's judgment of them.

My own judgment is that Iran-Contra was a mistake, a terrible mistake, and to understand how it happened is not to condone it. However, in order to understand it, one has to re-create the circumstances under which the decisions were made, and get inside the hearts and minds of the people who made those decisions. I have tried to do that.

Finally, this book is also an attempt to set the record straight about myself and my role in the affair. I would have preferred to do this in public testimony before the Iran-Contra committees, for many of the questions about me were raised in that forum. However, I was denied that opportunity. The parts of the book that deal with my activities contain the material I would have presented had I been given the chance to testify publicly.

Since a considerable amount of this book deals with my activities, a few words about myself are perhaps in order. I am a professional historian, with a doctorate in modern European history from the University of Wisconsin. I taught for a while at Washington University in Saint Louis, wrote several books on twentieth-century Italy, taught at the University of Rome, and, in 1974, was lucky enough to be asked to write for *The New Republic*. This required me to cover contemporary Europe, with an emphasis on Italian affairs, and led to a modest career in journalism, which eventually included a column for an Italian newspaper, and occasional commentary for Italian-language Swiss radio and television. It was a lucky time to be an Italianist, because Italy became a hot topic: Eurocommunism, Eurosocialism, and the

Red Brigades. Later I began to look at terrorism more broadly, including methods to combat it.

By late 1976, the Georgetown University Center for Strategic and International Studies (CSIS) asked me to be the first executive editor of the *Washington Quarterly*. While there, I was able to begin, on a part-time basis, some of the activities in which I was later involved during the period of this book: writing, lecturing, and some consulting about either Western Europe or terrorism. For example, I was hired by two Western European governments to help them with their crisis planning.

Later on, General Alexander Haig resigned his post at NATO and returned to the United States, and he took up residence at CSIS. When he subsequently became secretary of state, he offered me a job as "special adviser," and I accepted. The job involved considerable travel on Haig's behalf, mostly to Europe but occasionally to the Middle East. My main areas of attention were the Socialist International, Western Europe, terrorism, and some Soviet questions. For a while I was travelling so much that the joke around the department was that if General Vernon Walters was ambassador at large, I should be called "ambassador at small." When Haig resigned in the summer of 1982, I did, too, and returned to CSIS to write, lecture, and consult. Some people in government asked me if I were willing to do a bit of consulting work for them as well, and I did.

Part-time consultants are handy to have around for government officials. They don't cost very much by Washington standards (the top rate is about two hundred dollars per day), they can be asked to do useful research projects for which full-time employees simply do not have the time (full-timers are generally too busy moving paper and attending meetings to do basic research or step back and take a fresh look at issues), and they can travel and carry messages back and forth to officials of foreign governments.

From my point of view, I found the work interesting—as when I was asked to supervise the creation of a public archive of the documents captured by U.S. military forces in Grenada—and I enjoyed contributing to our efforts to understand and cope with such matters as terrorism. And there was the element of fascination with communication and perception in international affairs. This fascination may, I must admit, have had a particular resonance with me. To the despair of my parents and professors, I became a bridge fanatic at college and devoted an outrageous amount of time to the game until the early 1970s, playing professionally with Omar Sharif at one point and coaching the Israeli national bridge team to a third-place finish in the world championships of 1975. Bridge is a game in which communication, whether to one's partner or to one's opponents, is complex and every bit as important as the power position at the card table. It thus has some similarities to foreign policy, and my enthusiasm for bridge undoubtedly laid the groundwork for my fascination with some of the aspects of international strategy. Such aspects are always important in international relations, but they became particularly significant in the Iran-Contra affair.

While I hope this book makes the affair understandable, I have certainly not exhausted the subject. There are many reasons for this. First is the sheer volume of material. Although I have done considerable research (dozens of interviews, two trips to Israel and Western Europe, and reading as much as I have been able to find, including thousands of pages of newspaper articles, testimony, and depositions), I am certain that there is information that has escaped me. Some of it may prove to be fundamental. In short, this is a first attempt at understanding, certainly not the last word.

Second is my own limitations as an observer. Anyone familiar with the nature of evidence realizes that it is sometimes more difficult to understand something close-up than from a distance. I may well have been too close to some of the people and some of the events to present a balanced picture of them. I have tried to step back and look at them coolly, but I cannot guarantee that I have thoroughly succeeded. You will have to judge for yourself.

Third, having worked for the government, and having been granted security clearances, there are some things about which I cannot write. To the extent that I have written about sensitive information, that is the result of research undertaken after I left government. On the other hand, an enormous quantity of previously classified material has been made public by the committees, and I have drawn heavily on it. I have therefore been able to write freely about subjects I otherwise would never have discussed publicly.

I talked to as many of the participants as I could, and most of them were cooperative and forthcoming. A few declined, of whom the most important are North, Nir, and Secord—and most of the investigators and members of the Tower Commission and the congressional committees. Since I have not met Secord, and have had very little contact with Nir, the material on them is second-hand. Secord and North are facing trial, and Nir is under orders from his government to remain silent. Their concerns are about things more important than my deadline. I hope that if, as a result of their silence, I have been able to present only part of their stories, they will find it possible to provide a fuller version at a later date.

Many of the people I interviewed wish to remain anonymous, and I shall protect their identities. So with very rare exceptions, I do not identify my sources at all (printed sources are of course identified). In the last analysis, I have had to evaluate the information and decide who told the truth, and who attempted to mislead me. So I have simply written the story as I believe it happened, without referring to the interviews. In Washington, you can get two sources to confirm most any story, but that does not mean that the story is true. The issue is truth, not sources. Whatever mistakes have been made are my responsibility.

I owe debts of gratitude to several people who gave me help and encouragement. First and foremost, Barbara Ledeen, who, in addition to her work at the Pentagon, managed three children, one large and rambunctious Airedale, and an often difficult husband for the several months it took to write the book. Second, Dan Klaidman, my research assistant, who now probably understands it all better than I do. Third, my editor, Edward T. Chase. Good editors are as rare as good politicians, and Ned, as he is called, is the best editor I have had in the course of writing ten books. Finally, I am particularly grateful to Peter Rodman and Simon Serfaty for their helpful criticism of the manuscript.

When the scandal broke in November 1986, I never expected that I would spend the next year engaged in a seemingly endless series of hearings, depositions, and investigations. That is, unfortunately, what happened. In this day and age that means . . . lawyers. I was blessed to have one of the best, a man who understands foreign policy, and the problems unique to Washington, as well as the law. Were it not for him, that long year would have been even longer, and much less rewarding. He taught me a lot and saved me from countless mistakes. And when it was all over, he gave us a party. So I'm dedicating the book to him: Mr. R. James Woolsey, of Shea & Gardner. Thanks, Jim.

1. The Reagan Administration and the Contras

There was a day, relatively early in the Reagan administration, when the president slammed his desk, grabbed a pen with such force that the desk stand snapped in two, and wrote in capital letters on his pad, "NO TAX INCREASE." He brandished it at his top advisers, many of whom were trying to get him to frame his response to an anticipated press conference question in such a way as to leave open the possibility of future tax hikes. They all laughed, and feigned obedience. Within days, some of them were leaking rumors that the policy was not "set in concrete."

The president was deeply involved in tax policy, sent the clearest possible signal to his people, and rode herd on them when they vacillated. Even so, those who felt differently continued to work for their own views. Imagine how much more chaotic it was in the field of foreign policy, where the president was rarely involved in the day-to-day design and management of national strategy, and where he was relatively unschooled. And add to this confusion—what some like to call the inevitable chaos of democracy (and others prefer to describe by its proper name: lack of discipline)—the fact that everyone considers himself competent in foreign affairs, and you get a sense of the constant policy war within the administration, in which no battle was likely to be decisive. Every agency of government, and, it sometimes seems, every individual within government, feels entitled to make policy until some greater force imposes a different line.

In these foreign policy battles, the full range of political and bureaucratic weapons was brought to bear. Some of them are well-known, and emerged in full public view during the investigations into the

1

Iran-Contra scandal: leaks of secret information, decision making restricted to a handful of people, diplomacy conducted by private citizens, vitally important trips abroad kept secret from members of the cabinet, and so forth. Some of the others will be told for the first time in this book. But the basic point is the same: American foreign policy is made less by design than by struggle, and the struggles are between people of great passion and conviction, and of driving ambition. Ambitious people are of two varieties: those who seek to advance themselves, and those who seek to advance a cause. This means that the foreign policy struggles are sometimes over real substance, but often they mask conflicts between individuals maneuvering for personal advantage and power.

The intense fight over Central American policy certainly dealt with serious policy questions; but it also involved a very basic struggle for power within the new administration.

THE BIG PICTURE

When the Reagan administration took office in January 1981, several of its top foreign policy officials—including the president himself, Director of Central Intelligence William Casey, UN Ambassador Jeane Kirkpatrick, and Secretary of State Alexander Haig—wanted to strike a blow at the Soviet Empire as soon as possible. In their perception, ever since the fall of Saigon, the Soviet Union's power had been relentlessly expanding, and the United States had been thwarted, defeated, and humiliated in one crucial theater after another. If this pattern continued, there could be a decisive shift in the balance of world power in favor of the Kremlin.

The trend was impressive, from the establishment of Soviet-sponsored Vietnamese control over Laos and Cambodia, and the expansion of Soviet influence into the Horn of Africa, to the invasion of Afghanistan, and the establishment of pro-Soviet regimes in Nicaragua and Grenada. American impotence in international affairs had been dramatically underlined by the Iranian debacle, when the Carter administration stood by in virtual paralysis as one of America's most powerful and important allies—the shah of Iran—fell to Ayatollah Ruholla Khomeini. For actual and potential friends on the margins of the Soviet Empire—from Pakistan to Morocco, and from Thailand to Australia and New Zealand—the lesson was simple: If the Americans could not protect such an important ally as the shah, how could countries of lesser strategic importance count upon Washington?

The expansion of Soviet power and influence had been one of the central themes of the 1980 elections, and Ronald Reagan had promised to restore American strength and prestige after the weakness of the Carter years. After a lifetime in broadcasting, movies, and politics, Reagan was quick to recognize that international affairs are as much a matter of people's perceptions as of the real facts about the world, and America's friends and allies were asking some anguished questions. Was the United States capable of reversing this alarming trend? Would the new administration be able to contain the seemingly irresistible expansion of the Soviet Empire? If not, Reagan and many of his aides believed it was only a matter of time before countries in the middle of the East-West conflict made their peace with the Kremlin.

Indeed, the process had seemingly already begun. Several foreign leaders were quietly "taking out insurance" with the Soviets. Pakistan, for example, which was exposed to the might of the Red Army in Afghanistan, sent a clear signal when President Zia ul-Haq transferred his distinguished Ambassador Yaqub Khan from Washington to Moscow. And American efforts to find local bases for the Rapid Deployment Force in the Middle East were fruitless, since pro-Western Arab regimes, shaken by the failure of the Carter administration to support the shah against the radical Shi'ite revolution, were loath to join publicly in a military alliance with the Americans. In Western Europe, the vital core of America's worldwide security system, there was alarming talk of accommodation to Soviet demands, ranging from a great reluctance to accept the deployment of American missiles to a rush to cooperate with the Kremlin in economic ventures—and even to provide the money to fund them, at bargain rates. The buzz word of the late seventies was "Finlandization," the process by which Western countries came to accept the objectives of Soviet policy, and ended up making them their own. The United States itself had occasionally fallen victim to this dangerous form of self-delusion, most notably when Secretary of State Cyrus Vance announced that Jimmy Carter and Leonid Brezhnev "shared common dreams." The Carter–Brezhnev bear hug at the Vienna summit symbolized this process.

Experts in international affairs, as well as many who had voted for Reagan out of concern about foreign policy, were well aware of the gravity of the moment, and hence of the necessity for the new administration to shore up the resolve of America's real and potential friends around the world. And Ronald Reagan, although neither skilled in foreign affairs, nor particularly interested in the subject, understood the general principle quite well. His general understanding was reinforced in the days prior to his inauguration by an encounter worthy of Hollywood at its best. The president-elect was given a somber warning from one of the few colorful figures in the shadowy world of international spycraft: Count Alexandre de Marenches, until recently the head of French foreign intelligence (the SDECE, technically a military intelligence sevice, actually corresponds to our CIA). The count was a perfect interlocutor for Ronald Reagan, for he seemed to be typecast for the role he played. A flamboyant personality with the body and demeanor of Sydney Greenstreet in *The Maltese Falcon*, Marenches was the product of a French aristocrat and an American mother, spoke fluent English with a vague East Coast accent, possessed a sharp Gallic wit, and delighted in staging melodramatic scenes. His spacious office on the outskirts of Paris was replete with the standard props of the spymaster's role, featuring a huge wall map of the world with colored pins stuck into various crucial locations. He became a legend in Washington early in the Carter years when the new director of central intelligence, the hapless Adm. Stansfield Turner, went to visit him. "Things are much better at the agency," Turner reported, and Marenches, somewhat skeptical, asked for further detail. "When I arrived, I discovered that there was some spying on American citizens, but this has now stopped."

"My dear Admiral," the Frenchman is said to have replied, "what do you think I am doing here, anyway?" When Turner requested the answer to Marenches's rhetorical query, the acerbic reply came: "I am personally tapping the telephones of the highest officials in the French government."

"Why on earth are you doing that?"

"Because I know they are trying to tap mine, and I thought it was best to get a head start on them."

This is one of those stories about which the celebrated Italian phrase, *se non è vero, è ben trovato* (if it's not true, it's still well founded), was undoubtedly crafted; true or false, it captures the personality of the man who tried to initiate Ronald Reagan into the secrets of international intrigue in the weeks prior to his inauguration.

Marenches had watched with alarm as French president Valéry Giscard d'Estaing first opened the floodgates of French credits and technology to the Soviet Union, then, in a dramatic confrontation with Marenches himself, refused to order a bombing raid against a Libyan column marching into Chad. Such behavior, in Marenches's view, resulted at leat in part from the conviction that the United States

4

was no longer capable of a forceful response to the Soviet challenge, and he told Reagan in Santa Barbara in December 1980 that even such a solid ally as France would find itself wavering unless there were a clear signal from the new administration that things had indeed changed. He recommended to Reagan that the United States move quickly against the Soviets in the outer reaches of their empire: Angola, Afghanistan, Cambodia, or the Caribbean. In many ways, the advice from the French master spy was the precursor of what later came to be known as the Reagan Doctrine, and it fit nicely with the suggestions that would shortly come from Haig and Casey, and would later be reinforced and amplified by UN Ambassador Jeane Kirkpatrick and National Security Adviser William Clark. Indeed, insofar as *any* single idea remained central to Ronald Reagan's foreign policy throughout the constantly changing cast of characters in Washington, it was the notion that the hour had come for the United States to directly challenge the expansion of the Soviet Empire.

Marenches had a second recommendation to make, one which seemingly was tailor-made for the personality and skills of the new president: that the United States reenlist in the war of ideas, and take steps to combat the substantial efforts of the Soviet Union to "disinform" the world community. The Frenchman stressed that words mattered greatly in international affairs, and that one should be careful to use language as an effective weapon. He urged Reagan to speak of the "Soviet Empire," rather than "Soviet Union" (after all, it is neither soviet nor a union), in order to convey the nature of Soviet foreign policy, and he warned the president-elect to beware of ambiguous diplomatic language that could be exploited by the Kremlin for its own purposes.

Although one would have expected Ronald Reagan to have been enthusiastic about the notion of a systematic challenge to the Soviet Union, and while there were occasional rhetorical sorties (the "Evil Empire"), the struggle to define American policy showed fairly soon that there would be no sustained crusade against the Kremlin, at least in the first couple of years. This was not because the president was opposed to the notion of an anti-Soviet crusade; it was one of his basic convictions. But foreign policy was quickly relegated to a secondary position. Reagan and his key advisers—James Baker, Michael Deaver, and Edwin Meese—were determined to reshape the national economy and reduce the dimensions of the welfare state. And they were unwilling to have public attention diverted from this task by heated discussion of foreign policy.

To this basic decision on the supremacy of domestic over international considerations, there were three additional factors that made it impossible to carry out the activists' foreign policy. The first stemmed from the kind of government Reagan wished to install in Washington; the second was the result of the particular personalities with whom he surrounded himself; the third was the nature of the president.

Everybody knew that Ronald Reagan was unskilled in international affairs and would not give constant, hands-on attention to the details of foreign policy. Indeed, even in areas where he felt completely at ease with the basic issues—tax policy, welfare, and the like—he had made it clear that he preferred to play the role of chief executive, giving overall guidance, but leaving policy design and management to his cabinet officers. For such a system to work effectively, there had to be effective coordination among the various cabinet agencies, and the president's wishes, once expressed, had to be rigorously enforced on the government bureaucracy as a whole. It did not work well in foreign policy, both because the key instrument for policy coordination and management—the National Security Council staff —was deliberately weakened and filled with people whose skills were not equal to those of their bureaucratic antagonists, and because several key people in the White House held views very different from those of the president himself and the activists in the administration. Among those who favored a "soft" approach to foreign policy—and who fought against efforts to describe the Soviet Union in harsh terms, as well as against any attempt to challenge Castro and the Soviets, even in the Western Hemisphere—were Michael Deaver, the man who controlled the president's schedule, James Baker, the chief of staff, and Nancy Reagan, the person with maximum access to the president's heart and mind.

Although many suspected it at the time, few imagined the degree to which Michael Deaver—and, if Deaver's memoirs are to be believed, the First Lady as well—wished to avoid international conflict. Neither person based their view of foreign policy on the substance of the issues themselves; neither was sufficiently knowledgeable to do so. The Baker/Deaver/Nancy Reagan view of foreign policy derived in part from their desire to see Ronald Reagan go down in history as a particular sort of president, one who presided over the revival of the American spirit, and who ushered in a new era of peace and harmony. Here is the way Deaver described Nancy Reagan's view in his book, *Behind the Scenes*:

She lobbied the president to soften his line on the Soviet Union; to reduce military spending and not to push Star Wars at the expense of the poor and dispossessed. She favored a diplomatic solution in Nicaragua.[1]

This point of view also served their desire to curry favor with the media and to advance both their own personal fortunes and those of the administration.

Like many people who believe in slogans (like "one cannot make peace by preparing for war") that betray a fundamental misunderstanding of the causes of conflict and the efficacy of deterrence, these intimate associates of the president constantly labored to undermine any effort to mount a sustained challenge to the Soviet Empire, whether by an aggressive policy or clarity of language. They generally favored "negotiations" rather than confrontation, wherever conflict existed, and they bemoaned speeches like the "Evil Empire" proclamation. Deaver even claims to have played a decisive role in shaping administration policy during the Lebanese war of 1982, when his opinions were almost entirely shaped by the pictures on the evening television news broadcasts.

Since power in Washington is directly proportional to the amount of time one gets to spend with the key decision makers, Baker, Deaver, and Mrs. Reagan—along with the loyal Meese—were far and away the most powerful people in the government throughout Reagan's first term. Of these figures—the White House *troika* and the First Lady —only Meese favored an aggressive foreign policy. And their convictions meshed nicely with those of another powerful group in Washington, who were perfectly positioned to advance the personal ambitions of the *troika* and their allies throughout the system: the media. The opponents of activism—people like Baker, his deputy Richard Darman, Deaver, and their allies—soon became known as the "pragmatists," as opposed to the "ideologues" who favored strong moves against America's enemies. And the alliance between the pragmatists and the media was a most effective one. The pragmatists provided the media with good copy, and the media gave the pragmatists a good press.

This is not to say that the activists did not leak (in Washington, leaking is done by all factions and by virtually every ambitious person), but some leaks are more effective than others. Leaks from the center of power—the White House—are going to get more attention than leaks from the Pentagon or the State Department. And the most skilled

1. Michael Deaver, *Behind the Scenes* (New York: Morrow, 1988), p. 39.

7

leakers in the White House were opposed to the notion of an aggressive campaign against the Soviets and their allies. Indeed, as Larry Speakes's memoirs show, even the White House Press Office was solidly on the side of the pragmatists. The struggle was an unequal one from the start, as people like Haig, Casey, and Kirkpatrick would soon discover.

Consequently, despite the president's often strident rhetoric, the Reagan administration—from the very beginning—was not about to embark upon an activist foreign policy. There were too many powerful people opposed to it, and the president was altogether too nice a man to insist upon it over their objections. On occasion, his temperamental sweetness would even overcome the best efforts of his advisers to get him to be tough.

The most telling example of Reagan's inability to be mean came in the autumn of 1981, at a time when Haig, Casey, and Secretary of Defense Caspar Weinberger were enraged at the financial and military support being given by the French government to the Sandinistas, and even, according to some reports, directly to the Salvadoran guerrillas. Mme Mitterrand was a well-known supporter of the Salvadoran insurgency, and spoke publicly at their rallies in Paris. Something had to be done, and it was arranged to have Mitterrand fly in quietly on the Concorde to meet privately with the president. Reagan was drilled on the details of French actions in Central America, and was urged to take the sternest possible tone with Mitterrand. But when the critical moment arrived, Mitterrand entered the Oval Office, broke into a warm smile, and gushed, "My dear Ron." Reagan melted. "My dear François," he responded. They embraced. There was no harsh lecture on French Central American policies.[2]

This attractive human characteristic was one of Ronald Reagan's many great strengths, for his visitors invariably came away charmed by the president. Not only was he a spontaneously warm man, but he had sound instincts and some intellectual strengths that have often been underestimated. Although he rarely immersed himself in the details of foreign policy problems, there were a few exceptional cases, and one of these was Central America. Felipe Gonzales, now the Spanish president, told me after his first meeting with Reagan that he was astonished at the depth of the American president's understanding of the Central American situation, and the Portuguese prime minister (now president), Mario Soares, had the same reaction. The

2. Like so many policy initiatives in the Reagan administration, this one took far too long to execute. It was not until 1984 that the French were convinced to drop their support for the Sandinistas.

problem with Ronald Reagan was not lack of talent, it was a combination of the president's basic ignorance of, and lack of enthusiasm for, the subject, and his advancing years. One could never be entirely certain that the president would be in good form; and when he was off form, some rather bothersome problems arose.

It may not be possible to tell the full story of Ronald Reagan's presidency for several years, for some of his closest associates have guarded the truth very closely. But there is considerable evidence that the president was an intermittent force within his administration. Already in 1981, Secretary of State Haig had been forced to awaken the president during a "one-on-one" conversation with Prime Minister Spadolini of Italy, and again when the president fell asleep while talking with the Pope. With the passage of time, Reagan's ability to concentrate for extended periods declined even further, to the point where leading administration officials were often uncertain whether he had understood the range of points they were making. On other occasions, they were quite certain that he had not.

Among themselves, Reagan's top advisers wondered if "the old man" would be able to continue to stage his legendary public performances up to the end, or whether the advance of old age would eventually make it necessary to confront the problem in some other fashion. When the president was gearing up for his first press conference on the Iran-Contra scandal, for example, he badly flubbed a crucial question during the "dry run" that always preceded one of his public appearances. When asked whether any third countries were involved in the sale of arms to Iran, Reagan said "no." Afterward, he was reminded that Israel was deeply involved, and that he must change his answer. Another dry run was held, and again the president answered "no." Prior to the real press conference, he was once again reminded of the importance of giving an accurate answer to the "third country" question. He nodded his understanding. Yet, for the third time that day, he answered the question incorrectly—this time on national television.

Still, on many occasions he was fully in command, alert, and most definitely vigorously engaged. And he had a knack of rising to challenges. According to those actually present, his performance at a series of consecutive summits with Mikhail Gorbachev was impressive, and on a variety of issues, including some of the most complex and subtle ones, he asked penetrating questions, faced the questions logically, and made intelligent decisions. Yet at other times he seemed almost totally disengaged, and often left his aides in some doubt as to what had actually occurred in private meetings, even on subjects about which he felt quite passionately. For example, in early 1985, the president learned that a friendly country—according to press accounts, Saudi Arabia—was doubling its funding of the *contras,* from $1 million per month to $2 million. But when the president briefed McFarlane and George Shultz, he neglected to report this fact, and when McFarlane subsequently learned about it, he sent the president a note. The president expressed "gratitude and satisfaction." Had the president forgotten? Or was he determined to keep the decision in total confidence?

So we had a president who was not fully engaged on foreign policy, and who sometimes had lapses of memory and concentration, attended by people, many of whom did not share his view of the world, and who worked actively to advance their own notion of a very low-key approach to international affairs. In retrospect, it is surprising that such an administration mounted any sort of effective challenge to America's enemies around the world and, in fact, with the exception of the Central American campaign, American action was usually limited to brief outbursts like the Grenada, Libya, and *Achille Lauro* affairs, and the problematical engagements in Lebanon and the Persian Gulf. But it took some time before foreign-policy activists like Haig, Kirkpatrick, and Casey recognized the true nature of the president's agenda, and they set out in the winter of 1980–81 to design a program to first thwart, and eventually roll back, Soviet expansion.

Just as generals are invariably preparing to fight the last war, the foreign policy activists within the new administration were determined to erase the most recent symbols of American failure of will and power: Vietnam and Iran. In each of these catastrophes, the United States had abandoned an ally under attack, and they vowed that this would not happen again. In relatively short order, the new team discovered to its delight that there was a tailor-made opportunity to demonstrate that things were going to change under Ronald Reagan: the Central American crisis.

Central America

Central America seemed too good to be true, an archetypal communist effort to subvert American national interests in our own hemisphere. For here was a clear case of Soviet sponsorship of a guerrilla movement in El Salvador, through the intermediaries of Castro's Cuba and the new Sandinista regime in Nicaragua. The intelligence was surprisingly complete. We had captured guerrilla documents and agents among the Nicaraguans and the Salvadoran guerrillas, along with the usual array of sensitive technical intelligence. Best of all, the information had been collected by the Carter administration, and could not be written off as ideologically inspired (indeed, the intelligence showing Nicaraguan support for the Salvadoran insurgency was so convincing that Carter had cut off the American aid program to Nicaragua just a few days before leaving office).

We had a remarkably thorough picture of a Soviet–Cuban plan to bring the leftist insurrection in El Salvador under centralized control. Just as the opponents of Nicaraguan dictator Anastasio Somoza had been brought under a Sandinista umbrella organization—the FSLN —as a result of Cuban instructions (Castro threatened that there would be no further support to the guerrillas unless there were a single organizational structure), so the disparate radical groups in El Salvador were centralized under the mantle of the FMLN (Farabundo Marti Liberation Front) in 1980 at a meeting in Havana. Even though there were genuinely democratic groups and individuals in both the Salvadoran and Nicaraguan guerrilla movements, the superior strength and political ruthlessness of the Cuban-controlled parties guaranteed that the democrats would have little chance of prevailing in the political struggle that would follow the fall of the existing government. This preordained drama was already under way in Managua by the time Ronald Reagan came to office. In October 1979, despite Castro's entreaties to his Nicaraguan protégés to keep their real intentions secret as long as possible, the Sandinistas' hard-core supporters had been given an astonishingly candid printed statement[3] of the new regime's objectives:

- Talk about pluralism was frankly described as a ploy to deflect or at least delay potential opposition from other countries (particularly the United States).
- Plans were revealed for the creation of "an army politicized without precedent." By 1983, the Nicaraguan armed forces were far and away the most powerful army in Central America (fifty thousand men, with public plans to increase the number to a quarter of a million in the near future and a covert plan for more than double that figure).
- Nicaragua was explicitly described as a fully engaged player in the "world revolution."

In short, if the Communist leaders of the Sandinistas had their way—and the democratic forces in the Sandinista Front were clearly

---

3. This is known as the "72-Hour Document," since it was presented to the Sandinista faithful over a three-day period. It was translated and made public by the Department of State.

not up to this sort of challenge—there would be a "Seond Cuba" in the hemisphere. If the guerrillas in El Salvador were to win, it would bring the number of pro-Soviet states in the region to three, all dedicated to the struggle against "Yanqui imperialism," all living examples of the continuing success of the Soviet Empire. A victory for the Salvadoran guerrillas would lay the groundwork for an expanded guerrilla war against Guatemala and Honduras, and eventually into Mexico, a game plan that was found repeatedly in captured guerrilla documents. Not only would this vastly increase Soviet power in Latin America, it would give further luster to Castro himself, and Fidel was a particularly indigestible nettle for the new American secretary of state.

The problem of Fidel Castro was, of course, not new; the necessity of an effective anti-Cuban policy was a mainstay of American plans ever since the Bay of Pigs. And if Castro were considered a threat to American national interests in the early 1960s, he was far more menacing by 1981, having played a key role in the Soviet successes in Africa by sending combat troops into the bush in Angola and the Horn of Africa. Men like Haig were horrified at the thought that further Cuban advances might take place in the first year or two of the new administration. And the Salvadoran guerrillas had announced the "final offensive" in January, just prior to Reagan's inauguration.

Haig had already witnessed two American defeats at the hands of the Soviets and the Cubans: the installation of a Communist regime in Angola in 1975, following the cutoff of American support to the two non-Communist liberation movements; and the spectacular East African operation, shifting the Cuban military contingent from Somalia to Ethiopia. Although Ethiopia eventually became an economic and political albatross around the Soviet neck, the military operation provided the Kremlin with the best port facilities in East Africa, and a potential staging base as well, and this military potential, like that on the opposite side of the continent in Angola, deeply worried Haig. They occurred when he was the Supreme Allied Commander of NATO forces.

Haig would have felt passionately about Castro even if he had remained a military officer throughout his career, for the new secretary of state had very strong feelings about countries that launched military operations at the expense of the United States of America. His feelings were intensified by the knowledge that he had once been in an administration that had planned to avenge previous humiliations at the hands of the Cubans. Few people realized how intensely Nixon, Kissinger, and Ford felt about Fidel Castro, and fewer still were aware that Ford and Kissinger had planned vigorous action—including the possibility of a blockade of Cuba—if the presidential election of 1976 had been won by the Republicans. This never came to pass, and the frustration of the missed opportunity was augmented by the bitterness surrounding Carter's narrow victory. Haig was privy to these plans, and he fumed from his Belgian command post as Carter reversed course, and attempted to normalize relations with the Cuban dictator.

Like many powerful personalities, Haig is a difficult man to understand for those who have not worked closely with him. The hard-charging, seemingly tireless man of action has a richness of character and a personal sensitivity that have eluded the public at large. For all his high intensity and his love of firmness, Haig showed himself at NATO and again at the State Department to have a spontaneous grasp of international affairs, and a natural affinity with sophisticated foreign leaders, often of political persuasions quite different from those ascribed to him. Paradoxically, for a man who has been almost invariably placed firmly on the right of the political universe, Haig developed close personal and political ties with the Center-Left of European politics. His closest friends, and most reliable political allies—from Germany's Helmut Schmidt to Portugal's President Ramaldo Eanes —more often than not came from the Social Democratic and even Socialist parties of Europe, rather than from the groups further to the right. Similarly, in Washington, when Haig most needed straight talk and a kindred spirit, he would often closet himself with Joseph Califano, a brilliant Washington insider and former official of the Kennedy, Johnson, and Carter administrations. Haig's world view was far more diverse than many of his critics suspected.

Moreover, Haig had a rare ability to laugh at himself. In one of the most embarrassing moments of his tenure at State, a young Nicaraguan defector by the name of Tardencillas had been brought to the State Department after extensive questioning by the Central Intelligence Agency. The CIA had pronounced him a genuine defector and a reliable source, and the young man seemed eager to "go public" with highly damaging information about the activities of the Sandinistas. This was highly appealing to those State Department officials who were frustrated at the lack of public support for the administration's Central America policy, and a session was arranged for a handful of Washington correspondents to meet with the defector. At the time I was special adviser to the secretary of state, and fully agreed with the decision to let Tardencillas go public.

It turned out that Tardencillas was playing a deep game, and no sooner had the briefing begun than he came forth with a story that had clearly been concocted back in Managua: he had been harshly interrogated by the CIA, he had been forced to confess, it was all a lie, he had nothing bad to say about his government, but he was full of venom for the United States, and on and on. The briefing, which was supposed to provide a first-hand account of Nicaraguan misdeeds, instead became a highly charged attack on us.

Someone had to bring the bad news to the secretary of state, and this was not likely to be a pleasant task (bearers of bad news have never fared well, and Haig's temper was well-known to all of us). The first one in the door was Lawrence Eagleburger, the under secretary for political affairs, and an old friend of Haig's, having served with Henry Kissinger both on the National Security Council staff and at the Department of State. As everyone waited for the deletable expletives to flow, the secretary broke into a big grin, slapped the table, and began to laugh: "He sure made monkeys out of us, didn't he!" It was a remarkable response to a situation which Haig knew had been mishandled (the CIA's screening had obviously been poor, and we at the State Department could well have staged a trial run to see how the boy would have actually performed), but he had served notice on his staff that he knew errors would be made, and that life would continue nonetheless.

But while Haig understood the importance of maintaining morale in the Department of State, he had little patience for those who ignored what he considered the foreign policy imperatives of the early eighties. Haig knew from past experience that a new administration has a limited period of time to launch new policies, and he was eager to get the Reagan era underway.

To this sound political insight, there were personal elements that intensified Haig's drive for action beyond the bounds of prudence. Haig had recently undergone heart bypass surgery, and there is a body of evidence suggesting that some people emerge from that operation with a heightened drive, and less tolerance for disagreement. Haig would later poke fun at this theory when his old colleague, Henry Kissinger, entered the hospital for the same surgery. Haig warned Kissinger's family and colleagues that the former secretary of state would become highly suspicious, intensely protective of his turf, and personally aggressive (characteristics which Kissinger of course already notoriously possessed in great abundance). Yet there may be something to the theory. Even Haig's closest friends found him quite different—more "hyper"—as secretary of state than he had been at the Nixon White House or at NATO.

Haig himself had a somewhat different explanation, although he granted the accuracy of the assessment. He *was* different at Foggy Bottom, he said, perhaps because, after all the things he had lived through, he had simply run out of patience. He felt he knew what had to be done, he was deeply convinced that he was uniquely qualified to do it, he believed the president shared his convictions, and he wanted to get it done before time ran out.

Despite his great talent, he made a fatal mistake. Reagan may have shared Haig's general view of the world, but he did not share Haig's sense of absolute urgency. And the president's men, along with the president's woman, did not take kindly to someone who appeared to consider himself the real commander in chief. The celebrated "I'm in charge" pronouncement to the press while the president was under the surgeon's knife after the assassination attempt in early 1981 seemed to confirm the worst suspicions of Haig's colleagues in the cabinet. In the excitement of the moment, he had confused the Constitutional order of succession with the rank order of cabinet secretaries, and had charged into the press room without properly preparing what he was going to say. It was an unforgettable gaffe, and the damage it did to Haig's relationships with his peers in the administration was beyond repair. While the purpose of his remarks was exaggerated by the media—whatever else he was trying to do, the secretary of state was not attempting a coup d'etat in the Situation Room of the White House—Haig had made such exaggerations almost inevitable by his earlier demands to be treated as the man entirely in charge of foreign policy. Having antagonized so many so early, Haig had few allies to defend him when he came under attack.

THE CENTRAL AMERICAN DEBATE

Haig wanted to "go to the source" in Central America, which in his view meant Cuba. If, as the abundant intelligence showed, the Salvadoran crisis was fueled by the Cubans and their Nicaraguan protégés, it followed that a durable solution required that Castro come to terms with the United States, and cease his support of the Salvadoran guerrilla movement. Haig argued for a combination of military and political pressure on Cuba, making it clear that the United States was not prepared to tolerate continued Cuban subversion in Central America.

Haig's proposed policy—which foresaw that Castro's obduracy might eventually force the United States into adopting the old Ford/Kissinger option of blockading the island—rested not only on the logic of the situation, but also upon considerable information concerning Fidel's state of mind and his relationship with his Soviet benefactors.

The American government knew quite a bit about Castro, and one of the tantalizing bits of information that reached Washington in early 1981 was that Fidel was worried about the reliability of his Soviet protectors. Like most everyone else, Castro foresaw that the Kremlin would have to take steps to crush the Solidarity trade union movement in Poland, and he believed that the United States would take the opportunity to respond in some way. What better way than to settle the old score with him? Castro had let it be known, in private conversations with other Communist leaders, that he suspected the Americans would move against *him*. The only doubt in his mind was *where* the American strike would come: in Angola, in Ethiopia, or in the Caribbean itself. Furthermore, the Cuban dictator feared that in such circumstances the Russians would leave him to his fate.

Castro was most probably correct in his assessment of the Kremlin: Haig gently raised the Cuban question with Soviet foreign minister Andrei Gromyko and with Ambassador Dobrynin, and each indicated that whatever happened was a matter between Cuba and the United States. There was no stern warning of dire consequences in the event of a Cuban–American confrontation.

But Castro was quite mistaken about the resolve of the Reagan administration. It was simply out of the question to ask the new team to take forceful action in the Caribbean. Not only would such a decision have diverted attention in Congress and in the public at large from the economic issues the president and his men considered their top priority; it would also have flown in the face of the "conventional wisdom" about Reagan's chances for a second term. Most of the political experts believed that Ronald Reagan's Achilles' heel was a vague fear that his bellicosity would get the United States engaged in war —a "second Vietnam." To give credence to these fears at the very outset of the first term would unnecessarily jeopardize his reelection prospects. Moreover, if Haig's views prevailed, his own position within the administration would have become strengthened, and there was considerable opposition to the secretary's policies on those grounds as well. Finally, of course, the Bakers, Deavers, and Nancy Reagans simply did not want any confrontation with the Soviet Union, regardless of considerations of first and second term, regardless of who might derive political benefit from it, and regardless of electoral tactics.

In addition, there was the determined veto of the secretary of defense. Caspar Weinberger was a single-minded man, virtually immovable once he had set on a course, and he thought he had learned a basic lesson from the Vietnam years: Do not commit American military power without a solid national consensus. This "lesson" undoubtedly came from the armed services, through the Joint Chiefs of Staff, and although it was superficially attractive, it was wrong. The Weinberger theory was simply a variation on the misguided notion that policy should be made on the basis of public opinion polls, and it did not gain in logic by being pronounced by such an august personage. The very case from which the theory presumably derived showed how silly it was, for the Vietnam War had great popular support for quite some time (and was certainly broadly endorsed at the beginning), while there was great reluctance to enter the Second World War. Such solid national consensus did not make the Vietnam policy right, or American participation in the war against fascism wrong. Weinberger and the service chiefs had forgotten that good leaders must often go against the conventional wisdom or popular views. The policy evaluation must be done on the merits of the case, not on the presumed popularity of the line of action.

In the end, luck is often more important than brilliance, and there are times when good policies fail, while poor ones succeed. Given the choice, any public official would rather be lucky than smart, and this is often the case in foreign policy. But the Weinberger/Joint Chiefs position on this issue was extremely shortsighted, because popularity at the outset of a policy neither guarantees its success nor shields its framers from condemnation if it fails. Successful policies are always praised, and failures are rarely popular. But the secretary of defense was deeply opposed to Haig's calls for vigorous action.

The combination of Weinberger, the Chiefs, the White House *troika,* and the First Lady was unbeatable, and the State Department was instructed to find a policy that mitigated the Communist threat in Central America at the same time that it kept the new administration out of a potentially explosive all-out confrontation with Castro.

The "point man" on Central America was Thomas Enders, a man whose talents and ego were of a size equal to his own impressive six-foot eight-inch frame. Enders had been deputy chief of mission (the number two man in the embassy) to Cambodia in the early seventies, where he so impressed Kissinger that he was given the same rank—FSO-1—as the ambassador of the moment. Enders headed the embassy group that made the official recommendations on bombing targets, and he not surprisingly acquired a reputation as a super-hawk.

Ironically, he would eventually lose his post as assistant secretary of state for inter-American affairs because of White House suspicions that he was too soft on communism in Central America.

Like so many of the characters in this saga, Tom Enders seemed to have walked out of a film from a somewhat earlier time, for his appearance and behavior were reminiscent of the diplomatic stereotypes of the World War II period cinema. He spoke in the clipped language of the top levels of Connecticut society, dressed impeccably in elegant suits right out of Cary Grant movies, and dazzled his colleagues by mastering the Spanish language within a few months of taking charge of the Latin America post. Moreover, Enders understood the bureaucracy as few others, and had learned through bitter experience during the Vietnam period that anything committed to paper may eventually find its way into the hands of opponents, whether in the department, the Congress, or the media. Accordingly, once he began the Central American operation, Enders gave orders that the meetings of his "core group" would be attended only by "principals" (high-ranking officials from the Pentagon, the NSC, and the CIA, along with a couple of others from State), and that no notes would be taken. This had the double effect of leaving no documentary record of what had transpired, and compelling the participants to concentrate carefully on what was going on, since they would be unable to refer to printed minutes at a later date.

As his modus operandi became clear over time, Enders became the target of those who felt they were being cut out of the decision-making loop. Nothing irritates a government official more than not knowing what is really going on, and Enders was one of the few people in the foreign policy establishment who actually kept secrets. Within a year, there were articles in the press suggesting that Enders was running his own State Department. He wasn't, of course; first Haig, then Shultz—along with a select few in other agencies—were kept fully informed of the policy and the operations on the ground. But there were not many others who knew what was happening.

Meanwhile, the Central American policy was taking shape. After a few weeks of speeches and interviews in which Haig announced his intention to "go to the source" of the Central American matter, he was told by the White House to quiet down. This effectively killed any possibility of a visible, large-scale military, political, and economic challenge to the Cuban dictator. Nonetheless, there was no disputing the facts, and even the "pragmatists" shuddered at the possibility of a rising tempo of Communist success in our own hemisphere. What could be done?

18

If the administration were not prepared to deal with the Central American crisis in toto, it was certainly prepared to address the immediate crisis in El Salvador. The first order of business was to give the tenuous Salvadoran government (symbolized by the figure of José Napoleón Duarte) some breathing space by an infusion of military aid and some technical advice. Second was to nibble away at the supply lines of the guerrillas. Casey proposed a harassing operation, designed to interrupt the flow of weapons and intelligence from Nicaragua— where the operational headquarters of the Salvadoran guerrillas was located—to the fighters inside Salvador. Haig argued vociferously that the program was doomed to fail: if it were to amount to anything, the operation was too big to hide, and would become the object of public debate. On the other hand, since it did not address the central problem, but only one part of the crisis, a limited, covert operation could not fully succeed, thus making it subject to the kind of partisan political debate that had riven the country during the Vietnam War. The Congress would eventually terminate the funds, and we would be forced to abandon another ally under pressure from a Soviet client.

Haig's words were prophetic, but the president and his political advisers opted for the compromise solution.

Enders was thus given fairly narrow parameters within which to work, and he understood the political requirements of the White House. The bottom line was that the Reagan administration would not commit itself to removing the Sandinista regime in Nicaragua. For some— like Baker and Deaver—this represented their best political judgment. But for others—from Meese and Casey to Weinberger and Richard Allen, the national security adviser—it was a tactical retreat. For the latter group did not believe that the Sandinistas would ever come to terms with the United States or abandon their support for subversive movements elsewhere in Central America. Their support for the limited policy was based on political calculation: Congress would not support a full-fledged effort to bring down the Sandinistas, let alone take the fight "to the source." The most that could be accomplished was a defense of Salvador. The line would be drawn right there: There was to be no further expansion of communist power in Central America. It was a prescription for an uneasy stalemate, at two levels: internationally, we could bring pressure to bear on Nicaragua but would not be able to win; while domestically, we would ask Congress for middling support but never enough to resolve the crisis.

Enders reasoned that it might be possible to shift the focus of the political debate from Salvador to Nicaragua. After all, the Duarte government had been installed by a coup of progressive military lead-

19

ers the previous year, had promised a new constitution and free elections, and was in the process of carrying out one of the most radical land reform programs in Latin American history. Nicaragua, on the other hand, was well on the road to the creation of a Cuban-style Communist dictatorship, and with every passing month the evidence mounted: press censorship, crackdowns on private businesses, the arrest of political opponents, harassment of the Catholic Church. So just on the merits of the case, the American government should be able to educate the public, and direct primary attention to the activities of the Sandinistas. This would make it easier to support Salvador, and to mount some sort of campaign against Nicaragua.

Moreover, if the CIA could organize an effective guerrilla movement against the Sandinistas, Enders hoped that the Soviets and the Cubans could be convinced to abandon the Sandinistas. The maximum he thought possible was a defanged Nicaragua, deprived of operational support from the Soviet Empire, unable to spread subversion northward toward Mexico, and our southern borders.

If this policy were going to work, it would require considerable money from Congress, for both Salvador and some sort of anti-Sandinista force would have to be funded. In order to demonstrate that the United States was simply trying to shore up the fragile democratic experiment in Salvador (and not attempting to remove the Sandinista regime), Enders from the first embarked upon a "two-track" policy in the region. We would bring pressure to bear on Nicaragua through paramilitary, economic, and political means, but also open a diplomatic channel to Managua, Havana, and, ultimately, Moscow so as to be able to negotiate the neutralization of the Sandinistas as an active force in Central America. At the same time, Enders enlisted the European Bureau of the State Department to assist in explaining our Central American policy to the West Europeans, so that they would cooperate in linking their financial assistance programs to Nicaragua with the Sandinistas' behavior toward neighboring countries. In that manner, American policy would be seen as working for a peaceful resolution of conflict in Central America by those who feared the expansion of the fighting, at the same time that the Cubans, the Soviets, and the Sandinistas would see that if they did not come to a reasonable agreement with the United States, they faced a conflict that they could not hope to win.

Enders travelled to Managua in August 1981 to offer the Nicaraguans a deal: if they would renounce their support of guerrilla movements elsewhere in Central America and agree to limit their military buildup to reasonable levels, the United States would restore the aid program, issue a guarantee of non-interference, and crack down on the handful of anti-Nicaraguan groups that were operating in south Florida. The Sandinistas did not buy it; no answer came from Managua for nearly two months, and by that time the level of anti-American rhetoric was so intense, and the subversive campaign so active, that the rejection of the offer was clear to all. Enders had laid down the rails for the first track of his policy. We were willing to negotiate a peaceful solution to the Central American conflict. It was the Sandinistas who insisted on a military course. Thus our covert program—which was not drafted until November—was launched only after diplomacy had failed. And the diplomatic track remained open throughout Enders's tenure in office.

This diplomatic enterprise was bitterly contested by the activists within the Reagan camp. From Haig (Kirkpatrick became an active player in Central American affairs early in 1983) to Constantine Menges (the national intelligence officer for Latin America at the CIA, later NSC official in charge of that region), Nestor Sanchez (originally chief of the Latin American division at CIA, later deputy assistant secretary of defense for the area) and Fred Ikle (under secretary of defense for policy), they argued that only countervailing force could compel the Soviets to step down from the guerrilla war in Central America, and that we ought to have learned from Vietnam that a gradual escalation in such conflicts permitted our opponents to adjust to our every move. Furthermore, they felt that Vietnam had taught a second lesson: The American Congress (and, to a lesser extent, the American public) would eventually tire of prolonged conflict. If one were going to challenge a Soviet proxy, it should be done with sufficient power to win the confrontation cleanly.

The corollary to this axiom was that any negotiated settlement with the Sandinistas was suspect, for it would simply enable the Nicaraguans to gain precious time, consolidate their domestic power, and eventually return to the program of subversion. The activists were not content to force the Sandinistas to sue for peace (and did not believe it could be achieved); in their hearts, they wanted victory, a rollback of the Soviet beachhead on the Central American landmass. But they never convinced the president to take such a policy to the Congress, or the public at large. So while the activists may have believed that our Central American policy was "really" designed to overthrow the Sandinista regime, they, too, hewed to the public line that we were only defending El Salvador, and were perfectly willing to negotiate our differences with Managua.

In other words, the activists believed that the United States was committed to a policy that the president never enunciated, and for which adequate resources were never requested. The major figure in this group was Judge Clark, originally the deputy secretary of state, then Allen's successor as national security adviser. Clark knew the president's innermost wishes as well as anyone, and he was personally committed to an aggressive Central American policy. There was therefore a great tension within the Central American policy debate, for anyone who simply attempted to implement the announced policy was condemned by the activists as "failing to follow the president's policy." Yet although he constantly pushed for a tough position in every meeting at which the matter was discussed, the president never formally approved the activists' policy, even in very small meetings, nor did he ever sign a National Security Decision Directive that would have indicated his desire to see the removal of the Sandinista regime.

The notion that the president had decided against a campaign to overthrow the Sandinistas was hard to accept, even though it became increasingly evident with the passage of time. But by 1987, even an all-out opponent of the *contras,* Aryeh Neier, was taking it seriously:

> Even before the first Boland Amendment in December 1982 required that overthrowing the Sandinistas should not be the purpose of the war, the CIA may not have believed a *contra* victory was possible. When the war was being launched in 1981 and 1982, the agency may only have wanted to bleed Nicaragua as an object lesson to the Sandinistas themselves, and to anyone else with thoughts about establishing a leftist government in the Western Hemisphere. Getting the *contra* war started may have mattered more to the CIA than making certain it would ultimately succeed.[4]

This was precisely the point, although the decision was made in the White House, and not at CIA's headquarters in Langley, Virginia.

THE CREATION OF THE CONTRAS

The anti-Sandinista operation—the least covert "covert action" in American history—was approved at a White House meeting on the 21st of November 1981. Within hours, the *Washington Post* had been tipped off that something had happened, and we can now read the article on the twenty-second as a carefully crafted leak to present the covert program as a reasoned response to a serious policy dilemma:

4. Aryeh Neier, "The Contra Contradiction," in *The New York Review of Books,* April 9, 1987.

The Reagan administration is approaching a crucial decision on whether to take actions against Nicaragua to prevent that country from becoming "another Cuba," according to senior officials. . . .

The pressure to act arises from a widely held assessment throughout the top ranks of the administration that Nicaragua is increasingly becoming an armed camp from which leftist revolution can be exported to neighboring El Salvador, Guatemala, Honduras and Costa Rica. . . .

. . . they view the most urgent problems as military ones: a continuing sizable arms buildup in Nicaragua and the improved fortunes of Cuban-trained guerrilla forces in El Salvador and other nearby states . . . the private comments of high officials conspicuously left open the possibility that the U.S. response will likewise involve military actions. . . .

The decision had already been taken, and William Casey had his first major operation.

CASEY

William Casey was one of the two most powerful directors in the history of the CIA. Like Allen Dulles—the DCI during the Eisenhower administration—Casey enjoyed a close personal relationship with his president, a consuming interest in spycraft, and the high respect and personal affection of his top officers at the agency (including those who disagreed with some of his decisions). Above all, he was an unforgettable character. To look at him, you would have sworn he had stepped out of a P. G. Wodehouse novel, with his few remaining wispy white hairs eternally out of place, his tie knot sliding down toward an abundant expanse of belly, clues of past meals scattered on his shirt, tie, and jacket, and his pants somewhat askew. His suits were custom-made, but he was the despair of any tailor.

To this air of the eccentric country gentleman was added a charming incompetence when it came to anything mechanical. In the fall of 1986, a new telephone system was installed at the CIA, and Casey's personal phone looked like something out of "Star Trek": the receiver sat in the center of a clear plastic sheet, surrounded by multicolored buttons. It was supposed to be a triumph of modern technology, but one day as we were discussing counterterrorism, the phone beeped. Casey grabbed it, grunted something to the person at the other end of the line, jabbed one of the buttons, and said "Hello." Nothing seemed to happen, for he punched another button, and tried again:

23

"Hello," he cried. He glared at me, jabbed the air with his free hand (the right one), pushed another button, and yelled, "I can't get the goddamn thing to work, get him on the line." He hung up, turned back to me, laughed heartily, and exclaimed, "Once upon a time there was Bell Telephone Company. It was the wonder of the world. I used to have two phones on this desk, a regular phone for normal talking and the secure phone for the rest. Now they give me this masterpiece, and I can't get the fucking thing to work." A minute or so later, it rang again. He made a face, picked up the receiver with care, and gave it a pleasant "hello." He smiled and relaxed. His secretary had put the call through to him on the one line he had mastered.

One could have concluded from such amusing events that Casey was the prototypical absentminded professor, and his legendary mumbling would have augmented this impression. But, curiously, his friends never had any trouble understanding him. Only those Casey did not wish to enlighten found him virtually incomprehensible. He used the mumble as a defense mechanism, encouraging people to believe, as the joke in Washington had it, that Casey was the first DCI in history who did not need to use a scrambler when he spoke on the telephone, for nobody understood him anyway.

In reality, Casey was one of the smartest and most disciplined men in the administration. A voracious reader and a tireless worker, he exhausted his colleagues both physically and intellectually. He invariably returned from foreign trips loaded down with new books (and he read them), and was constantly looking for new ways to look at the world. Casey's door was always open to people with bright ideas, and I dare say that no previous CIA director ever met with so many "outsiders" as he. For Casey had learned one of the basic lessons of large organizations: Bureaucracies have a built-in tendency toward intellectual paralysis. Once certain rules have been established, they become institutionalized, even though the world may have changed. And Casey was determined that the CIA keep pace with the rapidly changing world. Even if the system lagged behind, he raced happily ahead, searching for new insights, new ways of gathering information, and new models of explanation.

One of Casey's lifelong passions was the study of revolutionary movements, from the American Revolution to the present. Both his historical studies and his wartime experiences in the OSS (where he was in charge of clandestine operations in Europe) led him to think deeply about one of the most interesting of all subjects: How can a small force defeat a powerful nation? While this was an intriguing issue for anyone, it was a vital one for the head of the West's most important intelligence service. In concrete terms, Casey wanted to be able to evaluate the possibilities of bringing a direct challenge to the Soviet Empire. Since it was unthinkable for the United States to bring about a military confrontation with the Soviets, the only possible method was to use some smaller quantum of power—an anti-Soviet liberation movement—to achieve this goal.

At the same time, Casey was one of the most clear-eyed realists in town and was keenly aware of the limitations of the organization he had inherited from Adm. Stansfield Turner. The operational capacities that Casey believed the country needed were not to be found in the Central Intelligence Agency, and the senior officials in the Directorate of Operations (DO) were survivors of the catastrophes of the mid-seventies, when the Church and Pike committees first, and Adm. Stansfield Turner later, had savaged the agency, driving most of the top clandestine agents into early retirement.

On the Directorate of Intelligence (DI) side of the house, there was a parallel deterioration. Given the flood of leaks over the past decade, many sensitive sources had dried up, people with crucial information in foreign countries were unwilling to cooperate with American agents, and the bureaucratic policies of the government—which encouraged professionals to change jobs at regular intervals—meant that there were few genuine experts in regional or country affairs. Just as there had been no full-time Farsi speaker current on Iranian affairs at the time of the shah's crisis in 1978–79, so there was no experienced Iran hand in the DI in the mid-eighties providing a thorough analysis of Iran. Occasionally, some senior official like Graham Fuller, the national intelligence officer for the Middle East, would weigh in with an opinion on Iranian affairs, but Fuller had numerous other responsibilities and could not sustain a tight focus on Iranian questions. Thus Casey was reluctant to ask the CIA to undertake difficult and complex operations, and his experiences at the agency did little to encourage him. On one occasion, a Soviet émigré came to Casey with a brilliant concept for an operation inside the Soviet Union, and Casey commended him for the idea and then said, "whatever you do, don't work with the CIA. They'll screw it up and get you into trouble." And this was well before the catastrophes of the Reagan era. As will be seen in chapter 7, during Casey's tenure at CIA a top "case officer" for the Moscow station defected to the KGB; repeated Soviet, Israeli, and even Chinese penetrations of the intelligence community were uncovered; and a high-ranking Cuban defector named Florentino Aspillaga revealed that virtually every one of our agents in Cuba was secretly working for Castro.

The image of Casey as an impetuous adventurer in investment banker's garb was thus far off the mark. Casey was a realist, and had no patience with people who urged him to do things he believed were beyond the capacities of the CIA. Yet he was also convinced that the Reagan years were a potential turning point in the history of the East-West struggle.

Casey had broken with tradition, and brought in several outside experts to help with the analyses at CIA. Among these were Dr. Henry Rowen, a brilliant economist from California; Herb Meyer, a highly original strategic thinker from New York; and Constantine Menges, an unconventional political scientist whose published work had ranged from Turkey to Central America and Mexico. Rowen oversaw the preparation of the intelligence estimates, Meyer served as a personal assistant to Casey, and Menges was named national intelligence officer for Latin America, and later, for a time, became the key person on Central American policy on the NSC staff. All of these, as well as the Deputy Director for Intelligence Robert Gates, believed that the Soviet Union was showing signs of structural crisis. There was a discernable cash-flow shortage; the failures of Soviet technology were so grave that the KGB had had to mount a massive foreign espionage effort to steal enough of the West's technology for the Soviets to hold their own, and there was evidence of serious tension within the satellites. Under these circumstances, Casey reasoned, if it were possible to deal the Kremlin a military defeat at the fringes of the Soviet Empire—say, in Angola, Afghanistan, Cambodia, or Central America—there might be extraordinary internal political repercussions.

Thus, Casey believed, the Central American operation had an importance far beyond the regional threat to American security. If we could roll back the Soviet thrust into the Western Hemisphere, there might be a devastating payoff within the Soviet Empire. And so, while the *contra* program started small, Casey always had his eye on the big prize: the possibility that it might grow into something powerful enough to threaten the Sandinista regime itself. Casey therefore determined that he would put his very best people to work on the Central American account.

The task of organizing the anti-Sandinista guerrillas was given to Duane ("Dewey") Clarridge, the new chief of the Latin American Division in the Operations Directorate of the Central Intelligence Agency.

In a CIA that had been decimated and demoralized for nearly a decade, Clarridge was an extraordinary talent. Hundreds of top officials of the Directorate of Operations had been driven into early retirement during the mid-seventies congressional investigations into illegal CIA activities, and Turner's internal housecleaning in 1977. Clarridge was just below the line of fire, having served for years in various posts in the Middle East, and then in Europe. He was an imaginative, aggressive officer, with the kind of flamboyant personal style that quickly endeared him to Bill Casey. A smoker of fine cigars, an eccentric dresser who favored white suits, and a gourmet who resorted to a pasta diet when his appetite placed his wardrobe in jeopardy, Clarridge was Casey's personal choice for running the Central American operation, even though he had had no Latin American experience. If Enders was out of a Cary Grant movie, Clarridge could have played *Our Man in Havana*.

Casey knew what he was doing, for Clarridge quickly learned the ins and outs of Latin American affairs, and he had another quality in terribly short supply: he was one of the few senior officials in the DO who was not afraid of taking risks. Almost all those in the upper echelons of the agency who had been lucky enough to survive the purges were determined that anything was better than a replay of those catastrophes, and the organization that Bill Casey inherited was little inclined to take risks. Once a beehive of activity, the CIA in early 1981 was a relatively quiet place, and most of the top officials had little interest in aggressive new enterprises. That is why Clarridge, who had no such reticence, was selected to head the largest single covert operation in the Casey years, as he would later be asked to take charge of a new directorate to combat international terrorism.

Clarridge's mission, as defined at the November 21st meeting, was to organize an anti-Sandinista movement that would simultaneously ease the pressure on Salvador, and make life difficult for Nicaragua. It was a daunting task. First of all, he had to get himself "up to speed" on Latin American affairs and the Spanish language (he never did learn Portuguese). Then he had to gain the confidence of regional secret services. There is a tendency to believe that secret operations are so common that any CIA official can pick up the (secure) telephone and organize vast undertakings at will. This was never true, and it was even more difficult for the CIA to gain the cooperation of foreign intelligence services in the early 1980s, following the revelations of prior secret operations in the mid- and late-seventies. No country likes to see its secrets on the front pages of the American press, and friendly

27

intelligence services were not about to embark upon sensitive adventures with the CIA without some assurance that things had changed.

Yet the active assistance of Latin American intelligence services was indispensable to the anti-Sandinista effort; one could not simply set up guerrilla camps and anti-Nicaraguan operations in Salvador, Honduras, and Costa Rica without the express approval of the governments involved. In the end, Clarridge won out because he was able to develop a personal relationship with the key people in Latin America. His personality and flair were perfectly suited to his new theater of operations; the Latinos preferred his natural ebullience, with the added fillips acquired in Europe, to the staid efficiency of the standard-issue American official.

The first bit of support for anti-Sandinista guerrillas came from Argentina, even before the inauguration of Ronald Reagan. The murderous military junta that ruled that unhappy country was deeply concerned about a revival of terrorism in the hemisphere, having experienced repeated waves of violence over a period of twenty years. The Argentine generals knew that Nicaragua had become a haven for terrorists from Europe and Latin America, that Libya and the PLO were well represented in Managua, and that members of the Italian Red Brigades and the Spanish Basque terrorist organization, ETA, were at training camps in Nicaragua. They were eager to contain and, if possible, remove this threat.

The Argentine generals were running a program in Honduras along with the Honduran military (at the time firmly in control of the government), to train some of the earliest groups of anti-Sandinista guerrillas. The Honduran government, which shared the concerns about the Sandinistas, provided some training facilities. And even before the administration had decided on a major anti-Sandinista program, Nestor Sanchez, Clarridge's predecessor as the CIA's chief of Latin American operations, flew down to Tegucigalpa to talk to General Guttierez, the Honduran military strong man of the period. Sanchez encouraged Guttierez to throw his full support to the guerrillas. Guttierez was outspokenly skeptical and told Sanchez he didn't trust the Americans: "You'll get me out on a limb with this thing, and then walk away from me." He knew his North Americans, but went along with the program. The CIA funded the Argentines' training of anti-Sandinista Nicaraguan rebels in Honduras, which lasted until the fall of the junta in 1983, in the aftermath of the Falklands War.

The secret connection with Argentina undoubtedly raised one of Haig's more difficult problems, for by taking Britain's side in the conflict, the United States obviously risked retaliation by the Argentines—in the form of termination of the *contra* project. Yet the secretary, and the president, along with CIA director Casey, all opted for vigorous support for Mrs. Thatcher's government and its principled position that aggression could not be tolerated.

A joint operation with Argentina to train anti-Sandinista Nicaraguans was politically controversial, both within the executive branch and in the Congress. To many, it was attractive to harass the Sandinistas, but unpleasant to do so with such a notoriously repressive regime as Argentina's. Yet within short order the covert project was approved by Congress, through the "oversight" committees, and was not seriously challenged thereafter (although the Argentine participation was leaked to the press within a year). Why was there not more opposition? There were at least three reasons.

- First, Reagan had just been elected by a landslide, and controlled the Senate. The Democrats in Congress were not inclined to challenge a president with such an electoral mandate in the first year of his administration.
- Second, the evidence of Sandinista subversion was thoroughly convincing, and there was general agreement to the need for some kind of containment program.
- Third, although the actual manpower came from Argentina, it was privately endorsed by leaders throughout Central America. This would remain a constant pattern of behavior: the other regional leaders would invariably tell Americans in private that they wanted an aggressive campaign against Nicaragua, while in public they would often denounce the very same campaign. But when the Kissinger Commission travelled to Central America in late 1983, they were told by every Central American leader (except the Sandinistas, of course) that democracy would probably not survive in the region if the Sandinistas consolidated their Communist regime.

The operation was initially designed to train and equip a force of five hundred to one thousand men. But the world does not always conform to the plans of the American government, and Clarridge discovered to his surprise and delight that the program was far more popular than had been imagined. Precise numbers are hard to come by, but by 1983 the Nicaraguan Resistance had reached about four thousand; in 1984–85—the period of the Congressional cutoff of funds and the White House efforts to find alternative sources of money—it was up to twelve thousand. By late 1987, there were more than fifteen thousand armed men fighting against the Sandinistas inside Nicaragua, with another five thousand or so serving as a support network in Honduras and Costa Rica.

The easiest way to appreciate the significance of these numbers is to compare them with the Sandinista armed force that drove Anastasio Somoza from power in 1979. At that time, there were at most five thousand people in the Sandinista organization, with approximately fifteen hundred of them engaged in the armed struggle against the dictatorship. Thus, within eighteen months the CIA found itself supporting a mass movement two to three times the size of the revolutionary movement that had driven the Somozas into exile, and twenty to thirty times as big as the movement envisaged by the American government in the late autumn of 1981.

The rapid development of the anti-Sandinista operation surprised even its most optimistic supporters, and transformed Dewey Clarridge from one of the most respected operatives within the shadowy world of CIA's clandestine services to a central figure in the foreign policy debate in the United States. Within the annals of covert operations, this ranked as one of the most successful. There had been nothing to compare with it in recent American history since the days when the CIA created an anti-communist movement of tens of thousands of Hmong tribesmen in Laos in the late 1960s and early 1970s.

In time, Clarridge's Central American campaign became the largest secret operation in CIA history, and he was in a position of which the vast majority of secret operatives only dream. He was waging a secret war, with a complete army under his command. The *contras* had it all, ground forces, a political arm, a tiny navy, and even a fledgling air force. Under his command, the *contra* armed forces bombed military and strategic targets, mined Corinto harbor, and occasionally engaged Sandinista regulars.

How had he done it? For one thing, Clarridge discovered that there were several Latin American countries—beginning with Argentina, but including virtually every other country in Central America—who were willing to help with expertise, information, and occasional services. Thus the original covert program provided for the allocation of funds to "third-country governments" to thwart Cuban and Nicaraguan plans for subversion in Central America. While under the guidance of the CIA, the men who actually trained the first *contras* were Argentines and Hondurans. This multinational cooperation permitted the creation of a small paramilitary group of several hundred, for the most part drawn from the ranks of the Nicaraguan exile communities elsewhere in Central America (primarily Honduras and Guatemala) and the United States (where they had been training—without official U.S. government support—ever since the fall of Somoza).

This operation accounts for the existence of a *contra* movement, but not its size and commitment. As the critics of the American policy would subsequently note, several of the key military commanders were former *Somocistas,* as were some of the early political leaders. They worked well with the Argentines, for there was a commonality of political outlook—distrust of mass movements, opposition to democracy, and a belief that the peoples of the region were incapable of rational self-rule—as well as a shared strategic objective.

Had the *contras* and their supporters remained primarily counterrevolutionary and antidemocratic Nicaraguans, Hondurans, and Argentines, the Reagan policy would have failed, and rightly so. For it would only have been a matter of time before the American people rejected a close working relationship with former *Somocistas,* Honduran military men, and Argentine mass murderers. But, from the very beginning, the picture was considerably more complex. For one thing, the worst of the hard-core *Somocistas,* who were based in Guatemala for the most part, were excluded from the operation. They were judged too extremist, and their participation would have instantly discredited the entire undertaking. This proved to be a farsighted decision, for in relatively short order a dramatic change took place as thousands of young men streamed across the Honduran and Costa Rican borders to join the anti-Sandinista resistance.

The transformation of the covert operation into a mass movement was not anticipated by the Americans, and it was a bit baffling to many of them. The policymakers of the United States were not used to thinking in terms of spontaneous anti-Communist insurrectionary movements, for much of our policy in the past twenty-five years was designed to thwart *anti-American* movements of this sort. Yet, according to the most attentive observers of the *contras*—from both the United States and Central America—the resistance came to be a movement of peasants and small landowners—*campesinos,* who, together with the Indian tribes along the northern coast, were willing to risk everything in a fight to the death against the new Nicaraguan regime.

As Robert Leiken, who originally opposed American policy in Central America but later came to support its basic objectives (if not always the methods adopted), wrote in March 1986:

31

. . . the popular base of the resistance has grown enormously. There are some 20,000 armed insurgents in a Nicaraguan population of three million, of which the FDN makes up some 12,000. The FDN claims that 40 percent of its troops are former Sandinista soldiers and fewer than two percent are former National Guardsmen. . . .

. . . FDN fighters are peasants with deep economic, political, and ideological grievances against the regime. They have maintained high morale despite a lack of military equipment and training—and sometimes boots and food. The FDN, in short, is a movement with a peasant base, populist middle-echelon officers, and a mostly reactionary leadership imposed and maintained by the United States. . . .[5]

The *contras* were catalyzed by the United States, but they were already present in the Nicaraguan test tube. The *contra* mass movement was the result of Sandinista policies:

• The forced draft. This was enormously unpopular in the countryside (somewhat less so in the cities). The draft was enforced by draconian measures, including the denial of food rationing cards to families whose children had not signed up for the army.

• The steady decline of the economy. Although accelerated by some of the *contras'* actions, economic decline was already a clearly established pattern by 1981. According to the Sandinistas' own figures, there was a drop of nearly 50 percent in gross GNP from the time of the revolution to 1987, which is unprecedented in modern times.

• The growing political consciousness of the *campesinos* themselves. This was paradoxically the consequence of some of the land redistribution programs of the Sandinista regime. By giving land to the peasants, the Sandinistas hoped to smash the old landholding class, and give the *campesinos* a greater stake in the future of Nicaragua. They succeeded all too well: the *campesinos* didn't want their children dragged off into the army (they were needed to work the land), and felt directly threatened by the disastrous economic policies of the Sandinistas. The establishment of rigid price controls after the revolution made agriculture a losing proposition (production costs were higher than the prices set by the government), and this inevitably convinced the *campesinos* that they had been deceived by the new regime. Moreover, the anticlericalism of the Sandinistas upset the *campesinos,* and gave a crusading overtone to the *contra* movement.

By late 1982 and early 1983, the operation that was supposed to frustrate the Cuban and Nicaraguan effort to subvert El Salvador was

5. Robert Leiken, "Reform the Contras" in the *New Republic,* March 31, 1986.

causing considerable anxiety in Managua. The American plan to bring pressure to bear on the Sandinistas, and change the focal point of the American domestic debate from the Salvadoran civil war to the nature of the regime in Nicaragua, was succeeding beyond the expectations of its supporters.

THE WAR AGAINST THE REAGAN DOCTRINE

The problem, of course, was that the *contra* operation was not designed to remove the Sandinistas, since no one—from Reagan and Haig to Enders, Casey, and Clarridge—believed that this could be achieved without the commitment of American military power. Yet the *contras* quickly became strong enough so that, even though there was no real possibility that the *contras* would seize power, the Sandinistas and their supporters reacted as if it were a mortal threat. In one of the many paradoxes that run throughout the Iran-Contra affair, an administration that set out to finesse a major problem ended by having to deal with an even greater one. Thus, a White House that ordered its hyperactive secretary of state to conduct a quiet Central American policy found that the "secret war" was a very noisy affair. Even though Baker, Deaver, and Mrs. Reagan didn't want a confrontation with Castro and the Ortega brothers, once the machinery was set in motion there was no way to avoid it.

And here, as so often happens, illusion became far more important than reality. It is difficult for Americans to appreciate the extent to which Washington dominates the thinking of foreign leaders, no matter how small or remote their countries may be. Many foreign leaders imagine that the president of the United States follows their every action with Machiavellian concentration, scheming how best to maintain American interests in every corner of the globe, every hour of every day. This is particularly true for the enemies of the United States, who least understand the chaotic functioning of this sprawling democracy. They, far more than our allies, take our rhetoric quite seriously, particularly when it is aimed against them and their ambitions. So it was that Reagan's aggressive campaign rhetoric, and Haig's early pronunciamentos on the need to "send a message" to the Kremlin and its friends—to "go to the source" of problems from Central America to international terrorism—convinced the Castros, the Ortegas—and the Qadaffis—that we would shortly bring the full force of American might to bear on them.

So it came to pass that while the Reagan White House strove mightily to finesse the Central American crisis (as it did with foreign policy problems generally), the anti-American forces refused to believe it. Castro expected us to move against him once the Russians had acted in Poland; the Sandinistas were morally certain that the marines would land in Nicaragua. Castro warned them not to antagonize the *yanqui* giant, to pretend they were friendly to us, to mask their Leninist convictions. All to no avail; the Sandinistas repeatedly announced that they were part of the world Communist movement and that they would carry the struggle against the United States throughout the region.

The Sandinistas' refusal to effectively conceal their true ambitions became a leitmotif of the entire affair, to the great despair of their defenders. On more than one occasion, the Reagan policy was saved, not by the brilliance of administration strategy, but by the pigheaded behavior of the Sandinistas themselves. Sometimes Daniel Ortega's actions were so spectacularly self-defeating that one had to wonder if he wasn't secretly in the employ of the American government. On one occasion he saved *contra* aid by leaving for Moscow within days of an initial congressional rejection of Reagan's request; on another, the Sandinistas invaded Honduras on the eve of a crucial vote.[6] Over and over again, the Sandinistas would find a way to make our own case for us, even when we failed to do so ourselves. They publicly stated their contempt for democratic elections; they repeatedly censored *La Prensa,* the only large-scale independent publication in the country; they singled out the Catholic Church, far and away the most popular institution in Nicaragua, for venomous attacks, and concentrated their bile on Cardinal Obando y Bravo, perhaps the most popular man in the country. And when the pope visited Managua, they staged a spectacular effort to "jam" his speech by playing noisy patriotic music over the loudspeakers that carried the pontiff's words to the vast crowd. All of these disasters effectively ended any hope of attracting great public sympathy for the Sandinista cause in the United States, or, for that matter, in Western Europe.

With such enemies, and with an increasingly attractive resistance movement, the Reagan administration should have had an easy time with Congress in supporting the *contras*. Why, then, was it so difficult to obtain the necessary public and congressional support—indeed, so difficult that Oliver North had to be instructed to find extraordinary means to keep the *contras* alive, "body and soul"? The explanation is fourfold: first, the Sandinistas' propaganda was a lot better than their

6. I found this pattern of behavior so striking that I wrote a satirical article for the *American Spectator,* suggesting that Gorbachev was a CIA agent. See "Our Man in Moscow," August 1986.

performance, and they gained a remarkable degree of support in American public opinion. Second, many Americans thought it was wrong as a matter of principle for the United States to wage a secret war against the Sandinista regime, seeing in this policy a replay of the worst aspects of previous American actions in Vietnam, Angola, and Cuba. Third, there were many members of the United States Congress who did not want to see the Reagan administration's policy succeed in Central America. Finally, the refusal of the administration, from the president on down, to be candid about their true assessment of the importance of the battle for Nicaragua, meant that there would not be an honest debate.

A war was underway in Nicaragua, but the decisive battle for the future of Central America was conducted in the corridors of the House and Senate. And since the administration lacked the courage and candor to present to the Congress a serious program that would have stipulated the conditions under which the United States was prepared to accept the Sandinista regime, along with a plan to change that regime if the conditions were not met, the votes were not on the basic questions. The issues were falsified from the outset, and the position most commonly attributed to the president—the Sandinistas must fall—was not presented to Congress until Oliver North appeared to argue the case in the summer of 1987.

2. The Contra War, and the War Over the Contras

The congressional opposition to the Central American program was symbolized by three New England Democrats: Thomas ("Tip") O'Neill, John Kerry, and Christopher Dodd. All were Catholics (although Dodd had broken with the Church on some major theological issues: he had obtained a divorce and had voted in favor of abortion even though expressing his personal opposition to it), and all tended to view Reagan's Central American policies in the light of their own personal involvement in previous American foreign adventures. Kerry's attitudes were profoundly shaped by his Vietnam experiences, Dodd's by his years in the Peace Corps in the Dominican Republic, and O'Neill's by the involvement of friends and relatives in Nicaragua itself. All three shared the position and the emotions of the Latin American bishops' Puebla Document:

> From the depths of the countries which make up Latin America, a cry is rising to heaven, growing louder and more alarming all the time. It is the cry of a suffering people who demand justice, freedom and respect for the basic rights of human beings and peoples. . . . the Church has affirmed its own need for conversion and has tried to respond to cries of the poor by seeking to identify with its people in their struggle for true justice.

From the young Vietnam veteran to the old Boston pol and the aristocratic gentleman from Connecticut, all saw the Central American issue in moral terms. None could accept the administration's claim that the Sandinistas, along with their Cuban and Soviet-bloc supporters, represented a major security threat to the United States and

36

a mortal danger to the future of democracy in the region. All were exceptionally effective politicians, and Kerry was a particularly charismatic speaker. Together, they led the opposition to the Reagan policies.

House Speaker Tip O'Neill was a romantic on Central America. His attitudes toward this geopolitical issue were shaped by two personal experiences, one when he was a teenager in Boston, the second an even earlier family event. The first came about when a friend of O'Neill's named Eddie Kelly was sent into Nicaragua during the U.S. Marine campaign against Sandino in the first half of the century. Kelly returned with a stab wound and told O'Neill, "We're taking care of the property and the rights of United Fruit. I got stabbed for United Fruit." It is the sort of experience that shapes adult perceptions, and O'Neill thought he had learned a basic lesson: "We kept that nation in servitude for years, we exploited them."[1]

O'Neill's second encounter with Nicaragua came through the experiences of his aunt, Annie Tolan, who was one of the original members of the Maryknoll order of Catholic missionaries. When she joined the order in 1919, she took the name of Sister Eunice, and remained an active member until her death in 1983. So the Maryknolls were a basic source of O'Neill's world view throughout his adult life, and the Maryknolls were among the most active American supporters of the Sandinistas. The order's monthly magazine, *Maryknoll,* has long been an advocate of liberation theology and support for revolutionary movements throughout the Third World. In a typical article on Nicaragua in July 1982 an American missionary in Matagalpa, Father Stanley Banaszek, summed up the order's attitude toward the Sandinistas:

> Maryknoll's priorities in Nicaragua are to accompany the revolution. It means not being paternalistic but rather being a brother, being one with the poor and identifying with them as Christ did.

Maryknoll's one-time editor, Donald J. Casey, became the Sandinistas' chief public relations consultant in New York shortly after the 1979 overthrow of Somoza.

It was no surprise, therefore, when Tip O'Neill threw in his lot with the Sandinistas, for he believed everything that came to him via the Maryknollers. Even after his aunt died, O'Neill had another friend in the order in Nicaragua, an intensely pro-Sandinista woman named Sister Peggy Healy, with whom he corresponded. "[The Maryknollers

1. Quoted in the *Washington Post,* June 5, 1985, p. A29.

are] only there doing God's work," O'Neill told the *Washington Post* (June 5, 1985), "and I have faith and trust when they come and talk to me. I have complete trust."

For the speaker, Reagan's Central American initiative was morally wrong, and, in a departure from his usual approach to politics, O'Neill attacked the president personally: "I just feel the president is determined, because of a Class-B movie attitude, to get our boys down there."

John Kerry was a very different sort of personality, but his attitudes were the same as O'Neill's. Kerry exploded onto the national political scene in the spring of 1971 as the head of the Vietnam Veterans against the War. A highly decorated Navy lieutenant in Vietnam, Kerry led a mass protest on the Mall in Washington, and appeared, in widely reported testimony, on Capitol Hill. It was inevitable that he would view the covert program in Central America in terms of his Vietnam experience. "I see the same sense of great victimization," he once said. "The little kids staring wide-eyed and scared. It really hits home the same way as Vietnam."[2]

O'Neill was a traditional pol, who worked his way up the ranks. Kerry and Dodd were a new breed, men who came from good families, went to good schools (Kerry was a Yale grad), and arrived in Congress while still in their twenties or very early thirties. They were in a hurry to make their mark on Washington, and it did not take long. Kerry, I am sure, could ask for no more eloquent tribute to his effectiveness than the repeated appearance of his name in North's notebooks. There were two reasons for North's preoccupation with the junior senator from Massachusetts. First was Kerry's staunch refusal to compromise on the question of Central America: he was opposed to any substantial American involvement in the region, aside from economic assistance. Kerry opposed military aid, whether to the *contras* or the beleaguered Duarte in Salvador, found the Ortegas sympathetic, and insisted on holding the *contras* accountable for any and every violation of the highest legal principles (in 1985 he offered an amendment to the foreign aid bill that would have cut off *contra* funding if they were found to have violated international law). Second, some of Kerry's investigations were getting alarmingly close to some of North's operations.

The third member of the anti-*contra* trinity was Senator Chris Dodd, the son of a two-term senator who had been censured for misuse

2. Quoted in the *Washington Post*, April 23, 1985.

of campaign funds. Chris was a lawyer, having earned his degree at the University of Louisville Law School in 1972, and was elected to Congress just three years later, at the age of thirty-one. Tall, slim, elegantly good-looking, Dodd early showed a soft spot for historical conspiracy theories, as when he participated in a three-man House investigation of the John F. Kennedy assassination. At one point in their investigation, Dodd, Louis Stokes, and Richardson Preyer spent four and a half days in Cuba, but would not reveal if they had met with Castro.

Like O'Neill and Kerry, Dodd's opposition to American efforts to fight communist movements and regimes in Central America was total, and, like the other two, Dodd believed that the basic cause of political conflict in the region was economic. "I've lived with the people in this region . . . they can't afford to feed their families when they're hungry," he said in the *Washington Post*, August 5, 1982. On this basis, Dodd proposed an amendment to the 1981 foreign assistance bill, stipulating that the president could not continue aid to Salvador unless he certified—every six months—that the country was making progress in achieving social, political, and economic reforms. He continued his campaign in 1982, when his amendment withheld money from Salvador unless the implementation of the land-reform program was vigorous.

By 1983, Dodd had achieved a perfect score on the Americans for Democratic Action score card and was widely perceived to be one of the central figures in the Democrats' fight against Reagan's Central American policies. This picture was confirmed when he was selected to deliver the Democratic response to Reagan's nationally televised speech on Central America on April 27th of that year. Dodd erupted with an emotional tirade, accusing the president of condoning Salvadoran security guards who murdered people "gangland style—the victim on bended knee, bombs wired behind the back, a bullet through the brain." The level of brutality in Salvador was well known, but to equate that with the president's support of the moderate Duarte was an outrage. Even leading members of his own party were offended, and in the *Washington Post* of May 8, 1983, Jim Wright—later to carry out much of what Dodd had hoped for—denounced the Dodd speech as "as destructive as the McGovern view of Vietnam."

Dodd's sympathy for the Salvadoran guerrillas and the Sandinistas was not a purely abstract matter, for he developed close personal ties to some of them. In the early 1980s, he was a frequent escort of Bianca Jagger, the Nicaraguan former wife of rock singer Mick Jagger, and

39

Dodd often travelled to Nicaragua, where he was always accorded a warm reception. Dodd became one of the Sandinistas' favorite Americans, and they later rewarded him for his support. When the Sandinistas decided to release Eugene Hasenfus—the lone survivor of the shoot-down of one of the resupply planes from the North–Secord network—the person to whom they released Hasenfus was Senator Dodd.

There were others who played important roles in the fight against Reagan's policies, and some—like Representative Michael Barnes or Senator Tom Harkin—would have considerable importance in eventually undoing the Reagan program. But Kerry, Dodd, and O'Neill were the Big Three, the men who fought tirelessly to keep the country out of what they viewed as a second Vietnam. At the beginning, they feared that the president, with his huge electoral victory, a Republican-controlled Senate, and a seemingly bottomless reservoir of goodwill among the American people, could do whatever he wanted in Central America. In all probability, the president could have been far more aggressive if he had chosen to take his case to the public at the outset of his first term. But it was not until late in 1981 that the policy was defined, and by that time political activists, church groups, a considerable chunk of the media and therefore many members of Congress had come out against any American involvement in Central American affairs. There was little support for aid to Duarte, let alone an effort to challenge the Sandinistas. Reagan would have to sell his program, and that would take even more time.

Meanwhile, the Sandinistas and their supporters had not been idle.

THE SANDINISTA CAMPAIGN

The model for the Sandinista revolution was Cuba, and Castro was its prophet and guide. During the war against Somoza's dictatorial regime, Cuban intelligence agents were constantly at the sides of the Sandinistas in Costa Rica. The Nicaraguan people were justifiably delighted to see Somoza defeated, but their joy was short-lived. A new, more disciplined dictatorship replaced the old one, thanks to the guidance of Castro. When Somoza fell, the Cubans moved quickly into positions of authority within the new regime. The chief of state security—the Sandinistas' KGB—was a man named Lenin Cerna, who was trained by Castro's own intelligence service, the DGI.

The Cubans had learned that American public opinion could be manipulated at the expense of the American government, and they enlisted the Nicaraguans in this effort. It was a good partnership, for educated Nicaraguans have long had a love-hate relationship with the United States. They love us for what we stand for, and the openness of our society, while they resent us for our wealth, the easiness of our lives, and our habit of deciding the outcome of their frequent civil conflicts. Either way, American culture was fairly well known to the Sandinistas, and they made good use of their knowledge.

The campaign to create an attractive image of Nicaragua was supervised by two of the most important Sandinistas: *comandante* Bayardo Arce, and Interior Minister *comandante* Tomas Borge. Arce was a former journalist for *La Prensa,* and one of the most toughminded Sandinistas. After the revolution, Arce explained the FSLN's notion of "freedom of the press" in a memorable sentence: "We support freedom of the press, but, of course, the freedom of the press we support will be a freedom of the press that supports the revolution." Borge, a highly independent and intelligent man who had survived several years in El Chipote, the nastiest of Somoza's prisons, set about the creation of a mechanism for the systematic deception of foreign visitors to Nicaragua. We owe a good deal of our information on this subject to a Sandinista defector by the name of Alvaro Baldizon.

Baldizon defected in 1985. For just over two and a half years, he had been chief investigator for the Special Investigations Committee of the Interior Ministry, a sensitive post he earned through years of service to the revolution (mainly in the police forces), including a span of ten months in Moscow studying criminology.

The Special Investigations Committee was created by Borge in response to accusations of human rights violations. In the course of his investigations, Baldizon discovered that the Sandinistas had carried out a systematic reign of terror and had concealed all evidence of their actions. They had assassinated political opponents (both in prison and at large), massacred groups held to be subversive (primarily, but not exclusively, the Indian tribes along the northern border), and had beaten, raped, and tortured presumed enemies of the regime.

Baldizon's findings were suppressed. Only in the rarest instances was any action taken against the perpetrators of the illegal acts. When Baldizon despaired of achieving any improvement, he discussed the possibility of finding other work, only to be told that the information he had uncovered was so sensitive that he would have to spend at least a year in military detention before finding another post. Realizing that he was part of the problem he was ostensibly working to solve, and that if he remained he would become hostage to his own knowledge, Baldizon crossed the border to Honduras and made his way to Washington.

The Sandinistas had good reason to be concerned about the explosive nature of Baldizon's discoveries, for he had confirmed the direct involvement of leading members of the regime, including Defense Minister Humberto Ortega and Borge himself. In mid-1981, for example, there was a riot at the Zona Franca prison. Borge went to the prison and promised that if the rioters returned to their cells, no reprisals would be taken against them. But Borge had set a fatal trap; the eight ringleaders of the uprising were taken behind a prison block and executed as Borge and Ortega watched. The Interior Ministry then reported that the eight had died in the course of the riot.

In 1983, more than three hundred farmers in Jinotega and Matagalpa departments were executed by the Sandinistas. Baldizon's investigation confirmed the event, but only four minor officials were tried, sentenced to brief prison sentences, and released almost immediately. The highest-ranking of these officials was then sent off for further study to Bulgaria, and the Interior Ministry again suppressed any information about the massacres.

In 1984, a Miskito Indian village was taken over by a company of Sandinista soldiers who locked all the men in the church and then, over the course of a month, raped and beat the women, sacked most of the houses, and slaughtered most of the cattle. Again, reports were censored, commanding officers were briefly arrested and then set free, and no further action was taken.

To his astonishment, Baldizon discovered that these actions were not random, but had been officially sanctioned by a secret edict signed by Borge, requiring that no reference be made to murders or killings but rather to "special measures." Baldizon discovered the existence of this edict, along with the policy of suppressing all information about the "special measures." He also found evidence confirming the Cuban, Libyan, East German, Bulgarian, Soviet, and even North Korean involvement in the day-to-day operations of the regime.

The accuracy of Baldizon's accounts was confirmed by the Inter-American Commission on Human Rights of the Organization of American States (OAS), but relatively little attention was paid to his story. I interviewed him in 1986 and asked the obvious question: Why, if his stories were true, had they not been found by the small army of foreign journalists, visitors, church representatives, and diplomats travelling across Nicaragua. He explained that the regime systematically deceives foreign visitors. Sometimes the Sandinistas use hired mobs (the *turbas divinas*) to prevent citizens from providing visitors with unwanted expressions of criticism of the regime. On other occasions, Borge deployed paid agents, a practice refined to the level of comic opera in Borge's office, where half a dozen mendicants were constantly on call so that Borge could stage scenes of bogus generosity for the benefit of foreign visitors.

There were other reasons as well. First, there were so many "internationals" helping the Sandinistas that a person with a foreign accent was quite likely to be a pro-Sandinista activist, and hence hostile to anyone telling unpleasant stories about the regime. Second, all foreign media people were kept under surveillance, so that anyone meeting with a foreign journalist would be reported to the state security apparatus. Third, there was a certain reluctance on the part of the American media to report the story. When Baldizon first came forward in early 1986, he was interviewed by Shirley Christian of the *New York Times,* one of the few American journalists with enough experience in Nicaragua to evaluate Baldizon's testimony. She found him convincing, and filed an article of some one thousand words. The *Times*'s editors reduced this to four short paragraphs, half of which were denials provided by the Nicaraguan Embassy in Washington. Over time, as the nature of the Sandinista regime became clearer, the reportage improved, but American journalists never mounted the sort of investigation of the Sandinistas that had been aimed at the Salvadoran death squads or, later on, Gen. Manuel Noriega's drug trafficking.

Finally, there is the silence that grips the vast majority of citizens living under a repressive regime, a phenomenon that many Americans are reluctant to accept. Nearly two years after the American invasion of Grenada, I travelled there with an ABC television team to prepare a documentary on what had happened under the Communist regime headed by Maurice Bishop. One afternoon, Tom Jarriel—the ABC news reporter—interviewed a Grenadian about the violence and torture to which he had been subjected. Toward the end of the interview, Jarriel asked why no one had heard about such things during the four years of Bishop's rule. "If you had asked me at the time," the Grenadian replied, "I would not have told you. I can only speak of such things now."

THE DECEPTION OF AMERICANS

But while the Sandinistas did much within Nicaragua to produce a distorted image of their regime, that alone could hardly explain the astonishingly gentle treatment they received from the press and from a considerable body of public opinion in the United States. Some of it was, of course, political: many Americans were so sympathetic to the goals of the revolution that they simply did not wish to hear the true story. In her excellent book on the Sandinistas, Shirley Christian recounts a 1982 encounter with José Esteban Gonzalez, the national coordinator of the Permanent Commission for Human Rights until September 1981, and one of the heroes of the struggle against Somoza. Gonzalez had been driven into exile by the Sandinistas and had travelled to the United States to tell his story. During the Somoza period, he had been warmly received by human rights organizations and church groups, but now he found a very different atmosphere:

> . . . he expressed his amazement at the change in attitude he had found among American church people since he had traveled to Washington in early 1979 to reveal the sins of Somoza . . . now that he was talking about the sins of the Sandinistas, the reception was very cool, even hostile.
>
> "My impression is that among these organizations there exists a very simple attitude, even naive . . . over what constitutes a revolutionary process. I said that the FSLN has not complied with democratic processes, and a nun said that democracy has nothing to do with a revolution."[3]

Having invested so much emotional energy in the fight against Somoza, many Americans were reluctant to accept the fact that the revolution had been hijacked by the Sandinistas, and that Nicaragua might be headed for a tyranny far worse than anything Somoza had imagined. And their reluctance was actively assisted by an extremely professional campaign mounted by the Nicaraguan government. The Ortegas became the darlings of the Hollywood jet set, flying to California for weekends at the most exclusive Beverly Hills and Bel Air mansions, charming the movie crowd and wowing the media. Unlike the old-style Latin dictators, the Sandinistas were able to provide young, handsome representatives who were not only elegant but even sexy. This was the case of Nora Astorga, the Sandinistas' UN Ambassador who died of cancer in late 1987. In one of the most widely publicized events of the revolution, Astorga had lured a Somoza National Guard official to her bedroom, where he was captured and brutally murdered by a Sandinista unit.

But above and beyond the personal charms of the leadership, the

---

3. Shirley Christian, *Revolution in the Family* (new York: Vintage, 1986), pp. 328–29.

political blinders of some Americans, and the systematic deception carried out within Nicaragua, there was another factor whose importance is more difficult to gauge, because we do not yet know the full story. That is the campaign of deception carried out within the United States.

Shortly after the revolution the *comandantes* ordered the preparation of a systematic study of American political culture, in order to pinpoint groups and organizations that could be targetted for propaganda and disinformation operations. One of those who worked on the study was Alessandro Bendana, a former Harvard University student who eventually became the official interpreter for Daniel Ortega's meetings with American officials. Another was Arturo Cruz, Jr., the son of the director of the Central Bank.

Julio Lopez, an ex-Trotskyite who became the head of the International Relations Department of the FSLN, was put in charge of creating a propaganda apparatus inside the United States, and within a year, Lopez's group was hard at work. One of the most spectacular successes of the Sandinistas' disinformation campaign was the forged "dissent paper," ostensibly about El Salvador (but actually designed to serve the purposes of the Managua regime) that circulated in Washington and overseas beginning in the autumn of 1980. The twenty-nine-page document was allegedly written by American officials from the NSC, the CIA, and the State and Defense departments. It was circulated by hand, and by mail, and reached dozens of journalists, think-tank intellectuals, and members of Congress, and was actively pushed by the left-wing Council on Hemispheric Affairs in Washington, which challenged Reagan's Latin American policies from the beginning to the end.

The central theme of the forged document was that the Carter administration had mounted a covert program to train Salvadorans in secret bases in Panama, in order to fight the guerrilla movement in their country. Moreover, other countries were participating in the program, including Argentina, Guatemala, and Chile—the usual collection of right-wing regimes. Well into the text, the Sandinistas' principal agenda emerges. The document claimed that a group of Honduran military leaders, with tacit support from the Pentagon, was encouraging Nicaraguan exiles to operate against the Sandinista regime and "believes it could win a military confrontation with Nicaragua."

The recommendations of the authors of the document were simple: no military or paramilitary action in Central America would work, only negotiations could resolve the conflicts in the region, and these should be handled by Central Americans, not *yanquis*. In a phrase, "U.S. out of Central America."

The document failed to attract any significant response in the mass media in 1980, but finally caught on in early March of the following year. In Europe, the lead was taken by Germany's most popular news-weekly, *Der Spiegel*. The main American victim of the deception was the *New York Times*'s distinguished columnist Flora Lewis, who devoted her column of March 6, 1981, to the "dissent document." She praised it in glowing terms:

> The Reagan administration would do well to listen to the paper's authors before the chance for talks is lost, and then make sure Salvador's ruling junta knows that the U.S. seeks a political and not a military settlement.

The Salvador Dissent Paper was a Nicaraguan disinformation operation. It was written by one Nicaraguan with the assistance of four Americans: a journalist from a leading national weekly magazine, a think-tank intellectual, and two graduate students in Washington. The document was distributed through various channels, the most successful of which was the Black Caucus in the Congress. It was not a professional job, for the markings on the document could easily be recognized as phoney. As the *New York Times* was forced to remark the day after Flora Lewis's article, the document carried a tag, "ESCATF/D," which supposedly stood for "El Salvador Central American Task Force." There was no such task force.

ARTURITO'S ODYSSEY

The identity of the dissent paper's principal author was revealed by none other than Nicaraguan Foreign Minister Miguel d'Escoto, who happened to be at the United Nations General Assembly meetings when the story broke. In a press conference, he was asked about the document, and he downplayed its importance, saying that the Sandinistas did not consider it a significant document, since it was written by "a Nicaraguan who is living in Washington and doing graduate studies at Johns Hopkins." It was a dead giveaway. The student in question was a scion of one of the most distinguished Nicaraguan families: Arturo Cruz, Jr., the son of the Nicaraguan Ambassador to the United States. Cruz, Sr., had fought Somoza since his graduation from the Georgetown University School of Foreign Service in 1947. That very summer he participated in one of the many failed coup attempts, and spent four months in jail. By the time the Sandinistas came to power in 1979, Cruz, although not a Sandinista, was an integral part of the Front, and took over the Central Bank. When Alfonso Robelo resigned from the junta, Cruz replaced him, and later in 1980 became ambassador to Washington, where he concentrated his energies on enlisting the support of liberal politicians like Chris Dodd. Arturo, Jr.—or Arturito, as he came to be known around Washington—was an invaluable asset in this campaign.

Arturito was the Golden Boy of the story. With the classic good looks of a Latin movie star, exceptional intellect, and spontaneous personal charm, he was an instant hit on the Washington social circuit. The nation's capital was familiar to Arturito, for he had lived there for years and attended American University and Johns Hopkins, as well as spending an interlude at the left-wing Institute of Development Studies in Sussex. His English was perfect, as was his understanding of American political culture. In his other incarnation—his Nicaraguan persona—Arturito was on first-name terms with the *comandantes,* as well as with the leaders of the opposition, from the businessmen at the Superior Council of Private Initiative (COSIP) to the journalists at *La Prensa*.

He had it all, all but sufficient age to be taken seriously by the top people. At the time of the "dissent paper" operation, he was a mere twenty-seven years old. Had he been ten years older, Arturito might well have provided the Sandinistas what they so badly needed: a charismatic leader capable of selling the revolution to a skeptical world. Instead, he went on a political odyssey from one end of the political world to the farthest pole. From an agent of the Sandinistas, he expanded his activities to collaborate with the Cubans in an effort to blunt Reagan's Central American thrust. Then, mirroring his father's political evolution, Arturito changed sides, and became a *contra*. Along the way, he befriended Oliver North, became a key American liaison to maverick *contra* leader Eden Pastora in Costa Rica, and fell in love with Fawn Hall. No Hollywood screenplay could have been more beautiful. But then, Hollywood would have provided a happy ending. Arturito's story, at least to his mid-thirties, was a failure. The romance ended, the Southern Front collapsed, Pastora left the world stage, and the *contras* came to terms with the Sandinistas.

Cruz, Sr., resigned his ambassadorship in November 1981 following the arrest of three Nicaraguan businessmen—including his close lifelong friend, Enrique Dreyfus—by the Sandinistas. He took a job as assistant treasurer of the Inter-American Development Bank, and over the course of a year, became the most eloquent critic of the Sandinista regime. Early in 1982, he was phoned by Pastora from Costa Rica, and in March Cruz flew to Cuernavaca to meet with *Cero,* and helped draft the speech with which Pastora declared war on the Sandinistas the following month. Later in the year, he wrote a devastating article in *Foreign Affairs* in which he explained what was happening to his country. As he explained to Shirley Christian, Cruz had read the memoirs of Carlos Franqui, the close collaborator of Castro who had been forced to flee Cuba as the Communist dictatorship was established in Havana. As he read, Cruz realized that the Cuban and Nicaraguan stories were frighteningly similar, "chapter by chapter."[4] He realized that he had been used by the Sandinistas to provide a moderate cover for their Leninist enterprise.

Most men in the position of the elder Cruz would have thrown themselves pell-mell into the *contra* movement, but he was a prudent person, ambivalent about the Honduran-based FDN, and did not get along well with its leaders, Adolfo Calero and Enrique Bermúdez. Calero had managed a Coca-Cola bottling plant before the revolution. Bermúdez had been a colonel in Somoza's National Guard and was a military attaché in the Nicaraguan embassy in Washington when Somoza was driven out of power. Neither was on the same cultural level as Cruz, Sr., and Bermúdez's involvement in the National Guard made him politically unattractive. So Cruz, the father, played the role of independent critic, above the fray, yet fully engaged in the political debate both in Washington and inside Nicaragua. Unwilling to become a *contra,* he launched a quixotically courageous campaign for the presidency in 1984, finally joined the leadership of the *contra* organization UNO the following year, and then gave up the fight in 1987.

By the time Cruz, Sr., left the Sandinistas, Arturito was installed in Managua as an adviser to the Sandinista Department of International Relations, specializing in tactics for dealing with the United States. It did not take long for him to see that all the talk about wanting good relations with Washington was a stalling tactic. "Whenever the Sandinistas negotiated with the United States, they were only buying time to consolidate their power."[5] And this was the least of it; Arturito was shaken by the blind obedience shown by the Sandinistas to the Soviet foreign policy line. He was uncomfortable with the endorsement of the invasion of Afghanistan, and the condemnation of the Solidarity trade union movement in Poland. And he saw old

---

4. Shirley Christian, *Revolution in the Family,* p. 323.
5. Arturo Cruz, Jr., "Notes of a Counterrevolutionary," in *Los Angeles Times Magazine,* April 19, 1987.

family friends driven into exile, locked away in prison, or simply disappear. Finally, when his father resigned, Arturito heard rumors that the *comandantes* were planning to use him to discredit his father. It was the final straw.

Arturito did not have his father's reservations about the *contras*. Like his father, Arturito came to understand the Leninist nature of the Sandinistas, and he could not stand apart from the struggle. If his father was content to provide editorial comments on Pastora's public declarations, Arturito wanted a more direct involvement. He resolved to fight for the true revolution, left Managua, and joined Pastora on the Southern Front. Commuting between Costa Rica and Washington, Arturito became a kind of cultural interpreter between two groups that barely understood each other: the American government, and Eden Pastora and his men.

THE METAMORPHOSIS OF THE CONTRA: THE PASTORA AFFAIR

Eden Pastora was the symbol of the Sandinista revolution, a military hero, a charismatic leader . . . and one of the most difficult, egotistical, and undisciplined individuals imaginable. Handsome, blessed with an instinctive flair for leadership that made him the only true *caudillo* among the Sandinista *comandantes,* Pastora was the sort of man for whom women would kill and men would die.

The event that defined Pastora as a great revolutionary took place in August 1978, when he secretly entered Managua and went to the home of a clandestine Sandinista supporter named Leonel Poveda. From Poveda's home, Pastora arranged to disguise two truckloads of men in the uniforms of the hated National Guard. The two trucks, leaving from opposite sides of Managua, arrived simultaneously at the National Palace, where the Congress was in session. With a couple of volleys, the Sandinistas seized the Palace, held more than one thousand people hostage for nearly three days, and negotiated the release of political prisoners, the payment of a substantial amount of cash, and safe passage out of the country for the guerrillas. It was the kind of action for which men are celebrated in song and story, and Eden henceforth passed into legend as *comandante Cero*—Commander Zero (every Sandinista cell identified its members by number, with zero going to the leader of the group).

After the exploit, several hundred of the Sandinistas headed for training in Cuba, while others took refuge in Panama or Venezuela.

49

Pastora went to Panama, where he established a close friendship with President Omar Torrijos, and thence to Venezuela, where he befriended President Carlos Andres Peres. Both of these leaders would later throw their support to the Sandinistas (and Torrijos would back Eden after his rupture with the Sandinistas in 1982).

Had he possessed even a modest quantum of managerial skills to go with his explosive personality, Pastora would have been irresistible. As it was, he was judged sufficiently dangerous that, in 1979, Juan Manuel Rivero, the top Cuban intelligence officer working with the Sandinistas in Costa Rica, suggested to Humberto Ortega that it would be better for everyone if it were arranged for Pastora to die in battle. For if he lived, Rivero said, Pastora would create political problems later on. This information was provided to me by Florentino Aspillaga, a former DGI officer who defected to the United States from his post in Prague, Czechoslovakia, in 1986.

Humberto told the Cubans not to worry, that Pastora was a dear personal friend and a great fighter, and that the Sandinistas knew how to handle him. In the end, both were right. After the seizure of power in Managua, a "cult of personality" grew around Pastora, But the Sandinistas were careful not to elevate him to their top ranks. Despite his nickname, he was not a true *comandante,* and he was not made a member of the Sandinista National Directorate—the politburo that actually ran the country.

They made him deputy interior minister, and he hated it. Eden was a man of action, ill-suited for a desk and a chair, no matter how well padded. When I went to Managua in the spring of 1988, several of the top Sandinistas told me that if Pastora had been named minister of defense, he would never have caused any trouble. As it was, he served a year and a half, and suddenly resigned his post on the 9th of July 1981, announcing that he was leaving in order to pursue his revolutionary vocation: "I am going to the trenches where the duty of an international combatant leads me." He returned to Costa Rica, and maintained an uncharacteristic silence for ten months, only to erupt once again on April 15, 1982, to denounce the Sandinistas, the Soviet Union, and the United States. Nicaragua, he said, was being turned into a totalitarian state, armed by the Soviet Union, and hence becoming a pawn in the East-West struggle. He revealed that he had created an anti-Sandinista movement, the Democratic Revolutionary Alliance (ARDE), which had already conducted some raids into southern Nicaragua.

He was not alone in Costa Rica. ARDE's political director was

Alfonso Robelo, formerly the head of the Nicaraguan businessmen's organization COSIP, and a leading political figure in his own right. Robelo was part of the Sandinista umbrella organization prior to the revolution, and had served in the junta after the fall of Somoza. There was also Carlos Coronel, a brilliant if enigmatic politician who had been one of the original *Terceristas,* the moderate, middle-class component of the Sandinista Front that had given a patina of respectability to the Sandinistas in the latter days of the Somoza period. Within six months others would join, including former comrades-in-arms like Leonel Poveda, the much-admired *comandante Comanche* who had been one of the leaders of the 1978 seizure of the Congressional Palace, and had been one of the key commanders of the Southern Front in the war against Somoza the following year.

With such an impressive entourage, and help from his friend Dewey Clarridge, Pastora quickly built up a fighting force of several thousand (as usual, figures vary wildly, but he probably had two thousand by the autumn of 1982, and may have reached a peak of seven thousand to eight thousand in late 1983 or early 1984), and carried out some cross-border operations from his bases inside Costa Rica. But although the Sandinistas had operated unhindered out of Costa Rica during the struggle against Somoza, within two months of his announcement, Pastora was thrown out of the country. President Luis Alberto Monge declared he would not tolerate the presence of guerrillas trying to overthrow a neighboring country. But a few months later he was back again, bigger than life, waging his endless war.

Thus began the saga of the Southern Front, a rich and melodramatic tale that awaits its historian. Whoever writes the story will need considerable gifts of wit and wisdom, for what I have been able to learn lends itself more readily to comic opera than to military history. In the first place, there was the relationship with Costa Rica. President Luis Alberto Monge hated and feared the Sandinistas, whom he properly regarded as a mortal threat to the independence and easy-going democratic institutions of his country. Costa Rica has no army, and its police force was no match for the armed might of the People's Army to the north. If Costa Rica supported the *contras,* she risked reprisals from Nicaragua. But if there were no armed threat to the Sandinistas, it was only a matter of time before Costa Rica would have to bend to the will of the *comandantes.* In the best diplomatic tradition, Costa Rica vacillated, and Pastora, Robelo, Alfonso ("El Negro") Chamorro, and the other Southern Front leaders came and went according to the political winds in San José.

Second was the Costa Rican milieu, as different from the Nicaraguan scene as San Francisco is from the Pittsburgh of the 1950s. Nicaragua is not only a poor country, but a gray one. Unless one has been to Managua, it is hard to imagine a Latin capital so utterly devoid of verve as this one. The town center was never rebuilt after the devastating earthquake of 1972, and much of the rubble, gutted buildings, and empty spaces remains to this day. The result is a city with no center, no *plazas* in which people congregate, and very little of the spontaneous vivacity for which Latin cities, from Rome to Rio, are known and loved.

Not so Costa Rica, the most prosperous country in Central America, with a capital—San José—that bursts with energy by day and carries on at a lively pace by night. The president at this time, Luis Alberto Monge, may be taken as a symbol of the place. A short, unimpressive figure, Monge was a bubbling pot of ideas, wit and *joie de vivre,* whose liberal approach to life extended to the cultivation of some of the most beautiful women in Central America. According to the apocrypha of the day, there came a moment during one of Monge's conversations with National Security Adviser Robert McFarlane at Monge's San José residence when a gorgeous woman, barely clothed in quasi-transparent garments, entered the room and sat down on Monge's lap. Not only did this bring an abrupt halt to the diplomatic proceedings, but her presence placed McFarlane—a man noted for his rigid sense of propriety—in an exceedingly unfamiliar and uncomfortable position. The woman, widely rumored to be deeply involved in spookery with Cubans and Nicaraguans, stayed long enough to demonstrate her affection for the Costa Rican leader, and then departed.

Such a place provided the perfect backdrop for Pastora's political spectacles. But it was also a country of profound corruption, where a person could not hope to exert political influence without considerable sums of money, and where the entrepreneurs of the region, from the narcotics dealers to the gunrunners, from the coffee, sugar, and cotton shippers to the bankers and nightclub owners, gathered for recreation, good food, and beautiful women. And, unfortunately for ARDE, this, too, was an appropriate backdrop for Pastora, whose revolutionary fervor was matched by an avidity for dollars and women.

Third was the relationship with the United States. From the moment of his resignation, Pastora was wooed by the CIA, for Clarridge was quick to recognize that *comandante Cero* had the potential of driving a political stake in the heart of the Sandinista regime. No other man in Nicaragua had the capacity to split the military ranks, take with him a substantial number of trained soldiers, and simultaneously lead a political insurrection. On this last point, Clarridge was certainly right, for Pastora's revolutionary credentials were impeccable. Unlike most of the *contra* leaders in the north, Pastora had not the slightest tinge of Somoza to dull his revolutionary colors, and when he branded the Sandinistas traitors to the cause of true revolution, it was political dynamite. Calero, Bermúdez, and the other leaders of the FDN were good men, but they lacked flair. No one could imagine Calero, the former manager of a Coca-Cola bottling plant, leading a triumphant procession of desperados into Managua, but Pastora was born to play that part—if only one could guarantee that he would be there that day, and could find the armed column.

The bad news was that there was an aspect of futility to this colorful character. Pastora was undisciplined to the point of near-total chaos. From the CIA officers who worked with him, to the fighters who risked their lives under his leadership, all testify to a mounting frustration with Pastora's inability to organize a coherent fighting force, design a strategy for victory, or even mount effective military operations. As time passed, he acquired a reputation as the Pink Panther of the *contra* movement: elegant, dashing, but an operational catastrophe. North once recounted to me how Pastora had set out to sabotage the telephone line that ran from Costa Rica to Managua, only to cut the wrong cable and briefly isolate parts of Honduras from international communications. Pastora's own *comandantes* in the south complained that his basic concept of the armed struggle was fatally misguided, for Pastora argued for a *guerra popolar permanente,* an ongoing insurrection based in the south along the banks of the San Juan River. This was suicidal, for their line of retreat would be blocked by the river behind them.

The upshot of it all was that while Pastora might well have been the most charismatic man in Nicaraguan politics, he lacked the discipline and tenacity to lead a successful military campaign against the most powerful military force in all Central America. Those who knew him well—from Arturito to *Comanche*—told the Americans that Pastora needed a political and psychological baby-sitter, someone to stroke his sensitive ego, speak to him of his world-historic significance, and whisper good advice in his ear. This could not be imposed upon him, for Pastora would not share power at the top of "his" ARDE (even though it was Robelo who gave some semblance of order to the organization, and, in the end, proved to be the most reliable figure in the top leadership in the south). It had to be done by guile.

53

Unfortunately for the future of the Southern Front and the Americans, there was already a supremely guileful baby-sitter on the premises: Carlos Coronel. And Coronel's credentials were ambiguous, to say the least. Coronel had been one of Pastora's key advisers during the anti-Somoza struggle and had been with Pastora throughout the fighting on the Southern Front in 1979. He had been a principal channel between Pastora, the FSLN *comandantes,* and Castro, and had tried to get Pastora named a member of the Directorate. But that was only one side of Coronel's fascinating personality, for he had also been a primary channel for the CIA to the *Terceristas*—the "moderate," non-Marxists created by the Sandinistas to give an appearance of respectability to the Front—in the prerevolutionary period, and he was very likely a CIA channel to Pastora in 1981 as well. Which side was Coronel on? Indeed, was he on any side at all? The questions needed answers, for the future of the Southern Front might well depend upon them. No one knew Pastora better than Coronel, and no one had so much influence over the mercurial *Cero*. To those—and they were numerous—who believed Pastora lacked the brains for political strategy, Coronel was the Dr. Svengali who manipulated Pastora. Time and time again, Coronel was invoked in an effort to explain the actions of the leader.

There was much in Pastora's behavior that defied explanation. Although he said he had broken with the Sandinistas, it seemed more like a trial separation than a true divorce. Early in 1982, after Pastora's original break with the regime, *Comanche* went to visit him in Mexico, and was horrified to find Pastora on the telephone, talking warmly with Jaime Wheelock, a key member of the Directorate. *Comanche*'s concerns deepened when Pastora explained his plans: he wanted Poveda to go to Guatemala to help the local guerrillas in their fight against the military dictatorship. Poveda protested, saying he had not the slightest intention of risking his life in a country he did not know, and in behalf of a group with which he was unfamiliar. He wanted to fight, yes, but for the future of his own country.

Pastora was torn between two violently conflicting emotions. On the one hand, he detested the Sandinistas, both for what they were doing to Nicaragua, and what they had done, or rather failed to do, to him. He demanded revenge, and ARDE was to be the instrument of his vengeance. On the other hand, he could not bring himself to believe that it was all over between him and the Sandinistas. For Pastora seemed to believe in his heart of hearts that the revolution was *his,* and they had somehow deprived him of his just rewards. He continued to nurture the hope that some day they—or perhaps Castro—would see the error of their ways, ask him back, and put him in charge. Meanwhile, he would fight the Sandinistas a bit, play at revolution throughout the region, see if the world at large recognized his talents, and follow where destiny led him.

At first, it led him to the CIA and Clarridge, who hope to make of Pastora the Che Guevara of the *contra* movement. Pastora got a budget—roughly $50,000 per month to start—some technical assistance, intelligence about the military situation inside Nicaragua, and considerable encouragement. At first, it was hoped that Pastora's actions would lead a substantial number of military officials to leave Nicaragua and sign up with the *contras*. These hopes were quickly dashed, in part because the Sandinistas exercised increasingly effective control over the armed forces, and in part because Pastora's luster had dimmed considerably since the glorious days of the Palace raid and the Southern Front. Furthermore, there was a question of ARDE's effectiveness; until Pastora showed he was a credible threat to the Sandinistas, recruitment—at least at the upper echelons of the armed forces—would be difficult.

But if the early hopes for a sudden rupture within the Sandinistas' ranks were quickly dashed, and although his military abilities were disappointing, Pastora proved to be a man of incalculable importance for the political side of the *contra* struggle. For he provided the *contras*—and the United States—with an unchallengeable source with which to attack the Sandinista regime. Pastora was the only credible *contra* leader with progressive credentials. The others were either tarnished by their *Somocista* past or unable to deal on the same cultural level as their foreign interlocutors. If a Calero or a Bermúdez denounced the Sandinistas, European socialists or American academics could shrug it off, at least for a while. But when Pastora accused the Ortegas of installing a Leninist dictatorship in Managua, that had to be taken seriously, from Mexico City to Madrid, and from Bonn to Harvard Yard.

Indeed, Pastora quickly became a hero to several leaders of the Socialist International. This was thoroughly understandable in cases like the Spanish, the Portuguese, and the Italian, for there was an instant affinity between Pastora and men like Felipe Gonzales, Bettino Craxi, and Mario Soares. But his charisma worked on the central and northern socialist parties as well, even the old German Social Democrat, Willy Brandt.

Pastora's international travels led to a reduction in European financial and political support for the Sandinistas, and a bit of money and moral support for himself and his men. Indeed, as late as 1986, after Pastora had left the field, the remnants of ARDE were still getting some financial support from European socialists. However, the political payoff was considerably more important, for Pastora was extremely effective in discrediting the Sandinistas among European and Latin socialists and social democrats. He apparently converted Panamanian president Omar Torrijos to his view, and when Torrijos's plane crashed on July 31, 1982, during a flight on which Pastora had been scheduled, Pastora concluded that the Sandinistas had tried to murder them both. Whether or not it was true, it made sense, because Pastora knew that he had damaged the *comandantes*. What followed made this point even more dramatically.

Immediately after the announcement of Torrijos's death, Pastora was contacted by Colonel Noriega, at the time the head of Panama's military intelligence, and the power behind Torrijos's throne. Noriega told Pastora that the former president of Venezuela, Carlos Andres Peres, had come to Panama to talk, and Noriega sent a private plane to pick up Pastora at a rural airstrip. But when Pastora arrived at the rendezvous, his host was Borge, who extended an invitation to Pastora for a vacation in Cuba. It was an offer he could not refuse, and Pastora was flown to Havana, where he was held under luxurious house arrest for several weeks, until the situation in Panama quieted down. By the time Pastora returned to Costa Rica in late August, he had drawn the obvious conclusion: it was not safe to talk too much about Torrijos.

Despite Castro's heavy-handed treatment, Pastora was fascinated by, and attracted to, the Cuban dictator. For nearly two years after his break with the Sandinistas, Pastora continued to believe that it was only a matter of time before Castro purged Arce, Borge, and the other hard-liners, and replaced them with "moderate Sandinistas." It was nonsense. Arce and Borge were two of Castro's most trusted men in Nicaragua, and he was not about to deprive himself of such exceptional talent. Nonetheless, Pastora continued to jump at the bait offered by Castro, and when a request for talks arrived from Cuba at the end of 1983, Carlos Coronel secretly went to Havana on Pastora's behalf to see if a rapprochement could be worked out between Castro and Pastora. Coronel sneaked out of Havana via Mexico, only to have the news of the mission—and its total failure—leak almost immediately.

The discovery of the secret mission to Cuba sent a shock wave through Pastora's followers, and through the CIA as well. How was it possible that Pastora's closest associate was meeting with the power behind the Sandinista throne? The CIA began to consider the possibility that Pastora might be a Soviet, Cuban, or Sandinista agent, sent to divide the *contra* movement, demoralize its followers, and trick the Americans. The case was never more than circumstantial, but many in the CIA believed it. Clarridge did not, and, like Elliott Abrams, he believed that Pastora's political importance was so great that we should support him, despite the problems he created. But Clarridge was taken off the Central America account in mid-1984, and his successors, along with Oliver North, took a far darker view of this question. As Elliott Abrams testified during the hearings:

> Basically, Colonel North and the CIA hated Pastora with great passion. They had concluded, on the basis of their dealings with him, that he was not only untrustworthy, but conceivably disloyal. And they wanted to have literally nothing to do with him.

The debate over Pastora was one of the nastiest, and most divisive, in the history of the *contra* movement, and will probably continue for years. It is complicated by the fact that while the suspicions about Pastora's loyalties are circumstantial at best, there is apparently considerable damaging information about Carlos Coronel. Most knowledgeable Americans, and those *contras* from the Southern Front with whom I spoke, are convinced that Coronel was working closely with the Nicaraguans and the Cubans. This did not prevent him from cooperating with the Americans as well, from time to time, but for those who were serious about fighting the Sandinista regime, Coronel could not be trusted. Coronel's basic loyalties, in their opinion, clearly lay with Castro and the Sandinistas.

By mid-1984 the CIA officials who worked on Central America had concluded that, whatever advantages he brought to the movement, Pastora was more trouble than he was worth. For three years, they had asked Pastora to coordinate his activities with the FDN in the north, so that the Nicaraguan people would see a unified guerrilla movement at work. He refused, claiming that Calero, Bermúdez, Bosco Matamoros and the other *contras* operating out of Honduras were too closely linked to the old Somoza crowd and to the United States. Furthermore, while Pastora constantly denounced the FDN for taking CIA money, he himself was enormously expensive. At one point, his monthly delivery from the agency ran to several hundred thousand dollars. His performance didn't seem to be worth that sum, and the agency had been told by Pastora's own courier that a percentage of that money was being deposited in Miami banks.

Pastora alway denied receiving CIA money (saying he didn't know where all the money came from, and didn't care), while condemning Calero and the FDN for receiving agency funds. This prompted Calero, a man not normally noted for grace of expression, to deliver one of the memorable one-liners of the time, remarking that Pastora got his money and supplies "from the same place we get ours—Santa Claus." It was the kind of remark that suggested a bright political future for Calero.

Finally, there was the question of control. It was obvious that while the CIA would finance Pastora, it would never be possible to "run" him. In the agency's jargon, he could not be recruited. He would not be an American agent. Such people are always viewed with suspicion by intelligence agencies. Like Ghorbanifar in the Iran initiative, Pastora had a lot to offer, but the attitude of most of the professional officers in the Operations Directorate was that if the CIA could not control him, they were opposed to working with him at all.

Men like Clarridge and, later on, Elliott Abrams, believed that the United States government should support Pastora despite his refusal to take CIA guidance. But the bureaucratic approach prevailed, and by the early spring of 1984—just about the time that the appropriated funds for the fiscal year were running out—the CIA decided to stop financing him. But, like an operatic soprano who will not die until the final coda has been played, Pastora hung on, raising funds in Europe, leading raids across the border, giving brave speeches. It was not until 1987 that he went back to the Costa Rican fishing village which he had left to fight Somoza in the 1970s, and returned to his previous career as a shark hunter on the Pacific Coast.

THE MIRAGE OF THE SOUTHERN FRONT

The Southern Front had its moments—particularly in late 1983 and early 1984—but it could not be sustained. It may well be that it was beyond the capacities of the United States and our Nicaraguan friends. First Monge, then his successor Oscar Arias, periodically expelled the *contra* leaders, only to let them reenter Costa Rica a few weeks later. This deprived the movement of continuity. The on-again-off-again approach of the Costa Rican government also made it difficult to arrange for the movement of military materiel, and on one occasion

McFarlane had to intervene personally to get the Costa Ricans to release an arms shipment that had been blocked in the harbor.

Without the full cooperation of Costa Rica, it was exceedingly difficult to keep the Southern Front well supplied. And when, in later 1984, the CIA was taken out of the game, it became virtually impossible. During the entire period of the North/Secord resupply operation, only a very few drops were made to the Southern Front. It was a long trip from Honduras, the plan for a private landing strip produced a runway that trapped Secord's aircraft in mud, and the far larger—and politically favored—FDN fought against any assistance to the difficult Pastora. The Southern Front burst into occasional activity, but it reflected the personality of its founder. Like Pastora, the Southern Front produced individual acts of great courage and even great significance, but its main value was tactical and inspirational, not strategic. ARDE was the only *contra* force to capture and hold, albeit briefly, a Nicaraguan municipality: San Juan del Norte, on April 14, 1984. But ARDE was also lightly regarded by the Sandinistas, who were able to concentrate the bulk of their forces against the FDN without fear that a major disaster would befall them in the south.

With all their problems, however, the Southern Front continued to grow, perhaps as much a tribute to the evils of the Nicaraguan regime and the recruiting skills of Pastora and Clarridge as to the talents of the ARDE fighters or those of the Americans who "advised" them. Indeed, the *contra* movement was expanding dramatically, and by mid-1983 it had the Sandinistas quite worried. The military actions of the second half of 1983 suggested that the movement was destined to expand further. At this crucial moment, the two superpowers acted to thwart the *contras:* the Soviet Union sped up its deliveries of helicopter gunships in order to provide the Sandinistas with the ultimate anti-guerrilla machine, and, at the same time, Congress moved to reduce military assistance. It was a serious blow to the resistance, and provided the Sandinistas with breathing space. It sent a message to the *contra* leaders that the United States would not be a thoroughly reliable source of support, and dragged the *contras* directly into domestic American politics.

All this happened at a moment when Pastora was taking his first tentative steps toward cooperation with the FDN, and the vision of a unified opposition force was beginning to take tangible form. Given the political obstacles within the *contra* movement, the military strength of the Sandinistas, and the intensity of the Congressional opposition, it might have failed in any event. But there were distinct chances for success as well. We shall never know what might have been, for the actions of the Congress guaranteed that the *contras* would be put on hold until the resumption of official American aid in 1986.

THE MINING OF THE HARBORS

By late 1983, the more optimistic CIA officials involved in the *contra* program were beginning to believe that the Sandinista regime was tottering, and only needed another substantial shove or two to go over the brink. The combined FDN/ARDE attack in September against Sandino International Airport in Managua and the oil terminal at Puerto Sandino had demonstrated that the *contras* could strike anywhere in the country. The economy had been severely weakened, thanks in large part to the Sandinistas' own version of economic Stalinism, and in part to the *contra* assaults against power stations and highways. This combination of economic malaise and signs of *contra* power had encouraged the domestic opposition, and the Sandinistas' response—intensified repression, censorship of *La Prensa,* and the shutdown of the Church's radio station—provoked statements of criticism even from such foreign supporters as the Dutch Labor Party.

Finally, an event of enormous psychological importance had occurred in October when American armed forces invaded the tiny island of Grenada, removed a Communist regime, and restored democracy. It was the first time that a regime recognized as a member of the world Communist movement had fallen, and this marked the end of the Brezhnev Doctrine (according to which once a country had become Communist, the process was irreversible). It also suggested that the United States was henceforth prepared to use military power to advance its objectives, and the Sandinistas were terrified. Among other things, the American troops had killed and captured several hundred Cubans, who had returned to Havana in disgrace (their leaders were sent to Angola as punishment). The same conditions that had existed in Grenada were in effect in Nicaragua as well, and the *comandantes* were convinced that within weeks, or at best months, the marines would remove them as well. Clarridge knew all this, and hastened to push his advantage.

At this very moment, however, Congress was moving to slash the funding for the *contras*. In October, it was decided to limit funding to $24 million for fiscal year 1984, and while it was possible for the CIA to use some other funds in its "reserve," and other accounts, it was evident to the administration that the clock was ticking on the Nicaraguan resistance. In the words of the Minority Report, "the *contras* might well be cut off completely if there was a slight change in the climate of opinion. The *contras* knew it; the Sandinistas knew it; and the U.S. Government knew it." Casey concluded that if it were possible to intensify the pressure on the Sandinistas in a short period, that should be done.

Realizing that the *contras* were in no position for a decisive military thrust (only Pastora spoke of a conventional military assault against the Sandinista army), Clarridge and his colleagues searched for a way to interrupt the shipping into Nicaragua's major harbors. If there were a state of war, this could be achieved by traditional military means, but under the undeclared and unconventional war going on, this was impossible. Among other problems, many of the ships in Corinto and Puerto Sandino belonged to our European allies, and we did not wish to do anything that would damage those ships or, worst of all, cause loss of allied life. Was there some halfway step that would stop the ships from sailing to Nicaragua without life-threatening acts of violence?

If one could find a way to induce the major international insurance companies (almost always Lloyd's of London) to withdraw their coverage of ships headed for Nicaragua, very few shipping companies would be willing to run the risk of entering Nicaraguan waters. But the only obvious way to frighten Lloyd's was to show that the risk in Nicaraguan harbors was unacceptably high, and that seemed to require acts of violence . . . which the United States could not commit.

If no act of genuine violence could be committed, what about a symbolic one? According to CIA experts, there were some mines available (so-called firecracker mines) that would make a very loud noise, frighten ships' crews half out of their minds, but not cause any serious damage, and certainly not kill anyone. Perhaps this was the answer. It was brought to Casey, who loved it. He chuckled at the thought of the dramatic explosions in the Sandinistas' ports, and the economic panic it would produce in London, Rotterdam, and Hamburg. He instructed Clarridge and the others to brief Congress, and this was done on several occasions, to both Oversight committees, and to the Senate Armed Services Committee.[6] In one of these hearings

6. According to a CIA press release, there were at least eleven separate briefings on this subject. See Henry F. Hyde, "Can Congress Keep a Secret?" in *National Review*, August 24, 1984.

61

a CIA spokesman expressed some reservations about the program. "You know," he said, "we have often had bad luck with this sort of thing. As often as not, when we put mines in harbors, the next ship to sail in has hundreds of vacationing nuns and schoolchildren on it." There was no objection from any of the committee members,[7] and the program went ahead.

The mining program was every bit as effective as its sponsors had hoped. Insurance was cancelled, ships ceased to sail into Nicaraguan harbors, and the Sandinistas faced economic catastrophe. While the *comandantes* launched their usual accusation that the CIA was at the root of all their troubles, little credence was given to their claims in the American media until April 5, 1984, when Senator Barry Goldwater, who had either forgotten or had failed to pay attention to the briefing he had received on the subject,[8] grabbed a classified memorandum on the mining operation, raced to the Senate floor, and began to read the secret information. The next morning, the *Wall Street Journal* had a report on the subject, and within a few days the CIA's role in organizing the mining was on all the front pages. It was a major political crisis, and several Senators, quick to recognize the dangers of being associated with the operation, denied any knowledge of these actions.

The most visible of the retreating Senators were Goldwater and Moynihan, each vigorously denying they had been briefed on the matter. Goldwater was so incensed he wrote a celebrated "I'm pissed off" letter to Casey, demanding an explanation for having kept Congress in the dark, and Moynihan resigned his position as the vice-chairman of the committee. Moynihan's resignation was particularly bizarre, since, as Congressman Henry Hyde noted, "Moynihan had reportedly requested a legal opinion from the State Department on the mining question a week before the Senate vote on assistance to the Nicaraguan resistance forces."[9] And Senator Leahy observed wryly that several members of the Senate

7. Not only were the committees briefed, but there had been private briefings as well. Senator Leahy of the Senate Select Committee on Intelligence had been out of town for his father's funeral, and had received a detailed briefing on the mining upon his return, well before the public disclosure of the CIA's role.

8. Bob Woodward suggests that Goldwater may have been "medicated" with cocktails at the time of the briefing. Goldwater was still in pain from some surgery, and Woodward may be right. But if so, he adopted a partisan position, for no such suggestion was offered to explain Senator Daniel Patrick Moynihan's selective memory on the subject. See Bob Woodward, *Veil* (New York: Simon and Schuster, 1987), 319 ff. for Woodward's version of these events.

9. Hyde, "Can Congress Keep a Secret?" p. 46.

voted one way the week before (the revelations) and a different way the following week who knew about the mining in both instances and I think were influenced by public opinion, and I think that's wrong and that is a lousy job of legislative action.[10]

Leahy was right—he had received a private briefing, having been out of town for his father's funeral during the committee session—but the Senate insisted on its prerogative to change the historical record as it suited Senators' political purposes. On April 26, Casey appeared in closed session before the Senate Select Committee, in one of those Washington scenes right out of Orwell. Although he firmly believed that the CIA had briefed the Senators (and other congressional committees), and although anyone reading the newspaper coverage of the mining incident would conclude that even the cynical Washington journalists recognized that the information had been provided, Casey had come to apologize. The Senators' claim that they had not been briefed was thereby given an official stamp of approval, and Senator "Jake" Garn of Utah, a devout Mormon, was upset by the hypocrisy of his colleagues. When Casey began his apology, Garn said, "You shouldn't be here to apologize to us. We should be apologizing to you for pretending we weren't briefed." Nonetheless, Casey continued, and went through his ritual apology.

Afterward, when Casey had gone and a handful of Senators remained in the room to discuss what had happened, Garn erupted. "You're all a bunch of assholes!" he declared. Moynihan glared at him. "Smile when you call me an asshole," he barked at Garn. The Utah Senator gave his New York colleague a big grin, and, between clenched teeth, replied, "O.K., asshole."[11]

The story made its way onto the front pages of the Salt Lake City newspapers on a Sunday when the Mormon elders were gathered for a meeting. Garn expected trouble, for Mormons are enjoined from using words of the sort he had directed at his Senate colleagues. And, sure enough, one of the elders came up to Garn that day, and mildly said, "I read about your remarks in the newspaper, Jake." Garn winced, but admitted having pronounced the offending words. "Well," continued the Mormon elder, "I don't care for the language. But I certainly share the sentiments." Garn received lots of mail about the incident, and while some complained about his choice of words, the overwhelming majority of his correspondents praised his stand.

10. Hyde, "Can Congress Keep a Secret?" p. 46.
11. There is a slightly different account of the incident in Woodward, *Veil*, pp. 337–38.

The mining incident galvanized the anti-*contra* members of Congress, and led directly to the third Boland amendment (October 1984),[12] which declared it illegal for the CIA "or any other agency or entity of the United States involved in intelligence activities" to send appropriated funds to the *contras*. Some have subsequently argued that this veto extended to the NSC staff, and even to the president himself, but the legislative history of the Boland amendments suggests the opposite. Two points show why:

> • Boland IV (August 1985) authorized $27 million in humanitarian aid for the *contras,* permitting the president to decide which agency should administer it, but the president was "precluded from using an intelligence agency." Nonetheless, the National Security Council was *required* "to monitor implementation of the proposal." Thus, the very wording of the Boland amendment showed that the NSC was not lumped in with the "intelligence agencies."
>
> • If Congress wanted to ensure that no agency of the government could spend any money on the *contras,* it had only to say so. There is a time-honored way to do such a thing, which is to use the ritual text, "Notwithstanding any other provision of law, no funds may be appropriated under this or any other act for the purpose of . . ."[13]

Further, there were several amendments introduced each time Boland came up for a vote. Some of these would have explicitly cut off *all* activities on behalf of the *contras* from any governmental agency. These amendments were always voted down. The conclusion is inescapable: Congress knew what it was doing, and did not wish to totally cut off the *contras*. The attitude of the congressional Democrats is documented by one of the best of all possible sources: the Majority Report of the Iran-Contra committees.

> Congress was unwilling to bear responsibility for the loss of Central America to communist military and political forces. So Congress compromised, providing in 1985 humanitarian aid to the Contras.[14]

12. There is a lot of confusion about Boland amendments. I have used Gordon Crovitz's decipherment. Boland I was 1982–83, and prohibited spending money for the overthrow of the Sandinista government. Boland II authorized $24 million in military assistance to the *contras* for 1983–84. Boland III (1984–85) was the most famous, prohibiting the CIA, the Pentagon "or any other agency or entity of the United States involved in intelligence activities" from spending money to help the *contras*. Boland IV (August 1985 to March 1986) gave $27 million in humanitarian aid.

13. These two examples are taken from the excellent article by G. Gordon Crovitz, "Crime, the Constitution, and the Iran-Contra Affair," in *Commentary,* October 1987.

14. *Report of the Congressional Committees Investigating the Iran-Contra Affair,* Majority Report, p. 15.

Bolands III and IV had two major effects. First, they took the CIA out of the *contra* game. However, there was a small window in Boland IV through which the agency was permitted to climb back in. Under its provisions, the CIA could share information with the *contras,* and the agency—with explicit approval from the congressional Oversight committees—interpreted that to mean they could give all manner of military intelligence. In practice, that meant helping with flights of military materiel and medical and other nonlethal supplies from Honduras to drop sites inside both Nicaragua and Costa Rica. This assistance was provided to the *contras* while Secord and his colleagues were running the resupply operation in 1985 and 1986.

Second, Bolands III and IV drastically reduced the amount of money available for the resistance movement, and it was generally believed this would mean the death knell for the *contras,* for the resistance budget was by now running along at between one milion and two million dollars per month. Where could such funds come from, once the Congress had prevented Uncle Sam from providing them? And, equally important, with neither the Pentagon nor the CIA permitted to train or advise the *contras,* how could they be expected to hold their own against a Sandinista army that was armed by the Russians and trained by the Cubans, the Bulgarians, the East Germans, and the rest of the bloc?

3. The Birth
of Project Democracy

There were at least three main battlefields for the Central American war: Nicaragua itself, the halls of Congress, and the corridors of the executive branch. This last was at once the bloodiest and the least noted, for both administration supporters and opponents imagined a bloodthirsty unanimity of purpose that never existed. If it had, the president's aggressive rhetoric would have been matched by requests for equally impressive action; as it was, the intensity of the rhetoric was considerably greater than the size of the aid requests, and the president was invariably prepared to compromise with the congressional critics. The last time the White House stood its ground was in 1983, when an early version of the most restrictive Boland amendment was introduced into the Continuing Resolution. If passed, it would have prohibited the administration from providing assistance to the *contras*. Sen. Ted Stevens, the Republican floor leader, asked Judge Clark what he should do about the amendment, and Clark told him that if it was not removed, Stevens should kill the entire bill. Reagan would not sign it. Stevens conveyed the message, and the amendment was defeated, but that was the last time the White House took such a stand.

The State Department was supposed to take the lead on foreign policy, but the activists in the NSC, the CIA, and the Pentagon felt that Tom Enders was overly enchanted with the second (diplomatic) element of his two-track policy. It was hard for them to judge Enders's real intentions, because so much of what he did was kept from the others. From time to time he did something totally unexpected. For example, the celebrated August 1981 trip to Managua, when Enders offered the Sandinistas a deal he thought they would not refuse, had not been cleared through the White House. The pattern held throughout 1982, as meetings of Enders's "core group" (Enders, Clarridge, Gorman, and their top aides) were kept secret from the rest of the bureaucracy, and nobody took notes.

This offended Judge Clark, and that was a political liability it was hard to pay off. Clark was the James Stewart of the Reagan administration: tall, lanky, a man of few words and little visible emotion, but whose demeanor bespoke an inner calm and an unyielding loyalty to his leader. Clark was not an intellectual, and didn't have the international experience a national security adviser should, but he had qualities that, in retrospect, made him the best of Reagan's national security advisers. Above all, he had good character. He was not afraid to make a decision, and, once he felt that the president had defined his stance on an issue, was not the least bit reluctant to crack the whip on cabinet members if he felt they were dragging their feet. Clark was a hard worker, studied problems carefully, listened far more than he spoke, and developed a good "feel" for several of the most important issues. One of these was Central America. Those people who used to make fun of Clark's amateurishness in foreign policy often forgot that while Europe was a distant place for the judge, Mexico was next door, and Clark—like the president—had spent time there, believed in the importance of good relations with our southern neighbors, and felt comfortable with Latinos. It was only natural that the judge would choose Central America as one of those issues in which he was going to play a major role. And he didn't much like it when Tom Enders kept his cards so close to his chest that not even the president and his national security adviser knew what was going on.

A person like Enders, both taller and smarter than most of the people around him, and not ashamed to point it out, automatically makes enemies, and he added another quality that did not endear him to his colleagues. He had a tendency to pursue his own sense of what was best, even when some of his superiors felt that he ought to be doing something rather different. Several of his peers maintain that Enders simply ignored a series of policy decisions, even when they had been incorporated in NSDDs (National Security Decision Documents). In 1981 and 1982, the president had instructed State to prepare a variety of economic measures against Nicaragua. Details are hard to come by, but they are known to have included various sanctions against the import of Nicaraguan cotton, sugar, and coffee, and other similar steps. Enders didn't think much of them, and they vanished into the black hole of the State Department bureaucracy. Nothing happened.

At the beginning of February 1983 the NSC staff, working with Pentagon and CIA analysts, had prepared its latest White Paper on Central America and passed it to the State Department. It took nearly four months for the department to release it, even though the debate over *contra* aid was raging in Congress. This was taken as further evidence of Enders's unwillingness to fight the good fight over Central America, and the activists complained to Clark that Enders was not carrying out the president's policy. This was a bit unfair, since Enders was behaving as White House Chief of Staff Jim Baker (and Nancy Reagan, supported as always by Michael Deaver) preferred. Baker and Deaver even fought against proposals to have the president launch a vigorous public campaign in 1982, arguing that it was best for him to stay out of it and try to resolve the disagreements with congressional leaders behind the scenes. But the president disagreed, and said he wanted to speak out. Baker and Deaver gracefully shifted gears and tried to get as low-key a text as they could.

It was Judge Clark who forced the issue, and during his term as national security adviser he accomplished a minor miracle by getting the president actively involved in the formulation of foreign policy. Only Clark, with his intuitive understanding of how to work with Ronald Reagan, could have managed this. None of his successors found the secret method. By early 1983, there was a confrontation between Enders and Clark at a National Security Planning Group meeting in the White House when the judge went down a list of seven or eight steps that he had expected Enders to take, none of which had been carried out. Shultz was astonished, and promised to attend to the problem.

It was the beginning of the end for Enders, but his final demise was prompted more by his personality and bureaucratic style than by policy disagreements *per se*. On February 9th, UN Ambassador Jeane Kirkpatrick was sent on a fact-finding trip to the region, visiting Salvador, Panama, Honduras, and Venezuela over a ten-day period. She returned with the conviction that the Sandinistas were a threat to democracy throughout the region, and that a new "Marshall Plan" for Central America might be called for. Henceforth, she would be a major player in the Central American debate, and she became one of Clark's closest allies. She reinforced Clark's conviction that the administration was way behind the power curve on Central America, that dramatic steps might be necessary in the near future, and that if the president wanted a vigorous program, he would have to educate the American public on the nature of the problem. She also brought back personal messages for the president from several of the diplomats and chiefs of state with whom she had spoken, asking or implying that Enders should be removed. He had, probably unknowingly, offended their sense of dignity, and they did not want to deal with him any longer.

Clark got the message. In late May, Enders was fired (in what would become a regular ritual, he learned of his fate from a colleague at the department, who had heard the news on the radio while Enders was being driven back from a White House meeting), and replaced by a political appointee, Langhorne (Tony) Motley, hitherto the ambassador to Brazil. In July, the president announced the creation of the Kissinger Commission on Central America, a group of prestigious national leaders (including leading Democrats like Robert Srauss and AFL-CIO head Lane Kirkland) who would, it was hoped, be able to establish the importance of Central America to the satisfaction of the media and the public.

As the Kissinger Commission was coming into existence, Clark created an Office of Public Diplomacy in the State Department.[1] While housed in State, the Office was viewed as part of the NSC system, with direct access to the White House, and was supposed to have more clout than just another bureau in Foggy Bottom.

The upshot of it all was that Clark was taking charge, a quite unexpected (and from Shultz's standpoint, quite unwanted) development. Clark had had it with the State Department, and while it was all to the good that Enders was leaving, Clark did not intend to let the State Department gain a new stranglehold on Central American policy, even though Shultz immediately tried to do just that. The little-publicized conflict between the two is documented in a classic exchange of memoranda around the time of Enders's departure.

Just two days before Enders's firing was made public, Shultz sent a memo to the president on Managing Our Central America Strategy. After running through the main elements of the program (protect Salvadoran democracy, win the public debate within the United States, push reforms in Salvador, "must not sell out the Nicaraguan patriots," push negotiations within both Salvador and Nicaragua), Shultz laid out his management plan:

---

1. This later attracted the suspicions of House investigators. For a more detailed discussion, see chapter 7.

We will set up a structure so that I can be your sole delegate with regard to carrying out your policies.

. . . there will be an interagency committee, but it will be a tool of management and not a decision-making body. I shall resolve any issues and report to you.

Meanwhile, I shall keep you and Bill Clark and others in the White House fully informed.

The president's reply (drafted by Constantine Menges and others at the NSC, and forwarded by Clark for the president's signature) was a rebuke to the Secretary of State:

I have studied your thoughtful memorandum . . . NSDD-2 provides that the policy process will function through the IG, SIG, NSC framework. . . . It provides that if the agencies agree at the IG level then the issue need not be elevated further, but that if there is disagreement, then it is raised to the SIG and if necessary through the NSC to me.

. . . Success in Central America will require the cooperative effort of several Departments and agencies. No single agency can do it alone nor should it.[2]

It was an assertion of NSC authority over the State Department, and served notice that Clark would not tolerate a replay of the Enders methods. He wanted policy to emerge from the interplay between the various agencies, to be approved and codified by the president, and coordinated and managed from the NSC. To this end, a Caribbean Basin Initiative Steering Group was created, and eventually became a principal forum for serious discussions of Central American matters.

It was a good try, probably the best that could have been made, but it could not succeed with the cast of characters in the Reagan administration. Even under the best circumstances, with a fully engaged president, a White House staff that defers to the foreign policy experts, and cabinet members that strain to work together, the American system of government is a ponderous one. But none of these potentially helpful conditions existed in 1983.

To begin with, there was the personal conflict between Shultz and Weinberger, a rivalry so intense that some government officials wondered openly how Bechtel Corporation had survived the presence of the two men at the same time. Added to the built-in rivalry between

2. The two documents have been recently declassified. I am indebted to Dr. Constantine Menges for showing them to me. For those unfamiliar with the acronyms, IG and SIG stand for "Interagency Group" and "Senior Interagency Group."

State and Defense, the personal antipathy between the two secretaries encouraged each to seek his own channel to the president, in an attempt to get Reagan to approve something before the other cabinet secretary could find out, and oppose it.

The primary practitioner of this bureaucratic end-run around established procedures was Secretary of State George Shultz, and in his defense it must be said that it seems to go with the job. Certainly Haig chafed at the necessity of having to convince Weinberger of the wisdom of Haig's (and the State Department's) view of the world, and the conflicts between Vance and Brzezinski, and Kissinger and Schlesinger, are well known. Some of this derives form the great self-confidence of the personalities involved, and some of it comes from the nature of the Department of State. The best characterization of the department comes, oddly enough, from Great Britain, in a television series entitled "Yes, Minister" (and its sequel, "Yes, Prime Minister"). There one sees a foreign minister and a prime minister trying to make foreign policy, only to discover that the Foreign Office insists on its *own* policy. And the civil servants at the Foreign Office have a seemingly bottomless bag of tricks that they can play in order to stymie any policy initiative with which they do not agree.

The American Foreign Service has many of these characteristics, and one of the great strengths of the Foreign Service professionals is their ability to gradually assert their own views against those of the political appointees who enter the building with each new administration. Having coopted the new arrivals, the department then applies the same methods to the White House. The Central American issue gives us a textbook example. Enders undoubtedly believed in the importance of the "military track" in Nicaragua, but as time passed one heard less and less of this, and heard and saw almost exclusively signs of diplomatic activity, some of it quite worrisome to those who wanted the issues clearly defined. For if we were to be constantly engaged in negotiations with the Sandinistas, it would be difficult to justify the "secret war." This point was made by several administration officials, most notably Kirkpatrick, who argued that we should break diplomatic relations with Nicaragua. This would both clarify our attitude toward the Sandinistas, and make it easier to discuss such measures as economic embargo and aid to the *contras*.

But the State Department, almost to a man, was horrified at this proposal, as it is horrified at the suggestion that our diplomatic presence be reduced anywhere on earth (that, by the way, is why so many of our officials remained in Beirut in the early 1980s, where they served as targets for terrorist attacks). It was not until 1985 that we declared an economic embargo against Nicaragua, even though it was clearly a logical step as early as 1981.

So Enders was purged and replaced by Motley, a gregarious, feisty man with a flair for dashing clothes, a quick wit and a very keen sense of gamesmanship. One could imagine Motley a winner in a cutthroat poker game, or even a successful prizefighter. Unlike many in Washington, he had few intellectual pretensions, did not use long words, and gave the impression of a straight-talking, no-nonsense, highly efficient manager. He viewed the Central American question in simple, unemotional terms. The *contras* had to be supported, but there was no confidence that they would overthrow the Sandinistas (and, given the political realities of Washington, no effort to achieve that). We didn't like the Nicaraguan regime, but we were going to have to live with it. The point was to bring them under control. In State Department language, we had to "make the situation manageable."

He liked Clarridge, and supported the mining of the harbors. When the scandal erupted, he was typically unapologetic, once commenting to a congressional committee that "more people died at Chappaquiddick than at Puerto Corinto." He was bluntly unromantic about the *contras,* and when the money began to run out in the spring of 1984, he remarked that "since they were born on the tit it was hard to get them off the tit."

So he had a job to do, and he didn't waste much time on deep thoughts or diplomatic niceties. He viewed people like Kirkpatrick and Kissinger as "kibbitzers," and he attempted to "clear the decks" of such irritants as quickly as he could. He also gave short shrift to one of Clark's inventions, former Florida Senator Richard Stone, who had been appointed as a special negotiator for Central America. Motley and Stone didn't like each other, for Motley felt Stone was yet another nuisance that didn't belong, while Stone viewed Motley as a turf-crazy bureaucrat who wasn't paying enough attention to the president's wishes. There was no contest, for Motley had the killer instincts of a street fighter, and Stone acted as if he were entitled to the deference due to a former member of the world's greatest deliberative body. Motley made mincemeat out of Stone. There came a day when Motley flew off to Managua to talk to Daniel Ortega, and during the course of the conversation he explained to the *comandante* that if Nicaragua expected a working relationship with the government of the United States, it would have to be worked out through the Department of State. Stone finally saw the futility of it all, and resigned.

Motley fully agreed with Shultz that the State Department should run the policy, and the others should do whatever State thought necessary for successful implementation. Above all, he and the secretary wanted to make sure that nobody, not even the president, could do anything without their knowing about it. In a desperate effort to insure total control over the ambassadors in the field, Motley had Shultz add a carefully worded paragraph to the standard letter from the secretary of state to new ambassadors. This bit of language emerged during the testimony of Elliott Abrams in June 1987, under questioning from Arthur Liman's deputy, Mark Belnick:

BELNICK: At the end of that letter (Shultz to Tambs) the secretary states . . . "I know that in the course of your duties you will have contact with many officials on a variety of matters and you will receive solicited and unsolicited advice and counsel on actions you should take. I want to emphasize that the line of authority runs from the president through me to Assistant Secretary Abrams."

Sir, was that your understanding as well of the line of authority?
ABRAMS: That is right. I should state that is known as the Motley clause. Assistant Motley, Assistant Secretary, had trouble on at least one occasion with ambassadors reporting to the White House. And he had adopted the practice of asking the secretary to put that clause in letters of instructions to ambassadors in the Latin America/Caribbean region to make sure they undersood exactly how they were to report.[3]

All of this was disturbingly reminiscent of Enders. It was also fatuous, for ambassadors are the president's representatives to foreign governments, not the State Department's. Every modern president has established back channels to certain ambassadors, keeping the State Department in the dark. The same would happen to Shultz in 1986, when our man in Beirut, Ambassador John Kelly, worked with Poindexter and North on the hostage question. Shultz knew nothing. And, even without being able to document it, you may be sure that it happened with other ambassadors as well.

Shultz's efforts to make sure nothing happened outside his turf (efforts that were, after all, the same as Haig had made at the beginning of the administration, and for which he had been roundly denounced) were what the Foreign Service wanted, but they were not the best way to solve the problem. By insisting that he run everything, Shultz

3. Abrams, unpublished testimony before the joint meeting of the Senate and House Select Committees investigating the Iran-Contra affair, June 2, 1987, morning session, pp. 45–46.

guaranteed that the White House would cut him out of the action on some sensitive undertakings.

Of course, the department played tit-for-tat, and Motley took to arranging trips without informing the White House. Once, as the plane lifted off from Andrews Air Force Base just outside Washington, his staff cheered at the realization that the NSC had been informed of the trip (to Managua, among other places) too late for Menges to make the flight. Shultz was a full participant in these little games, and once made an unscheduled side trip to Managua at the very last minute, again informing the White House too late for anything to be done to stop it.

Clark, Kirkpatrick, and Casey wanted pressure, pressure, and more pressure on the Sandinistas, so that the *comandantes* would either fall or sue for peace on American terms. Shultz and Motley instead fought for the State Department view that, whatever the differences between the United States and Nicaragua, they would ultimately be resolved through the diplomatic process. Thus, the centerpiece of American policy had to be negotiations, negotiations, and more negotiations. It was the old "two track" policy all over again, with an even more explicit tilt toward negotiations, and a lack of visible confidence in the long-term possibilities of the *contras*.

Clark was probably the only person in Washington who could have kept Ronald Reagan firmly in the foreign policy saddle, and found a way to get the old man to ride herd on Shultz, Motley, and the department. But the balance of power was tilted against the national security adviser. Arrayed against him was not only the secretary of state, but the unbeatable trinity of Baker, Deaver, and Nancy Reagan.

The judge had come to Washington at the beginning of Reagan's presidency with a firm understanding that he would stay for two years, and then go back to his California ranch. After a year at State, and a year as national security adviser, Clark gave Reagan a letter of resignation at the end of 1982, in keeping with their agreement. The president asked him to stay on, and told Clark with a grin that "this is the first resignation I haven't accepted." But the judge hated the continual infighting within the bureaucracy, and by the fall of 1983 found himself physically and emotionally exhausted, a victim of "Washington burnout." On a Friday afternoon in mid-September, he asked the president to let him leave the NSC, but noted in passing that Secretary of the Interior Jim Watt was clearly destined to leave. If the president thought it useful, Clark said, he would be willing to take Watt's job for a while. Over the weekend, Reagan called from

Camp David and told Clark, "I know you want to go back to your California ranch, but that Interior Job is really the biggest ranch in the country. I'd like you to go to that ranch instead."

Shortly after being named interior secretary, but still acting as national security adviser, Clark went up to the Oval Office one day to accompany the president to a meeting in the Situation Room. While riding the small elevator down to the ground floor of the West Wing, Reagan told Clark that he intended to make an announcement later that day: Jim Baker was going to be the new National Security Adviser, and Dick Darman, Baker's assistant in the White House, would become the number two man at the NSC. It was all set, the president said, and even the press releases were printed and ready to be handed out later that day.

Clark was dumbfounded, and, with only seconds before the elevator door opened, pleaded with the president to hold off on any public announcement before Clark had had a chance to discuss it with him.

After the meeting, Clark invited the president to the national security adviser's office on the ground floor of the West Wing, and implored him not to put Baker in a position for which he had no background, especially since Baker's political views were at odds with those of Clark, Casey, Kirkpatrick, Meese, and the basic Reagan constituency on Capitol Hill. Casey, Meese, and Weinberger weighed in, and the Baker and Darman nominations were buried. Casey proposed Kirkpatrick as Clark's replacement, but Shultz vetoed it. Without much time to organize a campaign for someone outside the immediate circle around the president, Clark, Casey, and Meese (with the approval of Weinberger and Shultz) proposed McFarlane, and the president accepted it.

McFarlane knew how his selection had been made and realized that he had been a compromise candidate. He also recognized that Baker's frustration would almost certainly lead Baker to search for ways to thwart McFarlane, and to enhance the intensity of their disagreements on strategic issues (McFarlane's instincts were distinctly hawkish, while Baker was one of the most dovish of the White House advisers).

There was also the question of what the president wanted. Casey, Kirkpatrick, and the other activists were frankly baffled at Reagan's behavior. How could it be, they wondered, that the old man seemed equally happy with quite active engagement in the policy process (as when Clark lit a fire under him on the *contra* issue), or with the more common good-natured detachment he practiced on other occasions? He clearly cared about the outcome of foreign policy, but did not seem to care much about how decisions were made and whether his instructions were carried out. The only pattern that they could discern was that, so long as Clark was there, the president was actively involved. Once Clark left, there were the good days and the bad days. Was it the phase of the moon? The aging process? They did not know. And neither did McFarlane.

While McFarlane knew the system cold, he could not possibly play the sort of aggressive role that Clark had. The most that could have been expected of him was to keep the Central American policy on track, with all of its problems. But history played a joke on Bud McFarlane. Instead of coolly managing and coordinating policy, he would soon find himself having to improvise under the most trying circumstances, trying to find a way to sustain the *contra* war without the CIA, without congressional funding, and without the logistical resources of the Department of Defense. This burden was thrust upon him by the Congress, and by the president's now deep-seated conviction that the *contras* must not perish. As the vote for Boland II approached, the president confided in his advisers that he was deeply disturbed. Was there nothing to be done? He would keep going back to Congress for *contra* funding, but in the meantime, he asked McFarlane to find a way to keep the *contras* alive, "body and soul."

It was at this moment that McFarlane turned to Lieutenant Colonel North for help.

The North Phenomenon

Elias Canetti once wrote that the greatest feeling of power a man can experience is to survive when others are dying all around him, and North had had that aphrodisiacal experience twice already in his short lifetime: first in Vietnam, then in the White House. And he sought out that feeling, like a moth fluttering toward a flame, in Central America, where he had become the supreme commander of the *contra* forces fighting against the government of Nicaragua.

There are two kinds of ambitious people: those who are driven by a need for personal aggrandizement, and those who strive to fulfill a mission or ideal. North's ambition was of the latter sort. As Robert Timberg has written,[4]

> Ollie has been called a zealot, and I think that's true. But he was not, in the final analysis, an ideological zealot; he was a zealot about the mission, whatever it was.

4. Robert Timberg, "The Private War of Ollie and Jim," in *Esquire*, March 1988, p. 155.

By January 1986 North had survived three national security advisers (Allen, Clark, and McFarlane) and two assistant secretaries of state for Latin American affairs (Enders and Motley). From his modest post as deputy director of political-military affairs at the NSC he had amassed unprecedented power, and an independent political base. He was a masterful bureaucratic warrior, skilled in the use of back channels and an extended network of friends throughout the government, and quite ruthless in using gossip and even deceit in defeating his political opponents. North regularly received, and brilliantly used, some of the most sensitive intelligence within the government, whether signals intelligence from the National Security Agency, raw intelligence reports from CIA agents in the field, or stories whispered in the corridors of the Old Executive Office Building. Above all, he had mastered the technique of letting it be known that he was beloved of the president himself, and there were few who could gainsay him.

Not least of the sources of his growing strength within the goverment were his close ties to McFarlane, which the national security adviser himself publicly compared to a father-son relationship. Aside from Don Fortier and Poindexter, North was one of very few senior staff officials at the NSC who could see McFarlane any time he thought it necessary, and the mutual affection of the two men for each other was palpable to anyone who saw them working together. It was therefore no surprise that when, in the spring of 1985, North came under criticism from Congress for his Central American activities, McFarlane responded with a rare declaration of personal accountability. Whatever North had done, McFarlane said, he had done under instructions from the national security adviser. And if anyone had any questions, McFarlane said, they should address them to him. It was difficult for anyone to remember the last time any American official had so forthrightly assumed responsibility for the behavior of a subordinate, and McFarlane's declaration was a tribute both to his own sense of honor and his strong personal feelings for North. The lesson was appreciated by Washington insiders: North had the personal protection of the security adviser and was not a man to be trifled with. To challenge North was to challenge McFarlane.

North thus became a formidable personage, and the combination of McFarlane's support, and his own institutional skills and personal charm and charisma, made him a force to be reckoned with. The only question was how far he could go.

The fire in North's belly was fueled by the Central American operation—Project Democracy, as North referred to it. Like everything else he did, North threw himself passionately into organizing help for the *contras* . . . and organizing the *contras* as well. It was the sort of mission that North loved, a chance to fight Communists in Central America, a return to the battlefield, and a chance to avenge the defeat in Vietnam. Just as he had heroically led a platoon into battle in Southeast Asia, he now threw himself into the war for Nicaragua. In Vietnam, North had been in situations where canteens, boots, and ponchos had to be taken from the bodies of his dead marines, in order that the living could continue to fight effectively. As a fellow platoon commander from the Vietnam days, Don Moore, said,

> When you're talking about Ollie North and the *contras,* you're talking about Ollie North and Mutter's Ridge. He knew what it was like not to have beans, boots, Band-Aids, and bullets.[5]

Believing that the president had personally given instructions to save the *contras,* North's friends outside the government mobilized hundreds of conservative loyalists around the country to organize fund-raising events. At the beginning, North remained in the background, but as time passed, he found that his speeches were more effective than those of his associates, and he began "going public," always speaking in the president's name, always stressing the supercharged nature of the conflict in Central America and the potentially mortal danger to the United States if the Sandinistas were permitted to win. At the same time, he repeatedly went to Honduras, sometimes with the CIA men in charge of the operation, later on when the various Boland amendments took the agency out of it, by himself. He returned with renewed fervor, showed everyone interested dramatic photographs of *contra* children, military operations, and training, and the emerging leadership of the movement, and redoubled his efforts on their behalf.

His methods were the same in every aspect of his life: get as close to the edge as possible and run the greatest risk, so that the thrill of survival would be as intense as can be. I sometimes felt that North wanted to die in the course of Project Democracy, for even before he got involved in the Iran project, his work for the *contras* was all-consuming. He virtually abandoned his family, often sleeping a couple of hours on the couch in his Old Executive Office Building office, and there were many occasions when he did not sleep at all. He found that it was possible to take a late-night flight to Miami, meet with *contra*

5. The quotation comes from Timberg, "The Private War of Ollie and Jim."

leaders and/or supporters in the early hours of the morning, and catch the first flight to Washington, in order to be at his desk by the time most people were arriving at work after a night's sleep.

North's total immersion in his work made it impossible for him to have anything approaching a normal family life, and other men in such circumstances often seek some kind of relief from the tensions of their jobs in sex, drugs, or alcohol. But none of these tempted North. It was inevitable that rumors would circulate suggesting a romantic liaison between North and his gorgeous secretary, Fawn Hall, but anyone who knew them realized that such a relationship was unthinkable. North's fulfillment came from his work. He did not need, or seek, wine, women, or other such diversions.

He did go to church, and took religion seriously, although his Christianity was rather unorthodox. He was a born-again Catholic who was drawn to the evangelical preacher Pat Robertson. At the time of the congressional hearings, we would learn that North had asked Robertson to pray for him on the eve of one of North's trips to the Middle East.

There was one other recurring pattern in North's life that warrants attention: throughout his adult career, he developed a series of son-father relationships. This began at the Naval Academy, first with his boxing coach, then with Bill Corson, a colonel in the marines. At the NSC, he was adopted by McFarlane. If his testimony is to be believed, Bill Casey became something like a spiritual mentor to him (although Casey was more likely to have played the role of favorite uncle than father). At the end, according to some members of the congressional committees who became fascinated by this pattern, Gen. Richard Secord may well have played a similar role. The pattern is not unusual for men who love the military. North's mentors were all military men, save for Casey, and Casey's background in the OSS (the World War II precursor of the CIA) gave him sufficient military credentials to pass muster.

North was a man of great capacity, but for all his unquestioned talents and limitless energies, North lacked the intellectual background that usually underlies sound foreign policy judgment. He was not familiar with the history and culture of Latin America and did not speak Spanish, which made it difficult for him to make independent evaluations of people and the exceedingly delicate political decisions he faced in the Central American project. He knew virtually nothing about Iran, one of the most complex cultures in the world. This left him at the mercies of the "experts" who advised him, and some of them gave him bad advice. And he was initially unskilled in the important area of intelligence, which sometimes led him to overstate the significance of individual reports. It also made it possible for him to be misled by professional intelligence officers, for, like most people who deal with intelligence sources and methods for the first time, he tended to place excessive trust in the mystique of spycraft. As will be seen, when he was in charge of the Iran initiative, he followed the lead of CIA professionals who convinced him to take a path virtually guaranteed to wreck the undertaking.

The other big problem with Ollie North was that he had a great deal of difficulty distinguishing between truth and fantasy. He constantly told colleagues—even close associates—stories that turned out to be false, and these stories ranged over a wide range of subjects, from his alleged dinner partners to supposed secret intelligence data. A few examples will suffice to indicate the pattern:

- North told friends that he had personally gone to the Philippines to escort President Marcos from Manila to Guam, and had staged a deception against Marcos to lure him to the airport. Nothing of the sort took place.
- He claimed credit for the October 1986 arrest of Mehdi Hashemi in Tehran. Hashemi was one of the bloodiest supporters of Khomeini, and had apparently been involved in the bombing of the Beirut U.S. Marine headquarters in 1983. In fact, Hashemi was arrested as the result of an internal Iranian power struggle. North was not involved.
- He claimed to have come under Sandinista attack while flying in a helicopter on one of his inspection tours of the Nicaraguan front. It never happened.
- He claimed to have had a long, chummy conversation with Israeli Defense Minister Ariel Sharon on Sharon's ranch shortly before the Israeli invasion of Lebanon in 1982. Yet the records of the Defense Ministry show no such meeting, and neither Sharon nor other top officials of the ministry remember it.

Many of the stories were of a traditional sort, clearly designed to enhance his own importance (as in the now famous PROFs note to Poindexter in which he claimed—falsely—to have called Costa Rica's President Oscar Arias, and induced Arias to remain silent about the secret landing strip at Saint Helena). But the number of the stories, and the ease with which North reeled them off, were worrisome.

This pattern of behavior has led some to brand North a liar, but this is unfair, for North himself was firmly convinced of the truthfulness of these stories, and he misled himself as effectively as he dazzled his audience. Assistant Attorney General Cooper spoke eloquently of this phenomenon when he told the Select committees that he was unable to detect any difference in North when he told the truth, or when he was being deceptive.

North's friends—not to mention his critics—had been aware of this growing tendency as early as 1984, and they approached McFarlane to suggest that it was time for the talented lieutenant colonel to be moved out of the NSC to a less-stressful position for a while. They knew that North had performed magnificently, mastering a vast body of information about the world and the inner functioning of the national security system. But they also pointed out the clear signs of worrisome behavior: the addiction to endless hours in the office and the increasing inability to distinguish between what was true and what he wished to be true.

THE MEN WHO WORKED IN THE HOUSE THAT NORTH BUILT

North and McFarlane shared a desire to avenge Vietnam, and a horror of abandoning the *contras,* as the South Vietnamese had been abandoned ten years before. The president's wishes corresponded with their own. Furthermore, they regarded the president's request to find some way to keep the *contras* going a legitimate order.

Had they been trained as lawyers, McFarlane, North, Poindexter, and, later on, Secord might have spent more time studying the fine print of Boland II. It is debatable that such a study would have changed their view of the matter (there is enough legal opinion on both sides of whether the involvement of the White House in private fund-raising for the *contras* was permissible that most any course of action would certainly have found at least some support in the legal community), but the important point is that they did not dwell overly long on the question. Their focus was rather on what they viewed as the *moral* issue, whether it was right for the United States to abandon the *contras*.

As we look back on the people who made the key decisions in the affair, one fact stands out above all others: The major players were all military officers, they all came from small-town America, and they all went to military academies.

• McFarlane was born in Washington, D.C., the son of a New Deal congressman from Graham, Texas (population 8,000). His mother died shortly after his birth, and Bud was sent back to Graham to be raised

81

by his brothers and sister. He moved back to Washington for high school, then entered Annapolis, graduating in 1958 with a B.S. in electrical engineering.

• North was born in Philmont, N.Y. (population 1,570). His father had served under Gen. George Patton in the Second World War. He grew up in Philmont, graduated from the local high school, and went to Annapolis. His graduation from the Naval Academy was delayed a year by a near-fatal automobile accident, but he overcame it and graduated in 1968 at the age of 24 and joined the Marine Corps.

• Poindexter was from Odon, Indiana (population 2,000). His father owned the town's only bank. He went to high school there and graduated as valedictorian and school president. He went to Annapolis, graduating first in his class in 1957.

• Secord was born in Larue, Ohio (population 842), went to high school in Columbus, and went to West Point, from which he graduated in 1955. He immediately entered the Air Force.

All four, then, spent most of their lives—and the entire, crucial, formative period of early adulthood—away from the tough and tumble existence of the big cities. They had very little firsthand experience with the American political system. This came later, and primarily in Washington. They knew the military bureaucracy, a closed system with its own rules. They were all "mission-oriented" men, used to receiving and giving orders, highly motivated to achieve the objective assigned to them. And they were all inclined to look at the world in terms of "us and them," the "us" all working to achieve the mission, the "them" trying to prevent it.

It would be unfair to suggest that they saw the world in black-and-white terms, for they were all intelligent, and they had all learned the art of compromise. But the tendency was there, particularly when it came to the national security of the United States. Here, they all felt, there should be no compromise, and they all were terribly frustrated by the constant intrusion of partisan politics, bureaucratic turf-fighting, and petty self-interest into the vital questions of America's role in the world. They were especially frustrated when these maddening actions came from within the government itself, whether other elements of the executive branch, or the Congress. And the worst—something akin to treason—came when details of sensitive operations were leaked to, and publicized by, the media. Opposition, even if carried out in a devious manner, was something they understood, sometimes respected, and could always live with. But the underhanded

leaking of secrets was something that went against their most fundamental convictions. It seemed to them profoundly unpatriotic, lacking
in both courage and virtue. If they could have found a way to stamp
it out, they would have done so with the same grim enthusiasm with
which heresy is eliminated by the believers.

To be sure, this zealous attitude toward leaks and leakers did not
apply to what they would term "authorized leaks," that is to say,
strategic leaks of information designed to advance the mission itself.
To varying degrees, all had been party to such leaks. In North's case,
it was done with panache and enthusiasm. McFarlane leaked in an
orderly and disciplined manner. Secord undoubtedly enjoyed it, but
had few opportunities to practice. Poindexter probably got cramps
every time he did it. But such leaks were different, they were part of
the mission. The unauthorized leaks were the problem.

All of them had been involved in secret operations (North for the
first time at the NSC) and had been trained to do everything in their
power to maintain operational security. In other words, no leaks. And
they were familiar with the dictum of Benjamin Franklin (which I
once saw, in Italian, on the wall of the office of the head of Italian
Military Intelligence), "three people can keep a secret if two of them
are dead." In short, they did not believe that every decision and every
operation of the United States government should be exposed to maximum discussion and the widest possible examination. Quite the contrary. They believed that there were many decisions, and some
operations, that were best made and carried out by a handful of people,
and that they should be shielded from public view.

This was of a piece with their upbringing, and with their careers.

It was entirely understandable that when the president asked that
something be done to sustain the *contras,* the immediate reaction of
McFarlane, Poindexter, and North was that whatever happened, the
program had to be closely held. And this meant keeping its existence
secret from all those who were likely to oppose it and summarily kill
it by disclosing its existence to the world at large. That is why Secretary
of State Shultz did not learn the details of third-country assistance to
the *contras* until well into 1986 (interestingly enough, even the president withheld from Shultz information about money from foreign
countries). And it is why Donald Regan (a man thoroughly despised
by the senior members of the NSC staff, both because, as we shall
see, he brought down McFarlane, and because he and his staff were
viewed as a major source of press leaks) was never brought into the
inner circle.

Finally, there is the question of the morality of the undertaking itself. It is true that Congress had left a loophole through which the president could drive his "body and soul" operation, but should he have done it that way? It was arguably legal, but that is not enough for the president of the United States. Was it an unacceptable violation of American standards of political behavior? Was it, in other words, a foolish political risk?

There was at least one fairly recent precedent for the secret assistance to the *contras,* and that was Franklin Delano Roosevelt's secret (and illegal) cooperation with Great Britain between 1939 and 1941. Roosevelt was Reagan's hero, and Reagan was aware of the story, since he had read the best-seller *A Man Called Intrepid,* which chronicled the affair. *Intrepid* revealed that Roosevelt had not only provided material assistance to the British (in direct violation of congressional legislation), but had cooperated with British intelligence in setting up an extensive espionage network within the United States, through which the British were able to operate against Nazi agents in America. It could obviously only have been done in secret, so very few officials knew about it, and some of those involved were private citizens. Had Congress found out about it, Roosevelt could well have been impeached, and the resulting political backlash could have cost the West the war.

Reagan may have thought about the *contra* program in much the same terms. Like Roosevelt, he felt strongly about a cause, but found his ability to act throttled by a hostile Congress. Like Roosevelt, he found that several allied countries were urging him to act, even if it meant taking a significant political risk. Like Roosevelt, Reagan was not afraid of tough decisions, or risky actions. So he went for it.

It was a tough problem, and it is easy to second-guess the president at this late date, but it proved to be a mistake. Things had changed since the 1940s, even if much of Regan's worldview had been unalterably shaped by those earlier events. The apt comparison was not 1939, but 1975, when Kissinger, in defiance of Congress, secretly funded anti-communist guerrillas in Angola. The result was disclosure, cutoff, and, for a while at least, the defeat of the guerrillas and the installation of a communist regime in Luanda. It would have been better for Kissinger to have accepted the congressional cutoff of American support for the guerrillas, and taken his case directly to the country. He might well have lost a national debate, but he would have left no doubt about congressional responsibility for the outcome, and made it possible for the country to learn its lessons in less than the decade that passed between the cutoff and the restoration of aid to Jonas Savimbi in the mid-1980s. Instead, he went for the covert "fix," and lost both the political debate and the war on the ground.

The same applied to Reagan a decade later. If he had accepted the Congress's cowardly isolationism, instructed his people to make sure nothing reached the *contras*, and taken his case to the country—demanding, at long last, a serious program of support for the resistance—he might well have lost. But, as with Kissinger in the 1970s, it might have been a tactical defeat that laid the groundwork for a strategic advance in the near future. But Ronald Reagan never fought the kind of open, political battle on Central America that the issue demanded, and the country deserved. He chose the *Intrepid* model instead. And we would do him an injustice if we forget that he did not think of the problem in purely strategic terms. He was a romantic on the *contras*, and he did not want to see them defeated by the first continental Communist government in the Western Hemisphere. As I said, it was not an easy call.

McFarlane found a solution: after being turned down by the Israelis, he went to a country that had previously helped out with financial support for the anti-Soviet forces in Afghanistan. He explained the situation, and found instant understanding. In short order, the country offered to help the *contras*, to the tune of a million dollars a month, starting in June 1984. Early the following year, it was approached again, and it agreed to double its contribution. In all, $32 million went to the *contras* from this country. Until well into 1985, this was all the *contras* could depend upon for their survival.

North was brought into the picture by McFarlane in order to arrange the money transfer to the *contras*. North, who by then was on good terms with Calero and the other FDN leaders, got a bank account number from the FDN leader, and passed it on to the country's embassy in Washington.

It was only the barest beginning. The congressional cutoff had come precisely when the *contras* were beginning to establish themselves as an effective fighting force. And, in keeping with the principle that everyone loves a winner, their ranks had swelled substantially in the latter part of 1983 and the first several months of 1984. This bit of money might sustain them, but it would not permit the *contras* to clothe, equip, and train the mounting numbers of volunteers. A man like North was not content with a holding operation; he wanted to win. And that required still more money. So he began scouring the world for possible sources, sometimes doing it directly, on other occasions enlisting the assistance of colleagues at the NSC like Dr. Gaston Sigur, the senior staffer in charge of the Orient, and Howard Teicher, who worked on the Middle East. At the same time he lobbied friendly Central American governments for favors: the use of airfields, storage facilities, and so forth. It was the start of a two-year long project to keep the *contra* army in the field. North would call it Project Democracy.

THE UNFOLDING OF PROJECT DEMOCRACY

Meanwhile, Calero was complaining about the prices he had been paying for weapons, as well as their quality. As Secord testified, hand grenades had blown up in their hands, and weapons were not functioning.[6] If they were to be kept together "body and soul," something needed to be done about this as well. But North could not do this one on his own. He turned to retired Gen. Richard Secord for help.

North had met Secord back in 1981, when North had been seconded to the NSC in order to help sell the AWACS-to-Saudi Arabia program to the Congress. North's role didn't amount to much, and he was decidedly the most junior member of the team, but it was where he got his start in the White House, and one tends to remember those people who are there at the beginning. In early 1984, North had asked Secord for some professional advice. In keeping with the normal rotation of military officers, North had been advised by the Marine Corps that it was time to move on. He had been recommended for the usual step up: a tour at the Naval War College in Newport, Rhode Island. It was flattering, but North was not interested. He had developed an appetite for being where the action was, the terrorism account was getting busier, and he was consumed by the *contra* passion. He asked Secord what he should do. Secord told him that he should go to Newport. In the summer, North, still at the NSC,[7] called again.

This time he wanted to talk about Central America. The congressional funding was gone, and the *contras* needed help. Would Secord pitch in? Secord said he'd be happy to do what he could. North arranged for Secord and Calero to meet, and, once Secord had heard the problems faced by the FDN, he offered to try to find a new source of arms for the *contras,* hopefully with both better quality and lower

6. Secord, published testimony, p. 50. I heard similar stories from *contras* who fought on both the Northern and Southern fronts.

7. The Marine Corps does not take kindly to officers who "go political," and do not return to the fold when they are asked to do so. North's long stay at the NSC irritated some people at the Corps, and this was probably why, a year later, McFarlane was unable to obtain a military command for North.

prices. He had two partners at this stage, Albert Hakim, an Iranian-born American citizen with whom Secord was involved in various business ventures, and Rafael Quintero, a former CIA officer whom Secord had known for many years. Later another ex-CIA official, Tom Clines, was brought in to assist with the arms purchases for Calero.

In his public testimony, North claimed that Secord's name was suggested to him by William Casey. While anything is possible, there are several reasons to doubt this claim. First of all, there was no personal relationship at that time between Casey and Secord. Second, and more importantly, if Casey had asked his top deputies at the CIA about Secord, alarm bells would have rung all over the agency, because Secord's name had been associated with two fairly major scandals in recent years. And although the several investigations never led to any formal charges, the habit in Washington is to shy away from such people, particularly on sensitive projects.[8]

Under the circumstances, why should Casey have recommended Secord? It is far more likely that North, who had worked for Secord before, and who had already shown his respect for Secord's judgment by asking him for help with a major career decision, made the choice himself.

Secord's record suggested that he was the ideal person for the sort of work North had in mind. In the late 1960s and early 1970s, Secord had worked on one of the most secret of all American military projects in Southeast Asia: the clandestine war in Laos. The management of the Laotian operation was located at Udorn Air Force Base in Thailand, where Secord was stationed. He worked there in a special compound, as a staff officer detailed by the air force to the CIA. His responsibility was designing the funding for upcoming operations, and he soon became expert in secret funding methods for fifteen Special Guerrilla Unit battalions. His budget ran to $13 million for a six-month period in 1973. He emerged from the campaign with a greatly enhanced reputation, not only for efficiency and brains, but also for his discretion.

[Secord was] a brilliant clandestine operative who handled the operational and logistical side of the U.S. Air Force's involvement in the

---

8. Not only was Secord under a cloud—and I repeat, so far as I know, or anyone has proved, all the accusations were dropped for lack of evidence—but so was Clines, who had had a working relationship with the infamous renegade CIA official Ed Wilson, who had worked for Qadaffi in the mid-70s and is now serving a major jail sentence. When Donald Gregg, Vice President Bush's national security adviser, learned of Clines's involvement in the *contra* support program, he was horrified.

secret war. . . . Secord, known among his West Point classmates as "the Fat Man," had previously been awarded the Distinguished Flying Cross for a rescue mission in the Congo and had also flown two hundred secret combat missions in fighters in South Vietnam before his arrival in Thailand in 1966. He became known as "the Buddha" among the secret warriors, because he was perceived as inscrutable, the fount of great secret powers, and round.[9]

Later, he served in Iran as the top air force officer in the Military Assistance Group in Tehran, and was generally highly regarded. In Washington, he was considered one of the most talented members of the military, a man who had demonstrated skill in both managerial and combat positions, and furthermore a man with considerable skill in all manner of covert operations. He seemed the ideal person to manage the "body and soul" operation.

But this was not Laos, and there was no infrastructure, no worldwide communications net, and a distinct shortage of money. By the summer of 1985, Secord, Quintero, and Clines had managed some four shipments to Calero. While there was some dispute about the quality of the weapons and the level of the prices,[10] the weapons had arrived (albeit on some occasions with several months' delay).

It was not good enough. Despite the money and the arms, the *contras* were grinding to a halt. The Sandinista army was benefitting from Cuban and other Soviet bloc training, advanced attack weapons, and improved intelligence. On the *contra* side was a *campesino* movement thrown back on its own relatively meager skills. The results were easily predictable.

Money alone does not keep an army in the field. Armies need food, arms, intelligence, communications, and strategy. And they need "the sinews of war," logistics. People and materiel had to be moved, in timely fashion, from their bases to the battle zones. The *contras* themselves did not seem able to do all this, and fighting units inside Nicaragua sometimes found themselves as much as thirty days' march from their base of supplies. From the summer of 1984 to the following autumn, there was little or nothing in the way of useful intelligence from the CIA or any other American government agency, and no private organization, regardless of the talents of its members, could

9. Christopher Robbins, *The Ravens* (New York: Crown, 1987), p. 124.
10. Calero compained about both, as did Felix Rodriguez, another former CIA officer who had helped set up an airfield in Salvador for Secord. Retired Gen. John Singlaub, who was similarly engaged in buying arms for the *contras,* also complained about pricing. It is hard to evaluate these complaints, although some of Rodriguez's accusations have been proven false.

fill that gap. The situation was improved somewhat in the summer and autumn of 1985. In August, Congress voted $27 million in "humanitarian aid" to the *contras*. In order to avoid the taint of militarism, Congress required that the State Department administer the money. It was a bizarre, if typical, decision. Congress wished to avoid being blamed for a Communist success in Central America, and therefore voted the money. On the other hand, Congress wished to avoid being blamed for getting America involved in "another Vietnam," and therefore insisted that the aid be for "boots, Band-Aids, and beans," and be supervised by the department least qualified to do so.

In November, Congress agreed to permit the CIA back into the secret war, but only a half step. The agency could henceforth provide intelligence to the *contras,* and help them with communications. But they could not get involved in military operations of any sort.

Early in July 1985, North gathered his brain trust for a meeting in a Miami hotel. On the American side were North, Secord, Clines, and Quintero. For the *contras,* the big two: Calero and Bermúdez. North began with a stern lecture. There were stories that individual *contras* had been pocketing some of the slender resources that had been given to them. That had to stop. Any such activity would discredit the movement in the eyes of the American public, as well as deprive the fighting forces of the wherewithal to wage war. That was point number one.

Number two was the urgent necessity of organizing an airlift capability. The *contras* inside Nicaragua needed to have supplies dropped to them on the ground, and the existing airplanes and crews were not up to the task.

> . . . there were a very small number of very old, poorly equipped aircraft that were operating out of their main headquarters . . . these aircraft, we were told, could only fly in daylight hours, and could not penetrate into Nicaragua any significant distance, because they couldn't fly at night, they weren't properly equipped, the crews weren't properly trained, and the Sandinista air defense, of course, had gotten much stronger.[11]

Point number three was the requirement of trying to reconstitute the Southern Front.

Finally, a broad strategic point: the *contras* had hitherto operated almost exclusively in the countryside. They now had to find a way to

11. Secord, published testimony, p. 58.

penetrate the cities. For while the Sandinistas might be greatly upset by a substantial insurrection in the mountains and forests of the country, their power would remain secure until and unless the *contras* reached the regime's strongholds in the cities on the Pacific coastal plain.

Secord agreed with the analysis, and he and North discussed the possibilities. It was a daunting task, requiring several million dollars in start-up money alone. But if it were not done, the *contras* were finished. And in the eyes of Secord and North, that would have been Vietnam all over again, with another American ally abandoned on the battlefield. Although he was full of misgivings, Secord agreed to try to organize the airlift for a two-front war against Nicaragua. To plan and manage it, he recruited yet another member of the old boy network from Vietnam days: Col. Richard Gadd, a veteran of the Air Force Special Operations Office who, after his retirement in 1982, had remained active in the field of covert paramilitary activities. He had quickly negotiated a one-million-dollar contract with the Army's Special Operations Division to provide round-the-clock transport service. By the end of 1983, he was managing some $5 million in contracts with the army, and had demonstrated his skills by quickly moving some helicopters from California to Barbados in October 1983 in preparation for the invasion of Grenada. He had done it in forty-eight hours with no advance warning, and everyone associated with the project was impressed.[12]

Secord now had his team, and they set to work on the airlift resupply operation. It would take almost a year before it was operational, ample testimony to the difficulties they faced. To complicate matters even more, within a few months North invited Secord to help out on another secret project: the Iran initiative.

12. For further details, see Steven Emerson, *Secret Warriors* (New York: Putnam's, 1988), pp. 143–47.

4. Iran I:
The Origins of the Initiative

Iran's geography is her destiny. She sits between Russia and the Persian Gulf, blocking Moscow's centuries-old ambition to acquire warmwater ports and thereby achieve direct access to the Middle East. For those who fear Russian expansion, Iran has always been—and will most likely always be—a country of supreme strategic importance. In like manner, Iran's foreign policy is dictated by the necessity of dealing with the menacing Russian presence to the north and east, and Persian leaders have always found ready Western allies who share their preoccupation with the Bear's voracious appetite.

For the first half of this century England played the major Western role in helping Iran contain Soviet power, but with the exhaustion of Great Britain after the Second World War, this vital task fell to the United States. American involvement with Iran began with the Truman Doctrine—which was designed to block attempted Soviet expansion in Iran and Greece in 1945—and continued with the celebrated covert action in tandem with British intelligence to remove the radical government of Mohammed Mossadeqh and replace the young shah on the peacock throne in 1953. Thereafter, until the Shi'ite revolution that overthrew the shah in 1979, Iran and the United States worked intimately on a variety of projects, from domestic Iranian development to maintaining security in the Persian Gulf to supporting Anwar Sadat in Egypt.

All this changed abruptly with Khomeini's seizure of power. Whereas America had been a favored ally under the shah, now the president of the United States became the Great Satan. With the shah on the throne, Americans had free run of the country, and American businessmen, diplomats, journalists, scholars, and military men engaged in all manner of activity throughout the nation; with Khomeini in power, the American presence disappeared virtually overnight. Yet Iran's destiny had not changed; she still shared a border of two thousand miles with the Soviet Union, and she was still a nation of vital strategic importance for the West. And now the Red Army, one hundred thousand and more, was engaged in combat with the *mujehedin* in neighboring Afghanistan.

The shah's Iran was a mighty military force blocking the Soviets' path to the Gulf. Khomeini's Iran was rather weaker militarily, particularly with the passage of time, but it was far more threatening to the Soviet Empire. For the Shi'ite revolution that brought the Ayatollah to power in Tehran was potentially exciting to the millions of Muslims within the Soviet Union, and Khomeini was no less anticommunist than Shah Mohammed Reza Pahlavi had been. The Russians thus had a double incentive to attempt to weaken Iran: the historic enmity between the two countries, and the danger that Khomeini might subvert Soviet control over Islamic areas of the Empire. And if the Russians were doubly concerned about the new Iran, the United States automatically had reason for anxiety as well. We were not concerned about Khomeiniism reaching our shores, but we faced the potential danger that the Soviet Union might find a way to destabilize Iran, thereby either turning it into a larger and more violent Lebanon or replacing the Ayatollah with something or someone more amenable to Soviet desires.

There was another, more immediate and even more fundamental, reason for an active American policy toward Iran. Khomeini had preached a violent sermon to the Islamic world. In essence, his message had been: If we wish to have our way with the West, it is necessary to unleash a terrorist onslaught against them. In time, they will bend to our will. And so it had been. First, the terrorist onslaught, from Tehran—with the humiliation of the Carter administration during the long agony of the hostage crisis at the American embassy—to Lebanon, as Iranian and Syrian-backed terrorist attacks were launched against military and diplomatic targets, from the French and American Marine Corps barracks to the American embassy in Beirut. And in each case, the Shi'ites triumphed: Carter was driven from office with a reputation as a weakling, and a few well-timed bombs drove America, France, Israel, Britain, and Italy out of Lebanon in less than two years following the Israeli invasion of 1982.

If the Western world did not deliver some effective blow to Khomeini before he died, then the Ayatollah would pass into legend with mythic qualities and a dangerous lesson: kill enough Americans, and they will do what we wish. It was therefore a matter of considerable strategic urgency to demonstrate that Khomeini's path would not succeed; that the power of the West was sufficient to thwart his megalomaniacal plans for the expansion of radical Shi'ism throughout the world.

To be sure, we could try to make our peace with Khomeini, and work toward a normalization of relations. But this was probably impossible in the first years of the Ayatollah's rule, since hatred of America was so central to the society he was attempting to create. For Khomeini's loathing of the United States was based on what we represented: modernity, a nonreligious society, an equal role for women, and toleration of various points of view. His ideal society was one where women were subservient and wrapped in *chadors*—with only their eyes visible—and where the priests—the mullahs—laid down a stern Islamic discipline. Jews, Baha'is and Sunnis were oppressed, tortured and killed. For Khomeini, America was the symbol of corruption and evil in the modern world. He wished to return Iran to a pristine, medieval state. It was hard to imagine a rapprochement with such a regime.

Our policy concerns were easily stated, but it was exceedingly difficult to formulate any reasonable American policy, because our intelligence was very poor. This was not new. At the time of the Khomeini revolution, neither the CIA nor the dozens of Foreign Service officers in Iran had any meaningful contact with the Ayatollah or his followers, and none of them had any inkling of what was to come. As late as the summer of 1978, when the Israeli government sent directly to President Carter a report concluding that the shah was doomed, the intelligence community reacted with scorn. And even after the Shi'ite seizure of power, when the American embassy in Tehran was overrun, the CIA had been so lackadaisical that hundreds of classified documents remained in the files.

Bad as the situation was in 1979, it was even worse by the time the Reagan administration came to office. Even the most elementary information was hard to obtain, and such bits and pieces as reached us through travellers, foreign governments, and the occasional Western journalist were hardly sufficient for serious policy. The CIA seemed unable to develop adequate sources of reliable information, and when I later learned in detail just how bad our intelligence was, I couldn't resist the suspicion that no one at CIA really wanted to know anything about Iran. For when I finally met the CIA officer in charge of Iranian affairs for the Directorate of Operations (we met in December 1985), he turned out to be a man who had spent his entire career in Latin America, spoke not a word of Farsi, had never worked in the Middle East, and did not recognize the names of many of the leading figures in the Khomeini regime. This was the man upon whom the CIA—and hence the government of the United States—depended for its understanding of one of the most strategically important areas of the world.

So throughout the first term, American officials wanted to do something, but didn't know what to do.

The first encounter between the Reagan administration and Iran had taken place in the last days of Carter's presidency, as the old team worked frantically to achieve the release of the American hostages in Tehran. The Persians are cynical masters of the art of negotiation, and had dragged the process out to the last minute, hoping to gain the maximum advantage from an exhausted president desperate to free his countrymen before leaving the White House. The constant shifting in the Iranian position suggested that the Ayatollah might judge it best to wait for the new president. Secretary of Defense Harold Brown and National Security Adviser Brzezinski communicated their concerns to the transition team, and Haig sent a stern message to Tehran. His words were brutal: once Reagan was inaugurated, the curtain would fall on the hostage question. Reagan would not negotiate, would not pay a cent, would not make concessions. He even hinted at a military option. So if there were to be some sort of deal for the hostages, the Iranians had better take it now, from Carter. After midday on January 21st, 1981, all negotiations would cease. Khomeini accepted the Carter deal.

There was no follow-up to this terse communication from the new secretary of state, but for the next several years there were numerous efforts to get the United States involved in Iran. Some were of a familiar sort: "walk-ins" at the various agencies of the government in Washington, people claiming to possess unique access to the highest levels of the Iranian government, offering to bring an end to the poor state of relations between the two countries. Sometimes they asked for money or other acts of largesse from the Americans, sometimes not. Each case was examined; none offered any real hope.

Other efforts came from more serious quarters. Leaders in the region, from Arab monarchs like Hassan of Morocco to elected presidents and prime ministers from Turkey to Italy, approached the White

House or the State Department, urging us to reestablish contacts with the Iranians. Even some West European foreign ministers quietly suggested a resumption of "dialogue." But despite a cautious show of interest on our part, no legitimate channel was opened.

In the autumn of 1981, the State Department received Señor Hector Villalon, who, it will be recalled, was one of the two intermediaries between Hamilton Jordan and the Iranian regime during the Carter hostage crisis. Hector Villalon is a genuine rarity in the political universe: a social democratic Peronist. He is also one of those unforgettable characters who inhabit the margins of international affairs. He looks somewhat like a cherubic Salvador Dalí, with an ebullient personality and an irrepressible imagination. One can easily understand why Hamilton Jordan enjoyed dealing with him, for Villalon is an engaging fellow, and great fun to be around. Not surprisingly, Villalon had spent very little time in recent years in his native Argentina, and divided his schedule between the more attractive watering places of Western Europe. He came to inform us of the possibility of an anti-Khomeini coup in Iran, headed by Sadeqh Ghotbzadeh, the one-time foreign minister in the immediate postrevolutionary period. I met with him, explained that my duties did not include Iran, spent an hour or so in an extremely interesting discussion of the state of social democracy in Latin America, and introduced him to the experts at the Near East Bureau. He was not received with enthusiasm, but his information proved right.

Several months later, I met again with Villalon, and he again started in on the story of the imminent coup in Iran. He said that he would know a couple of days before it was scheduled to take place and would call to tell me. I told him that he absolutely must not call, that my telephone calls were undoubtedly listened to by the KGB, and that any such phone call would be terribly dangerous.

High officials of the United States government are aware that the KGB intercepts all microwave communications in and out of Washington, D.C. (that is why they were so pleased when they were granted permission during the Kissinger era to build their embassy on the highest point in the city). These are then analyzed by high-speed computers, which print out conversations, telexes, and telefaxes which might prove of value to the Soviets. Since most telephone conversations in the United States are transmitted by microwave, rather than carried by land line, it is safe to assume that any given conversation is being recorded. For that reason, I—like all governmental officials who discuss sensitive matters—made it a point to ask my interlocutors not to talk about potentially delicate subjects on open telephone lines. Villalon got the standard sermon on this subject.

To no avail. A few weeks afterward, I returned to the office one day after lunch and my secretary gave me the bad news: Villalon had called—in French, since his English is quite poor—to talk about an imminent coup in Iran. Once she had understood what he was saying, she brought the conversation to a quick conclusion. I have no way of knowing whether this indiscretion was noted by the Soviets and then passed to the Iranians (Iran has quite good internal intelligence, after all), but Ghotbzadeh was arrested, tortured, and executed. There had not been the slightest American involvement, but this did not prevent some of the more inventive publications from writing that we had been engaged in some way or other. Incredibly, I was later accused by some Iranian emigres in France of having betrayed Ghotbzadeh to the Ayatollah, a charge that was cheerfully picked up by a variety of left-wing publications in Europe and the United States.[1]

Aside from such events, and the dozens of unfulfilled promises from self-proclaimed "channels" to Iran, the American government did virtually nothing on its own prior to the second Reagan administration. Nonetheless, many people believed that the United States had been involved in Iranian affairs, from the Ghotbzadeh "coup" to the defection of a senior KGB agent. This occurred in October 1982 when Vladimir Kuzichkin, the Soviet vice-consul in Tehran, defected to Great Britain. Kuzichkin proved to be a reliable source of information about the KGB's Iranian network, and within a few months eighteen Soviets were expelled from Iran and over one hundred Iranians— believed to be members of the underground Communist party, Tudeh—were arrested, and later tortured and executed. It was widely reported at the time that the information had reached Iranian authorities from the CIA, but it was not so. The British had done it themselves.

Thus, despite the rumors, nothing much was going on from the American side. The one notable exception to this rule had nothing to

---

1. See, for example, "The Invisible Man," *In These Times*, January 21–27, 1987, p. 9, which says, *inter alia*, "Ledeen accompanied Robert McFarlane on his secret mission to Tehran last May 28, former Iranian President Abol Hassan Bani Sadr told *In These Times* . . . Ledeen could expect a warm welcome, since he is considered by Iranians to be 'the man who sold out Sadiq Ghotbzadeh to Khomeini.' . . . According to Bani Sadr, Ghotbzadeh sent a messenger to inform the U.S. government that 'something was going to happen' (a coup d'état) in Iran, and asking the U.S. not for help but simply to remain neutral. The messenger spent three hours waiting for an answer and finally was sent word from Ledeen that the Ayatollah's regime in Iran was anti-Communist and the U.S. was opposed to a coup to overthrow it." Every assertion in this account is untrue.

do with an American initiative, but rather with the relationship between Iran and Israel.

THE ISRAELI CONNECTION

During the shah's rule there had been a close working relationship between Iran and Israel, particularly on defense matters, and Israel had developed an efficient information-gathering network inside Iran. In part, this network utilized the relatively small but prosperous Jewish community in Iran, but even more important were the hundreds of close contacts developed in the Iranian defense establishment. Following the revolution, many of these contacts remained in important positions, and hence the Israelis were able to keep at least a small window open into the Ayatollah's world.

While there was some disagreement on the best course of action among Israeli policymakers (unanimity among Israelis is undoubtedly an oxymoron), there was a general consensus on the desirability of keeping open channels of communication and trying to remain active inside Iran. This view was quite bipartisan, and was shared by men from Prime Minister Peres (1984–86) and Foreign Minister Yitzhak Shamir, to Defense Minister Yitzhak Rabin, his predecessor Ariel Sharon, and top regional experts like former Israeli ambassador to Tehran Uri Lubrani. Most Israelis believed that, with the passage of time, the revolution would spend its fanaticism, and that Iran would become a "normal" country once again. And when that day came, Israel wanted to be able to resume the good relations that had existed before Khomeini. In order to keep the channels open, the Israelis believed it wise to respond positively to the requests for arms sales that arrived in Jerusalem from Iranian officials. The Shi'ites' hatred of Judaism did not prevent them from buying weapons from the Jewish state. For Israel, even more than the United States, an interest in keeping Iran strong as a buffer against the projection of Soviet power into the Gulf area.

The end of keeping the Israeli hand active in the Iranian game was worthy enough, but what were the most effective means to achieve it?

In the Middle East, arms have long been the lubricant for good relations between countries, and this is particularly so during times of open conflict. Iran faced serious problems, first withstanding the Iraqi blitz, then retaking the territory that Saddam Hussein's armies had occupied, and finally attempting to fulfill Khomeini's long-standing threat to destroy the Iraqi regime. But to prevail in the war, Iran had to deal with the two great strengths of the Iraqi armies: tanks and aircraft. The Ayatollah's armed forces thus needed effective antitank and antiaircraft weapons. In the fullness of time, TOW antitank missiles and HAWK antiaircraft missiles would become the currency of the transactions between the United States, Israel, and Iran.

But the United States was opposed to the sale of arms to Iran, and actively lobbied third countries to do likewise. The United States has enormous leverage in such matters, for third countries are permitted to purchase American military technology only after agreeing to restrict its resale to such buyers as Washington approves. And while it is not all that difficult to outwit the requirements of the formal "end user's certificate," countries that are caught flouting American wishes are likely to find themselves locked out of the American market for their own products, as well as denied permission to obtain the most modern American weapons in the future. Thus, Operation Staunch, as it came to be called, gravely restricted Iran's ability to buy weapons on the open market. Under these circumstances, the Iranians were prepared to purchase weapons from the devil, even the hated Israelis. From the earliest days of the Reagan administration, there were contacts between Tehran and Tel Aviv, testing the possibilities of doing business. And while the public evidence is skimpy, it is known that at least some business was done. In early 1982, for example, Israeli Ambassador Moshe Arens publicly stated that Israel had sold weapons to Iran, with implicit American approval.

On other occasions, the American press carried stories of Gen. Ariel Sharon selling airplane tires to the Iranians, and there were some tales that verged on the fanciful. Perhaps the most entertaining is the celebrated pistachio nut caper. According to this account, which made the rounds of the Hebrew-language press in Israel, some Israeli arms dealers negotiated a deal with Iran for the sale of Israeli weapons and spare parts. They loaded a ship with the merchandise, sailed out of Eilat, and delivered it to Iran. Once there, they found that their customers were unable to pay the full price in cash, but could offer part cash, part pistachio nuts. The Israelis accepted, and returned to Eilat with a shipload of pistachios, with which they flooded the Israeli marketplace. Within days, the price of pistachio nuts had dropped by 50 percent.

The story, alas, turns out to be false, but its near universal acceptance shows how widespread was the conviction of a flourishing arms trade from Israel to Iran. In fact, while there was indeed a series of weapons sales between 1979 and the mid-1980s, this commerce was not nearly so extensive as some have suggested, and the question of American knowledge and approval was somewhat more subtle than is generally suggested. The basic American demand was that Israel refrain from shipping arms which had come from the United States or were covered by American end-user certificates. And while the United States was not enthusiastic about sales of Israeli (or other foreign) weapons to Iran, the American government never went to the Israelis with a firm demand that all such shipments be stopped.

So the flow of Israeli arms to Iran, which had been so substantial under the shah, continued under the revolutionary regime, with one period of interruption. When Carter discovered that the Begin government had sent arms to Iran shortly after the Iranians overran the American embassy in Tehran, he sent a stern message to Begin. How could Israel do such a thing while our hostages were being held? Begin promised to stop it, and for the duration of the hostage crisis there were no further shipments. But they resumed again once the hostages were released and Reagan took office.

While some American officials suspect that the Israeli arms traffic to Iran after Reagan's inauguration was more substantial than the Israelis have admitted, Israel willingly acknowledged that it was going on. On some occasions, American Ambassador Samuel Lewis was informed by the Defense Ministry, and he restated the American position: We were not enthusiastic about it, and rather wished it would stop. But there was no clearcut veto. And the matter was raised in general terms with Secretary of State Haig on two occasions: once during Haig's trip to Israel in the fall of 1981, and again on the occasion of Defense Minister Sharon's visit to Washington the following spring. Accounts of the American response vary somewhat, but they are unanimous on one point: there was no stern American condemnation of the practice.

Since they were not told to stop, the Israelis continued, assuming that the Americans had accepted the Israeli assessment of the advantages that derived from the Iranian deals:

• It kept channels open, in keeping with the theory that Israel—and the West as a whole—wanted to be involved inside Iran, hoping for better days to come.
• It helped the condition of the remnant of the Jewish community in Iran, and by 1985 Khomeini had eased the restrictions on Jewish

99

emigration, so that it was significantly easier for Iranian Jews to leave for Europe, Israel, and the United States.

• It was a source of money, particularly attractive in the mid-eighties when the Israeli economy was in very difficult straits.

• It prevented Iraq from winning the war. Israel was far more concerned about Iraq than about Iran, since Iraq had participated in the Arab wars against Israel and had long financed the Abu Nidal terrorist organization. Iran, at least in the short run, posed no comparable threat to Israel.

The arms traffic between Israel and Iran continued to produce some useful Israeli contacts inside Iran. In part because of these contacts, and in part because the old Israeli network was never totally dismantled by the Ayatollah, Israel had by far the best understanding of the internal Iranian situation. I was told of this by one of the smartest and most experienced intelligence officials in Western Europe in the winter of 1985.

There are certain kinds of secret information that move between friendly countries quite outside the routine channels of government. In the modern world, where "secrets" are routinely published on the front pages of Western newspapers, governmental leaders have had to revert to some old-fashioned methods of communication, of which the most common is the personal courier. Experienced leaders know that anything committed to paper—as well as anything transmitted electronically—is likely to leak, and so they ask trusted envoys to carry verbal messages to their counterparts overseas. Typically, such messages are passed between heads of state, foreign ministers, or intelligence chiefs, with the request that the information not be written down. The bearers of these messages can be anything from businessmen and journalists to actors and trusted personal assistants; they are rarely top officials themselves. Frequently, their names do not even appear on official calendars or appointment schedules; they are slipped in between the formal appointments, or they are ushered in to the leaders' private residences on weekends or after dinner.

As of the end of 1984, I was on the lists as a part-time consultant to the National Security Council, reporting to Robert C. McFarlane, the security adviser. From time to time, I was asked to carry such messages overseas, or to discuss sensitive subjects with foreign leaders with whom I had become friendly in the past. When I was asked to meet with this particular intelligence official in early 1985, I could not have imagined where this perfectly routine conversation was going to lead me. We had a wide-ranging discussion of some of the hotter topics of the day, and since my friend was quite tan, at a certain point I asked him if he had been skiing. "No," he said with the sort of smile such persons produce when they are about to reveal a particularly delicious piece of secret information, "I'm just back from Iran."

It was as surprising an answer as I could have imagined, but no more surprising than the description of his trip: he had travelled throughout the country, had met with a variety of people, from entrepreneurs in the bazaars to leading officials in the regime. His conclusion was typically concise and to the point: "the situation is very fluid, there is a lot of internal conflict, and the country is wide open. It is a good time for you people to get involved again." But how, I asked, could we be usefully involved in Iranian affairs when we knew nothing about the country? "Talk to the Israelis," he replied, "they know all about it."

There is a surprisingly widespread belief, which exists even at the highest levels of Western governments, that the Mossad knows everything that everyone else wants to know, but doesn't. The Israeli intelligence service is less than one-tenth the size of the CIA, and almost all of its attention is devoted to the potentially fatal threat from neighboring Arab countries. There is very little left over for the rest of the world, yet many people, even experts, insist on believing that Israeli intelligence has unique information about remote areas of the world, even including the Soviet Union. My own limited experience in conversation with Israeli intelligence officials has led me to believe that these are myths. Mossad is a good, professional organization, but one which has undergone the same dreadful process of bureaucratization and politicization as most Western intelligence services in the past two decades. It is not nearly as good as it should be, and falls far short of its reputation.

In any event, it certainly stood to reason that the Israelis would know a lot about Iran, whatever the qualities of their intelligence services. For there had been a considerable emigration of Iranian Jews in recent years, and they would have provided the Israeli government with first-hand accounts of the situation. When one added to this the knowledge gained through the weapons sales, and whatever Mossad had been able to come up with, the Israeli understanding of Iran should certainly have been far better than ours. How good was it? Specifically, did they have sufficient understanding so that one could base an intelligent policy on it? To find out, we would have to ask.

Accordingly, I reported the conversation with the European official to Bud McFarlane a couple of weeks later, and suggested that if he deemed it desirable, I could raise the Iranian question with Israeli Prime Minister Shimon Peres, whom I had gotten to know during my tenure at the State Department as special adviser to Secretary Haig. Back in those days, I had been asked to deal with the leaders of the Socialist International, and Peres at the time was the head of the opposition Labor party. We had met four or five times, had gotten along well, and I thought, as did McFarlane, that it might be easier for a part-time consultant to raise this matter with Peres than if the query came through formal channels. After some discussion with the NSC officers responsible for Middle Eastern questions, the trip was approved, and scheduled for the first week in May.

I met Peres alone in his office in Jerusalem (it is probably the only governmental office building in the Western world where you are invited to check your personal weapons with the attendant as you enter), and explained the nature of my visit. We were interested in Iran, but unhappy with the state of our knowledge. We had heard that Israel had first-class intelligence on the subject. Was it true? And if so, would they be willing to share it with us? Finally, in the event that the answers to the previous questions were "yes," did they have any bright ideas about Western policy toward Iran?

As usual in these conversations, I was surprised at the response. Peres's words were low-key, even downbeat: Israeli intelligence was not particularly good, he said. He was personally dissatisfied with it. He suspected it was better than ours (a slightly sardonic smile here), but it was nowhere near sufficient for policy purposes. However, he added, the subject was certainly an important one, and he suggested that we work together to produce a joint assessment of the Iranian situation. Perhaps by pooling our knowledge we might arrive at a satisfactory picture.

The words were not exciting, but the body language was quite different. For when I put the questions to him, Peres—who is normally an extremely relaxed and low-key individual—was visibly charged up. He snapped upright in his easy chair, and spoke with unusual animation. I could not figure out the reason for his excitement. It was only later that I discovered that the first contacts with Ghorbanifar had been made within the past two months, and that the Israelis were wondering whether to bring this matter to our attention.

There were two concrete developments as a result of the conversation with Peres: he asked Shlomo Gazit, the president of the Ben Gurion University of Beersheva (and former chief of military intelligence), to meet with me and arrange the intelligence-sharing on Iran;

and he asked me to convey a request to McFarlane. He had recently received a request from Iran for some artillery shells. Israel was prepared to do this, but only if there were no American objection. Would I ask? I was not eager to do this, since I had always stayed away from such questions, and I told Peres that I preferred not to be the channel for this request. But he insisted, and I agreed to pass the message to the security adviser (McFarlane subsequently approved the sale, provided that it contain no spare parts for aircraft, and stipulated that this was a one-time transaction. He stressed there was no American blanket approval for arms deals with Iran).

After Peres, I met with Gazit, outlined the project, and agreed to try to get our evaluation of Iranian matters within a month and then meet with him for further discussion, at which time we would compare notes. McFarlane also agreed, and asked me to coordinate this matter with Don Fortier, the number three man on the NSC staff. Don was one of my oldest friends in Washington, a longtime staff assistant to the House Foreign Affairs Committee and a student of the brilliant California strategist Albert Wohlstetter. He was also one of the gentlest souls in government, an exceedingly easy man with whom to work, and a person upon whom McFarlane first, and later Poindexter, depended heavily. His untimely death at the hands of a vicious liver cancer the following summer was a terribly damaging blow to the NSC.

Fortier quickly arranged to have the CIA prepare a Special National Intelligence Estimate (SNIE) on Iran, which was in hand later in May. This was to provide me with the basis for the follow-up conversation with the Israelis. But during this process, there was a political incident that set back the program for some time: Defense Minister Yitzhak Rabin informed Ambassador Lewis of my visit, and Lewis of course relayed the notice to Shultz, who was off in the Orient. The secretary of state, who was one of the most tenacious turf protectors in the government, fired off an angry cable to McFarlane, demanding to know why I had been sent behind Shultz's back to Israel. McFarlane replied that there was nothing to be upset about, since I had gone to Israel "on my own hook." It was, of course, not true. I had travelled on a ticket issued by the White House, under McFarlane's detailed instructions. And McFarlane had told me before I left that he was going to inform Shultz of the trip (so when Peres asked me who knew about the visit, I had responded that I believed the secretary of state was witting). For one reason or another, McFarlane had not been able (or had not chosen) to brief Shultz, and when the secretary raged at him, he evidently decided it was easier to blame me than get into an intercontinental explanation with an angry Shultz. Some time later

Shultz was brought up to speed on the conversation with Peres, and McFarlane told me that by early summer the follow-up conversation could be held.

But in the meantime, Manucher Ghorbanifar had entered the scene, and the entire nature of the Iran initiative was due to change.

ENTER GHORBANIFAR

Ghorbanifar is probably the most fascinating person in the entire Israel/Iran-Contra saga, and for those of us who came to know him, he is barely recognizable in the one-dimensional caricatures of him that have emerged from the press coverage and much of the testimony. His is a rich personality, as befits his Persian heritage. Blessed with quick wit and intelligence, he is the Iranian version of the self-made man. His father was a policeman in Tehran, and Ghorbanifar attended public school and later university in the capital. He then worked his way up in a series of businesses, ultimately becoming the managing director of an Iranian shipping company that had two foreign partners: an Israeli and an American Jewish businessman from Detroit. Like many Iranian businessmen, Ghorbanifar cooperated with SAVAK— the secret intelligence service—on counterintelligence matters in the 1970s, and acquired a certain facility with the craft of intelligence.

When the revolution came, Ghorbanifar was thrown into prison in Tehran, and much of his wealth was confiscated. In time, he managed to buy his way out, and moved himself and his immediate family to Europe. From there, he joined up with some of the leading émigré figures, who were trying to organize some way of removing Khomeini. Ghorbanifar worked with Shahpur Bakhtiar, the former prime minister who lived in Paris; and with General Ariana, a distinguished old man who had established a modest military organization divided between France and eastern Turkey. Neither organization amounted to much, and like most émigré movements, they rather soon became places for nostalgic reminiscing and unrealistic dreaming. Both Bakhtiar and Ariana were good men, but with the passage of time Ghorbanifar became disenchanted, and left the émigré organizations. By early 1983, he had left; within two years we find him deeply involved with some of the most radical members of the regime.

What had happened? Was he, as some have suggested, an infiltrator within the ranks of the émigrés, who then went back home after the discovery and elimination of a Bakhtiar-planned coup attempt in 1982, when more than one hundred conspirators were executed in Tehran?

Was he simply looking for useful contacts in the hopes of reviving his business career, and was willing to do business on either or both sides of the Iranian political divide? Or was he a man with a fairly consistent political agenda, constantly searching for some way to change the policies of the Iranian government, fearing that his country might become permanently detached from the Western world, and might therefore fly off into a dangerously eccentric orbit of its own, too far from any decent tradition to permit civilized life to continue? We do not know the answers, and the very fact that even those who worked quite closely with him wonder about his real identity, testifies to the complexity of his personality and the cunning of which he is capable.

Of Ghorbanifar, two statements could be made with some confidence as of the time we met him in 1985: He knew a great deal about Iran, and he knew virtually nothing about arms. For despite the near-universal label "arms dealer" that everyone from the journalists to the congressional investigators have hung around his neck, Ghorbanifar had no substantial involvement in the arms business prior to this period. Alas, events would bear this out, and his lack of knowledge contributed to one of the major debacles in the short history of the affair: the HAWK missile fiasco of November 1985.

Ghorbanifar entered the story in the late winter–early spring of 1985, thanks to the flamboyant Saudi Arabian billionaire, Adnan Khashoggi. In many ways, Khashoggi was the originator of the entire enterprise, for, contrary to the widespread theory that the Iran initiative was purely an Israeli plan to advance its own interests by luring the United States into supporting Israeli arms sales, it was Khashoggi who realized that the shortest route for Ghorbanifar to reach Washington lay through Jerusalem. This was not a guess on his part, for he had been one of the major international "back channels" between the Middle East, East Africa, and the United States for the better part of two decades. And while many of his interlocutors—especially those in Washington—winced at his flamboyant life-style, Khashoggi was a man to be taken seriously in Western capitals. And he was man well known to certain segments of the Israeli government.

Back in the days when David Kimche was a top Mossad officer, he had hit upon the idea of opening a secret channel to the Saudi royal family. The requirements for such a channel were twofold: reliability and deniability. Khashoggi was the perfect candidate on the Saudi side, and the Mossad soon worked out an arrangement whereby Khashoggi would meet regularly with a designated Israeli intermediary, and they would exchange information and policy ideas. In this

105

way, the Saudi businessman not only enhanced his own business prospects (his access to such information gave him an obvious advantage over most of his competitors), but also made him a man of considerable value to several governments. It was obvious to everyone who knew of his activities that the royal family must have been aware of what he was up to (and approved at least a good deal of it), and this reinforced his outreach; as his knowledge and extraordinary contacts became known to other countries, his access at the highest levels of the Western world—including Washington—grew proportionally. By the time of our story, he was guaranteed a hearing in the White House most any time he wished. His interlocutor there was Bud McFarlane.

Khashoggi combined keen intelligence, a childlike passion for fun in almost any form (although he had a strong preference for sharing his fun with gorgeous women), and a rare combination of Western sophistication and Eastern cunning. He once encountered a troupe of Indian fortune-tellers, and immediately hired them all. That year, he gave them away as year-end presents to several of his friends, including heads of state and powerful international businessmen. Khashoggi knew that such men might tell things to a fortune-teller that they would never share with their personal friends or business associates, and he arranged to have the fortune-tellers report to him at regular intervals. He thus created a first-class international intelligence-gathering network, consisting of a ragtag collection of bearded soothsayers. It is probably not the first time this has been done, but it is a contemporary rarity.

The story of Adnan Khashoggi is a fascinating one, but not quite as extraordinary as might appear at first blush. Governments need deniable intermediaries, and it is easier for the Saudi royal family to use a Khashoggi for this function than to employ a relative of the king or an official of the government. Furthermore, a man like Khashoggi has a degree of mobility and universal access that few government officials can hope to achieve: if Khashoggi had to travel on the spur of the moment, he had three private aircraft at his beck and call, as well as a pleasure yacht so luxurious that it was used in the James Bond movie *Thunderball*. Finally, he had that most precious of all qualities for secret diplomacy: cover. Khashoggi could show up in almost any world capital, and his presence would not arouse suspicion. He always had a credible motive for being someplace: he was making more money, or attending some fantastic party. He was the perfect discreet courier.

On his side, Khashoggi welcomed the role, and not only because it was potentially profitable. At a certain point in their careers, virtually

106

all highly successful businessmen (as well as the odd actor or television newsperson) yearn to participate in life's biggest contest: international affairs. So men like Gianni Agnelli of Fiat, and Henry Grunwald of *Time* come to the conclusion that they have accomplished whatever they could in their chosen professions, and—successfully in Grunwald's case (he is now American ambassador to Austria), unsuccessfully in Agnelli's—seek to enter the great international game of diplomacy. Khashoggi is no different, and he threw himself into the game with typical enthusiasm, imagination, and nerve. To be sure, he was always on the lookout for ways to cash in on these activities, but there were many times when the game itself was the thing.

The most interesting story about Khashoggi's diplomatic activities is one concerning the Arab–Israeli conflict, and it is one that at least two of the principal characters in the tale have not denied. According to this account, once Peres became prime minister, Khashoggi decided to take a stab at working out the conflict between Israel and the PLO. As he saw the matter, each side was frozen in its public position, and neither dared to take the first step. If Arafat recognized Israel without first gaining some guarantee that he would thereby achieve some meaningful concession, he would be murdered; if Peres recognized the PLO without previously gaining a guarantee that Arafat would acknowledge Israel's right to exist, he would be thrown out of office. So Khashoggi, with years of experience in business deals between parties who profoundly distrusted each other, proposed to act as the middle man in the transaction. He would draw up two pieces of paper addressing the basic questions, and the concessions that each side would eventually have to make. Peres would be given a document to sign, saying, "if the PLO recognizes the right of Israel to exist and renounces its war against us, I will recognize the PLO and enter into negotiations with it for the resolution of the Palestinian question." Arafat would sign something saying, "if Israel recognizes the PLO and enters into negotiations for the resolution of the Palestinian question, I will acknowledge Israel's right to exist, and will accept United Nations Security Council resolutions 224 and 338."

Khashoggi asked both Peres and Arafat if this were acceptable. If each signed, Khashoggi would be the holder of the documents, and each would have the right to demand that the documents be made public at any time. That way, the process would only begin once each had signed; neither would risk exposure without the other side accepting the same risk. They both said they would sign. Khashoggi drafted the documents, and went first to Peres, who signed his pledge. But when Arafat was asked to fulfill his side of the bargain, he backed off, promised to consult his council, and eventually failed to sign.

It cannot be said with absolute certainty that the story is true, although neither Peres nor Khashoggi has denied it (Arafat can be expected to deny it, whether true or false). With regard to Khashoggi, the story rings true to me, for it captures both the kind of imagination he is able to bring to international diplomacy, and his willingness to assume a personal risk if he believes the cause is worthwhile. Thus, whatever one's feelings about the endless revelling in which Khashoggi has indulged, his nerve, his contacts, and his imagination have enabled him to frequently play a positive role in international affairs.

When Kimche established the Khashoggi channel, he also managed to find an ideal Israeli counterpart: Al Schwimmer, the long-time president of Israel Aircraft Industries. Schwimmer was an American by birth, but at a young age became active in the Zionist movement, and immediately following the Second World War became one of the men who scoured the West for money and weapons for the fledgling Israeli state. So effective was Schwimmer—even to the point of smuggling weapons out of the United States to Israel on the eve of the War of Independence—that the American government deprived him of the right to vote.

Schwimmer became Khashoggi's chief interlocutor for the Israeli government, a relationship that lasted for more than fifteen years, until the mid-1970s, when the top leadership of Mossad decided that it was potentially corrupting for Israel to have such a relationship with a man whose monetary and sexual profligacy had become legendary. But although the Mossad had opted for an uncharacteristically moralistic stance with regard to Khashoggi, the channel was too important to be abandoned altogether, and we may presume that the relationship continued, this time out of the office of Shimon Peres. For Peres was Schwimmer's closest personal friend, the man for whom Schwimmer had labored for so many years with unfaltering loyalty and a devotion so intense that it produced a story in Israel that Mrs. Schwimmer had once asked her husband to choose between her and Peres . . . and he had instantly chosen Peres. The story is undoubtedly false, but its message is a true one.

So it was perfectly understandable that when Khashoggi decided to introduce Ghorbanifar to the Israelis, he turned to his old friend Schwimmer. And this was indeed the first occasion on which Ghorbanifar met with the Israelis, despite the numerous claims—many of which were endorsed in the Majority Report of the joint Iran-Contra committees—that there had been earlier contacts. Some of the claims indicated an old connection between Ghorbanifar and Yakov Nimrodi, a former top Israeli intelligence official who had served for more than two decades in Iran, and who subsequently became a leading arms dealer; others—from North to CIA Director of Operations Clair George—went so far as to state that Ghorbanifar had been an agent of Mossad. According to a staff member of the Select committees, the CIA believed that Ghorbanifar had been the object of a "false flag" recruitment by the Israelis. The CIA claimed that Ghorbanifar had once been imprisoned during the shah's rule, and that an official of SAVAK counterintelligence offered to get him out of jail if Ghorbanifar would work for him. Ghorbanifar allegedly agreed, and did some counterintelligence work for SAVAK. But, the CIA told the Select committees, the SAVAK official was also an Israeli agent, and "ran" Ghorbanifar for Mossad.

It is an intriguing story, but even if it is true, it does not show that Ghorbanifar was an "Israeli agent" in the normal sense of the term. At most, one might argue that he was unwittingly being used by Israel. But even this claim was strenuously denied by the Israelis at the time of my first contact with Ghorbanifar. I asked several senior Israeli officials—including some who had been deeply involved in the relationship with Iran under the shah—if the Israeli government had had any previous contact with Ghorbanifar, and, if they had, what evaluation they gave him. To a man, they said there had been no previous contact, and in the spring and summer of 1985 they had a difficult time deciding if he was reliable.

So far as I have been able to establish, there was no contact between Ghorbanifar and any of the Israeli participants in the Iran initiative before 1985. The first contact was in Hamburg, in March 1985, at the Four Seasons Hotel, and resulted from Khashoggi's connections with Schwimmer. Consequently, Ghorbanifar was brought to Peres's attention, and from there, inevitably, to the intelligence community.

The evaluation of a man like Ghorbanifar is a daunting task for an intelligence service, yet it is precisely in such cases that the spooks earn their keep. The Israelis were skeptical, for a whole series of very good reasons. They didn't like the Khashoggi channel, since they suspected that any proposal that came from him was likely to be a business scheme masquerading as geopolitics. Second, Mossad knew Ghorbanifar had been involved with the Bakhtiar group in exile, and had information that Ghorbanifar was on a "wanted" list in Tehran. How could a wanted man be an effective channel to the topmost levels of the Ayatollah's regime? Then there were the Ghorbanifar contacts in Europe and Great Britain, which constituted a very mixed bag indeed, ranging from anti-Khomeini exiles to Iranians involved in unpleasant activities like drug running, weapons smuggling, and even terrorism.

Finally, there is an unknown: Did the Mossad take into account the CIA's extremely negative evaluation of Ghorbanifar? There had been at least two contacts, one in 1981 in London, the second in Germany in 1984. On each occasion, Ghorbanifar had offered assistance to the Americans (the second time he claimed to be able to help gain freedom for captured CIA agent William Buckley). And each time, the CIA had offered him money, and given him a polygraph examination. Ghorbanifar refused the money (he was offered four thousand dollars, and he laughed, saying "with me you have to start at ten million") and flunked the polygraphs. As a result of these experiences, and the conviction that Ghorbanifar had been the source of false information associated with Libya, the CIA issued a "burn notice" in the autumn of 1984. A burn notice is a warning, circulated to friendly intelligence services, that the individual in question is considered to be a dangerous fabricator and is not to be trusted. Under normal circumstances, the Mossad should have received this warning, and it should have been part of their evaluation of Ghorbanifar. But if they were aware of the burn notice, they did not inform any of the Israelis who ended up working with Ghorbanifar on the Iran initiative, and I heard nothing of it either from the Israelis or from the CIA.

Both Mossad and Military Intelligence worked on the problem, and between the time of the original contact with Schwimmer and Nimrodi, and the date in early July 1985 when the Israelis decided to bring Ghorbanifar to the attention of the American government, there were two test cases which enabled the Israelis to reach at least a tentative conclusion about the Iranian. The first, of which the American government remained ignorant throughout the history of the Iran initiative, was an attempted arms shipment to Iran in April; the second, of which only a very few Americans were aware—and those only in 1986—was Ghorbanifar's role in the happy resolution of the TWA hostage crisis in June.

The March 1985 meeting arranged by Khashoggi took place in Hamburg, a city in which there is a surprisingly strong Shi'ite community. Organized around the Hamburg Mosque, these Iranians constitute a sort of forward position for Khomeini's revolution; their center is a place where various Iranian officials travel from time to time. And of course, in keeping with the traditions of their country (and those of the celebrated German seaport), some fascinating commercial ventures are launched by the selfsame religious zealots. For example, there is a bonded warehouse down by the docks which contains some of the most beautiful Persian carpets in the world; some of them used to be the property of the shah himself. Khashoggi fancies such carpets, and when, in a subsequent meeting, the discussions of the future of Iran were completed, he went down to the warehouse to admire—and eventually purchase.

The Israelis admired, but did not purchase (although Nimrodi, a veteran of twenty years in Iran himself—and not without financial resources—was interested); they were intrigued by the conversation. The meeting was attended by Khashoggi, Ghorbanifar, Schwimmer, Nimrodi, and an important official of the Khomeini regime. Totally fluent in Farsi, Nimrodi was able to monitor Ghorbanifar's translation into English. The conversation was the first of many that would take essentially the same form: first, an analysis of how the internal Iranian situation was worsening, to the point where many of the leaders of the revolution felt that they must attempt to improve the relationship of Iran with the West; second, suggestions on how best to achieve a better relationship; third, proposals for certain kinds of commercial transactions. Both Ghorbanifar and the Iranian official stressed that it was possible to achieve real changes in Iranian policies, even including a cessation of terrorist attacks, provided that Tehran is permitted to move out of its pariah status. And the only way to demonstrate a greater Western willingness to accept Iran was through the sale of weapons.

I do not know if the Israelis were aware that there was a curious diplomatic background to the Ghorbanifar initiative. By late 1984, Khomeini had come to the conclusion that Iran was under severe strain; Iraqi planes bombed major Iranian cities at will, and while Iran was slowly recapturing lost territory from the invaders, the rate of advance was measured in one or two kilometers per year, and was accomplished at a terrible cost in human life and economic sacrifice. If Iran were to have any chance of winning the war, she would need modern weapons and spare parts. The best weapons, like the spare parts for the crippled Iranian arsenal, were American. Thus, in the late autumn or early winter, the Ayatollah informed his foreign diplomats that Iran would seek some form of contact with the West for this purpose, and particularly with the Great American Satan. They were to seek out channels to the Americans, in order to begin the process.

Ghorbanifar was aware of this decision, and his own activities were

111

designed to achieve the double objective of the regime: better relations with America, and the purchase of American arms. Although the Israelis were unaware of it, Ghorbanifar had tried to find a channel to the government of the United States a few months earlier.

Through a former SAVAK official, Ghorbanifar had arranged a meeting in November 1984 with Theodore Shackley, a former high-ranking CIA officer who achieved distinction for his operations in Southeast Asia in the sixties and seventies. Shackley retired from the agency shortly after Stansfield Turner took it over, and devoted his resourceful mind and considerable energies to activities in the oil business. As part of those activities, he maintained contact with some former Iranian intelligence officers, and one of these arranged the November meeting with Ghorbanifar, and, as luck would have it, a high-ranking Iranian official whom I would meet nearly a year later.

The discussion between Shackley, Ghorbanifar, and the Iranian official ranged over several subjects, from Iranian affairs to business ventures,[2] but one subject raised by the Iranians immediately caught Shackley's attention: Ghorbanifar said he believed it was possible to bring about the release of William Buckley, in exchange for the payment of a certain amount of money.

Shackley promised to bring the information to the attention of the proper persons in Washington, and early in December he reported on the meeting to Gen. Vernon Walters, the ambassador to the United Nations. Nothing came of it. In May 1986, during a luncheon conversation, he told me about the November meeting, without naming the Iranian with whom he met. I asked if the offer still held. Shackley inquired, and the reply came back: "negative." He wrote up a summary of his encounter and gave it to me. I passed it to North without reading it, and there it ended. Or so I thought. When the affair erupted at the end of the year, I read an article in the *New York Times* that informed me, for the first time, that the Iranian with whom Shackley had met was . . . Ghorbanifar.

This, then, was the third effort by Ghorbanifar to establish a channel to the American government, and in all probability it failed for the same reason as the other two: the CIA wanted nothing to do with a man they had declared a dangerous liar and had twice failed to recruit. Yet if their evaluation of Ghorbanifar was based on his claim to be

2. There was a passing reference by Ghorbanifar to an Iranian interest in TOW missiles early in the conversation, but it was never followed up. This later excited the interest of investigators from the Tower Commission and the congressional committees, since they believed it to be the first mention of TOWs in the entire affair. But their curiosity remained unfulfilled, since Shackley had no involvement in either the Iran or the Contra affairs, and his reports on the November meeting produced no response from the government.

able to help in gaining the release of American hostages in Lebanon, we are entitled to a certain skepticism about the accuracy of their assessment. For, whatever the ultimate decision about his motives, Ghorbanifar has achieved an impressive track record in the hostage-release field. At least six Americans and five Frenchmen owe their freedom to his role as intermediary. He can hardly be said to have lied about his ability to help in such matters.

Many have interpreted the Iranians' behavior as a cynical attempt to deceive the United States, falsely promising better relations (including hostage releases, an integral part of a better relationship) simply to obtain our weapons. They may well be right; but the time for that evaluation was some months in the future. At the moment, there were other questions that required answers: Did Ghorbanifar really have access to the top levels of the Iranian regime? And if so, were the messages he was transmitting from Tehran accurate, or was he delivering them with his own personal "spin"?

Finally, there was the extremely interesting question of the hostages. Most Western counterterrorist experts were convinced that the destiny of the hostages was firmly in the hands of local terrorist groups (such as the Hezbollah), and, to the extent that *any* government could effect their release, that government was Syria. It was hard to find a single expert who believed that Iran could do it, and yet this was precisely what Ghorbanifar was saying. This also needed to be checked, for if that claim proved accurate, then Ghorbanifar had somehow acquired a unique understanding of a situation which had baffled all Western intelligence services.

Accordingly, the Israelis decided to test the situation by asking Ghorbanifar to arrange a weapons sale through the office of the Iranian prime minister, Mir Hussein Moussavi. They listened in as Ghorbanifar spoke repeatedly on the telephone with a man in the prime minister's office. In time, this man became known to American officials as "the Australian." He was the right-hand man of the prime minister. Schwimmer and Nimrodi argued that the test should go ahead; the intelligence people were extremely dubious. Finally, Nimrodi agreed to provide a personal guarantee for the shipment of Israeli weapons and spare parts; if the shipment had been lost, he would have had to reimburse the Ministry of Defense for more than half a million dollars.

The ship was supposed to sail out of Eilat early in April, but as the date grew closer it was evident that there were problems in Tehran. Ghorbanifar claimed that the difficulties arose from the extraordinarily high prices the Israelis were asking; the Israelis thought it showed that his access to Iranian leaders was not nearly as good as he claimed.

In any case, the deal was cancelled at the last minute, and the ship had to be unloaded. To this day, the Israelis are not entirely certain why the deal fell through. Even those who doubted his connections at high levels of the Iranian regime are now fully convinced of their existence; and it was certainly in the interest of the Ayatollahs that they lay their hands upon additional weapons for the war against Iraq. Why, then, did the ship not sail?

It is another mystery—albeit a minor one—in a profile of a man who remains enigmatic to the present day.

This story—with all of its significant implications—was not told to us by the Israelis; it only came out during the various investigations after the fact. Had we known about it at the time we were introduced to Ghorbanifar, it might well have made us more cautious about him (which is probably one reason why the Israelis did not tell us the story). On the other hand, they did not immediately tell us about his role in the TWA skyjacking, and that was decidedly helpful to Ghorbanifar's cause. Had we known about *that,* we would have been considerably more enthusiastic about Ghorbanifar than we actually were.

When the TWA Tristar was taken to Beirut in June 1985, the American hostages from the flight were divided into two groups: the bulk of them was in the hands of the Shi'ite Amal militia, headed by Nabbi Berri, but a small contingent of four hostages was taken away by representatives of the fanatical Hezbollah. Very little was known about the Hezbollahis, and opinions varied as to whether or not they responded to guidance from Tehran. Ghorbanifar claimed that they did, and that he could be helpful in convincing them to give up the hostages. At this very moment, the effort to reach a negotiated solution to the hostage crisis had run up against the problem of the Hezbollah hostages. Syria had promised to compel the Amal to release their captives, but could not deliver cooperation from the more radical Shi'ites. The American government had no useful channel to the Hezbollah, and turned to Israel for assistance: Did the Israelis have a way? The Israelis had Ghorbanifar, with his grandiose claims that he could perform miracles with his Iranian compatriots and their Lebanese disciples. The Israelis were not convinced, but it was a way to subject him to a further test: they invited him to visit Iran and Lebanon. Within a few days, he emerged with good news. The Hezbollah had decided to make a gesture. The four Americans were released, a major obstacle to ending the crisis was removed.

The failure of the April weapons shipment was a blow to Ghorbanifar's credibility, but it was more than restored by his TWA performance. At this point, even the skeptics had to grant that Ghorbanifar had demonstrated that he could play a helpful role in the relationship between Iran and the West. Most of the Israelis were also willing to take seriously Ghorbanifar's claim that the Iranian government would use its influence to achieve the release of the American hostages in Lebanon, if it could be done as part of an overall move to normalize relations with the United States. And the release of the four Americans suggested that Iran could deliever.

On the other hand, the picture of Ghorbanifar was still a clouded one, and the Israeli intelligence community was not inclined to recommend any action that depended heavily upon him. They urged prudence, looking for additional information before committing the government to a potentially damaging policy initiative. It is the sort of recommendation that intelligence services normally make to political leaders, especially those who, like Shimon Peres, favor bold action. And Peres's response was entirely in keeping with this pattern: he decided to take a chance on Ghorbanifar.

Peres's life was one of great success, but the Labor party leader was not an upbeat personality. I got to know him as a brooding idealist, who dreamed great dreams of transforming the world at a single stroke. One of Peres's earliest memories was of his life in Eastern Europe, where he recalled getting up one morning to find his parents reading a newspaper. On the front page was the photograph of a man who had been murdered the night before. He never forgot that moment, for it brought home to the little boy the tenuous mortality of men, a lesson that was repeated over and over again, from the Holocaust through the several wars in which Peres was involved. Like many of his generation, he constantly searched for ways to reduce the threats to his people and his country, but he was destined to lead a country in constant danger.

His greatest strength was a willingness to take chances, even when the odds were heavily stacked against him. Against all the evidence, he steadfastly believed that King Hussein (and even Yassir Arafat) would sit down and negotiate a Middle East peace with him, and he pursued every possible avenue to bring it about. In like manner, he believed that the Iran initiative would lead to a major breakthrough, even though there were many reasons for doubt.

Dreamers typically resent the brutal intrusion of reality into their fantasies, and Peres hated the routine processes of government, particularly in foreign policy, where the foreign service functionaries constantly reminded him of the recalcitrant facts of international affairs. He got little encouragement for his dreams from his professional diplomats. So Peres, disappointed with and distrustful of governmental institutions, preferred to operate outside established agencies, with the assistance of a handful of trusted friends. Thus, when the possibility of an Iranian operation developed, he entrusted it to two friends (Schwimmer and Nimrodi) and one controversial professional (David Kimche). Later, when the first phase of the operation went badly, Peres turned to yet another outsider (Amiram Nir), a former journalist with no governmental experience, but with a driving ambition to make a name for himself.

This approach to foreign policy has become nearly universal in the West. I have yet to encounter a head of government who is happy with his or her foreign ministry, and the inevitable conflict between political leaders and policy professionals leads to the creation of a personal foreign policy team that is loyal to the political leadership.

McFarlane had worked for Kissinger at the National Security Council, and shared this atttitude with his former boss. In what would become an almost eerie pattern in the affair, the attitudes and personalities of crucial actors in different countries mirrored each other: Peres and McFarlane were strikingly similar in their attitudes toward their own governmental institutions. They did not trust them, and preferred, wherever possible, to operate outside the professional bureaucracy.

Hence Peres operated through trusted friends like Schwimmer, and preferred the advice of such people to that of his bureaucracy, and McFarlane took care that knowledge of the entire affair was kept secret from as much of the American foreign policy community as possible, above all from the CIA.

There was one further parallel: the three Israelis involved in the first phase of the initiative—David Kimche, Al Schwimmer, and Yakov Nimrodi—were all regarded critically by Mossad, while I had been repeatedly criticized by some of the professional officers at the CIA. Thus, an initiative in which the four of us were involved was likely to generate spontaneous opposition from both national intelligence agencies. And, on the other side of the coin, all four of us were tantalized by the prospect of contributing to a diplomatic success that our governments had been unable to accomplish.

THE OFFER THE PRESIDENT COULD NOT REFUSE

In the first days of July I received a phone call from Israel. At the other end of the line was David Kimche, a good personal friend

116

who, after his distinguished career in Mossad, had become the director general of the Israeli Foreign Ministry; in essence that made him the deputy foreign minister of Israel. He did his job very well indeed, but it was no secret that the Foreign Ministry was too confining for a man of Kimche's imagination; he yearned for the intelligence game, not least of all because he had been driven out of Mossad in a particularly unpleasant power struggle nearly a decade earlier.

Kimche's intelligence background played a role in the events of 1985, but not the one commonly assumed. His relations with Mossad were exceedingly poor, and it was taken as a given in Israel that anything Kimche proposed would be fought by his former colleagues. Even foreigners were caught up in this hostile cross fire; it was virtually impossible to be a good friend of Kimche's and have a close relationship with Mossad.

At a certain moment it appeared that his desires would be fulfilled, for in 1982 Begin announced to the cabinet his intention to appoint Kimche the chief of Mossad when the position came open later that year. It would have been approved, but Foreign Minister Yitzhak Shamir insisted upon one caveat: Kimche was, he said, indispensable to the ongoing negotiations with Egypt and with the Lebanese. Could he keep Kimche for one more year, and then yield him to the intelligence community? Begin agreed. It was to prove unlucky for Kimche; within a few months, the Mossad job was filled, and by the time it came open again, Kimche had become a private citizen, with the stigma of the Iran-Contra affair upon him.

Kimche's involvement in the Iran initiative was the result of happenstance. When, in early July, Peres decided to bring Ghorbanifar to the attention of the White House, Kimche was scheduled to travel to Washington for meetings with State Department officials. Kimche knew nothing of the initiative until that moment, and he was brought into the story simply because he was a convenient bearer of the message from the prime minister.

Kimche was a major talent, and there are some American officials who consider him one of the outstanding Israeli diplomats of his generation. Among these Americans was Bud McFarlane, who worked closely with Kimche during McFarlane's stint as special Middle East envoy prior to (and after) the Lebanon War. The two men had much in common: a strong sense of personal honor, and a recognition of the importance of candor and honesty in dealings among allies. Almost from the first, they liked and trusted one another. In time, the two became close personal friends. I, too, had become Kimche's friend.

I had dealt with him during my stint at the State Department, reporting on the reasons for my conversations with Israeli members of the Socialist International, and our wives and children had come to know and like each other. For someone with my passion for understanding how the world really works, Kimche was a treasure. I knew very few people anywhere with the range of his experience, and fewer still could match his intellectual wherewithal and philosophical temperament.

He called to say that a friend of his—Al Schwimmer—was coming to Washington in a couple of days; could I see him? I quickly agreed, Schwimmer called in the following day to schedule lunch, and less than a week after Kimche's call I met Schwimmer for the first time. He told me the Ghorbanifar story—or at least most of it, leaving out the unhappy story of the failed April arms deal and the happier one of the TWA hostages. He stressed that, according to Ghorbanifar, there were good chances to do various things:

- Establish contacts with high-level officials of the regime, in order to work toward normalization of relations.
- Establish contacts with opponents of current Iranian policies, in the hopes of strengthening such elements in Iran and eventually changing the policies themselves.
- Gain Iranian assistance for the release of the hostages in Lebanon. But such a gesture—which would be a step along the road toward rapprochement—would have to be accompanied by an American gesture of equal significance. Ghorbanifar proposed that we permit Israel to sell several hundred TOW antitank missiles to the Iranians. This would demonstrate that the president himself was committed to a new relationship with Iran (despite his formal public policy of Operation Staunch, which was designed to prevent anyone from selling weapons to Khomeini's regime).

This last was the most complicated, for it was possible to interpret what Ghorbanifar was saying in at least two different—and significantly contradictory—ways. The first was that the reciprocal gestures were part of the process of reconciliation between the two countries —in simple terms, we were coming to terms with Khomeini and he with us. The second interpretation was that we were working to strengthen the hand of those Iranians who wanted better relations with the West, and who disapproved of the more radical aspects of Khomeini's policies (such as the use of terror to advance the cause of radical Shi'ism). This was the point of the presence of the Iranian official at the Hamburg meeting: he and his supporters would presumably be credited with opening the channel to the West, and with obtaining the arms so desperately needed to fight Iraq.

Schwimmer brought with him a long typewritten analysis of the Iranian situation, which Khashoggi had prepared, based on talks with Ghorbanifar. And he brought the proposal that, as one of the first steps toward the new relationship, the United States should approve the sale of several hundred TOWs, and Iran would move to ensure the release of the hostages. Kimche had described the facts in a general way to McFarlane a few days before my luncheon with Schwimmer, and, although neither Schwimmer nor I knew it at the time, Khashoggi had sent a copy of the report to McFarlane through his own channels to the NSC.

I immediately reported this conversation to McFarlane, to whom it came as no surprise. Indeed, Kimche had asked him whether the American government was truly interested in pursuing the matter, and, if so, whether I was the proper channel. McFarlane had said yes to both questions, and Schwimmer had accordingly flown to the United States to brief me. I also took the occasion to introduce Schwimmer to the NSC official in whose office in the Old Executive Office Building I worked: Lt. Col. Oliver North.

I pointed out to McFarlane that my family had long since scheduled a mid-summer vacation in Jerusalem, and that it would be possible to meet Ghorbanifar during that time if it were deemed desirable. In the meantime, it was necessary to raise the question with the president. We could go one of three ways: we could decline the Israeli offer to pursue the matter; we could reject the proposed reciprocal gestures and limit our activities to a further pursuit of greater knowledge about Iran and investigations of useful political contacts; or we could decide to take the first steps toward an improvement in the relationship with Iran, including the proposed gestures, and see where they led. But such a decision could only be made by the president.

We were scheduled to leave for Israel on the evening of July 16th, less than a week away. The president was facing surgery at Bethesda Naval Hospital that very morning. McFarlane undertook to discuss this sensitive issue with Reagan prior to my departure, and did so on the morning of the 16th, after the president's surgery. As McFarlane described it to me early that afternoon, it was the first matter raised with Reagan after he emerged from anesthesia, and I suspect that this is one reason why the president's memory about the discussion has always been rather fuzzy.

119

Much has been made of the apparent contradiction between Operation Staunch and the president's willingness to sell weapons to Iran. How could Ronald Reagan, along with Casey and McFarlane, justify the Iranian arms sales at a time when secretaries Shultz and Weinberger were cracking down on friendly countries who were attempting to do the same thing? The question is a legitimate one, but the matter is not as clear-cut as the critics have suggested. Operation Staunch was created for a specific purpose: To bring sufficient pressure to bear on Iran so that the Ayatollah would feel compelled to change his policies (specifically, abandon the use of terror, and also show a willingness to come to terms in the war with Iraq). It was not intended to be a permanent policy of the United States, but would be changed when and if Iranian behavior changed.

The July 1985 proposal from the Iranian government promised just such a change in Iran's behavior (including an end to terrorism against Americans and American targets), and asked us—as a gesture of *our* willingness to change—to permit Iran to purchase some weapons that had been "staunched." If the process had worked as advertised by Ghorbanifar, there would have been more normal relations between the two countries in a few months, and movement toward an end to the Iran–Iraq war. Normal relations include commerce, and Iran would eventually have the opportunity to purchase American goods, including weapons. The TOW sales were seen as a part of that process, a demonstration of good faith and a sample of what would happen if Iran agreed to a rapprochement with us.

In other words, the president was asked to consider a first move in a complicated game that might lead either to an improvement in the relationship between the United States and Iran, or to a strengthening of pro-Western forces inside Iran. Given the recent history of conflict between the two countries, no one could expect a lightning breakthrough, but the possibilities were certainly intriguing.

I agreed with the president's decision to approve the sale of the original TOWs, and I still think it was reasonable. For if we were embarked on a policy of rapprochement with the Khomeini regime—with or without a parallel effort to strengthen pro-Western Iranians—we would eventually have to permit them to purchase our weapons, just as they, in turn, would have to gain freedom for the American hostages in Lebanon and put an end to the terror weapon. I thought the president was right to take a chance, for the strategic importance of Iran is so great that a leader is justified in taking risky steps.

120

THE FIRST ENCOUNTER

McFarlane's instructions to me were, as always, quite precise and prudent. The president was interested in principle, but there was to be no go-ahead until we had a better picture of what was involved. I was therefore authorized to meet with Ghorbanifar, collect as much information as possible, and then report back to McFarlane. My role was that typically assigned to part-time consultants: listen, ask questions, and then inform the policymakers in Washington. Part-time consultants are almost never involved in the actual policy discussions; indeed, their value to the government derives in no small measure from the fact that they are independent of the debates that divide the Washington community. I did not know, for example, that there had been an extended discussion within the government about the possibility of resuming limited arms sales to Iran, well before I had heard about Ghorbanifar's proposals.[3]

The discussions with Ghorbanifar were held in one of Nimrodi's extravagant houses in Savion, which is the Beverly Hills of Tel Aviv. Once again, the symmetry between Israel and the United States held: the house in which the discussions were held is known as the White House, for it is a replica of the president's Washington residence. So, whether in America or Israel, the Iran initiative was most commonly discussed in the White House.

By the time I got to Israel, Ghorbanifar and the three basic Israelis (Kimche, Schwimmer, and Nimrodi) had gotten to know one another quite well. Kimche had met Ghorbanifar in Hamburg for the first time on his way back to Israel following his meeting with McFarlane; for Schwimmer and Nimrodi, the European meeting was simply the latest in a long series.

The talks in the Savion White House ran over a two-day period, and Ghorbanifar went through a substantial part of his extended repertoire. We discussed the internal Iranian situation in some detail, pressing him for detailed explanations of the political infighting he

---

3. At about the same time that I went to Israel to meet Ghorbanifar, Graham Fuller, the national intelligence officer for Near East affairs at CIA, wrote a "think piece" for Casey, examining ways in which we could improve our understanding of Iran and increase our ability to influence future events there. One of the options he considered was that of reopening some sort of dialogue with the Khomeini regime, and the possibility of permitting the sale of weapons as part of this renewed dialogue was mentioned, along with other possibilities. Some saw in this evidence of either a sinister coordination between the NSC and the CIA, or even an effort to slant CIA analyses. Anyone who believed this obviously did not know Mr. Fuller, a highly independent thinker who would express his own views regardless of the political winds in the White House (or the agency, for that matter).

121

claimed was going on, as well as accounts of the war effort, the effect of the war on civilian morale and on the political and religious leadership of the country. The picture we got was of a country with severe internal tensions. Since Iran had no functioning night radar, the Iraqis were able to bomb Iranian cities at will once the sun had set, and Ghorbanifar told us (and we obtained confirmation of this from other sources) that there was a regular nighttime exodus of thousands of people from the major cities into the countryside, in order to avoid harm from the enemy air force. Moreover, the cities themselves had turned into a Hobbesian war of all against all, with members of the Revolutionary Guard (the *Pasdaran*) hiring out to individual leaders as private militias. Men—even mullahs—were murdered in the streets in broad daylight, and fighting between the groups of *Pasdaranis* was not unusual.

On top of all this, there were signs of popular discontent with the regime itself. By the summer of 1985, there were demonstrations in Tehran and Tabriz, and Ghorbanifar believed there had been some strikes by workers in the oil fields. The economic fortunes of the bazaar had long since taken a dramatic slide, adding another substantial group to the numbers of the disgruntled.

Against this background, it was easy to believe that some of the mullahs and ayatollahs, along with regular army officers and leaders from other traditional institutions, feared the disintegration of their country, a concern made particularly acute by the notorious appetite of the Russian Bear to the north and east. Those among them who favored better relations with the West had a growing stock of political ammunition to use against the radicals who called for an unrelenting holy war—an Islamic *jihad*—against the Western world.

So far as they had been able, the Israelis had checked Ghorbanifar's picture of Iran, and found it credible—as the CIA did later on. The issue was whether we could make a deal with the existing regime, or did we have to seek out—and support—its internal opponents?

This was to remain one of the murkiest of all the questions associated with the initiative. On the one hand, we might be interested in contacts with "conservative" elements in Iran—those who favored good relations with the West, opposed the export of Shi'ism by terror, and argued against the centralization of the economy. If these people proved strong enough, we might wish to find some way to support them, in the hope of changing the policies of the country.

On the other hand, it was unrealistic to believe that a faction—

especially a faction opposed to current policies—could bring about the release of American hostages in Lebanon, or the end of terrorist attacks against American targets. Nor could a faction receive and use TOW missiles; these would go to the government, and any military gain that Iran derived from the missiles would work to the government's advantage. Was the government—including the radicals—prepared to change its policies to achieve rapprochement with us? Or was this a clever deception, designed to get our weapons?

There was one further possibility: the deception, if such it was, could have been carried out at the behest of a foreign power, such as the Soviet Union. The Kremlin certainly recognized the strategic significance of Iran, and knew of our long-standing interests there. Would they not wish to know our intentions? And were they not capable of staging elaborate deceptions, just in order to find out our plans? It would not have been unusual for the KGB to have done so; their use of elaborate deception—against both foreign and domestic enemies—was one of their trademarks. Few intelligence services have resorted to deception with such regularity, and such zeal, as those of the Soviet Union.

The most famous Soviet deception was the Trust affair shortly after the Bolshevik Revolution. It began in 1921 and ran for six years. The central deception was something called the Monarchist Association of Central Russia, a presumed anti-Soviet subversive network inside Russia, which established contact with Western intelligence services, offering inside information and the capacity to subvert the Soviet system—even assassinate leading Soviet officials. The West fell for the hoax (it eventually cost the lives of dozens of top agents, including Sidney Reilly, the so-called Ace of Spies of the British Secret Intelligence Service), financed the Trust throughout its existence, and handed the Soviets a treasure trove of information about Western intentions. So the notion that Ghorbanifar might be part of a Soviet deception was not at all fanciful. Both we and the Israelis were alert to this possibility from the beginning.[4]

Before attempting any long-term decisions, at least some of the immediate questions needed to be resolved. If we went ahead with

4. Some members of the Senate Select Intelligence Committee staff apparently entertained the hypothesis that the whole thing was a Soviet deception, run by a KGB agent within the Israeli government, who in turn ran Ghorbanifar. This was only one step removed from the theory that Ghorbanifar had earlier been run by a SAVAK official who was in turn an Israeli agent. There was a steadfast determination on the part of many American investigators to reject what was in front of their noses: that Ghorbanifar was his own man, and that no intelligence service would feel comfortable "running" him.

the proposed reciprocal test—Iran taking steps to end terrorism, gain the release of hostages, and indicate a willingness to change, while we enabled them to get a small number of TOW missiles from Israel—many of these murky areas would hopefully become clearer. To be sure, there was not much enthusiasm in Washington for enabling the Khomeini regime to obtain the TOWs, and there was considerable opposition to it, especially from Shultz and Weinberger. However, there was also a general recognition that the issues were serious, and that a coherent Iran policy was badly needed. In the end, the president decided to swallow his instinctive dislike of the weapons side of the equation in order to obtain the possible benefits of freedom for hostages and a breakthough in contacts with Iran.

REAGAN AND THE HOSTAGES

There is no doubt that Ronald Reagan's passion for the release of the American hostages in Lebanon was a very strong emotion. On another occasion, Reagan demonstrated a great weakness on this matter. This occurred during the Nicholas Daniloff affair, when the KGB framed and arrested an American journalist in Moscow in response to the arrest of one of its agents in New York. The president was furious, enraged by the thought of an American citizen being held in a KGB prison, his every motion monitored by the all-seeing television camera mounted in the ceiling of his cell, his sleep interrupted for the ritual interrogations designed to make him confess to acts he had never committed. The rumors in the State Department were that Daniloff was nearing the breaking point, and that the KGB would soon be in a position to present his admissions of "guilt" to the world media. A deal was cut, the Soviet spy freed, and Daniloff returned to the United States. Although we unbalanced the equation by expelling a number of KGB officers, Reagan's willingness to bend his principles in order to rescue Americans held hostage was evident.

If Reagan was upset at the thought of a journalist in the hands of the Soviet Union, he was even more shaken by the spectacle of several innocent Americans in the hands of fanatics in the Middle East. For we knew a good deal about the treatment of Western hostages, and it was sufficient to shake even the most hardened observers. Governments like Iran and Syria specialized in torture, and had refined their methods over the centuries to the point where their unfortunate victims were quite quickly reduced to unrecognizable bundles of pain and terror. Limbs were amputated, eyes torn or burned out, electrical shock applied to the genitals, teeth drilled to the nerves. Middle Eastern torturers did not adopt the more refined methods of sleep deprivation or psychological torture made infamous by the Soviets and the Vietnamese. They stuck with the centuries-old methods of direct, physical violence. It is no wonder that those who fall into the clutches of such a regime are quick to "confess" to anything, hoping thereby to avoid the worst of the horrors their captors can inflict upon them. For particularly hated enemies, special treatments have been devised, as in the case of General Nasiri, the former head of SAVAK, the shah's secret police. This unfortunate man had been arrested for corruption in the latter years of the shah's rule, and hence was already in prison when Khomeini seized power. He was in a sense killed three times: first by being subjected to the most horrible tortures (including being compelled to swallow razor blades), then hanged—and cut down at the very last moment—and finally sent before the firing squad.

While we did not have reliable accounts of the conditions of the American hostages (the first detailed information came only with the release of the Reverend Benjamin Weir in September 1985), it was easy to assume that they were being subjected to one or another variation on the standard theme.

It is easy to understand the president's concern, but people have searched for singular explanations for his deep emotional involvement in the hostages' fate. There are stories, for example, about a tape recording of the torture of William Buckley, the CIA station chief in Beirut who was taken hostage by the Hezbollah in 1984. I know of no one in the American government who ever heard such a tape, and everyone with whom I have spoken is quite convinced that no such thing ever existed.[5] But there *was* information that Buckley was being tortured, and this had an effect on the top decision makers in Washington.

Buckley was an outstanding CIA officer, with detailed knowledge of the Middle East and a fine track record as a clandestine operative. But he was well along in his career and had developed attitudes that are typical of people who should not be sent out on dangerous missions. Buckley was afraid to return to Beirut. He was convinced that his identity had been blown years ago, that the KGB and several Middle Eastern terrorist organizations knew him, and that he would surely be murdered if he went back.

---

5. There was a videocassette of Buckley, to demonstrate he was still alive, but although he looked drawn and weak, there were no "live" torture scenes on the tape.

Buckley's fears were not merely those of a man who has lived a dangerous life and has reached an age where adventure has become less inviting. His name had appeared on a list in the early 1970s, published by a magazine founded by Phillip Agee, a former CIA officer who left the agency and devoted his life to attacking the CIA and its activities. The name of James Welch, the CIA's Athens station chief, was also on the list, and Welch was assassinated.[6] Buckley took this as an evil augury for himself.

William Casey had personally urged Buckley to go to Beirut. He knew of Buckley's anxieties, but he also knew that skilled talent and good judgment were in very short supply at the CIA. If not Buckley, who could do the job? Buckley, ever the good soldier, agreed, but old friends who visited him in Beirut found him melancholy and brooding, convinced that he had been fingered, and awaiting his fate. It is a mind-set that often leads to disaster.

When Buckley was grabbed, Casey was deeply shaken, for he knew that without his intervention, Buckley might well not have gone to the Middle East again. The CIA director called for action; the agency went all out to try to locate and rescue their captured colleague, and Casey informed the president of the situation at regular intervals, thereby reinforcing Reagan's strong passions about the Lebanon hostages.

The details of the Buckley case explain Casey's feverish activities, and also the willingness of Vice President Bush (who, when CIA chief, had known and liked Buckley) to support the arms-for-hostages policy, but are not required to understand the president. Furthermore, despite the Tower Commission's conclusion that the president's hands-off management style led to the kind of error that characterized the Iran initiative, in fact the very same mistakes were made by other national leaders—with management styles no one would characterize as "hands-off." Reagan's behavior was not unique; it was part of a Western pattern. Leading Israeli, French, and German officials all abandoned their strong public stance against dealing with terrorists in favor of making clandestine deals to ransom their hostages.[7]

6. For more on Agee and the assassination of Welch after his name was published by *Counterspy* (Agee's publication), see S. Steven Powell, *Covert Cadre* (Ottowa, Ill.: Green Hill, 1988), pp. 65–67.

7. Both Mitterrand and Chirac opened secret channels to Iran and negotiated at length for the release of French hostages. Under Mitterrand, French arms were sent to Iran (there are claims that Mitterrand himself was witting, although he denied it. Defense Minister Hernu was certainly involved in the chain of command, however), along with considerable quantities of money. Under Chirac, secret negotiations led to "unfreezing" more than $300 million when French hostages were freed in 1987. The Israelis released more than fifteen hundred convicted terrorists in exchange for four hostage Israeli military men. And the Germans established a secret channel to Tehran in 1987, thereby obtaining the release of one of two hostages in Lebanon, in exchange for business concessions.

126

From Begin, Peres, and Sharon to Kohl, Chirac, and Mitterrand, all these men were moved by personal appeals from the families of the hostages. These were deeply emotional encounters. At one of them, in Jerusalem, the mother of an Israeli soldier in the hands of Palestinian terrorists hurled herself on the floor in front of the prime minister, wailing with grief, grabbed his ankles, and begged him to redouble his efforts to save her boy. Such scenes were repeated in Bonn, Paris, and Washington, and no chief of government was able to resist; each promised to do everything possible to save the hostages.

Reagan was certainly no tougher minded on this question than Ariel Sharon, François Mitterrand, or Jacques Chirac, none of whom could be accused of governing his country with a Reaganesque "hands-off management style," or a laid-back approach verging on absent-mindedness. And although they have all been accused of political opportunism, I doubt that this played much of a role in their calculations. Indeed, each had reason to expect that his decision would be politically unpopular; French and Israeli public opinion was solidly behind an uncompromising toughness toward terrorism, while Reagan had the example of Jimmy Carter to draw upon.

Reagan made the same decision, even though he fully recognized the political risks. In a candid moment he indicated a suspicion that his subordinates might have to go quite close to the line of legality in order to fulfill his instructions; but he said he was fully prepared to accept responsibility for their actions. At the NSC meeting in the White House on December 7th, 1985, at which he discussed the future of the Iran initiative with McFarlane, Poindexter, John McMahon (Casey's deputy), Shultz, Weinberger, and Regan, the president listened attentively to all the arguments against pursuing the matter any further. McMahon spoke passionately against working with Ghorbanifar, and Shultz and Weinberger reiterated their opposition to the entire undertaking. Reagan was not moved, and, with a twinkle in his eye, told them: "I don't care if I have to go to Leavenworth; I want the hostages out." He joked that Thursday was visiting day, and brought the meeting to an end.

5. Iran II:
Hostage to the Hostages

The issue before the president in the summer of 1985 was not merely arms-for-hostages, although both arms and hostages were involved; it was a proposed set of reciprocal gestures that would enable the United States to test various propositions, ranging from Ghorbanifar's credibility as a channel to the highest levels of the Iranian regime, to the ability of the Ayatollah to control the destinies of American hostages in Lebanon. And there was the intriguing possibility of establishing a working relationship with pro-Western Iranians interested in changing the nature of the regime. Kimche flew to Washington immediately following our meetings with Ghorbanifar, and on August 3rd he briefed McFarlane on what we had learned, as well as on the proposed gestures. McFarlane promised to raise the matter with the president. By the time I returned to Washington from vacation in the middle of the month, the president had decided to give it a try.

The understanding after our meetings with Ghorbanifar was that the cessation of terrorist attacks would be effective immediately; that we would shortly begin to hear a distinct change in the public statements of leading Iranian officials; and that a total of five hundred TOW missiles would be sent to Iran from Israel. These would arrive in two tranches: an initial delivery of one hundred, then the balance. Between the two shipments, one or more hostages would be released, and the rest of the hostages would come out after the second missile shipment. But although Ghorbanifar swore that Prime Minister Moussavi had promised the Iranians would faithfully fulfill their side of the bargain, some of us were dubious. Israeli Defense Minister Rabin told me in a one-on-one meeting in his office in Tel Aviv that he believed

128

we were wasting our time. In his opinion, not a single hostage would be released, and Israel would simply have squandered hundreds of missiles to no good end. Kimche, Nimrodi, and Schwimmer held varying degrees of hope, but none of them believed that the test would prove fully satisfactory from our point of view.

McFarlane was aware of these different expectations, and fully realized that the test might fail. Yet he, along with all the Israelis involved (including Rabin), did believe that it was worth a try. For all the doubts, this was the best chance we had had to get involved in the future of Iran.

All the operational details were in the hands of the Israelis, the American role being restricted to one promise and one backup operation. The promise was that Israel would be able to replace the TOWs in short order. This was important because the gravest military threat to Israel came from Syria, and Syria had thousands of tanks massed along the northeast border. Israel could not deplete her antitank arsenal for very long without putting the country at grave risk. The promise was given by McFarlane to Kimche.

Ghorbanifar had reported that it was not possible to predict precisely where the freed hostage(s) would appear, and prudence dictated that we be ready for various contingencies. Accordingly, McFarlane instructed me to brief North, who was responsible for preparations for "extracting" hostages from various places in Lebanon: making certain that helicopters and/or submarines were in the area, specialized units ready to move at short notice, and the like. Meanwhile, the Israelis were asked to press Ghorbanifar for detailed information; the earlier we knew where to pick up our hostages, the better our chances for a successful extraction.

At McFarlane's instructions, I discussed all these matters with Kimche at London's Heathrow Airport a week after the president's go-ahead. At the same time, we agreed upon an elementary code to use on open telephone lines to exchange information about the progress of the TOW shipment and possible locations of hostages to be picked up. The use of such codes amused some of the members of the congressional committees, but, as North pointed out with some heat, they were absolutely necessary if the lives of the hostages were to be effectively safeguarded. Top officials of the governments of the United States and Israel know that virtually all of their telephone conversations—and every international call—are monitored by the Soviet KGB, and we were not eager to have the Soviets know of our activities. Since we could not risk speaking openly about these matters on normal international telephone connections, we needed a secure code. The safest kind of code is one which is generated at random, and used only once or twice, and this was what we did.

To be sure, it was theoretically possible to use the more sophisticated communications systems of the Department of State or the Central Intelligence Agency, but McFarlane was insistent that knowledge of this effort be restricted to the smallest possible number of people. There had been too many leaks of sensitive information during the Reagan administration, and most of them had come from members of the executive branch.

At the same time, North took steps to increase our ability to evaluate the Ghorbanifar channel, and instructed the intelligence community to monitor Ghorbanifar's movements, and, so far as was possible, his contacts with Iranian officials. The results of this surveillance are obviously sensitive, and cannot be fully discussed here, but it was possible to piece together an interesting picture of Ghorbanifar's relationship with the Khomeini regime, as well as of the ability of Iran to influence events in Lebanon and elsewhere. The Iranians may have been aware of our efforts to gather this information, and they are highly imaginative in finding ways to mislead observers about their abilities and intentions. As usual in the intelligence business, the watchers and the watched played a complicated game, in which the truth was rarely self-evident, and every presumed fact was frequently open to several interpretations. This effort was rendered even more difficult because, while the CIA was involved in the effort, agency officials did not know the true identities of Ghorbanifar and his interlocutors. They were given pseudonymns, and only became aware of the real names at the end of the year. It was indeed a tangled web. The only people in the government who were generally informed about the initiative at this stage were the cabinet-level people who dealt with national security affairs (Reagan, Bush, Casey, Shultz, McFarlane, Meese, and Weinberger), Chief of Staff Donald Regan, three senior members of McFarlane's staff (Poindexter, Fortier, and North), and I.[1]

The Israeli Mossad was likewise absent, once the basic evaluation of Ghorbanifar had been completed. Kimche had asked that the Mossad handle the operational arrangements for the TOW shipment, but

1. By the end of the year, if not earlier, Assistant Secretary of Defense Richard Armitage and some of his colleagues, along with Under Secretary of State Michael Armacost, Ambassador Robert Oakley, and a handful of State Department officials had been briefed on the initiative. Armitage, Armacost, and Oakley were instrumental in pushing for a general discussion of the issue, and appear to have played a role in bringing about the December 7th White House meeting just prior to McFarlane's departure for London that night.

the intelligence agency declined. Later on, senior Mossad officials would say that they should have been involved in the project, implying they had not been asked. But the decision to stay out had been their own.

The first one hundred TOW missiles were shipped on schedule in late August. Schwimmer, with backup from the Defense Ministry, arranged for a 707 with Latin American registration to fly to Israel, pick up the missiles, fly out over the Mediterranean, and then enter a standard commercial flight path to Iran. The pilot was skeptical about the willingness of air controllers to permit him to cross their air space without previous permission, but the Israelis' experience had been that this would be possible if the pilot simply announced that he was coming from Europe. And they proved correct; there was no challenge to the aircraft. Nor was there any problem from the Iraqi Air Force, which the Israelis considered the major threat to the mission.

The plane carried more than missiles; at the last minute, the Israelis insisted that Ghorbanifar personally accompany the cargo to Tabriz. The April failure had taught them a lesson, and they were not about to risk a second major embarrassment on Ghorbanifar's word. So, as they explained while pushing him steadily toward the aircraft at the military section of Ben Gurion Airport outside Tel Aviv, either he went on board, or the mission would be cancelled.

Ghorbanifar was not eager to go to Iran, for although he had developed effective channels to many of the top leaders, he was still a person who had worked with SAVAK, and who had supported elements in the anti-Khomeini émigré community. He therefore had enemies in Tehran and was not altogether certain that he would receive a totally friendly welcome. But there was no alternative; he had to take his chances.

The good news was that the TOWs arrived as promised; the bad news was that we had nothing to show for it. No sooner had the plane landed in Tabriz than the Revolutionary Guards seized the missiles and carted them off; and Ghorbanifar, his worst fears fully realized, was escorted to the offices of SAVAMA—the successor to the dreaded SAVAK—for interrogation. It cannot have been pleasant—the penalties for wrong answers being notoriously painful—but he passed. Early the following morning, he was in Prime Minister Moussavi's office, asking about the hostage releases. He quickly learned that no hostage had been freed, nor had anything been done to ensure any releases in the near future.

Had Ghorbanifar been tricked? Or had he been part of an Iranian deception of the Israelis and us? We knew that he had accurately reported to us what he had been told by people in Prime Minister Moussavi's office. Unless those exchanges had been part of a systematic effort to mislead us (and the Iranians were certainly capable of conceiving such a deception, although they would have been hard pressed to stage and maintain it for very long), Ghorbanifar cannot be considered to have been part of a deliberate scam.

The most likely explanation is that the Iranians themselves were surprised at what had happened. Remember that Ghorbanifar was merely one among scores of Iranians who claimed the ability to acquire advanced American weapons for the Ayatollah. Iran had been tricked many times in the past, paying millions of dollars for empty boxes or crates that were supposed to contain weapons, but turned out to be full of sand. As a result, the Iranians had grown profoundly suspicious of anyone who promised American weapons, and while Ghorbanifar had good connections in Tehran, he could hardly have been considered a man in whom the Ayatollah had total confidence. Indeed, the Iranians had refused to advance a single penny toward the purchase of the TOWs, until they were actually delivered to Iran.

The question of financing had created a minor crisis, for the Iranians refused to pay until after delivery, while the Israelis were unwilling to ship until they had been paid in full. The impasse had been solved by Khashoggi, who provided the "bridge loan" that got the transaction off the ground. Khashoggi paid a million dollars (100 missiles at $10,000 per missile) to Ghorbanifar, and he paid the Israelis, who then delivered the missiles. If Iran paid, there would be a commission in it for Khashoggi.

In other words, the Iranians were skeptical about Ghorbanifar's ability to deliver, and while they certainly encouraged him to go ahead with his project, they undoubtedly believed that much of what he was telling them was hot air. It was not as if he had delivered any weapons to them in the past, after all. Many American journalists, congressmen, and investigators have decided that Ghorbanifar was a long-time arms merchant, but so far as I can discover, this affair was the first time he had actually dealt with weapons. And the behavior of the Iranians was that of people who had no confidence in Ghorbanifar's ability to deliver. The evidence suggests that they were quite surprised when he arrived in Tabriz with one hundred genuine American TOW missiles. The Iranians had promised the hostages and a change in policy, but their promises had been given without any expectation that they would have to fulfill them. It was not until Ghorbanifar and the missiles landed, that they had to face the consequences of their commitments.

The seizure of the TOWs by the Revolutionary Guards effectively demolished one of the theories that Ghorbanifar had put forward. This was the notion that the pro-Western faction in Iran, by taking credit for obtaining the missiles, would be strengthened as a result of the arms sales. I was always rather skeptical about this theory, since it seemed to me that you couldn't deliver weapons to a faction, only to a government. No matter what gloss Ghorbanifar attempted to put on the transaction, it was still a sale of weapons to the Khomeini regime. And since I favored an effort to strike a blow to Khomeini and change the nature of the Iranian regime, I certainly did not want to strengthen the regime itself. Later, when I met with a representative of the pro-Western faction, he confirmed this view with considerable passion, and indicated that he, too, thought it was a great error to sell weapons. Nonetheless, the rationale of "strengthening moderates by selling weapons to the regime" continued throughout the initiative.

That brings us back to Ghorbanifar: to what extent did he know exactly what was really going on in Tehran? The most likely hypothesis is that he suspected that the prime minister and his associates had less than total confidence in Ghorbanifar's reliability. But he probably also believed that, once the missiles arrived, the regime would have to make good on its guarantees. His task was to initiate the process, drawing both sides into the dialogue and convincing us to take the first step. Thereafter, his understanding of the needs of both sides was such that he was confident an agreement would be reached. If that is correct, his judgment was accurate; the Iranians quickly moved to change their public rhetoric and to obtain the release of one of the American hostages.

With the missiles in Iranian hands, and Ghorbanifar cleared by SAVAMA, we began to see evidence of the promised shift in Iranian policy. In early September, President Khamenei delivered a speech on the anniversary of the 1978 uprising against the shah that presaged the fall of the monarchy. On every previous anniversary, the speeches had been full of venom for the United States; on this occasion there was no such rhetoric, and Khamenei instead reserved his harshest language for the Soviet Union. Furthermore, although it was too early to call it a clear change in policy, there had been no Iranian-sponsored terrorist attacks against Americans or American targets (and there would be none until the fall of the following year).

But the hostage question remained. At a day-long discussion in a suite at the elegant Prince de Galles Hotel in Paris in the second week of September, Ghorbanifar, Kimche, Schwimmer, Nimrodi, and I looked at the possible paths of action. Ghorbanifar transmitted the regime's proposal: send the remaining four hundred missiles and hostages would be freed. When we challenged him, he picked up the phone and called the prime minister's office. Nimrodi listened in on the extension and confirmed that this was indeed the official position of the Iranian government.

At the same time, we spoke at some length about organizing meetings with Iranians who, quite independent of the hostage question, sought to change the nature of the regime. It was conceivable, albeit unlikely, that the president might have opted to abandon the hostage question and pursue the political matter on its own merits, and I wanted to be in a position to provide first-hand information about the pro-Western faction. But Reagan's primary concern was for the fate of the hostages, and a week later, after a briefing from McFarlane, the president decided to go through with the basic test: the Israelis were authorized to send the remaining TOWs.

The same 707 was used, with the same flight path. Once again, European air space was traversed without difficulty, but this time two Iraqi fighters came after the plane as it headed for Iran. The pilot took evasive action and eventually landed safely, but the little adventure presaged more difficulties to come. On the return flight, the plane's radio went out, and, rather than risk a long flight without the possibility of ground contact, the pilot decided to improvise and fly directly to the one known safe haven in the area: Israel.

The unexpected arrival of the plane in Tel Aviv was of course observed by the world's monitoring systems, and within minutes air controllers had announced that an unidentified commercial airplane had flown from Iran to Israel. A couple of hours later, the notice had been picked up by the international wire services (I remember a Reuters bulletin, and there were also others), and Schwimmer had called in from Tel Aviv to ask if we could take measures to diminish the level of interest in the question. I informed North of the problem, and he busied himself with it for some time. Precisely how he managed it, I do not know, but somehow he convinced a lot of interested persons—from the Pentagon to the National Security Agency—not to delve too deeply into the matter. At the same time, Israeli journalists learned at least the essential facts about the mission, for the military censor "spiked" a story saying that there had been a flight to Iran as a result of a conversation between David Kimche and Bud McFarlane.

This little contretemps masked a deeper problem produced by the steadfast refusal of the Mossad to get involved in the operation. Kimche, Nimrodi, and Schwimmer felt that since Mossad had finally pronounced Ghorbanifar a reasonable risk—albeit with reservations— the intelligence service ought to help organize the mechanical details, such as obtaining the aircraft and the pilots. But the Mossad chieftains would not get involved. In part their refusal stemmed from the usual bureaucratic motives: it was not their operation, and they did not wish to play handmaiden in someone else's bridal party. Beyond that, there was the well-known personal animus between the top Mossad officials and the three Israelis.

When the scandal erupted, Mossad officials were quick to say that they had had reservations about the wisdom of the overall initiative. This was a bit of an overstatement. They had opposed it, as they opposed anything involving Schwimmer, Nimrodi, and Kimche. But this was a blind opposition to the three men, not a carefully reasoned critique of a policy. Kimche, Nimrodi, and Schwimmer had many talents among them, but they did not add up to a professional intelligence service. Mossad's decision deprived them of a vast quantity of operational expertise, as well as the possibility of ongoing professional assessments of the state of the initiative.

The Iranian regime now had to move on the hostage question, and it was not easy. In a peculiar way, the Ayatollah's rule was similar to Reagan's concept of cabinet government: the maximum leader tended to remain aloof from the day-to-day discussions and debates. Khomeini defined the overall direction of the country, and he intervened directly only when conflicts between his subordinates could not be resolved any other way.

The hostage question required Khomeini's direct involvement, for the fight between those who favored hostage release and those who opposed it was so intense that only the Ayatollah could decide. We had good intelligence, which showed that the faithful were gathered. The opposed factions in Iran, the leaders of the Hezbollah from Lebanon, and Ahmad Khomeini, the increasingly powerful son of the Ayatollah, came together to discuss the fate of the American hostages. After hours of debate, Khomeini directed the Hezbollah to release one hostage, and the Americans were given a chance to name him. This decision was communicated by Ghorbanifar to the Israelis, and Kimche asked McFarlane to choose a hostage. It was an easy choice —or so it seemed—and the national security adviser named William Buckley. Forty-eight hours later, the Reverend Benjamin Weir, a Presbyterian missionary who had spent some twenty years in the Middle East before his capture, was deposited in front of the British embassy in Beirut. It was one of the bits of evidence that led us to conclude that Buckley was dead.

I only learned that McFarlane knew in advance of the release of a single hostage when he testified before the joint Select committees in 1987, but I was awakened quite early on the morning of September 15th, 1985, by a phone call from McFarlane: "We have a delivery," he said, "a priest. Many happy returns."

Weir was an extraordinary character, and the Iranians had evidently chosen him with some care. It was hard to imagine that anyone could be held hostage for more than a year (with a full year in solitary confinement), and emerge full of hatred for his rescuers and unlimited praise for his captors and their cause. Yet Benjamin Weir was such a man. He was fully devoted to the Shi'ite cause in the Middle East, viciously denounced American and Israeli policies, and apparently believed he had been released because of humanistic impulses of the Hezbollahis. North, who had debriefed Weir at a military safe house in Virginia, was shocked at the Reverend's behavior, and that of his family. He told me that Weir's relatives were convinced that the Reverend had been taken hostage by the United States in an effort to discredit the Shi'ites, and refused to let any American official talk to him before they did, for fear that we would "deprogram" Weir, thus making it impossible for the family to discover what had actually happened.

The Iranians had chosen well: a hostage who would do their propaganda work in the United States.

Weir had been released in the middle of the Jewish high holiday period, and I had reason to reflect on the significance of his freedom. In the prayer book for Yom Kippur there is a passage that reads, "one who has saved a human life is judged to have saved all mankind." I wondered if this applied to a man who so deeply hated people like me, and would devote his life to support movements that wished to destroy Americans and Jews. A few days after Weir's release, Ghorbanifar called, and I asked him if it was possible for the Iranians to take Weir back, and send us a patriotic American instead. He laughed, and said it would be difficult to do that kind of swap.

THE POTENTIAL TURNING POINT

With the release of Weir, our basic questions had apparently been answered, and it seemed the president had made a good decision to approve the reciprocal test. Ghorbanifar was indeed a legitimate channel to the highest levels of the Khomeini regime, the Iranians could indeed determine the destiny of hostages, and there was at least some interest on the Iranian side in an improved relationship. We now needed to define the next step, and our worldwide travelling discussion now shifted to Washington, as Ghorbanifar, Schwimmer, and Nimrodi came to town the first week in October 1985.

We met all day on October 3 in a conference room on the third floor of the Old Executive Office Building. North had been invited. He did not attend, but met separately with Schwimmer and Ghorbanifar. At the discussions of the full group (Schwimmer, Nimrodi, Ghorbanifar and me), Ghorbanifar again reported that the Iranian government was asking for weapons. This time, however, they had moved into new categories: Harpoons, Phoenixes, Sidewinders . . . you name it, they wanted it. And for each bundle of advanced weapons, they were offering one or more hostages.

At the same time, Ghorbanifar confirmed that it had become possible for us to talk directly to spokesmen for the "conservative line" inside the country, and we were promised meetings within the next month.

I urged that we recommend to our respective governments that the hostage question be abandoned, and that we concentrate entirely on the political channels. My argument was that, if we continued to sell arms to the Iranians, we would never be able to evaluate their real intentions, since they would do almost anything in order to lay their hands on the weapons. If we could not accurately assess their intentions, we could not possibly design a coherent Iran policy—which, after all, I believed was the ultimate objective of the entire exercise.

The Israelis were upset at this suggestion, and while they were quite excited about the possibilities of the political contacts, they also argued passionately that it was wrong to abandon the hostages. It had emerged that the Israelis had a hostage problem of their own with Hezbollah: a dozen Lebanese Jews and two Israeli soldiers had been taken prisoner, and Israel was concerned. Thus, Schwimmer and Nimrodi were most likely upset at my position because they, like most Israeli officials, feel that it is incumbent upon a government to do everything possible to save its citizens in these circumstances. My attitude threatened *their* hostages as well. While they had access to American officials, they were clearly concerned that I, the only American present at the meeting, would recommend that we reject the Iranian government's proposal for an arms-for-hostages deal.

I asked Ghorbanifar what he thought, and to my surprise he calmly said, " if we continue in this manner, we shall all become hostages to the hostages." He was in favor of concentrating our energies on efforts to change the nature of the Iranian regime. If that could be achieved, the hostage question would be resolved as a matter of course.

Within a couple of days I briefed McFarlane on the meeting, underlining the disagreement with the Israelis, and Ghorbanifar's recognition that the hostage question was a trap for us all. But the Hawk deal went through nonetheless. If I ever knew who made this decision, and how it was communicated to the Israelis, I have forgotten it, and the testimony before the various committees has not provided any helpful detail. Despite the slight mystery, it is clear that it was agreed to have Israel sell eighty Hawk ground-to-air missiles, in return for which Iran was supposed to release the balance of the hostages. Here, for the first time, was a clear-cut arms-for-hostages transaction, for the only rationalization one could offer for proceeding in this fashion was the one that North would give at his testimony to Congress: the hostages were an obstacle that had to be removed before an improvement in the relationship could take place. He was accurately reflecting the attitude of the president and those advisers who supported the operation, but it was a topsy-turvy approach to the subject.

If the relationship between the two countries could be improved, the hostage question would automatically have to be cleared up in the process, for it was unthinkable that we would take dramatic steps toward normalization so long as the hostages remained in captivity in Lebanon. To concentrate our energies on the hostages was to invert the logical sequence. Worse still, it inverted the strategic priorities as well, for our relationship with Iran was, and is, a strategic issue of considerable importance, while the question of the hostages may be a deeply moving human drama, it is not—and should not be—high on the agenda of American strategic concerns. Whenever I asked Casey why we continued to act in this foolish manner, he replied, "because with this president we have to do the hostages first." So the president wanted it this way, and no one could convince him otherwise.

Yet the president might have made a different decision if he had known about the efforts we made to establish a working relationship with a group of high-ranking Iranian officials. For while the president considered the arms-for-hostages decision in October, McFarlane sent me to Europe to meet with a person who is identified in the records of the Iran-Contra committees as a "Senior Iranian Official." Having spent considerable energy urging the congressional committees that our Iranian contacts should not be named (to do so would almost surely result in unpleasant consequences for them at home, and lessen the likelihood of our ever establishing such contacts in the future), I shall not identify him further. The Senior Official claimed to speak for dozens of persons in Iran, whose positions in the government, the military, the clergy, and even such organizations as the Revolutionary Guards, were sufficiently impressive that they could make a credible claim of constituting an effective force for change. We understood that these were not people who were interested in sabotaging the Shi'ite revolution; none of them could be accurately termed "moderate" in the normal, commonsense meaning of the term.

But these were people who had many reasons for seeking out a better relationship with the United States, and for changing the policies of their government. In addition to their religious convictions, they were intensely anti-communist, and were united in their conviction that Iran could not long survive in total isolation from the West. They were therefore prepared to work for a moderation of national policies. In this sense, and in this sense alone, the term "moderate" could accurately be applied to them. "Pro-Western" is a more accurate description of their attitudes.

This was not the first time that the Senior Iranian Official had attempted to establish a channel to the American government. He had met in Hamburg with Theodore Shackley and Ghorbanifar in late 1984, and, along with Khashoggi and Ghorbanifar, he had talked with Schwimmer, Nimrodi, and Kimche in Europe in early July. This latter encounter took place within days of Kimche's conversation with McFarlane, at which McFarlane confirmed an American interest in pursuing the Iranian initiative.

The July 1985 conversations firmly established that the Senior Official was interested in pursuing a political dialogue with the United States, and not in obtaining weapons for Iran. In the second half of a three-hour conversation, the Israelis asked the Senior Official if he could help obtain the release of the American hostages in Lebanon. They told him that if this could be done, the Americans would be more enthusiastic about a dialogue with him and his supporters, and might even be willing to assist in the defense of his country against Iraq: "we can make the Iraqis dance to a different tune," he was told. The Senior Official was deeply concerned by what he had heard, and he told the Israelis, "you are making a mistake. If we try to solve this problem case by case we will come to a bad end," and he urged them to focus on the central issue: changing the nature of the Iranian regime. Without a better relationship with the West, and the United States in particular, the Iranian problem would remain a threatening one.

The October 1985 meeting—involving Ghorbanifar, Schwimmer,

139

Nimrodi, the Senior Iranian Official, and myself as the lone American—ran along similar lines, but by now the Senior Iranian had seen his advice rejected, and consequently had something to complain about. After the introductions and the ritual expressions of hope for a better relationship between our countries had been exchanged, the senior official launched into a bitter condemnation of the weapons shipments to date: "Why are you sending weapons to the regime?" he asked angrily. "Don't you realize that by doing so you are strengthening the most radical elements? How do you expect the policies to change if you reward the radicals with the weapons they need to wage the war?"

The Senior Official explained that the war had been going badly for Iran, and the radicals—who were leaders of the war party—were losing political strength as a result. Then, just as they were about to be repudiated, we had saved the radicals by providing them with precisely the kinds of weapons they most desperately needed to continue to wage war. He did not claim that the TOWs had made any great difference on the battlefield. But he said that the political effect of the TOW shipments had been enormous, for the arrival of the missiles had been used by the regime as a demonstration that the United States would support them. He was visibly shaken by this development, and he wanted us not to do such a thing again. I asked him if he wanted us to abandon the hostage question altogether, and he said it was difficult for him to tell us to give up on a humanitarian question, but pleaded that if we felt it was absolutely necessary, to bring it to an end as quickly as possible. His opposition to the hostage operation could hardly have been stronger.

Meanwhile, the leitmotif of the weapons sales continued to play in the background, and Ghorbanifar—in discussions separate from those with the Senior Official—was ready with the latest requests from the regime: the shopping list had now grown to include Phoenix, Sidewinder, and Harpoon missiles.

We then turned to the Senior Official's plan of action. He contended that so long as Khomeini lived, the nature of the regime would remain what it was, but Khomeini was sick, and many people in Iran were convinced he would soon pass from the scene. If that happened, it would be possible to change the nature of the government through political means, and he maintained that he and his supporters were close to a voting majority in the Majlis, the Iranian legislature. And even if Khomeini lived on, there were good chances to strengthen their "line." Once they had consolidated their political position, he said, they would be able to replace some of the key officials of the regime, and that would suffice to give him and his allies effective control over policy decisions.

To our surprise, he did not ask for financial support (although the Israelis and I had concluded that Ghorbanifar was helping him, and perhaps some other Iranian officials, from time to time), but asked instead for the development of an orderly working relationship. If we understood each other, he said, and compared notes as the Senior Official and his allies got closer to effective power, we would thereby establish the basis for a new kind of relationship between the two countries. He therefore wanted us to provide him with a secure communications system. Moreover, since he and his people could expect to come under attack from their political enemies, he asked for some small arms with which to defend themselves, along with some training in their use.

The conversations with the Senior Official went on for a day and a half, during which time he confirmed Ghorbanifar's picture of the progress of the war, the intensity of the internal conflicts, the morale of the population, and economic conditions around the country, as well as his own notion of what an effective cooperative relationship between the United States and Iran would look like. At one point, one of us observed that Iran had always been governed by a strong leader; who would the new leader be? The Senior Official agreed with the general theory, but said it was still too early to be able to say who would lead Iran after Khomeini. The evolution he advocated was going to take some time—at least a couple of years—and afterward one would be better placed to predict (and influence) the post-Khomeini succession. Meanwhile, it was urgent to strengthen the pro-Western forces inside Iran.

I was not entitled to speak for my government, but I was morally certain that we would find the Senior Official's basic proposition irresistible. To be sure, the same doubts that we had had about Ghorbanifar applied to the Senior Official as well: he could be part of a deception, whether Iranian or Soviet. But he was not asking for weapons for the war, his strong condemnation of the missile sales lent support to his claim to speak in the name of a group that wanted better relations with the West, and I could not imagine that we would be unwilling to investigate the matter further. After all, the entire Iranian initiative had begun because we were searching for some sort of workable Iran policy. And here was a man, claiming to speak for a powerful coalition of national leaders, trying to establish a working relationship with us. Were we not obliged to see if it was actually possible to do what he proposed? Did he indeed speak for such a group? And if he did, were they capable of the changes he envisaged?

They were difficult questions, but they were—at long last—serious, strategic questions. And I was so certain that the president and his advisers would insist upon following up this conversation, that I promised the Senior Iranian Official that we would meet again within thirty days, at which time I would have my government's response. It was a mistake; I had no authorization for such a promise, and it was not fulfilled.

I returned to Washington confident that we were finally on the right track, and when I briefed McFarlane on the talks with the Senior Iranian, I reiterated my conviction that we should get out of the hostage business and focus our attentions on the political possibilities. Now that we had begun to develop contacts inside Iran, I thought we should expand the number of contacts, and attempt to evaluate the Senior Iranian's proposals. It was extremely difficult to judge the truthfulness of a single man, but in this case, he had given us an hypothesis that we could attempt to verify: he claimed to speak for a large number of influential persons. It should be possible to check on at least some of them, to see if his claims were plausible.

This was easy to say, but in order to perform an assessment of the Senior Iranian and his associates, we needed a first-class professional intelligence service. The National Security Council staff could not possibly have done a task of such magnitude. But it was hard to believe that the CIA could do it, either. Their failure to learn anything of significance about Iran had provided one of the basic impulses for the initiative. And the Special Assessment on Iran in May had been a series of "we don't know," suggesting that our access to informed persons on things Iranian was so poor that the CIA might not be able to handle even this fairly elementary task. On top of this, McFarlane had a great distrust of the agency's ability to keep things secret. It was unlikely he would ask them to undertake this important task. Perhaps one of the military services could do it? Or perhaps we could turn to the British or the French, who had long had pretty good information about Iranian affairs, and who had the benefit of several of the leading émigré groups operating on French soil. Or it might be possible to talk the leaders of the Mossad out of their opposition to the initiative, and get some assistance from the Israeli intelligence service.

McFarlane was clearly interested, and promised to get back to me when the decision had been made. I underlined the fact that I had promised a response within thirty days. "Understood," he said. But he did not respond within thirty days; indeed, he never responded at all. The Senior Iranian's proposal was never seriously evaluated, the people for whom he claimed to speak were never subjected to the sort of analysis they warranted, and to this day no one can answer the questions he raised: Is evolutionary change in Iran possible? Can the United States exert some sort of leverage over Iranian affairs? Are there legitimate channels to pro-Western Iranians who are loyal to the revolution, but in opposition to its more extreme policies?

If the answer to some of these questions is yes, then we committed a great blunder in failing to pursue these (and other) promising contacts in the fourteen months that followed. For if there were indeed powerful people in Iran who wanted to move their country in a relatively pro-Western direction, we should have seized the opportunity and pursued it with all the energy at our disposal. If any meaningful rapport had been established with Tehran, we would be able to look to the future of that region with at least a modicum of confidence, instead of facing an almost totally uncertain situation when the Ayatollah finally passes into history. Alas, we do not know the answers to these vital questions.

When Shultz and Weinberger testified before the Select committees in the summer of 1987, both were quite confident in saying they believed there were no Iranian "moderates" with whom to deal. In one sense of the word "moderate," they were clearly right. All important figures in Iran are loyal to the revolution and, on many issues, what we would regard as fanatics. But in another sense—open to some shifts in foreign policy that would improve the chances for a better relationship with us—they were almost certainly too categorical. In any case, their strong feelings were hardly based upon detailed information. When I briefed Secretary Weinberger in the summer of 1986 on the contacts with the Senior Official, he was astonished, and demanded, "why did I never hear anything about this?" When, at Weinberger's insistence, I repeatedly offered to brief Secretary Shultz, the secretary of state replied that he was not interested in hearing about it. So far as I know, neither man inquired further about the Senior Official and the many Iranian leaders for whom he claimed to speak. Thus, despite the strong feelings of the two secretaries, the crucial questions remained unanswered.

We do not know the answers because Bud McFarlane was overwhelmed by his responsibilities and his own sense of personal burden in the autumn of 1985. He simply could not deal with the terrible weight that he felt on his shoulders. The Iran initiative—at least as I had understood it, and believed McFarlane had envisaged it—died stillborn between the beginning of October and mid-December. In that period, we walked away from the intriguing possibilities offered by the Senior Iranian Official, agreed to swap Hawk missiles for hostages, and then abruptly terminated the entire enterprise, only to revive it again within days of its ostensible shutdown. And for the next year, despite persistent opposition from people like Shultz and Weinberger to the policy conducted by the White House, the political option presented by the Senior Iranian Official was never pursued.

These abrupt about-faces, and the refusal to explore the real strategic possibilities that had been uncovered, can only be understood against the background of Bud McFarlane's anguish, and his relationship with the president.

ROBERT C. McFARLANE, THE FALLEN WARRIOR

Bud McFarlane was a loyal Republican and a devoted public servant. He had proven his adherence to Reagan's announced ideals through a lifetime of public service to famous men, first in the Marine Corps, then in the National Security Council under Henry Kissinger and Gen. Brent Scowcroft, in Congress under Senator John Tower, with Gen. Alexander Haig at the State Department and with Judge William Clark and then Ronald Reagan in the West Wing of the White House. Few men or women in Washington had served so long in the national security community, or achieved such distinction and respect.

McFarlane seemed an excellent choice for the kind of low-key, nonconfrontational national security adviser that Reagan favored, for McFarlane did not seem likely to seek the limelight, or to engage in a direct challenge to the senior members of the cabinet. In Reagan's style of government, the security adviser was to function as a manager, coordinating policy, informing the president of differing views, and sometimes riding herd on the bureaucracy to ensure effective implementation. He was not expected to be a major source of new initiatives or to emerge as an advocate of his own policy line. In short, he was expected to be a Scowcroft, not a Kissinger. And his managerial and intellectual skills, combined with his military discipline and legendary discretion, were obvious strengths for the position.

It did not work out that way, in part because he came to disagree quite strongly with Secretary of State Shultz and Secretary of Defense

Weinberger, in part because he became the victim of a campaign conducted by Chief of Staff Don Regan, and because he found it increasingly difficult to function as he had wished—as a trusted senior member of the White House team.

In many important ways, Bud McFarlane was totally different from his White House and cabinet peers in the Reagans' social world of California-on-the-Potomac. Unlike the president's close associates, McFarlane was a shy person. Laughter came slowly to him, and while Ronald Reagan was a man who greatly enjoyed telling anti-Soviet jokes (as well as more risqué stories), this was never one of Mc-Farlane's talents. From the time he became Judge Clark's deputy at the National Security Council, McFarlane felt ill at ease among the wealthy, country-club Republicans and movie stars who so often surrounded the president and the first lady. Every other top adviser to the president was wealthy and/or gregarious (Edwin Meese being the most conspicuous example of the nonwealthy chum); McFarlane and his schoolteacher wife Jondra were modest and quiet. But there were some who had known him for years who believed that McFarlane's stoic exterior and measured speech masked a spirit in profound inner turmoil, one which would never have found a peaceful haven, even in a less pressurized atmosphere than the West Wing of the White House.

Much of the inner turmoil undoubtedly came from a rage over the role he had had to play in Vietnam. McFarlane commanded the first unit of marines to go ashore at Da Nang, back in 1965, when he was in charge of protecting the arrival of American troops. A decade later, he was the man on the telephone in the White House, giving the orders to end the helicopter evacuation of Saigon. How could he not have been haunted by the pictures of the panicky race to the rooftop of the American embassy, the desperate hands reaching toward the departing aircraft? It was impossible that a man with McFarlane's sense of honor, and with his strong religious convictions, could have avoided a sense of personal guilt for the horrors that were visited upon South Vietnam after the Americans' departure, and he also understood that Vietnam was a major theme for his NSC colleagues as well. As he told Barbara Walters in an interview after the scandal erupted:

> . . . the people that went through [the Vietnam War]—and Colonel North surely did—you come away with the profound sense of very intolerable failure, that is, that a government must never give its word to people who may stand to lose their lives, and then break faith. And

I think that it is possible that in the last year we've seen a commitment made to human beings in Nicaragua that is being broken.

Beneath the stolid demeanor was a driven man. Vietnam could no longer be saved, but it could be avenged, if only America would act. If this is understood, the depth of McFarlane's frustration inside the Reagan White House can perhaps be appreciated. For his alienation meant not only a sense of personal unhappiness (a man of his outlook could have readily accepted *that*); it meant an inability to get things done.

McFarlane's malaise in Reaganite society was not merely a matter of feeling uncomfortable; it undermined his political position, and thus his ability to influence policy. Power in Washington rests on many pillars, and people rose and fell during the Reagan years because of their social graces, or lack thereof. Nancy Reagan viewed the White House as an area for well-dressed, well-behaved and charming individuals, and those who did not fit the pattern were driven to the margins of real power, which inevitably depends upon access to the president himself. Persons like Lyn Nofziger—despite decades of loyal service—found themselves excluded from the inner circles, in no small measure because they were deemed socially unacceptable, while ambitious men—like Richard Burt—rose in status when they married into the Reagan "club." Burt, whose intellectual talent was as distinguished as his personality was abrasive, married Nancy Reagan's social secretary, and rose from assistant secretary of state for Europe to ambassador to the Federal Republic of Germany.

It is easy to develop a sense of personal isolation in such a place. Unlike the corporate world, where new arrivals are subjected to a sort of ritual initiation and a support system is in place for those who need it, top-level Washington has little in the way of psychological or social safety nets. To be sure, there are always groups within each administration that band together (like the Georgians during the Carter administration, the Texans under Johnson, and Kennedy's "Irish Mafia"), but there is rarely any systematic effort to create or maintain an internal esprit de corps.

THE TRAVAIL OF THE NATIONAL SECURITY ADVISER

Things were hard enough for Reagan's national security advisers without the additional handicap of feeling excluded from the inner circle. Ronald Reagan had based his long run for the presidency on a rejection of Henry Kissinger's foreign policy, and during the period between election day 1980 and year's end, a transition team labored to produce the outlines of the new policy and the bureaucratic structure necessary to implement it. Not surprisingly, one of the basic recommendations of the transition team was to strike a major blow at the institution from which Kissinger had established his awesome power base in the first Nixon term: the National Security Council.

The entire structure of national security policy-making was designed in order to enfeeble the NSC. The symbol of this decision was White House Counselor Edwin Meese, who, despite his almost total lack of foreign policy experience, stood between the security adviser and the president in the new organizational chart. Meese announced that the NSC would no longer have its own spokesman or press office, and he took care to point out that Richard Allen (Reagan's first national security adviser) would function as "the referee . . . or," he added, "I should say, the enforcer. That's a better word."

Allen's weakness was demonstrated early on when he sent a memorandum to Defense Secretary Weinberger asking the Defense Department to chair an interagency meeting on whether the United States should attend an upcoming scheduled meeting with the Soviets in Geneva on compliance with the SALT II Treaty. Weinberger did not reply, and Allen received curt notes from Deputy Defense Secretary Frank Carlucci and Deputy Secretary of State William Clark, informing the security adviser that this matter was already under review, and that he would be informed when a decision had been reached.

When Allen departed the scene the first autumn, he was replaced by William Clark who, although a foreign policy novice, was by far the most powerful of Reagan's six national security advisers. Clark had maximum access, hence maximum power, firmly grounded on a friendship and close working relationship that extended back to the beginnings of Reagan's political activity. Clark was, after all, Governor Reagan's chief of staff in Sacramento.

Yet with all that, when Clark went to "the old man" in the fall of 1983 to complain about the constant meddling of Jim Baker and Mike Deaver in national security matters, Ronald Reagan did not move. This made a deep impression on McFarlane, who realized that if one of the president's oldest and closest friends could not prevail over the political clout of Baker (who had worked for George Bush in the 1980 primaries) and Deaver (who was Nancy Reagan's eyes and ears in White House meetings), then a former marine colonel with no long-standing friendship with the top man, and limited charisma to boot, would inevitably be a poor match for them. And McFarlane also knew that Clark had never been one of Nancy Reagan's favorites, so that when McFarlane fell out of favor with the first lady, it had a devastating impact.

Finally, above and beyond the problems of personality and style, all the national security advisers to Ronald Reagan had to find a way to overcome the president's basic lack of interest in, and substantive knowledge of, foreign policy and national security. McFarlane confided to intimates that he had a terrible time getting the president to focus on matters only Reagan could resolve. And it is a commentary on his state of mind that McFarlane interpreted this problem as a reflection of his own shortcomings, rather than a basic fact of life in the Reagan era. He concluded that he had the wrong personality for the job, and as his power waned, the daily briefings became an ordeal.

McFarlane could never effectively compete within the national security establishment. Despite his daily access to the president, McFarlane knew full well that he was *minimus inter pares*—the least of the top-level foreign policy and White House advisers. In any open debate, McFarlane's opinions would carry less weight than those of his opponents, as he learned from his frustrating experiences in the Middle East.

At the time of the bombing of the U.S. Marine headquarters in Beirut in October 1983, McFarlane fought hard to convince the president to respond militarily against the Iranian and Syrian-sponsored terrorist groups who had carried out the bloody massacre. He had impressive international support for his recommendations, for both Israel and France encouraged stern reprisals against the terrorists. But within the higher councils of the administration, he had an uphill battle, primarily against the secretary of defense. Weinberger had adopted the peculiar view of the military service chiefs, that the armed forces of the United States should never be deployed except in the case of a clear national consensus in favor of military action. In practice, this meant that we would use military force only when attacked, and then only when we could respond "in kind."

Even on those rare occasions when the Pentagon went along with the demand that the United States respond to armed attack, there was generally some way or another to prevent the use of American force. After the attack on the American marines and French paratroop barracks, for example, the French decided to launch military reprisals and invited the United States to join in a show of allied resolve. Shultz and McFarlane argued vigorously for an air strike against terrorist

Lt. Col. Oliver North is sworn in before the House Foreign Affairs
Committee on December 9, 1986. North cited his Fifth Amendment rights
and refused to answer the committee's questions involving the Iran arms
sale.

Former National Security Adviser Adm. John Poindexter contemplates a
question while testifying on July 15, 1987, before the joint congressional
committees investigating the Iran-Contra affair.

Former National Security Adviser Robert McFarlane on December 12,
1986, waiting to speak to the Senior Executives Association, where he
maintained that American overtures to moderate Iranians still represent a
viable strategy, but it requires the full support of Congress.

Former Air Force Maj. Gen. Richard V. Secord reviews his notes while testifying on May 6, 1987, before a joint House and Senate committee hearing on the Iran-Contra affair. Secord, the first witness during the joint hearings, traced profits from secret Iranian arms sales to Nicaraguan rebels.

Adnan Khashoggi, considered by many to be the richest man in the world, used his rare combination of Western sophistication and Eastern cunning in pursuing a significant role in international affairs. Khashoggi introduced Manucher Ghorbanifar to the Israelis via Al Schwimmer, long-time president of Israel Aircraft Industry and close ally of Shimon Peres.

Ayatollah Khomeini in April 1987. Khomeini rose to power in 1979 when his Shi'ite fundamentalist followers deposed the shah of Iran. Although hatred of America was central to the society Khomeini attempted to create in post-shah Iran, he realized that Iran must reconcile itself to the West as a potential source of arms and support in the war against Iraq.

Albert Hakim listens to a question while testifying before the Congressional committees holding joint hearings on the Iran-Contra affair. When Republican congressmen accused him of attempting to compromise former National Security Council aide Lt. Col. Oliver North by funneling money to his family, Hakim protested, "You are leaving a bad taint on me."

Manucher Ghorbanifar, the Iranian version of the self-made man, operated as the channel between the Khomeini regime and the Israeli government. At least six Americans and five Frenchmen owe their freedom to his role as intermediary.

Former director general of the Israeli Foreign Ministry, David Kimche leaves federal court in Washington on May 22, 1987, after appearing before a grand jury on a subpoena issued by Independent Counsel Lawrence Walsh, who wanted to question him regarding his conversations with Reagan administration officials concerning the sale of U.S. TOW missiles to Iran in exchange for American hostages.

Rev. Benjamin Weir in January 1987. As the first fruit of the Iran initiative, Weir was released in September 1985 after sixteen months. Ironically, Weir emerged from captivity full of hatred for his rescuers and with unlimited praise for his captors and the Shi'ite cause in the Middle East.

President Ronald Reagan conferring with CIA Director William Casey aboard *Air Force One*.

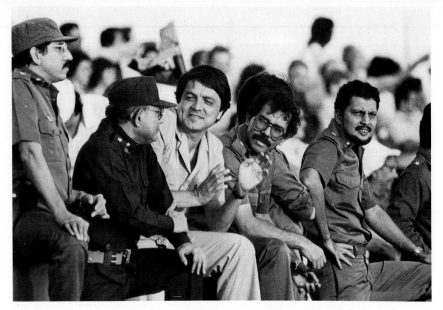

Five members of the Sandinista National Liberation Front directorate before a final campaign rally for the general elections in 1984: (*from left*) Defense Minister Humberto Ortega, Interior Minister Tomas Borge, junta member vice presidential candidate Sergio Ramirez, junta member presidential candidate Daniel Ortega, and Political Coordinator Bayardo Arce.

The leaders of the Nicaraguan *contras* met with Secretary of State George Shultz in March 1986: (*from left*) Alfonso Robelo, Eden Pastora, Shultz, and Adolfo Calero.

targets in the Bekaa Valley of Lebanon. After days of debate, it was finally approved. But the military had the last word, for the instructions from Washington to the Fleet Commander in the Mediterranean were such as to make it impossible for the sortie to be flown. The entire operation was to be micromanaged from the Pentagon; the fighter-bombers were to take off during daylight hours (thus maximizing the risk to the pilot and the aircraft); and certain crucial countermeasures, to protect against antiaircraft missiles, were not to be adopted. While the Pentagon technically carried out its orders to plan a bombing raid, they knew that no competent commander in the field would send one of his men to attack under such conditions, and they knew their man was a good one. McFarlane and Shultz were thwarted.

Over time, these frustrations drove McFarlane to adopt a course of action that was basically contrary to his own instincts: he decided that the best chance to advance programs in which he deeply believed lay in secrecy. If he could convince the president to undertake a course of action before the other members of the National Security Council weighed in with the old man, he had a chance to prevail. Increasingly, he resorted to this method, which reached its zenith in the Iran and *contra* policies.[2] As several of the better White House correspondents remarked, McFarlane began to issue instructions in the president's name, even without waiting for general discussions of the issues. This was interpreted as a sign of strength—it apparently bespoke a close relationship with Reagan—but actually it was a sign of growing weakness.

In all likelihood, McFarlane would have told the president about the secret Iranian contacts, but the period in which they developed was one in which McFarlane was undergoing a serious psychological crisis. Already an outsider in the inner circle, McFarlane was the victim of a subtle attack in the autumn of 1985. According to several senior members of the NSC staff, the prime mover in the anti-McFarlane campaign was chief of Staff Donald Regan, and the weapon was rumor—whispers that McFarlane was having two romantic affairs (with NBC White House correspondent Andrea Mitchell and NSC

2. The Strategic Defense Initiative—Star Wars—was presented to the president with McFarlane's active support before the Pentagon realized what was happening. As Hedrick Smith has written, McFarlane arranged for Edward Teller and other spokesmen for SDI to brief the president and enlisted the support of White House Science Adviser George Keyworth, without having the bureaucracy informed. Weinberger himself was apparently astonished when, just a couple of days before Reagan's public announcement of the initiative, he received a draft of the president's speech. By then, the president was committed to the project, and critics of SDI could only make minor changes in the text.

spokeswoman Karna Small). For some men in Washington, such ro-
mors would have been a source of bemusement or even pleasure, and
certainly would not have produced a major breakdown. But these
stories—which were widely believed, even though they were utterly
false—struck at the two weakest links in McFarlane's psychological
armor: his extraordinarily rigid sense of morality and self-esteem; and
the perception of him in the White House, especially the opinion of
Nancy Reagan.

For the first lady was widely reported to have believed the stories,
and did not approve of a wenching national security adviser. Mc-
Farlane was at a loss how to respond, and his humiliation was compounded by horrified astonishment that anyone could believe him
capable of such behavior. Thus, at a single stroke, McFarlane saw his
power undermined and his image besmirched. He could not cope with
it. Had this been the only blow, McFarlane could easily have dealt
with it. But it came as the culmination of a long ordeal. Tired from
years of lack of sufficient sleep, exhausted by the endless wrangling
within the national security community, and frustrated by his inability
to drive foreign policy in a coherent direction, McFarlane slowly ground
to a halt. By early November, when I asked David Kimche to come
to Washington to talk to McFarlane and try to strengthen his resolve,
it was clear that McFarlane was no longer functioning effectively.
"Some strong men are flexible, and bend in a hostile wind," Kimche
observed. "Others are too rigid, try to stand against it, and break.
Bud has broken." He went to the president and resigned. But within
hours, he was seized with remorse and wished he had remained to
fight to the end. So much had been left undone, and, inevitably, he
felt a personal responsibility for the crisis that later overcame the NSC.
His attempted suicide a year and a half later was the climax of the
dramatic tension; the tragedy had already begun in the fall of 1985.

With a strong and confident McFarlane in the White House, the
political contacts with Iran would have undoubtedly been expanded
and explored in depth. With an anguished and exhausted man at the
helm of the NSC, the initiative was stillborn. He kept it secret and
carried it away with him. Indeed, he blotted it out of his own memory,
for by the following March, when I asked him if he could help arrange
a visa for a high-ranking Iranian to meet with an American official in
Switzerland, McFarlane assumed I was talking about Ghorbanifar and
complained about it in a computerized PROFs note to North. It was
obviously a confusion, for a moment's reflection would have reminded
McFarlane that Ghorbanifar had no need of a visa to Switzerland; he

had a home there, as well as a close working relationship with some of the country's leading banks. But McFarlane did not reflect on the matter, nor did he respond to my entreaties that we reestablish contact with the pro-Western Iranians: he no longer remembered.

While the political opportunity slowly died, the president's persistent concerns about the hostages were again translated into policy: the Israelis were informed that they could go ahead with the sale and transfer of eighty Hawk antiaircraft missiles to Iran.

HAWKS

I cannot remember when I learned of the decision to go ahead with the Hawks-for-hostages deal and was not involved in any of the technical operations associated with it, but I knew it had been approved well before the disastrous delivery around Thanksgiving Day.

The Israelis were not eager to live through the anxiety of the second TOW shipment again. Twice they had flown a 707 loaded with antitank missiles across the breadth of European air space without challenge from the ground. It was not likely to go so smoothly a third time, especially since European air traffic controllers—and many others— had been keenly interested in the real story of the aircraft that took off from Iran, headed for Europe, and abruptly rerouted to Tel Aviv. If there were some easier way to do it, it would be gratefully endorsed by the Israelis. And there seemed to be a good alternative: North was now actively in the picture, and suggested that the Americans manage the details of the operation. Israel would provide the missiles, and the Americans would organize the transportation. This seemed better all around. The Israelis had only to worry about providing the right missiles, leaving the troublesome operational details to the White House.

North, too, was pleased. He had wanted to be involved in the planning stages, and he now had the authority he desired. So the auguries for the Hawk shipment were good, with everyone seemingly pleased about the arrangements. In the first half of November, North undertook to commission a jumbo jet that would carry the eighty Hawks from Israel to Iran. It is one of those tasks that seems like it ought to be elementary for a man as operationally savvy as North, particularly with Secord now actively engaged, but it proved beyond his capabilities. Had it been possible to use American government aircraft, it would have been elementary, but there was no official approval of the operation. The plane would have to be a private aircraft, and the entire undertaking had to be free of official footprints

151

from beginning to end. After days of unsuccessful attempts, North conceded defeat and went back to Schwimmer for help.

In a series of telephone calls—sometimes as often as five or six times a day—North at one end and Schwimmer (sometimes Kimche) at the other examined the problem and decided to compromise: if the Israelis could find a way to deliver the missiles to a European country, the Americans could pick up the cargo and carry it back across Europe to Iran. North further undertook to "fix" the situation in Europe so that no embarrassing questions would be asked about the movements of so many planes in and out of their principal airport. Assuming he could deliver on that promise, it only remained for each side to line up the necessary aircraft.

Hawk missiles are imposing pieces of hardware. Each one is more than five and a half meters long and weighs more than a ton and a half. With items of such size and weight, the most appropriate aircraft is a Cargo 747, with a "clamshell" nose that opens up to permit front-end loading. That way, the Hawks can be slid in from the front by mechanical lifters, rather than having to be maneuvered by ten or more men in several steps through a side bay that is shorter than the missiles themselves. Many of the larger commercial shippers have such 747s, but where were the Israelis to find shippers prepared to provide one on short notice, to fly a mission of obvious sensitivity, with a cargo of considerable danger, and keep the whole thing quiet? The Israelis inquired of some of their friends in the business and were told that while it might be possible to lease a jumbo for the mission, no Western insurance company would cover the trip. Consequently the shippers required a $50 million bond before they would provide the plane and crew. This was out of the question. Neither the Israeli government nor, needless to say, the private Israeli citizens were prepared to assume such a risk.

Time was running short, and delay might be fatal to the undertaking. A fragile, yet positive relationship of trust was developing with Tehran. After the initial, near total suspicion, the Iranians were now quite clearly convinced that the project was serious, and their interlocutors reliable. This was obvious from the way the payment for the Hawks was handled. When the first TOWs were shipped in August and September, the Iranians had refused to make any payment until the Israeli planes had landed and the weapons had been unloaded and examined. This had brought Khashoggi into the picture, thereby enabling the TOWs to be shipped. There were no such preconditions for the Hawks. The Iranians paid in advance, and Nimrodi was able to hand the Defense Ministry a check for $24 million before a single missile was moved out of Israeli inventory.

But this sign of Iranian trust could be undone in a single stroke. If there were a delay, the Iranians would immediately conclude that they were being cheated, with possible consequences ranging from long-term difficulties in the relationship with Tehran, to acts of violence against the hostages. Delay was a major danger, and the Defense Ministry suggested the use of a commercial Israeli jumbo, of the sort routinely used to deliver Israeli oranges, lemons, and grapefruit to the markets of Western Europe. The plane belonged to KAL, a subsidiary of El Al, and was clearly marked as such.

North was informed, and he assured the Israelis that everything was on track. And now a new actor was introduced: Mr. "Copp" (Secord) had by now made his appearance telephonically, and the Israelis were able to deal with North in Washington and "Copp" on the ground in a variety of European locations. I don't know where Secord got his *nom de guerre,* but readers of *U.S. News & World Report* on January 25th, 1988, could find a quotation from a certain E. Anthony Copp (identified simply as an "oil executive") which was very Secordesque. Speaking about life in Yemen, Copp observed "they carry a gun like we carry a wallet. It adds to the charm of the place." As happened so often in this tale, life came to imitate art.

On the Israeli side, everything was set for wheels up at noon on Friday, November 22nd. The plane was loaded, the fuel pumped, the crew—one of El Al's most experienced teams—in place. But with less than an hour to go, North called from the Old Executive Office Building. There was a glitch in Europe, but it should be cleared up momentarily. Please stand by. An hour later, he called again. There was still a problem. Don't panic. Another hour and another and yet another. As the afternoon dragged on, a new and very different kind of problem loomed ahead, for Israeli planes are rigorously forbidden to fly commercial missions on the Sabbath, and the sun was rapidly setting over the Mediterranean horizon. Rafi Har-El, the head of El Al, was not about to incur the wrath of the Orthodox rabbinate, and he informed the Israeli team at five o'clock that so far as he was concerned, the mission was finished. Not only did Sabbath regulations forbid the takeoff, but that very aircraft was needed to carry food to Frankfurt on Saturday evening. None of the three Israelis was in a position to give orders to El Al, and so the prime minister received an urgent phone call from Schwimmer: would Peres kindly promise El Al that

153

no rabbinical curse would be visited upon the national airline or Ben Gurion Airport if that plane flew on the Sabbath? The call was made; the flight was still on.

Finally, in the early evening, North called in from Washington and told the Israelis to go ahead with the flight. The plane lifted off in the early evening and headed west.

This was the first time, but not the last, that North would order a plane loaded with weapons destined for Iran to take off from Israel even though there was a high probability that the delivery would not take place. (The second, even more dramatic occasion was during the McFarlane negotiations in Tehran the following May.) North had given the go-ahead with full knowledge that the situation in Europe was anything but promising. Secord had been dispatched by North with orders to obtain the approval of the European government for the operation, and, for the first time in the history of the Iran initiative, the CIA had been brought into the picture. North had called Dewey Clarridge, now chief of operations for Western Europe, for help with the Europeans, and Clarridge had passed on the orders to the local CIA officials.

The European government was not happy to hear the American request that they facilitate a mysterious transshipment in the dead of night. Secord informed them that the United States needed help with a humanitarian mission: the shipment was headed for Iran and was involved with an attempt to free the American hostages in Lebanon. The Europeans wanted to know what was being shipped and asked for a written request from an American official. It was an awkward moment, and Secord could hardly have confided in his European interlocutors: Listen, we are keeping this secret from most of *our* people, don't expect us now to put this business in writing. However, the situation subsequently became so desperate that Secord informed the Europeans that there were "Israeli weapons" on board the plane. It was to no avail, and North was informed that the project was hopelessly stalemated in Europe.

Having been blocked in Europe, North moved another step up the chain of command, this time to McFarlane. The national security adviser was at the Reagan–Gorbachev summit in Geneva, his mind fully occupied with the deadly serious business of the future of East-West relations, when North phoned in from Washington with the bad news that the Europeans were being difficult. Reagan was preparing to deliver an address to Congress on the results of the summit. Geneva had been a singularly unpleasant experience for McFarlane—Regan had elbowed him out of the limelight, and acted as if he, rather than McFarlane, was the key White House person on foreign policy—and McFarlane had made up his mind to resign. He would stay behind in Europe for a few days after the president returned, brief the allies on the results of the Reagan–Gorbachev talks, and then fly to the Western White House to submit his resignation.

North's call was a reminder of the travails back in Washington: Could McFarlane kindly ring up the European authorities and get the thing back on track?

McFarlane started placing calls from Geneva to the foreign minister and prime minister of the country involved. By late afternoon, McFarlane reached the foreign minister. As he expected, given the traditionally good relationship between the two countries, there seemed to be comprehension of the American problem and eagerness to help.

In reality, the Europeans were irritated. Like all our allies, they had grown used to unexpected behavior from the United States, and were worldly enough to understand that it is sometimes necessary to make rapid decisions on matters of extreme urgency. But they also knew that one could not do things with the Americans and hope that the actions would long remain secret. They had seen too many sensitive operations exposed in American newspapers and on American television broadcasts. So they had learned what in Washington is known as CYA (for cover your ass) tactics: if they had to do something that might be embarrassing later on, they wanted to make certain that someone else was going to accept responsibility for the decision. And that meant that while they might honor a request from the American government, they were not about to do something sensitive on the say-so of a retired American Air Force General using a phony name.

So that while the Europeans continued to act with their traditional warmth, reassuring the embassy officials of their willingness to co-operate, they were asking for something that neither the CIA nor the National Security Council wanted to provide: a piece of paper that could later be produced as a "smoking gun." Back in Washington, North and Poindexter fiddled with the language of a request that could be given to the Europeans and eventually offered a compromise: they would ask for humanitarian assistance, but would not put the hostage question in writing.

It was not quite good enough for the Europeans, who insisted on a more explicit document. Meanwhile, the plane had reached the halfway point in its flight; beyond this moment the aircraft could no longer safely turn around and return to Tel Aviv. It had been loaded to near total capacity (it was, in fact, within a single ton of its maximum permissible load), and its tanks contained no excess fuel. There was no margin for error.

With no clear assurance that a workable compromise could be reached with the Europeans, a decision had to be made at once. If North waited any longer, and the plane still could not land, it would have to find some other European airport. Once on the ground, all kinds of embarrassing questions would be asked, to which neither the Americans nor the Israelis would have acceptable answers. In all likelihood, the entire operation would have been blown. So North called Schwimmer in Tel Aviv and told him to turn the plane around. Baffled and furious at the constant delays and now the inexplicable decision to abort the mission, Schwimmer gave the order. He was fortunate that the pilot was willing to turn around and fly straight to Tel Aviv without taking on further fuel. He was technically in violation of regulations, but it was one of those violations for which awards are given.

Nimrodi was sitting in the Noga Hilton in Geneva with Ghorbanifar, the "Australian" (from Prime Minister Moussavi's office), and two Iranian bodyguards, waiting excitedly for the successful conclusion of their biggest exploit. Instead, that Friday was the beginning of the worst period of the entire enterprise. When Schwimmer called with the bad news, Nimrodi informed the Iranians that, because of "technical difficulties" the plane had turned back to Tel Aviv. The Iranians were horrified. Why had this happened? What technical difficulties? Nimrodi speculated that an engine had failed. If that were so, they raged, why had the plane not landed in Europe, closer by? Why had it gone back? Had it not gone past the half-way point? Nimrodi could not answer. The Australian, dismayed at the course of events and alarmed at the certain reaction in Tehran, picked up the telephone to inform his masters.

Moussavi was displeased. Was this, as he had feared, the proof that the Americans and the Israelis were cheating Iran? Had the American promises turned to dirt? Was the world's greatest power unable to fly an airplane from one point to another? The Australian reassured Tehran: No, no, machines break down even for the most powerful, be patient. It will be good.

Meanwhile, Nimrodi had become a hostage in Geneva. The presence of the two Iranian bodyguards was not a matter of protocol; they were armed and clearly capable of violent action. It was clear to him that if the operation failed, vengeance was likely to be visited upon him and Ghorbanifar. And as the delay increased from a matter of hours to days, the tempo of telephone calls between Israel, Washington, and Geneva mounted accordingly.

In Tel Aviv, the Israelis were perplexed: North had told them to send the plane and had then turned it around. Had he, as it appeared, decided to throw the dice, putting the plane in the air in the hopes that things would work out? If so, they feared they were working with someone who was grossly inexperienced in this sort of mission. For only a super-optimist would have put 140 tons of explosive missiles in international transit "on spec." Errors were one thing, and all three of the Israelis had made their fair share of them, but this appeared to be rather more serious. They informed Peres and Rabin of their concerns. Rabin called North and asked that the matter be straightened out forthwith. North informed Schwimmer that he and Secord would arrange to send a plane to Tel Aviv and deliver as many Hawks as possible to Tehran within the shortest possible time.

There was considerable confusion, and at one point Copp suggested that an aircraft scheduled to carry ammunition to the *contras* be used for the Hawks instead. North sent a PROFs note to Poindexter reflecting the situation:

> Too bad, this was to be our first direct flight to the resistance field . . . inside Nicaragua. The ammo was already palletized w/parachutes attached. Maybe we can do it on Weds or Thurs.[3]

Two days later, a 707 arrived. The Israelis examined it and were shocked to discover that it was of American registry. North was called and informed. "We thought you didn't want anything with American papers." Right they were. Copp had apparently made a mistake. The plane was removed, and, three days after the initial fiasco, a second 707 arrived in Tel Aviv, with a German-speaking crew and Cayman Islands registry. But this one was not from Secord's business contacts or old boy network; it had been provided courtesy of the CIA.

A 707 is not well-suited to carry Hawks, and after considerable effort, eighteen missiles were loaded onto the plane. It was to be the first of five shipments. Once again, unexpected problems arose. As the loading was going on, North called to say that the plane would have to transit Cyprus, less than half an hour away. This displeased the Israelis for three reasons: it obviously increased the risk of the

---

3. *Tower Commission Report*, B-33.

mission, it imposed a new delay, since tons of fuel had to be emptied out of the plane's tanks (it had been supplied with enough fuel to reach Iran, a flight of several hours, and could not safely land in Cyprus with so much fuel on board), and it cost them money, for the plane's pilot informed Schwimmer that he had no money—and no credit card—with which to refuel in Cyprus. The Israelis had to go from one friend to another to raise ten thousand dollars in cash for the cost of the fuel.

Finally, the plane lifted off, with a worldwide sigh of relief from Washington, Geneva, Tehran, and Tel Aviv. But the satisfaction was premature. The melodrama had only just begun.

THE FIASCO OF THE HAWKS

It was assumed in Tel Aviv that North and Secord had made the necessary arrangements for the aircraft to transit Cyprus (after all, the instructions to go to Cyprus had come from Washington), but that turned out to be overly optimistic. A few hours after take-off from Ben Gurion, the plane's owner called Schwimmer to ask what was being done to get his plane and crew out of custody in Cyprus. Schwimmer, astonished that the White House had given his private telephone number to a man with whom he was not supposed to have any contact, mumbled that he did not know, but would find out. He then called North, who told him that the problem would soon be solved. In the meantime, the aircraft, with its explosive cargo, sat on the runway, a ticking political time bomb. A couple of hours later, the owner called in to say the plane had left.

When the aircraft landed in Tabriz, the first reports were cause for celebration. The plane was there, the missiles were being unloaded, and the crew was being treated to a caviar feast. But the celebration was premature. The Hawks were handed over to the military experts—men who had been instructed in the use of such missiles by American Air Force officers, perhaps including Secord himself. When they unpacked the Hawks, they were horrified: they were old Hawks, older even than the remaining forty or so in the Iranian inventory. Furthermore, they were covered with Israeli markings, even though Schwimmer and Nimrodi had given explicit instructions that all markings be removed (and they were subsequently charged several hundred thousand dollars for the cost of removal by the IDF). Later, one of the Hawks was tested and found to be defective. The crew was seized and told they could not leave for the foreseeable future. This led to still another of the bizarre telephone calls to Schwimmer from the plane's owner. Understandably, the owner was concerned at the silence from his pilot, and he wanted to know what was going on. Schwimmer was not keen to tell him that his plane and employees were in the hands of an enraged group of Revolutionary Guards, so he blandly said there had been some sort of delay, but things ought to be working again in relatively short order. The owner, who was sitting in Europe at the time, promised to keep in touch.

A more frightening situation could hardly be imagined for the three men sitting with two Iranian bodyguards in the luxurious suite in the Noga Hilton in Geneva, and the gravity of their situation was driven home during a telephone conversation between a top official in Tehran, on the one side, and Ghorbanifar and the Australian on the other. As the official erupted in a torrent of rage at the evident cheating and provocation by the Americans and Israelis, Ghorbanifar insisted that there must have been some mistake, that there was undoubtedly a misunderstanding, and that things would be put right. "We are here with him," he said, "and he will make sure it is done correctly." "That man," pronounced the official, "can go to hell." In the Islamic Republic of Iran, these words were tantamount to a death sentence. The Australian fell to the floor, unconscious. He was sent by ambulance to the hospital, where tests revealed no sign of stroke or cardiac arrest. Like a character in a nineteenth-century romantic novel, he had been overcome by his emotions.

What had gone wrong? The Iranian experts who examined the eighteen Hawks were entitled to be disappointed, for the Israelis had shipped them some of the oldest in their inventory. This may have been a conscious decision on the part of the Israeli military, either because they did not wish to see Schwimmer get credit for sending top-notch equipment to the Iranians, or because, like ordnance officers throughout the world, they preferred to ship older rather than newer weapons to their clients. If the latter, it was a routine, if unfortunate decision (and it should not be forgotten that these were, after all, Hawks that the Israelis were prepared to deploy in the event of war). If the former, it was a grave mistake.

There is another explanation: The Israelis may have seen this as an opportunity to get rid of old missiles and to replace them with new American models. At least one of the people present at the shipment of the Hawks from Tel Aviv heard two military men talking happily about "unloading" some older missiles on the Iranians. And the story was taken seriously enough for Schwimmer and Kimche to urge that

159

the missiles be in first-class condition, and to warn against sending inferior equipment.

Finally, there is the high probability that the whole thing was a simple misunderstanding. The only Iranian with whom the question of the Hawks had been discussed prior to shipment was Ghorbanifar, and he was no expert. It turned out that the Iranians wanted missiles to shoot down Iraqi surveillance aircraft, which flew at an altitude of some sixty thousand feet. Apparently the Iranians believed there was a new American Hawk which would reach that altitude, and they expected these to arrive in November. In fact, no Hawk flies that high, and even had the Israelis shipped the so-called I-Hawks (for "improved" Hawks), the Iranians would have been disappointed. But there were no I-Hawks in the Israeli inventory. The electronic components of these missiles were so advanced that only the United States had them, and it is highly unlikely that the American government would have approved the sale of such an advanced weapon to Iran.

Whatever the explanation, the arrival of these weapons in Iran, especially after the delays, returns in mid-flight, and cancellations of earlier aircraft convinced the Iranians that they were the objects of a deliberate hoax. Had the mission succeeded, there might have been a real breakthrough in the relationship between the United States and Iran. But with the arrival of the unacceptable Hawks, it required all of the negotiating skills of Ghorbanifar, and intense activity among the Israelis, to stabilize the rapidly degenerating situation. While the Australian received medical treatment in Geneva, Nimrodi and Ghorbanifar were on the telephone to Tehran, assuring the Iranians that the money would be promptly returned, and that the hated missiles would be quickly withdrawn.

If the situation were not resolved promptly, the Iran initiative was probably at an end. So the Defense Ministry was asked to transfer the $24 million to Nimrodi's account in Geneva, in order that the money could be refunded. At least that way, it would be clear that there was no attempt to defraud the Iranians. Within forty-eight hours that was accomplished (albeit with a deduction of a couple of million dollars for the eighteen Hawks that had been delivered, and attendant costs), and Tehran was calming down. Moreover, the Israelis promised that as soon as the next shipment had been arranged, the offending Hawks would be taken out. The Iranians were now talking about future arrangements, and the Israelis took the opportunity to demand that the aircraft and the crew be released. This time the threat of unspecified, dire consequences came from Tel Aviv: if the plane and pilots were held much longer, Iran would have to worry about the arrival of new aircraft from Israel, and they would not be carrying presents for the Iranian war effort. The message was understood; the airplane and crew were released. (In keeping with the bizarre lack of communication between Washington and Tel Aviv, Schwimmer and Kimche did not learn from North that the pilots and aircraft were safe, but from the owner, who called in to ask where he was supposed to send the bill. By this time, the plane had landed in Western Europe.) The Israelis believed the worst was over. From the standpoint of Nimrodi, Kimche, and Schwimmer, the initiative was back on course.

Nimrodi believed that a dramatic gesture was now required to re-establish trust after the Hawk catastrophe, and he suggested that several thousand TOWs be sold to Iran *at cost,* as a sign of good faith on the Israeli/American side. He felt sufficiently strongly about it to urge it be done unilaterally in the event the Americans did not agree. Secord and North cannot have been excited at the prospect of lower prices to Iran, but they agreed that the initiative should continue, for within a couple of days, there were meetings between the Israelis, Ghorbanifar, the Australian, and Secord in Geneva, and further conversations in Paris among the same people. All these discussions were about the "next step": how best to structure a new transaction sending American weapons to Iran for the release of the hostages in Lebanon.

Things were not so cheery in Washington. In the first place, the Americans' perception of what had happened was quite different from the Israelis'. North's reporting implied that each error along the way had been due to Israeli incompetence.[4] There was no suggestion that it was he who had worked hand-in-glove with the Israelis; instead he acted as if it all might have worked if only he had been given sufficient authority.

On the day the missiles arrived in Iran—the 25th of November— I received a frantic call from Ghorbanifar. I had seen him in high dudgeon before, but nothing that approached his current intensity. His voice cracking with the strain, he told me that a disaster had occurred, and that Iran had been cheated by the Israelis. He had a message for President Reagan from Prime Minister Moussavi: "We have fulfilled our every promise, and now you have cheated us. You

---

4. In a later memorandum, North blamed the debacle on joint incompetence shared between Schwimmer and me. This was part of North's campaign to discredit me, along with Kimche, Nimrodi, and Schwimmer, in order to gain control over the initiative for himself and Nir. In fact, I had nothing to do with any of the details concerning any of the shipments. These were all handled by the Israelis, or, as in the case of the Hawks, the Israelis and North.

must immediately remedy this terrible situation or else dire consequences will follow." Ghorbanifar explained to me what had happened: Moussavi felt Iran had been "cheated" by the defective Hawks,
and was enraged after the exertion of liberating Weir. I called the
White House, informing them that I would be coming in with a
message for McFarlane. I drove downtown and came into the West
Wing early in the evening. McFarlane was not available, but Poindexter would see me. I read him Moussavi's message and gave him a
brief explanation. He nodded and then abruptly informed me that I
was being taken off the project. "We need people with more technical
expertise," he said. I said, "Very well, but I want to remain engaged
in the other part of this project," and then named the Senior Iranian
Official. He stared blankly at me, not the slightest sign of recognition
in his eyes. He knew nothing about the political contacts with Iran.
Only McFarlane and North (and possibly Don Fortier) were privy to
this information. There was no point in any further conversation, and
I left the office. It was the last conversation I had with him. The
following year, when he became the national security adviser, I attempted several times to talk to him about the Iranian matter, but
always without success.

He had evidently concluded that I was unreliable, incompetent, or
both, and would not receive me. At the time, I was quite upset. I
believed deeply in the political initiative and feared that it was being
overwhelmed by the hostage matter. Later, I was grateful I had been
replaced at such an early stage.

THE CHANGING OF THE CAST

North was at one with the Israelis in wishing to see the initiative
continue, and—even in the fragmentary picture given in the published
documents—there was a regular flow of memoranda from him to Poindexter throughout the period between the Hawk fiasco and the presidential approval of the Finding in January 1986. His message was
typically single-minded: get the hostages out quickly, thereby clearing
the decks for serious discussion of the relationship between Iran and
the United States. And this would remain the basic impulse all the
way through to the end. North became the prime American actor in
November, during the preparations for the Hawk shipments. Thereafter he quickly took control over both the planning and the operational
aspects of the initiative. As a matter of fact, not only did he gain
personal control, but—in tandem with Nir—he achieved the replace-

162

ment of all the previous intermediaries. And this was no small undertaking, for Schwimmer was Shimon Peres's closest friend and an indispensable political supporter, Nimrodi was a highly respected expert on Iran and an intimate of Gen. Ariel Sharon and other key members of the Likud party, while Kimche was one of the most important people in the Israeli national security establishment. But this still lay in the future; at the moment, the pressing issue was whether the Iran initiative should continue at all, and if so, on what basis.

An overall American assessment of the Iran initiative was imperative following the Hawk disaster, and this took place in three stages: a high-level National Security Planning Group meeting in Washington on the 7th of December; a meeting in London with Ghorbanifar and the Israelis the next day; and the decisions made in Washington— ostensibly on the basis of the results of those two earlier meetings— shortly thereafter.

The NSPG meeting on the seventh provided the occasion for Shultz and Weinberger to express their reservations about the program, and while there are some differences about the intensity with which the two secretaries spoke, there is no question that they opposed any further swaps of weapons for hostages. It was decided to send McFarlane—now the former security adviser—to London for a potentially final session with the full cast. The stage was already carefully set, for North and Secord had already arrived in the British capital, where they were involved in discussions with Israeli Defense experts, Ghorbanifar, and Kimche.

If it was hoped that the day's preparation would guarantee a successful meeting on the eighth, these hopes were quickly dashed. For McFarlane—as he would be in Tehran five months later—was not in a mood for elaborate diplomatic charades. He came quite quickly to the point with Ghorbanifar: the United States was no longer going to barter with the Islamic Republic. If the relationship between the two countries was going to improve, Iran had to begin the process by releasing all the American hostages. There would be no American *quid* for this unilateral *quo,* except the expectation that, with the hostage issue eliminated, it would be easier to move toward some form of rapprochement.

Ghorbanifar could not believe his ears. After all the hours of hard work to convince the Iranians that the hostages should be released, that the Americans were reliable, and that America wanted a new relationship, he had seen his plans dashed by the Hawk catastrophe.

163

Now he was being told that Iran would have to make a unilateral gesture to get the process moving again. It was preposterous, and he told McFarlane so. The discussion continued quite heatedly, with McFarlane erupting from time to time in moral denunciations of the Khomeini regime.

As Ghorbanifar later told the Tower Commission:

> I said what are you talking about? You just left a mess behind and you want something else? I was tough. I explained, I explained to him that what is the situation inside Iran between the rival groups, between the politicians, what is this mess, what the hell a problem has brought this one, this issue has presented to this big policy.[5]

One could hardly imagine a more unlikely development than a charitable gesture by the Ayatollah, and Ghorbanifar told McFarlane that he could not possibly expect such a thing to occur. But McFarlane would not budge from this position. On the other hand, he stressed that the United States remained interested in the overall relationship with Iran, and for the first time since my conversation with him earlier in the fall, he picked up on the political initiative: he was interested in such contacts and would respond positively to any suggestion for future meetings, whether with the Senior Iranian Official or other leading figures from Tehran. But, he said, lacking some positive signal from Iran, the initiative was terminated, so far as he was concerned. This was the content of his report to the president upon his return from London. At the same time, North told me that the Iran initiative was terminated.

But the initiative was not dead at all. From the moment of his return from London, North urged Poindexter to go ahead with it, on much the same basis as Schwimmer, Nimrodi, and Kimche had proposed: send several thousand TOWs to Iran in an effort to get the project back on track. Within a month, the proposal was approved by President Reagan. But it soon became evident that there was one element in the new arrangement that the three Israelis had not anticipated: they too were going to be removed from action, and replaced by Amiram Nir, the prime minister's special adviser on counterterrorism.

5. *Tower Commission Report,* B-47

6. Iran III: The New Team

If it is true that opposites attract, while like personalities repel, the North/Nir partnership must be counted a curiosity, for they are so alike they could have been twins, and their careers up to the time of the Iran-Contra affair were almost eerily similar. Both served enthusiastically in their armed forces and performed well. Both entered civilian governmental service at a very high level, despite the fact that many of their colleagues considered them relatively inexperienced. Both had to overcome initial suspicion and hostility in order to acquire impressive political power and influence. And both managed to survive in power even though their original sponsors either left office or were replaced.

Amiram Nir

Of course, there were differences, even beyond those that obviously differentiate an American from an Israeli. For one, Amiram Nir came from a relatively well-to-do family. As a teenager he enjoyed privileges given to few Israelis: sporty cars, foreign travel, access to good society. But he early demonstrated the qualities that would make him and North such formidable political and bureaucratic forces: remarkable tenacity (to the point of obsessiveness), enormous raw intelligence and quickness of wit, along with a military discipline and an officer's ability to set an objective and devote all his energies toward conquering it. Generous as a child, Nir gradually developed a single-mindedness that would leave some of his early friends in doubt about his willingness to place fairness and friendship above ambition.

But these doubts came later, as they did about North; in the beginning, there was the skill, the energy, and the dedication. Like

165

virtually all Israelis, Nir served in the army. Unlike some, he loved it, perhaps because his military service was fulfilled as a journalist. Most Israelis limit their postdischarge military activities to the obligatory reserve duty, but Nir served enthusiastically in the reserves, attended officer's school, then went through an intelligence course, and stuck to it until he achieved the rank of major. (By the time he enters our story, he, like his American counterpart, was a lieutenant colonel.) All of this was done on his own time, in addition to his successful journalistic career. And along the way he married Judy Moses, a lovely woman whose father owned one of the most important newspapers in the country, *Yediot Aharonot (The Latest News)*.

Like North, he looked good in uniform and wore it proudly. His personal courage and single-mindedness emerged in the course of an automobile accident in which he lost an eye. The story they tell about him in Israel is that he picked up the eye and carried it, pressed into the bloody socket, as he drove at top speed to the Hadassah Hospital in Jerusalem. It's another of those stories whose truth may never be known, but which nonetheless gives us a fair picture of the man and his qualities.

In 1976, at the age of just twenty-six, Nir won a major journalistic award, the Agron Prize of the city of Jerusalem. The following year he became the official television journalist of the Israeli Defense Forces, one of the most prestigious and visible positions in national journalism. His departure from that post was even more spectacular than his entry and gave a hint of the political explosiveness that he would produce five years later: in March 1981 he resigned, shortly after producing a Friday night feature on the Begin government that was one of the most openly hostile broadcasts of the season. Within days of the announcement of his resignation, the newspapers were full of stories that Labor party leader Shimon Peres—at the time nearly thirty points ahead of Begin in the polls—had promised Nir the job as chief of the Prime Minister's Bureau if Labor won the upcoming elections. Was this Nir's first blatantly political operation? And was the television show a down payment to the Labor party? Labor's campaign manager, Aharon Harel, denied it: Nir, he said, had resigned simply because he wanted to participate in Labor's campaign efforts.

These theories were never tested because Begin unexpectedly won the June elections, and Nir entered academia, becoming one of the resident scholars at Tel Aviv University's celebrated Jaffe Center for Strategic Studies. There, under the tutelage of the brilliant former military intelligence chief Aharon Yariv, Nir worked on current Middle East problems, focusing his attention on Lebanon. It was of a piece with his destiny: Lebanon would remain at the center of his activities for many years.

At the same time, Nir quickly moved to the forefront of Labor party affairs, and in November was named Peres's spokesman. His political breakthrough came in 1984, with the formation of the coalition government, and Shimon Peres's accession to the prime ministership. Nir was named adviser to the prime minister for counterterrorism. He was a curious choice for the job, since he had never worked in the field and such a position notoriously depends upon good access to the Israeli intelligence community. If Nir were to have such access, he would have to earn it, and the experts were not pleased with his appointment. They let it be known that they were not about to fully cooperate with a man without the requisite background, and who was likely to return to journalism in a few years, where he could write about the sensitive information he had acquired during his brief stint as a political appointee. The *Jerusalem Post* quoted colleagues of Nir's criticizing his selection as "a symptom of the growing politicization of the Civil Service."

As if this were not enough of a problem for a person with no previous experience inside the political bureaucracy, Nir had other difficulties to overcome. These were not of his making. His immediate predecessor had been one of the most controversial figures in recent years: Rafi Eitan, a long-time intelligence officer who had played the central role in the recruitment and running of Jonathan Pollard, Israel's American spy in the Pentagon. The Pollard operation—undoubtedly one of the most foolish and disastrous decisions made by the Israeli government in the history of its relations with the United States—had been conducted by a little-known, but enormously powerful governmental organization known as *Lekem,* which had been in existence since the late 1950s. *Lekem* was charged, among other things, with the two most sensitive aspects of Israel's nuclear program: the research and development of the atomic bomb which was to be used as a "doomsday device" of last resort in the event of an impending military destruction of the country; and the acquisition of those materials necessary to construct the weapon itself.

It was clear that such functions had to be concentrated in some governmental office; but very few knew of the formal existence of *Lekem,* or that Eitan sat atop such an imposing structure. And what a structure it was! In a country of modest economic means, Rafi Eitan disposed of an annual budget that dispensed hundreds of millions of dollars (some knowledgeable Israelis put the figure as high as a billion dollars a year). In such a sea of money it was child's play to hide a small ripple of the dimensions of the cost of recruiting and running a Jonathan Pollard.

Eitan departed the prime minister's office before the Pollard scandal broke, and *Lekem,* with its vast budget, left along with him. *Lekem* was not part of the counterterrorism portfolio, and had been managed from that office simply because Eitan happened to be there. Following the Pollard scandal, *Lekem* was formally dissolved (and in any case no one was about to hand over this account to Amiram Nir). Nir thus took over a position which had been gutted of its effective power. Eitan distributed fortunes; Nir had only his own salary, one top military assistant—the loyal Gidon Mechanaimi, inherited from Eitan— and a couple of secretaries. It was not an auspicious beginning.

At first, relations with the intelligence community—Mossad, the domestic security organization Shin Bet, and Military Intelligence— were so poor that whenever some sensitive intelligence had to be sent to Peres through the counterterrorism office, it invariably went through Mechanaimi. Nir was simply cut out of the information loop. Worse, he was sometimes asked to endure the governmental equivalent of fraternity hazing: tag along on routine intelligence missions, carry messages of little importance to foreign officials, and the like. In the corridors of the Mossad, Nir's name was a source of mirth, and their derision was not confined inside the community. Trusted journalists knew. And they told their friends.

When a man of Nir's qualities finds himself in this sort of position, he does not go to the prime minister and complain. He digs in, prepares for a lengthy struggle, and goes to work. Nir had arrived without the knowledge and skills required to meet the standards of the intelligence community. Fair enough; now he would acquire them. He was not without resources, after all, and while Israeli insiders might consider him a useless appendage of Peres's office, his title was a good one. He made a good impression, and he could travel. One can sometimes prevail in a domestic political struggle by foreign achievements, and for Amiram Nir, Washington was the best place to win his foreign stripes.

Within countries allied with the United States, an official's standing in Washington counts for a great deal. Trips to America, whether taken by presidents or lower-level civil servants, are ostensibly for substantive discussions. In reality, they are primarily occasions for winning points back at home. That is why foreign visitors often spend so much time in America in blatantly political pursuits: photo opportunities, press breakfasts, honorary degrees, sporting events, and so forth. Such public events are ways in which foreign politicians make useful headlines back home.

Nir, of course, did not have this public option. In the past, he had achieved success through his public activities as a journalist and Labor party spokesman; now he had to act in secret, or at least in shadow. Any effort to become a celebrity in Washington would only add to his misery with Mossad and the Military Intelligence people. But the intelligence world has its own form of publicity, and Nir undoubtedly realized that his cause would be greatly aided if he could establish close working relations with some counterpart in the American government. So he travelled to Washington and sought out the experts on terrorism, from the Pentagon and the State Department to the CIA and the National Security Council. That is how he met Oliver North, and the two men came to realize that they had much to offer each other.

TERRORISM

By 1984–85, the period in which North and Nir developed their working relationship, North was seeking to enlarge his governmental portfolio. He had managed to become one of the major players in Central America, but he had not yet established himself as a heavyweight in counterterrorism. Moreover, unlike Central America—where he had been a total amateur at the outset, and where his passions grew as he learned more about the subject—his emotions were fully engaged when it came to terrorism. His own comrades-in-arms, the marines, had been the victims of brutal terrorist attacks in Beirut, and North had suffered with McFarlane the agonizing frustration of having been unable to prevent the massacres in Lebanon and then thwarted in efforts to avenge them. He had a score to settle. And he knew—as everyone involved in the program knew—that the United States was not up to the challenge.

Despite the aggressive rhetoric of two successive administrations, very little had been done to give the United States effective counterterrorist options. The first problem lay in the bureaucratic organization of the problem: the "lead agency" was the State Department, which meant that a State Department official headed the interagency groups that dealt with the problem. And it was obvious to everyone, even those of good will within the Department of State, that one simply couldn't run counterterrorism from Foggy Bottom. Effective counterterrorism depends primarily upon good intelligence and prompt response. Neither could be organized from State. The intelligence was in other buildings, and by the time it reached the Office to Combat Terrorism in the State Department, it had usually already been filtered, digested, and analyzed by the various intelligence community experts. True, the occasional piece of raw intelligence came into the Bureau of Intelligence and Research, but nothing like the quantity that was required to do a proper job. The intelligence community did not trust State with large quantities of highly sensitive material. Most intelligence officers regarded State as one of the prime sources of leaked information and did not wish to encourage the process. In that business, after all, a leak may mean death.

Nor could the State Department hope to direct the various special units in timely responses to terrorist attacks. That was the Pentagon's business, and the Department of Defense guarded its turf with the same vigilance as the Foreign Service. If military or paramilitary actions were called for, the key decisions were going to be made across the Potomac river in the Pentagon.

Finally, the very nature of the State Department's personnel system guaranteed that no real expert would ever manage the Office to Combat Terrorism. Throughout the Reagan years, a series of diplomats drifted in and out of the top counterterrorism slots; men with various degrees of brain and courage, but not a single one with any prior substantive background in the subject, or any first-hand experience with special forces.

In short, there was bureaucratic gridlock among the three key agencies (State, CIA, and Defense). And within the CIA and the Pentagon, there were further obstacles to an effective program.

At Defense, the prime responsibility in the field had been given to Noel Koch, a survivor of the Nixon White House with a solid military record in Vietnam and a varied background in political activities, ranging from the staff of Senator Robert Dole to pro-Israel organizations and speechwriting for Weinberger. Although he possessed considerable talent, he was also a man who engendered almost instant hostility in many quarters, particularly among the officers within the military services charged with the preparation of American special forces. Almost from the start, he was involved in a vicious bureaucratic struggle with the services, which, like all such battles within a government, involved both substance and turf. Koch recognized that the makeup of our special forces—JSOC, the Joint Special Operations

Command—was dictated by the demands of each individual service for its own special forces. The Navy had the Seals, the Army its Rangers, and so on. Each service was eager for its own "special force" to participate in any serious undertaking, yet was unwilling to turn over authority to the joint command. This was both wasteful and silly, for the country needed an efficient organization which drew upon the talents of all the services to create the best possible groups.

Koch knew what a good organization looked like, for one of his contributions to the Reagan administration was the development of good working relations with JSOC's counterparts overseas. So Koch had seen the work of the German GSG9, headed by the brilliant commander of the Mogadishu operation, General Ulrich Wegener; the celebrated British SAS; and of course the Israeli elite paratroop units of the sort that had been sent to Entebbe. All these countries —and others, from Portugal to Italy—had overcome the interservice rivalries and constituted special forces with high prestige and first-class training. In the United States, the competition between the services had left JSOC as the unwanted stepchild of the Department of Defense. It might be exciting to serve in the unit, and the training exercises and international competitions (which might be called the Clandestine Olympics) were great fun, but it was not good for one's career. This was hardly the way to get the best talent, let alone develop a team upon whom one could count in moments of desperate necessity.

So Koch decided to battle the service chiefs and demanded that an appropriate organization be created. It was an unequal contest from the beginning, and the combination of his unsubtle methods and his abrasive personality left him with little hope of success. It also meant that if and when the administration decided to get serious about terrorism, he would not be picked to take charge. In the end, this was all to the good, for later events would demonstrate that there were elements of his personality that made him ill-suited for a position of such responsibility.

Meanwhile, over at the CIA, terrorism had a relatively low profile; as the agency's struggle against Haig in 1981 had shown, the spooks had little enthusiasm for the subject. Furthermore, the CIA's method of organization virtually guaranteed that it would not be able to gather and evaluate intelligence rapidly enough to permit prompt action.

From its inception, CIA was designed to limit the damage of any hostile penetration of the American intelligence system. The theory was known as compartmentalization, and its champion was the long-time chief of counterintelligence, James Jesus Angleton. As befits a man whose chief obsession was the ability of the KGB to penetrate and deceive Western intelligence services, Angleton argued for an effective defense: the agency would be divided into various compartments, with each working independently of the others. Intelligence would be transferred between compartments only at the very top, and only on the basis of a strict "need to know." That way, if an enemy recruited an agent within the CIA, the enemy would only be able to spy upon a single compartment, not upon the system as a whole.

There was also an intellectual justification for compartmentalization: maintaining a strict division between the people who ran the actual spies (in the Directorate of Operations) and the analysts (in the Intelligence Directorate) who evaluated the spies' reports would help ensure that there would be no "contamination" of the intelligence-gathering process.

It is an attractive theory, but in order to gain the advantage of damage limitation, the CIA sacrificed speed and efficiency. There are many cases in which an active interplay between the collectors and the analysts is imperative—particularly in wartime—and the airtight compartments did not permit this timely exchange to take place. This lesson was driven home to Casey—and, significantly, to North as well—in the case of Central America. In the first years of the administration, the CIA's major task was to protect El Salvador from Nicaraguan and Cuban subversion, so agency and Pentagon experts were dispatched to Salvador to teach the locals how to conduct a counterinsurgency campaign. We soon learned that the Salvadorans lacked the equipment and the skills to figure out the guerrillas' intentions and maneuver quickly enough to defeat them. It was decided to do it for them, but we then learned that although the United States has an amazing ability to gather information, by the time it was given to the analysts, and their evaluations passed to the people who could then design countermeasures, it was often too late. We needed an integrated unit, and, at Casey's instructions, with North's enthusiastic support and input, such a unit was created. In many ways, the survival of José Napoleón Duarte's brave government in Salvador was due to the willingness of the CIA to abandon its previous theory, break down the boundaries between the compartments, and create an effective team.

So it was with terrorism, and the event which best demonstrated it was the one which had so terribly upset North and McFarlane: the murderous truck-bombing of the U.S. Marine headquarters in Beirut. For, when the intelligence community did its "damage assessment" of the event, it was discovered that we had in fact gathered sufficient information to have been able to predict the attack. But the information was not all in one place where smart minds could be brought to bear on it. Instead, it was divided up amongst the various compartments, so that the overall picture was as secure from our own understanding as it was from the Soviets. Like a jigsaw puzzle made up of human reports, photographs from outer space, words in the ether, and movements of significant individuals, the elements remained spread out over the CIA's vast table, and were not pieced together to form a picture.

To be sure, we did not require a sophisticated intelligence organization to recognize the virtual certainty that the marines would eventually come under terrorist attack. That was inherent in the nature of Lebanon in the 1980s and could have been thwarted if the marines had installed proper security. North recognized this and was enraged by the lax security measures, as well as by the shocking failure to hold the commanding officers accountable for the disaster. But North also recognized that there would undoubtedly be other, less obvious cases in which we would have sufficient information to save the lives of our people but would be unable to recognize the situation because of the inadequacies of our intelligence organizations.

Once it was seen that we could, that we *should* have seen the preparations for the bombing of the U.S. Marine headquarters, it was a short step to the demand that an integrated intelligence unit be created. And the parallel with Salvador held: the integrated unit on Central America enabled us to stave off a guerrilla assault against an ally; the antiterrorist unit could help us—finally—move against the killers of our people.

William Casey had had to ride herd on his own people to get the Central American unit up to speed, and he knew that it would be equally difficult to get an integrated group working effectively on terrorism. But he was not disposed to temporize; by the beginning of Reagan's second term he had been diagnosed with prostate cancer, and he was afraid that he wouldn't have time to finish the work he had begun at the agency. He ordered the creation of the new Directorate, and named Dewey Clarridge to head it.

Like Koch at the Pentagon, Clarridge quickly found himself in a head-on battle with the Near East Bureau people—the chief of the NE Division and his deputy. And they were usually supported by the deputy director for operations, Clair George. But unlike Koch, Clarridge was a professional, and it was much more difficult for the NE people to challenge one of their own than it was for the military men at the Pentagon to take on a political appointee like Koch. Furthermore, Clarridge had the full support of an activist director at CIA; Koch did not have similar support at DOD. Finally, Clarridge was one of the most highly respected men in the agency (he had a long string of successes in the Middle East and Western Europe before coming to the counterterrorist job), while Koch did not enjoy such esteem at the Pentagon. In the end, Clarridge succeeded where Koch failed.

To describe the potential of the new CIA unit is to sense the excitement that must have gripped North in those days. But putting together the scattered pieces at CIA was not enough; there was a larger puzzle to be solved within the government at large. To what avail the creation of a top-notch unit at CIA if the services spent more energy on the defeat of Noel Koch than in preparing to avenge our dead marines? And to what avail the creation of an effective counterterrorist force, and the existence of timely information, if the bureaucrats could not coordinate policy among the different agencies?

Two iron rules of American bureaucracy came into play: only a small group can quickly reach decisions; and only the White House can effectively drive policy among the participating agencies. A new group—the Operations Sub Group—was created in order to coordinate counterterrorist policy. It was small, including one State Department representative (generally Ambassador Robert Oakley), one or two Defense Department people (Koch, with Assistant Secretary Richard Armitage sometimes in attendance), Clarridge and Charles Allen from the CIA, and a top FBI official, along with North from the NSC. When the time came to act against international terrorism, this group would be at the center of the action.

THE ACHILLE LAURO AFFAIR

If there was one single event that made North one of the most influential and effective people in Washington, it was the *Achille Lauro* shipjacking in October 1985, and its spectacular aftermath in the Mediterranean skies from Cairo to Sicily and Rome. The facts of the incident are fairly well known: a group of four Palestinian terrorists with a considerable quantity of explosives and handguns boarded the ship in Italy, intending to disembark in Israel, where they planned a suicide-type attack on Israeli civilians. But they were sloppy terrorists, and one night while they were inspecting their weapons, a steward came upon them, thus discovering the nature of the group. This caused the terrorists to change their plans, and they took over the ship, ordering all the passengers to their quarters and performing the now ritual division of the passengers' passports between those with Jewish surnames and the rest of the world.

The terrorists' actions were communicated to Italian authorities by the ship's captain, and in less than an hour the Western world was on a state of alert.

The *Achille Lauro* affair was quite unusual for the American government: in every other terrorist incident, there had always been a fairly predictable division between those who wanted to act, and those who didn't. The NSC was invariably for action, with frequent support from the State Department, while the Pentagon and the CIA tended to be more cautious. Secretary Weinberger, in particular, was invariably in favor of waiting a while longer. But this time, everyone felt it was necessary to take action, and we quickly dispatched a team to the area.

Meanwhile, there was considerable talk with the Italians, who held nominal sovereignty over the ship, and therefore held a veto over any unilateral action on our side. The Italians were deeply divided, with Defense Minister Spadolini in favor of a paramilitary strike against the ship, and Foreign Minister Andreotti arguing for negotiation. Finally, Spadolini carried the day. However it was evident that Andreotti would attempt to reverse the decision as soon as possible, and the experts in the White House were convinced that Andreotti would prevail in relatively short order.

Meanwhile, the special forces were on the way, and we were preparing to send a team of underwater commandos to storm the ship, save the passengers, and neutralize the terrorists (either by capturing or shooting them). We hoped that the Italians' nerve held a few hours longer.

In the end, there was no assault on the ship, but not because of a failure of Italian nerve; it became physically impossible for us to carry out the planned operation. The men and equipment did not arrive on schedule; our experts lost touch with the *Achille Lauro,* and actually were in considerable doubt about its location for several hours. The situation was made even worse by the fact that Weinberger had given orders that no one was to discuss the question with the Israelis, thereby cutting us off from the best source of information. Things finally got so bad that McFarlane started talking like a real marine. By the time that our military experts had located the ship and organized themselves to rescue it from the PLO terrorists, there was no longer a diplomatic consensus for action. The Italians and the Egyptians had gotten in touch with the PLO, which in turn had issued instructions to the terrorists on board ship. A deal had been struck: the terrorists would permit the ship to come into an Egyptian port and would guarantee the well-being of the passengers. The terrorists would be given safe passage out of Egypt, and that would be that.

It was not known at that time that the terrorists had murdered Leon Klinghoffer, a paraplegic confined to a wheelchair, in cold blood and pushed his body overboard. That was first discovered when the ship's captain communicated laconically to his company in Naples that all the passengers were okay "except for one American Jew."

North, along with most of the NSC people who had been working on the case, were furious. Were we going to let these murderers simply walk away? Was there no way to make the Italians hold firm? The answer was no. Andreotti was one of the Arabs' best friends in Europe, was not about to take the side of the United States against the Palestinians, and was concerned at messages he was receiving from the Egyptians (Mubarak had given his personal guarantee for safe passage; if anything were to happen to the terrorists—or if we should not abide by his promise—the Egyptian leader could become the target of a future terrorist operation). Prime Minister Craxi was also very favorably disposed to the PLO and was not eager to humiliate Yassir Arafat. There was no chance that the Italians would help us undo the deal with the Egyptians and the PLO.

So there it was: the one time that everyone had agreed to act, we hadn't been able to do anything. It had been three days of little sleep since the incident began, and it was apparently about to end with yet another appeasement of terrorism. Our failure was manifest.

Then, early the following morning—October 10th—we got a reprieve: information came in that the terrorists had been promised an airplane from Cairo to Tunis for a flight later that same day. We knew everything: the nature of the plane, the tail number, the flight schedule, the names of the passengers and crew. North absorbed the information, thought briefly, and then picked up the phone in his OEB office for Poindexter across the drive in the West Wing of the White House: "Sir," he said, "I think we can do an Admiral Yamamoto."

Given a second chance, the system—thanks to North's unique abilities to get rapid action out of people, and the quick decision making of McFarlane, Poindexter, and the president—functioned to perfection. This was one of those rare times when working for the American government was a real thrill, and North was functioning at full bore. By mid-day the "Yamamoto" plan had been relayed to McFarlane and enthusiastically approved by the president, and in the late afternoon, the Egypt Air jet carrying four PLO terrorists (including Mohammed Abu Abbas, the leader of the terrorist group that had murdered Leon Klinghoffer) was intercepted by American fighter planes over the southern Mediterranean and invited to follow the American lead plane toward the Italian NATO air base at Sigonella, Sicily.

All afternoon, North had been pondering the problem of where to bring the captured Egyptian aircraft. His intention was simply to touch down briefly at some base, transfer the terrorists to an American military transport, and fly Abu Abbas and his henchmen to Washington, where they would be put on trial for murder. But things were not as simple as they looked, for many allied governments were very leery of being involved in such an operation.

Where should the terrorists' plane be forced down? Commercial airplanes generally have only enough fuel to reach their planned destination, so it was unlikely that the Egyptian aircraft would reach airports in West Germany or France. There is a British base at Akrotiri, Cyprus, but it was not likely that Mrs. Thatcher's government would give permission on such short notice. Israel was of course a possibility, but that would cause such a political firestorm that it was preferable to avoid it if possible. Greece was out of the question, for the Papandreou government was, if anything, more sympathetic to the PLO than to us. That left Italy. Would the Craxi government cooperate with such a dramatic action?

It might seem an easy matter simply to ask the Italians how they felt about the operation, but there were several good reasons why this could not be done. For one thing, there was such a close relationship between high Italian officials and a variety of Arab leaders (from PLO chief Arafat to Egyptian President Mubarak), that there was considerable concern in Washington that simply asking the question would lead the Italians to inform the PLO and the Egyptians of our intentions, thereby scuttling the operation. Moreover, there was a more general consideration: the likelihood of Italian cooperation was likely to increase if they were asked to go along with a *fait accompli*. They were much more likely to agree to let a plane land that was already over Sicily than they were to participate in the plan to skyjack an Egyptian aircraft. So, contrary to many published reports suggesting a closely held joint Italo-American operation, the Italians knew nothing of our intentions until the skies over the Sigonella NATO base

177

were full of unexpected traffic: the Egyptian airliner with its load of terrorists and Egyptian military men, the American fighter planes that had escorted the terrorists from their planned route northwest across the Mediterranean, and the two American military transport planes that hoped to carry the terrorists and our special forces to Washington to face a federal judge on murder charges.

At that point, a moment of comic relief broke the rhythm of North's frenetic day. Orders had been given for the American embassy in Rome to contact Prime Minister Craxi and ask him for permission for the planes to land, but Craxi was nowhere to be found. Ambassador Maxwell Rabb was the second consecutive American representative in Rome who had failed to develop the kind of personal relationship with Craxi that he desired, and, like his predecessor Richard Gardner, Rabb rarely saw Craxi and did not know the channels to use in order to find the prime minister under such circumstances. Each time he called Craxi's residence—the charming Hotel Raphael just off Piazza Navona in the heart of ancient Rome—Rabb was told that the prime minister was not there, and no one would admit to knowing where he was, or how he could be reached.

The American embassy may have suspected that Craxi was in fact in his penthouse apartment in the Raphael, and simply did not wish to be disturbed. But they were unable to break through the barrier of his loyal assistants, and the planes continued to circle Sigonella.

It was at this point that I received an urgent call from North. He knew that Craxi and I had been friends for nearly twenty years. When my wife and I lived in Rome in the first half of the 1970s, we occasionally visited Craxi on the rooftop terrace of the Raphael, and our baby daughter would sit on his lap and receive lessons in Italian politics. North knew that I might get through to Craxi even if the regular bureaucracy couldn't. "He's your friend," North ordered, "get him and ask him to give permission for the plane to land." I asked the White House switchboard (one of the true miracles of international communication) to get me the Raphael, and the call was instantly put through to one of Craxi's personal assistants at the hotel. It was slightly after midnight in Rome. "The prime minister is not here." I identified myself and told him in Italian that I was calling from the White House because there was a serious crisis. Lives were at stake. "If people die tonight because you refuse to let me talk to Craxi because he doesn't want to be disturbed, you will find your picture on the front page of every newspaper in the world tomorrow morning." Ten seconds later, Craxi was on the line, asking what the problem was. I explained:

"Mr. Abu Abbas, his right-hand man, and two terrorists from the *Achille Lauro* are on an Egyptian civilian plane. They are circling over Sigonella, surrounded by a certain number of American military aircraft, and they don't know where the hell to land."

"Why here?" he asked, for the first time realizing the gravity of the decision he was being asked to make.

"Because," I replied, hoping that a light-hearted approach was the most likely to gain a favorable response, "no other place on earth can offer the unique combination of beautiful weather, cultural tradition, and magnificent cuisine that Sicily can provide these people." He laughed, and said he would take care of it at once. It cannot have been an easy decision for him, but he was true to his word; a few moments later the terrorists were on the ground at Sigonella.

It was one of North's greatest achievements, but there was still a lot of work to be done. We knew that the Italians were not happy with the situation, and steps were quickly taken to ensure that the PLO terrorists did not fly their Sicilian coop. We informed the Italian government that we would shortly file a request for the extradition of the four terrorists, invoking the provisions of a recently signed treaty between our two countries which required the Italians to give us forty-five days to present our evidence.

The extradition request required the existence of an arrest warrant for the terrorists, and American law is predictably quite precise about the requirements for a warrant: the government has to present a federal judge with sufficient evidence—of a sort that can be introduced into evidence at a trial—to convince the judge that there is a reasonable case against the terrorists. In the *Achille Lauro* affair, most of this evidence consisted of sensitive intelligence, and a great deal of that was not gathered by us, but by the Israelis. Israel shared it with us during the crisis, but we were not entitled to declassify it; that authority rested with the government of Israel. If the information remained classified, it could not be presented as evidence at a trial, and that in turn meant that we would be unable to get an arrest warrant. Without the arrest warrant, we had no legitimate grounds to demand extradition, and that would permit the Italians to let the terrorists flee the scene, regardless of the forty-five-day provision of the new treaty. We needed an arrest warrant—fast!—and we could only get it if Israel agreed to release the information demonstrating that the men on the airplane were all part of a criminal conspiracy to perform terrorist acts.

So began hours of conversations with our government's legal ex-

179

perts, on the one hand, and with the Israelis on the other. We worked through two channels to Jerusalem: one ran through the Israeli embassy in Washington, the other, all through the night, was Amiram Nir in Tel Aviv.

Rarely have two governments cooperated as fully as America and Israel worked together that night. As our legal experts (under the guidance of Judge Abraham Sofaer at the State Department, with Assistant U.S. Attorney Lawrence Barcella doing almost all the detailed work) told us what the courts required, we relayed the information to the Israelis. In record time, the Israelis approved the declassification (without exception), and the evidence was presented to the judge. Early the following morning, Rome time, a flash cable was sent to our embassy so that they could present the request for extradition—along with a considerable amount of the supporting intelligence—to the Italian Justice Minister. In the meantime, Attorney General Meese (aside from McFarlane, the only cabinet-level officer who had actually showed up in the Situation Room of the White House during the crisis) had been on the phone from his box at the Kennedy Center to Justice Minister Scalfaro to alert him to the imminent arrival of our request. Calls were also placed to President Cossiga, Foreign Minister Andreotti, and Defense Minister Spadolini.

There was an important lesson that many of us drew from the events of that night: North was absolutely insistent that we operate within a context of strict legality. We were in constant touch with both State Department lawyers and the Justice Department; we rigorously conformed to their requirements. Thus, when North told me later on that he had confirmed the legality of his Central American activities, I never doubted it. After all, I had seen his concern for a scrupulous respect for the law in action when it came to hunting down terrorists.

North's original plan was to have American special forces take the terrorists off the Egyptian plane, force them onto one of ours, and take off for the United States. But we were not going to force the issue if the Italians insisted on keeping them in their own custody. The problem was a delicate one, because if we asked the Italians to turn over the terrorists, they would be forced to say no. Italian pride would not permit them to acquiesce to such a demand. On the other hand, Craxi might well wish to have us take the terrorists off his hands, and then lodge a violent protest over our "violation of Italian sovereignty."

The only way to find out was to send our paramilitary unit to the Egyptian plane and see what the Italians did. We needed to act seriously but be prepared to back off quickly in the face of resolute resistance from the Italians.

In the Situation Room in the basement of the West Wing of the White House, a handful of government officials lived through a scene worthy of the best of Hollywood. The technology was spectacular, so good that we heard the conversation between our men on the tarmac in Sigonella and the Italian officers who confronted them; a few minutes later, the commander of the American forces was able to listen to Larry Speakes brief the press in the White House. All this was "live," in "real time," while we received minute-by-minute reports from the intelligence community on what was going on in other capitals around the Mediterranean. We got up-to-the-minute reports on the frantic reactions in Rome, Cairo, and Tunis, as well as within the scattered command posts of the PLO. And through it all, Nir was working steadily with his intelligence people—above all, the chief of Military Intelligence, an extraordinary young general by the name of Ehud Barak—to give us the benefit of their information, sometimes several times an hour.

The Italians stood firm against our efforts to take the terrorists in Sicily, and we learned that plans were being made in Rome to spring Abu Abbas. I placed another call to Craxi (the third time I spoke to him that night), briefed him on the situation, and told him that the president would come on the line. The president was in his private quarters in the White House, while we were in the Situation Room in the West Wing. As the conversation between the two heads of government began, Craxi said he had trouble understanding the State Department translator, so I translated from English to Italian. After some initial pleasantries, Craxi asked Reagan for the identities of the men on board the Egyptian plane. I had already given Craxi this information twice, and realized that the president had not been briefed in detail on this matter, so when Reagan said, "I'm not sure we know who they all are," I took the liberty of saying (in Italian), "we know exactly who they are," and repeated the information I had previously given Craxi. Then, toward the end of the conversation, Craxi asked if the United States insisted upon the arrest of all four terrorists on the airplane. The president said pleasantly that it might be acceptable if the two main terrorists were put in jail, either forgetting or unaware that we had already demanded that they all be arrested, pending our request for extradition. So once again, Craxi got somewhat more in Italian than the president had spoken in English: "We want all four in prison." Craxi agreed. When Reagan heard what had happened, he

181

was delighted, and sent me a warm letter thanking me for my "helpful translation."

Despite the promise, the Italians could not keep the chief terrorist in their country. Mubarak insisted that he would be in danger if he were perceived to have reneged on his agreement, and Craxi and Andreotti wanted to remain on good terms with the Egyptians as well as with the PLO and their Arab supporters. Abu Abbas was permitted to leave Italy for Yugoslavia, whence he travelled to Yemen. But even though the chief terrorist of the Palestine Liberation Front got away, the American government had taken its first serious action against international terrorism. And North, thanks in part to his Israeli partner, was the star of the counterterrorist team. Henceforth, whatever the organizational charts might say, he was de facto in charge.

Five thousand miles away to the east, Amiram Nir could justifiably tell his superiors that he had been the key liaison between the White House and the Israeli government, and his privileged access to North suddenly gave Nir an enormous boost in status. Once again, there was an eerie mirror image between the two men's lives. In both Washington and Jerusalem, the *Achille Lauro* adventure provided a springboard from which North and Nir leaped to greater prominence. By the end of January 1986 the two would be in charge of the Iran initiative.

THE PURGE

The *Achille Lauro* affair enabled Nir to become a privileged Israeli interlocutor with the White House, but his contacts were with North, not McFarlane. No matter how good Nir's talents, it wasn't possible for him to replace Kimche as the main Israeli channel to the NSC. If nothing had changed in Washington, Nir would have remained a useful ally of North's, and would have slowly increased his prestige with the Israeli intelligence services. But the combination of McFarlane's breakdown and resignation, and the Hawk missile fiasco at about the same time, gave Nir his chance, and he exploited it.

We do not know precisely when and how Nir became aware of the Iran initiative (although, as will be seen, North probably told him about it in mid-November 1985 in Washington), but the method he used to get involved in it can now be told. In early December Nir became aware that the Palestine Liberation Organization (PLO) had approached CIA officers in the Middle East with an offer to negotiate with the Hezbollah for the release of the American hostages in Lebanon. This was highly threatening to the Israelis, for if the PLO were able to obtain the release of the remaining American hostages, particularly after the embarrassment of the Hawk affair in November, Israel's stock in Washington would tumble, and the PLO would gain a major coup.

Nir went to Peres to argue that Israel had to accelerate the efforts to free the American hostages. Peres agreed, and instructed Schwimmer to add Nir to the group working on the Iran initiative. Nimrodi briefed Nir on the 30th of December, in London, and Nir announced that he would leave almost immediately for meetings with North in Washington. He promised to inform Schwimmer—who was vacationing in New York at the time—so that both of them could attend the Washington meeting.

Once in the United States, Nir took his first move in the elimination of the original group. He wished to appear to be the special messenger of Shimon Peres to Washington, not simply a new member of the old team. Thus, Nir did not contact Schwimmer, and met alone with North and Poindexter on the 2nd of January 1986.

There are two documentary sources that enable us to reconstruct the conversation: Poindexter's fragmentary notes, and a memorandum from Poindexter (but actually drafted by North) to the president,[1] asking Reagan to sign a Covert Action Finding[2] that would permit the Iran initiative to resume. The memorandum began:

> This week, Prime Minister Peres of Israel secretly dispatched his special advisor on terrorism with instructions to propose a plan by which Israel with limited assistance from the U.S. can act in concert to bring about a more moderate government in Iran.

The key ingredients of the "Israeli plan" described in the memorandum were simple enough. Israel would send four thousand TOWs to Iran, and the five remaining American hostages in Lebanon "will be immediately released upon commencement of this action." This would represent a demonstration "of influence and good intent" on the part of the Iranian government.

1. The memorandum was published in the *Tower Commission Report* (B-58 and B-59), and Poindexter's notes were released along with Poindexter's depositions by the joint committees in 1987, at the time of Poindexter's public testimony.

2. By law, all covert actions undertaken by the U.S. government require formal approval from the president. The vehicle for this approval is a Covert Action Finding, and is usually a typewritten document, signed by the president to demonstrate his approval. However, in the course of the Iran-Contra affair, one finding was initialed by Poindexter (with a written reference indicating Reagan had given verbal approval), and Attorney General Meese argued that a "verbal finding"—with no written documentation at all—would be legally acceptable.

According to the memorandum, this shipment would enable Israel to achieve "a heretofore unobtainable penetration of the Iranian governing hierarchy," help produce "favorable long-term changes in personnel and attitudes within the Iranian government," and, last of all, create a dependency on the U.S./Israeli supply of weapons, "thus allowing the providor(s) to coercively influence near-term events."

The rationale was ostensibly the same as that for the original TOW shipment the previous summer, which had produced only a single hostage and had not noticeably strengthened the pro-Western forces in Iran. Moreover, the violent rejection by the Senior Iranian Official of a policy of selling weapons to Iran had evidently been forgotten or dismissed. And despite the previous experiences which had amply demonstrated that one could only sell weapons to the regime, and not to a group, the memorandum still spoke of Israel "selling military materiel to Western-oriented Iranian factions."

There was, then, nothing new in the plan described in the memorandum. But according to Poindexter's notes, there were some new elements in the verbal briefing Nir gave to North and Poindexter on January 2, 1986. One was the promise that Israel would arrange the release of some Hezbollah prisoners from South Lebanon, thereby sweetening the pot for the Iranians. According to North's notes of an earlier conversation with Ghorbanifar,[3] Nir's proposal to release Hezbollah prisoners had been made before Christmas, and he was simply confirming the offer to Poindexter.

There was one other new ingredient in the package that Nir brought to the White House in January. This was a promise from Nir that America could test the operation without risk. Israel would ship five hundred TOWs to Iran. If all the hostages were not released, America would have lost nothing, and would be under no obligation to replace the five hundred missiles.

It is hard to believe that Defense Minister Rabin approved this proposal. In fact, at this time Rabin was insisting that the United States immediately replace the five hundred TOWs that had been shipped in August and September. Israeli's national security was gravely jeopardized by the lowered inventory of antitank missiles, and by the time the plan was put into effect, this element was dropped. All four thousand TOWs were sold to Iran, even though no hostages were released.

---

3. These notes from North's personal spiral notebooks were released as part of the documentation accompanying Poindexter's depositions.

In early 1988 I asked Shimon Peres why he had sent Nir to Washington to revive the Iran initiative, and he replied that he had not. Peres told me he believed that the United States had already decided to go ahead on its own. Nir (who, after all, was supposed to have brought Schwimmer along with him) was merely supposed to assure the White House of Israel's continued willingness to assist, should it be necessary. Was North's memorandum an artfully crafted document, designed to credit Israel for something that the United States was determined to do in any event?

It is always difficult to read people's minds, but we do know that McFarlane and North always intended to blame Israel for the Iran initiative if it ever became public. David Kimche said publicly that McFarlane had made this a condition of U.S./Israeli cooperation at the outset of the initiative, and North's notebooks show that he went so far as to ask Nir if the Israelis would accept responsibility for the "diversion" of funds to the *contras* when the scandal broke in November 1986. The memorandum of January 6th might well have been written with an eye to building up this "cover story" later on.

Furthermore, there is abundant NSC documentation—from written memoranda to PROFs notes between North and Poindexter—that shows there was a constant effort to keep the Iran initiative alive, beginning promptly the day after McFarlane's London meeting with Ghorbanifar. It is tempting to conclude that the memorandum was deliberately designed to protect the president from later criticism if the initiative worked out badly.

There was probably an element of providing "cover" for the president, but that is only part of the story. Israel also had many reasons to keep the initiative alive. In addition to the fear that the PLO would bring about the release of the American hostages, there were at least three very strong motives for renewed Israeli interest in the initiative. They had made a major gaffe—shipping the "wrong" Hawk missiles to Iran—that threatened to undermine much of what had been achieved during the first several months. They wanted to set things right (hence the suggestion of a new TOW missile shipment, which Nimrodi, Schwimmer, and Kimche thought should be undertaken by Israel alone if the Americans were unwilling).

The second motive was the wish to obtain the release of the Lebanese Jews and the two Israeli soldiers held hostage by Lebanese Shi'ites. This was a very sensitive subject, for it was national policy that the Israeli government would not get directly involved in efforts to free non-Israeli Jews. The reasons for this policy were obvious: it is impossible for the tiny state to safeguard the Jews of the world. And if Israel acted as if she were the protector of world Jewry, then Jews everywhere would be at risk from Israel's enemies.

On the other hand, Israel could hardly remain indifferent to the plight of the Israeli soldiers and Lebanese Jews in the hands of Hezbollah and was willing to do what it could to help within the context of a broader initiative in which the United States was playing a lead role. Nir's proposal to release Hezbollah prisoners from south Lebanon was undoubtedly an element in this effort.

Third was the Pollard affair, which had exploded in the American press on the 21st of November, right in the middle of the Hawk crisis. Within weeks, the gravity of this matter was evident to the Israelis, who pushed harder and harder to obtain the release of American hostages, hoping thereby to pull out the sting of the Pollard catastrophe.

Finally, there is an unanswered question: was there a relationship between the Israelis' desire to keep the Iran initiative going and the secret talks about Israeli participation in a possible pipeline between Iraq and Jordan? On the Israeli side, both projects were being handled by Peres, typically using personal friends (Schwimmer in the one case, Bruce Rappaport, the controversial Swiss millionaire, in the other) as channels to the American government. The previous September, just after Weir's release, Peres had sent a message[4] to American Attorney General Edwin Meese in which he said that Weir's freedom had been obtained by Israel, that other hostages would soon be saved, and that the United States might well consider going ahead with the pipeline deal as a reward for Israel's actions in the Iran initiative. By the end of the year, with the Pollard affair throwing a dark shadow over U.S./ Israeli relations, Peres might have felt it desirable to support the Iran initiative in an effort to keep alive the pipeline—with its alleged capacity to generate substantial profits for Bruce Rappaport, one of the major contributors to Israel, and to Peres's Labor party.

In addition to these matters of national policy, Peres must have known—perhaps from Nir—that there was a good deal of unhappiness in the White House with the original group, and he probably also realized that with McFarlane's departure, Nir was one of the few Israelis who had any sort of personal relationship with Admiral Poindexter, the new security adviser. It would have made sense for Peres

---

4. The message was transmitted to Meese by E. Robert Wallach, a close friend of the attorney general. Wallach had been retained by Rappaport to help with the American side of the pipeline project.

to ask Nir to join Kimche, Schwimmer, and Nimrodi in the Iran initiative.

Nir realized that this was a chance to take over the Iran initiative. That is undoubtedly why Schwimmer was left behind in New York and not invited to the White House on January 2nd.

The Presidential Covert Action Finding, with its accompanying memorandum, therefore represented the desires of both governments, and the personal interests of Oliver North and Amiram Nir. North was by then firmly in charge of the American side of the initiative. Nir was on his way to taking charge of the Israeli side.

To this end, Nir undertook a campaign of deception against his own colleagues. On the 21st of January, Nir met with Kimche, Schwimmer, and Nimrodi at the Savion White House to discuss the future of the Iran initiative. He informed them that the Americans had decided to terminate the "joint venture" aspect of the initiative; whatever was going to happen in the future would be done by the United States alone.

This did not sit well with the others (although they had no reason to suspect Nir was lying), and Schwimmer proposed that they all go to Peres the next day to discuss Israel's future role. Nir, who had come to the meeting in uniform, said he could not possibly attend, since the next day he had reserve duty. It was a lie. Nimrodi had learned that Nir was scheduled to meet with Ghorbanifar in Frankfurt the next day, and in fact Nir flew at 6:30 A.M. to Germany.

This was not the behavior of a man who is confident of his authority. If Nir had Peres's blessing to act as the sole Israeli intermediary, he would not have had to invent stories for the other three. Instead, Nir wove a tangled web around the other participants, in an effort to appear to be the lone reliable interlocutor. On the twenty-third, Ghorbanifar called Nimrodi from London to say that Nir had promised to introduce him to Prime Minister Peres in the next couple of days. Nimrodi, who had become deeply suspicious of Nir, correctly saw this as a direct threat to his own continued role in the initiative, for if Nir were to bring Ghorbanifar to Peres, that could only mean that Nir had taken over. Nimrodi alerted Schwimmer, who flew to London and met with Peres. Once again, Nir's story was false; Peres had not approved an encounter with Ghorbanifar.

Finally, Nir and North whispered yet another lie, alleging that I was involved in a secret money-making arrangement with Ghorbanifar and some of the original Israelis. On January 16th, North sent a PROFs note to Poindexter:

... Ami (Nir) suspects that there is probably a secret business arrangement among Schwimmer, Ledeen, and Gorba that is being conducted w/o the knowledge of any of the three respective governments. ...

I have no problem w/someone making an honest profit on honest business. I do have a problem if it means the compromise of sensitive political or operational details. We might consider making Mike a contract employee of the CIA and requiring him to take a periodic polygraph.[5]

Eight days later, North sent a second PROFs note to Poindexter claiming that Casey "shares our concerns" because of some information indicating "what may well be/have been a financial arrangement among Schwimmer, Nimrodi, Gorba, and our friend."

A month later, North scribbled a note to himself: "Gorba got 13,200/ missile. Gets $260/missile Gives $50/missile to Ledeen."

It was all nonsense, as was confirmed by the joint congressional committees, and the investigators from the independent counsel's staff.[6] I never received a penny (aside from salary and reimbursement of expenses) as a result of my work on this project, and was never offered any money by Ghorbanifar, Kimche, Schwimmer, or Nimrodi. Interestingly enough, it is clear that nobody in Washington believed it either. I continued to work as a consultant on counterterrorism for nearly a year after the first bit of electronic gossip from North to Poindexter. No one ever asked me about it directly,[7] no investigation was ever carried out, and my status—and clearances—remained intact. If North, Poindexter, or McFarlane had believed the story, I would have been turned over to the FBI or, at a minimum, asked to take a polygraph (North's suggestion that I needed to be hired by the CIA in order to be subjected to polygraph examination was a bad joke; polygraphs were trotted out in the NSC on several occasions when there were suspicions of leaks to the press). Indeed, North testified to the joint Select committees that he had not believed it, and never saw any evidence to give it credibility. Nir has denied ever having said it to North, but according to Charles Allen of the CIA,

---

5. This PROFs message—a sort of electronic gossip—was published in the *Tower Commission Report* (B-70), as were the others to be quoted immediately afterward.

6. I was required to provide all documents on my financial activities for the past several years to congressional investigators and to a top Internal Revenue Service investigator working for Judge Walsh. This latter gentleman, after some months of pouring through my records, informed me that mine was the most boring set of financial records he had ever been asked to look at. I asked him not to tell me, but to report it to the *Washington Post*.

7. In the autumn of 1986, North mentioned to me that "some people in the Pentagon think you made money from the TOW sales." I told him it was nonsense, and would be delighted to sue anyone who said it publicly. That was the only time he ever raised the matter with me.

Nir was repeating the story to CIA officials as late as September and October 1986.[8]

The rumor circulated in both capitals, serving the purposes of North and Nir. The mere suspicion that Schwimmer, Nimrodi, and I were involved in a sleazy money-making deal with Ghorbanifar made it easy for North and Nir to argue that we should be removed from any activities associated with the Iran initiative.[9]

The rumors encouraged others to believe that Schwimmer, Nimrodi, Ghorbanifar, and I were doing what North and Nir were planning to do themselves: take money from the sales of weapons to Iran and use it for other purposes. Both Nir and North were very interested in laying their hands on some loose cash. The money was not for themselves, so far as can be ascertained, but for some secret operations that had not been carried out because of lack of funds. They had discussed the problem of raising money in mid-November, during one of Nir's trips to Washington. North's cryptic notes from the conversation[10] revolved around two issues: covert operations, and the need for money, at the rate of about $1 million per month. North's last conversation with Nir took place on the nineteenth, just as the Hawk shipments were about to begin. It is reasonable to guess that this was the first time North and Nir talked about the Iran initiative, and the possibility of using it to fund other activities.

We know from North's public testimony (and I have confirmed it with Israeli sources) that they worked together until November 1986 to generate funds for their own purposes. We do not know the details of the Israeli projects. On the American side, there was money for the *contras,* funds to purchase a boat and other equipment for an anti-Libyan propaganda campaign, salaries for General Secord, Albert Hakim, and their coworkers, and even a bit of profit for Hakim (Secord testified that he decided to forgo his share of profit).

THE MONEY QUESTION

As you would expect in an affair in which tens of millions of dollars were involved, many journalists, congressional and FBI

8. See Charles Allen deposition to the Select committees.

9. It will be recalled that I had been removed from the Iran Initiative in late November. But I continued to see Ghorbanifar on other matters (related to my responsibilities on counterterrorism), and North was concerned that Ghorbanifar would tell me what was going on. In his PROFs note of January 16 to Poindexter, North wrote, "it is my opinion, based on my meeting w/Gorba on Monday night [January 13], that Gorba tells Ledeen everything." (*Tower Commission Report,* B-70)

10. North's notes from the November 19, 1985, conversation with Nir were released by the joint Select committees along with Poindexter's depositions.

investigators, and even some of the participants suspected that huge sums of private profit were made. Having been falsely accused of taking money in this affair (if only by Nir and those who repeated his allegation), I am reluctant to repeat unsubstantiated gossip about others.

On the other hand, we know that the Iran initiative became a source of funds for other purposes, from support for the *contras* to Nir's covert operations, and this linkage suggests, inevitably, that at least some of the energies devoted to keeping the Iran initiative alive derived from a desire to spin off funds for the other programs. In other words, we have to try to answer the question: Where did the idea for the "diversion" come from?

In his congressional testimony, North claimed that the idea for the "diversion" of Iran revenues to the *contras* was suggested to him by Ghorbanifar in a bathroom conversation during the December 1985 London metting with McFarlane and the Israelis. That Ghorbanifar understood North's interest in money for the *contras* is hardly surprising. Anyone who spent time with North knew that much. But North had been on a worldwide search for *contra* funds for more than a year and a half by the time he met the Iranian businessman and hardly needed Ghorbanifar to tell him that there was money to be had in the Iranian business. In fact, he and Secord had already taken close to a million dollars in November from the proceeds of the original TOW transaction. In late November, North and Secord informed Schwimmer and Kimche that it would take a million dollars to "clean up the mess" in Portugal. The Israelis promptly transferred the money, but, as Secord later testified, only two hundred thousand dollars was required to cover the Portuguese expenses; the Israelis, in Secord's pun, had "made a contra-bution." It was the original "diversion."

But even this was not the first time it had occurred to North that joint activities with Israel might provide money for the *contras*. In September, he had organized a quiet breakfast meeting in Washington with three Israelis involved in an effort to sell Kfir jet fighters to Honduras. I have interviewed them all. Two remember North offering to help the project and asking if it was possible for the commission on the sale—which would normally be paid to an Israeli representative in Latin America, whether or not he was actually involved in the transaction—to be withheld. And one of the three told me that this request—to which no response was made at the breakfast—produced considerable consternation. Was North asking for a personal payoff? This Israeli (the only one of the three who had had previous conversations with North) was certain that North was investigating ways to obtain additional *contra* funding and was exploring the possibility that the commission might be given, or at least shared, with the *contras*. There was no follow-up meeting, and the Kfir sale fell through, so no additional evidence is available.

To be sure, there had always been a certain margin built into the Iran initiative. During the first TOW shipments, the Israelis had incurred substantial expenses: an airplane had been rented, pilots had been paid, and fuel had been purchased. Those costs had been covered by the price charged the Iranians. Later, when we met with the Senior Official, it was obvious that if, as we all expected, it was decided to pursue this matter further, money might have to be found for it. Where would it come from? In practice, this question was never pursued, for we did not see the Senior Iranian Official again, but Schwimmer and Nimrodi took a preliminary step: a bank account—separate from the one used to handle the funds from the TOWs—was opened in a Swiss bank. The account was never used.[11]

Some of the investigators for the joint Select committees and the independent counsel suspected that some additional revenues from the TOW and Hawk sales went toward covert Israeli projects (or even Israeli individuals or institutions). Their suspicions rest in part on a curiosity in the accounting between the original group and the Defense Ministry: the outstanding funds were not paid by Nimrodi (who was in charge of the bank accounts) until April or May of 1986. Why the long delay? The question is particularly intriguing in light of the concern expressed repeatedly by Defense Minister Rabin that the TOWs be "replenished." Rabin constantly demanded that the United States replace the five hundred-plus TOWs as soon as possible, and although McFarlane always agreed, this proved another bafflingly difficult task.

So it's surprising that it took so long for the accounts to be settled with the original three. Was it because some of the proceeds were

---

11. Inevitably, there were suggestions from investigators that money from the TOW and Hawk sales was used to pay off Iranian officials. So far as I can learn, there were no such payments. The account created at the time of the meeting with the Senior Official was never used, and his opposition to the weapons sales made it clear that he had no intention of profiting from the initiative. Whatever money may have gone to Iranians—and again, there is no documentation one way or the other—flowed outside the context of our activities. I believed, for example, that Ghorbanifar had given money to Iranian friends of his, but that was his affair, not ours.

191

being used for covert operations? Or, perhaps, for more mundane, personal (or party) objectives?[12] I do not know. But the failure of the Israeli government to demand its money earlier strongly suggests that if the money was being put to some purpose, at least some Israeli officials must have approved of it. This undercuts the suspicions that the money was going into private pockets.

Finally, there is the question of monies that allegedly went to Ghorbanifar. Like Schwimmer and Nimrodi, he certainly wished to recover his substantial expenses, and that was reasonable enough. His telephone bill alone would qualify him for favored treatment by the world's telecommunications companies, and there were periods when he virtually lived on airplanes. In addition, the rest of us concluded from various remarks he made that he felt obliged to support his friends in Tehran. I believed that he had done so out of his own pocket, not out of commissions or profits from the arms sales, at least in the early stages of the initiative, and he submitted a considerable quantity of documentation to the Tower Commission, the independent counsel, and the Iran-Contra committees to support his claims.

On the other hand, virtually everyone else in a position to know something about the cash flow has accused him of having earned commissions. That Ghorbanifar has an affection for money is beyond doubt. His life-style was the envy of most of those with whom he came into contact. And that he had a legitimate need to cover large expenses is also unquestionable. Whether or not he actually made money on one project or another is very difficult to establish, and I am personally convinced that, in the long run, he lost money on the initiative.

Ghorbanifar was accused of many things of which he is almost certainly innocent, from having been an agent of Israel to inventing

---

12. There is a cryptic remark in the *Report of the Congressional Committees,* Majority Report: "The middlemen in the [Hawk] transaction—Ghorbanifar and Al Schwimmer and Yaacov Nimrodi . . . had substantial monetary incentives to negotiate a deal in which large quantities of weapons and money would change hands." But no evidence is provided for the claim. And, while North wrote in his notebook that the proceeds from the sale of the original 504 TOWs "was used for other purposes," the Majority Report notes that the Israeli documentation does not support that claim.

The only first-hand knowledge I have of this question suggests that no profit was made by Nimrodi and Schwimmer from the TOW sales. In November, when Schwimmer was engaged in obtaining replacement TOWs from the United States government, he called to ask me how much TOWs cost. I got a figure, and called him back. He was astonished: "that's much too high," he said, "tell them it must be considerably lower." I suggested that this was properly done by his people and never heard anything more about it. But if Schwimmer was alarmed at the price, it suggested to me that he had charged the Iranians too little for the TOWs, not that he was wondering where to invest his profits.

lies at key moments of the initiative. In this melodrama, Ghorbanifar often seemed type-cast as the heavy, the Bela Lugosi of the affair. It was easy to ascribe to him motives that belonged to others, or blame him for errors that were not his own. There was a tendency, for example, to hold him responsible for unkept promises made by officials of the Iranian government, just as the regime in Tehran blamed him for errors and unkept promises made by the Americans or the Israelis. There was no possible escape from this role, and elements of his explosive personality (such as his constitutional inability to pass a polygraph) reinforced it.

Yet Ghorbanifar survived the first purge, and, as he would from beginning to end, remained a major player. The new team was now in place: North, Nir, Ghorbanifar, and Secord would shape the events of 1986. Up until that point, there had been two independent projects of the American government, run through the National Security Council staff: the Iran initiative and Project Democracy. The new team brought together the two hitherto separate strands to create the Iran-Contra affair.

7. The Iran-Contra Affair

As of January 1986, Project Democracy was finally flying, and with Secord, Gadd, Quintero, and Clines in charge of the resupply operation and the CIA back in business providing intelligence and communications support to the *contras,* there was hope that the military campaign would go better. Even the Sandinistas had lent their unwitting support, for just a few days after the House of Representatives had overwhelmingly rejected Reagan's request for a new aid package in late April 1985, Daniel Ortega left for Moscow. This produced a public backlash against the Congress, which promptly reversed itself and voted the new program of $27 million in humanitarian aid. The final vote was taken in August.

So, by early 1986, there was American government money for the *contras* again, and there was (as will be seen) a fair amount of private money coming in as well. Nonetheless, it was not enough. The *contras* did not have enough money to sustain an offensive, and the money would run out by spring. The administration was confident that, sometime in 1986, a new aid bill would be voted, and the president was asking for $100 million. But once again some bridge financing was needed to keep the *contras* going. North had seen this coming, and had, as we have seen, discussed with Nir as early as November 1985 ways of generating money for secret projects. This was the backdrop for the January Finding that resurrected the Iran initiative. According to Poindexter's deposition, shortly after the Finding was approved by the president, North came to the admiral with the news that "I think I figured out a way to provide some funds to the *contras* out of the Iranian project."

Listen to Poindexter for a moment:

I thought about it. I felt that it was in terms of supporting and implementing the President's policy, that it was entirely consistent.

The President really never changed his policy with regard to supporting the contras . . . I knew that it would be a controversial issue . . . I felt I had the authority to approve Colonel North's request. I also felt that it was, as I said, consistent with the President's policy, and that if I asked him, I felt confident that he would approve it.

But because it was controversial, and I obviously knew that it would cause a ruckus if it were exposed, I decided to insulate the President from the decision and give him some deniability; and so I decided . . . at that point not to tell the President.[1]

This was the decision that created the Iran-Contra affair. From that moment on, Project Democracy and the Iran initiative were intimately linked. For Project Democracy badly needed money, and the Iran initiative was a promising source of funding. Many people doubt Poindexter's testimony, preferring to believe that the president must have known about it, or that Casey somehow masterminded the whole thing. I believe Poindexter.

POINDEXTER: THE BOOKISH ADMIRAL

Rarely has a man been more poorly suited for a position than Adm. John Poindexter for the hot seat at the helm of the National Security Council. If McFarlane was shy, Poindexter was a virtual Trappist monk, eschewing not only contact with the media (the very thought of which was generally sufficient to send him grabbing for a pipe to chew on) but with his own staff. By tradition, the NSC is an organization that flourishes on the basis of esprit de corps and collegiality; the national security adviser not only listens to his staff, but he brings them before the president for direct briefings on their specialties. Such direct contact with the commander-in-chief compensates for the low pay, endless hours, and generally very low visibility in the Washington community.

Poindexter was temperamentally incapable of that sort of camaraderie and installed the naval chain of command. He brought in Comdr. Rod McDaniel as executive secretary, and McDaniel built a seawall between Poindexter and the staff on the one hand, and Poindexter and the outside world on the other. Henceforth memos were to be

1. Poindexter, Published Deposition to the joint Select committees, p. 1067.

sent forward according to preordained flowcharts or filed through the elaborate internal computer network that Poindexter had helped design (an overlooked, but delicious irony, of the entire affair, was that Poindexter didn't realize that the PROFs system had been designed so carefully that it was impossible to erase some of the vital documents from the system's memory, even for Poindexter himself).

Poindexter had always been an unusually bookish naval officer and was blessed with an extraordinary intellect. He graduated first in his class at Annapolis. He had earned a Ph.D. in nuclear physics from Cal. Tech., a major achievement for a full-time student, let alone a junior naval officer with other responsibilities, and he was a tireless worker, an amiable if reserved colleague, and a devoutly religious man. Indeed, the three key figures at the NSC—McFarlane, Poindexter, and North—were all deeply committed Christians who, to varying degrees, often viewed their own activities in a religious context. Poindexter's wife was an ordained minister and appeared at the hearings wearing a clerical collar.

Admiral Poindexter was well connected within the military establishment, and his position was strengthened when his old mentor, Adm. William Crowe, became chairman of the Joint Chiefs of Staff. But Poindexter had little experience with diplomacy, was devoid of foreign language skills, was unacquainted with foreign cultures, and tended to analyze foreign policy problems in the sort of abstract, balance-of-power terms in which he dealt with military matters. Moreover, his self-contained personality lent itself to manipulation, although he was a man with great personal integrity, and a uniquely low level of ego-involvement in his work.[2] In the case of the Iran initiative, Poindexter's reservations about the enterprise were overwhelmed by the force of North's powerful personality and an eruption of political support for North from the political Right, in the Congress and outside it.

Poindexter had long recognized that North was a time bomb within the NSC. His Central American activities had attracted considerable press attention throughout the second half of 1985, and several members of Congress—most notably Senator Kerry of Massachusetts—were calling for investigations. McFarlane had confided to Poindexter that North was under great stress and was behaving erratically. McFarlane recommended that North leave the NSC, take some med-

2. He put it perfectly himself, in response to one of Liman's questions: "I really am a very low-profile person. I don't feel that I need a lot of acknowledgement in order to get any sort of psychic income." Poindexter, Published Deposition, p. 1155.

ical leave, and take a cushy foreign assignment that would permit him to earn his pension and then go on to other things, but North resisted. McFarlane was unable to address the question before his resignation, leaving Poindexter with the unpleasant nettle.

The problem was a grave one, for McFarlane had misled Congress about North's activities, and Poindexter was aware of the cover-up. For McFarlane, the issue was both political and emotional. He was in agreement with North's plan of action to find ways of supporting the *contras,* even though he knew there would be a firestorm in Congress if the facts became known, but he hoped that he had compartmentalized the operation sufficiently to make the basic facts inaccessible to congressional or journalistic inquiry. Furthermore, as he testified, there may well have been some aspects of North's activities about which McFarlane was unaware. He and Poindexter never dreamed that North, who spoke the language of spycraft, and who had been involved in some of the most sensitive programs inside the government, had committed virtually every detail of the Central American operation to paper, thereby violating one of the basic principles of secret operations.

The emotional matter derived from the intimate relationship between the two men. When McFarlane told the press in the autumn of 1985 that North was like a son to him, he spoke the truth. North was, or appeared to be, everything that McFarlane could want in a son: handsome, brave, imaginative, disciplined, and tireless, as well as a devout Christian. It was virtually inconceivable that McFarlane, especially in the state of near collapse that characterized him in late 1985, could drive North out of the NSC. He urged Poindexter to do it, but Poindexter was out of his element.

Poindexter had risen to a level to which he could never have realistically aspired, and all his instincts cried out for a cautious course, avoiding potential crises. He was by training and temperament a manager, not a risk-taker, and he wished to put in two quiet years coordinating the foreign policy already in place, and then be awarded a final command in the navy. North was clearly a threat to this vision of routine administration, and Poindexter planned to shift North outside the NSC. In early spring, 1986, Poindexter asked North how he would feel about becoming military attaché in London. At about the same time, he informed North that he was taking him off the Central American "account," and put it in the hands of a member of the NSC Intelligence Directorate, Vince Cannistraro.

But North had unanticipated strength. He went first to his conservative friends—Andy Messing and Spitz Channell among others—and rallied support from "movement" Republicans as well as from the right wing of the Congress. He also spoke, at my suggestion, to Leonard Garment, one of the most influential Republican lawyers in Washington. The result of all this political activity was a barrage of phone calls to Poindexter, demanding that North be kept in his post. Poindexter was steamrolled by this political machine and abandoned the idea of replacing North. Unskilled in political maneuver and infighting, Poindexter lacked the tools and the allies necessary to remove North from the staff. He was left with the challenge of managing a crisis he knew would arrive; the only question was when, and in what form.

This helps explain Poindexter's decision to seal off the truth about North's activities from the president. For if Poindexter could not eliminate North, he could and did try to shelter the president from the inevitable fallout. His decision was not merely based on the explosive nature of the diversion of funds from the Iran operation to Central America, but rather to protect the president from North's activities across the board. Believing, as he did, that North would eventually become too hot for the White House to handle, Poindexter simply compartmentalized North's activities and resolved to be the "fall guy" himself.

A different national security adviser, in different circumstances, might have done it differently. For North, with all his problems, was a magnificent battle horse, and Poindexter might have tried to rein him in. This required a rider, however, and the only available candidate was the admiral himself. But North's projects were so complicated, and entailed so many decisions, that occasional oversight would not be effective. Poindexter would have had to devote a goodly percentage of his own time to managing North. But time was in terribly short supply, and the few extra minutes available to the admiral vanished at the crucial moment—the spring of 1986—when disease struck down Poindexter's deputy, Don Fortier.

Don had not felt well for some time, but like most overworked people, he concluded he was run-down or had a stomach ulcer and simply needed more rest. But rest is one of the pleasures of life that are systematically withheld from members of the NSC staff. The working day for senior staff members averages about twelve hours, and the top staffers—Fortier was number two, remember—work even more. So he plugged away, waiting for the next vacation to recharge his engines.

198

Poindexter relied heavily on Fortier. Don had long been involved in questions of nuclear proliferation and was one of the government's top experts on Pakistan and India. That quite logically had led him toward the Afghanistan issue, and he had contributed to administration policy in this area ever since his days on the Policy Planning Staff under Paul Wolfowitz. But even more importantly, Don was the key NSC person on congressional strategy, having spent years on the Hill working with Clem Zablocki, the long-term chairman of the House Foreign Affairs Committee, and with Dante Fascell, who succeeded Zablocki. So not only did he have to deal with several substantive issues, but he worked with congressional leaders on everything from arms control to Central America. Fortier was one of a small group of people aware of Ollie North's activities, both in Central America and in the Iran initiative. If his effectiveness were hampered, Poindexter would find it difficult to have someone else take up the slack.

Finally, in April 1986, Fortier's wife Alison convinced him to see a doctor. The first test results were bad. There was something wrong with his liver. The doctors diagnosed hepatitis, told him to rest, and continued their tests. He took some time off, and as the tests continued, something didn't add up. They decided to do some exploratory surgery, and the results were devastating: severe liver cancer, with a very poor prognosis for survival. Don and his family evaluated the options and chose drastic chemotherapy, knowing it would be an agony for him, but it was the only chance to live.

The fates toyed with Fortier, permitting him, along with his family and friends, to believe he was recovering before finally striking him down. He lost weight and hair, slowly recovering his strength between treatments, only to collapse again with each new dose of chemicals. But by early summer he was visibly stronger, and his zest for work had returned. Papers were delivered to his home in Maryland, and he undertook a light work load. Then, in July, his liver gave out. Within days of telling friends he was cautiously optimistic about "making it," he was dead.

Fortier was the first of his Washington generation to die, and his death had a profound effect on his wide circle of friends and colleagues. His good nature, his tireless willingness to sacrifice his time and energy to his work, and his deep commitment to restoring serious strategic principles to their rightful place at the center of American foreign policy made him a paradigm of the best elements of the Reagan administration's national security team. He was a student of Albert Wohlstetter, the dean of American nuclear strategists. He was a Democrat of the Scoop Jackson variety and had entered the administration along with other like-minded Democrats and close friends like Wolfowitz, Richard Perle, and James Roche.

The funeral produced a glittering assembly of distinguished Washingtonians, a dignified religious ceremony, and full military honors. His wife, several months pregnant with their second child, brought their two-year-old son to the small church in Arlington Cemetery. For those of our generation, it was one of those occasions on which the thought "there but for the Grace of God go I" was in every mind. McFarlane cancelled a trip to come to the graveside, and the entire NSC staff was present. With one exception: Poindexter remained in California with the president at the Western White House.

Poindexter's absence was unfairly misinterpreted by some NSC staffers, who believed that the national security adviser had felt it more important to stay on the job than to attend the funeral of his deputy. It was not true; the admiral wished to attend, but was talked out of it by Fortier's widow, Alison. She told Poindexter that this was purely a religious ceremony, that a memorial service was scheduled two weeks later, when other officials had returned from their summer vacations, and that that would be the occasion for him to attend. He respected her wishes, but in the corridors of the Old Executive Office Building there were many who felt it outrageous that Poindexter had not come to the funeral. It was a bum rap, but for some staff members, it stuck.

Throughout the period of Fortier's illness, Poindexter refused to appoint a new deputy, fearing it would give an appearance of finality to Fortier's departure, and possibly undermine his will to fight the cancer. It was the proper thing to do, but it had the effect of piling even more paper on Poindexter's desk and cramming more PROFs notes into his computer terminal. Under the circumstances, there was no way Poindexter could supervise North at close range.

THE GHORBANIFAR ENIGMA

In keeping with the president's decision to revive the Iran initiative, North took steps in the second half of January 1986 to arrange for the sale of one thousand TOWs to Iran. It was designed to accomplish two objectives, the release of the remaining American hostages in Lebanon, and the accumulation of substantial profits that would be spent for the *contras* and for covert projects that interested Nir. As before, the intermediary to Iran was Ghorbanifar, even though in the period between McFarlane's December 8th meeting in London and the president's approval of the new program, Ghorbanifar's credibility had been violently challenged by the CIA.

As Ghorbanifar had told me when I first met him in Israel, the CIA did not like him. He had twice before been given polygraph examinations and had flunked both (as he said, he did not wish to be an American agent and had no reason to tell them the truth about many of the questions they had asked). Yet the experience I had had with Ghorbanifar was quite encouraging. His overall view of the internal Iranian situation was coherent, and much of it was confirmed by the Israelis and later on by CIA analysts as well. Above all, his description of the process by which the release of Reverend Weir had been achieved checked out, and this overcame my initial skepticism and convinced me that, while he would probably never reveal to us the entire truth of who he was (in fact, it was evident that he would mislead us on occasion) and what his ultimate objectives were, he could be a very useful person for the American government. In addition to his knowledge of Iran, he had also helped me better understand the complex picture of international terrorism, and I was eager to have this information passed on to the CIA officials who headed our counterterrorism program: Dewey Clarridge (who we have met before in Central America and again during the Hawk affair) and Charles Allen, the national intelligence officer for counterterrorism.

Prior to December 1985 I had been under instructions from McFarlane to withhold any information about my activities from the CIA. Nonetheless, I had suggested to North that some of the information that I had gathered about terrorism should be given to the agency, and that had been done (attributing it to an unknown source). But when McFarlane resigned, I was told by North that the Iran initiative was over. I thought that the time had come to brief the CIA on what had happened and give them the opportunity to talk to Ghorbanifar about terrorism.

North approved this step, and I went to CIA headquarters at Langley to brief Clarridge and Allen about the Iran initiative and to suggest they might benefit from talking to Ghorbanifar. After the discussion, we agreed to meet again in a few days when I had returned from a European trip.

While in Paris, I had to go to the Air France office on the Champs-Elysées to change a ticket. As I walked in the door, I found myself wrapped in an enthusiastic bear hug. It was Ghorbanifar. We went off for a long, sumptuous dinner at a nearby Chinese restaurant and talked well into the early morning. I explained that I had been removed from anything having to do with Iran, and that in any event my impression was that the initiative had come to an end. He said he thought there was still hope that something could be done, but that in any event he was still willing to help out with the terrorism problem. But, I said, there would always be the problem of his previous encounters with the CIA. What could he tell me?

He expressed himself very strongly about the CIA officers with whom he had spoken in the past and pointed out that on one occasion they had concluded he was lying when he said he could be helpful in getting American hostages out of Lebanon. Was that not absurd? He had been instrumental in obtaining the release of Weir and would have gotten many more out had it not been for the Hawk disaster, and they called him a liar!

Fair enough, I said, but it would still be necessary to deal with the agency's reservations. "OK," he replied, "I am coming to America later in December in any case, and I will talk to them."

I reported the discussion to Allen, who urged me to tell the whole story to Casey. I did that on December 19th, bringing the director up to date on what had happened and also describing to him a scam that Ghorbanifar had proposed to run on Muammar al-Qadaffi, the Libyan dictator. The only credible opposition to Qadaffi was an émigré group headed by a man named al-Mugarieff, who seemed to spend most of his time in Cairo. According to Ghorbanifar, Qadaffi had spoken to some of Ghorbanifar's friends, saying that he would pay $10 million for the murder of al-Mugarieff, grant a substantial oil shipment at bargain prices to whoever did the job, and then make his own assassins available for the elimination of other people.

Ghorbanifar proposed that his friends accept Qadaffi's offer, and that the CIA help stage a bogus funeral for al-Mugarieff. It would then be possible to take the money and ask Qadaffi to identify his terrorists in Europe to carry out a presumed operation. Once that was accomplished, al-Mugarieff could appear, Qadaffi would be humiliated, his money taken, and his terrorists identified. The total risk to the U.S. government: ask a friendly government somewhere to stage a fake funeral and possibly provide relocation for a couple of Ghorbanifar's friends afterward.

I liked the idea. Humiliation and ridicule are effective political weapons, and in the absence of a vigorous response to terrorism, such weapons should be used enthusiastically. In addition, the Libya scam offered a chance to test Ghorbanifar in a way that didn't risk very much. If he were able to pull it off, that would enhance his credibility. If he failed, we might learn more about what made him tick. Finally, if the scheme worked, we would have weakened Qadaffi's prestige and strengthened his opponents.

Casey loved it and asked the Operations Directorate, headed by Clair George, for an evaluation. But he also said that, if anything was going to be done in tandem with Ghorbanifar, he would have to clear up the problems associated with the earlier polygraphs. Would he be willing to take another lie detector test to resolve the unanswered questions? I said I thought he would, something Ghorbanifar confirmed by telephone a couple of days later.

When Ghorbanifar came to Washington toward the end of the month he met several administration officials, including North and Charles Allen. There was also a gentleman from the CIA who called himself "Patrick." It is not his real name, but I will abide by his wishes and refer to him that way. Patrick was a tall, gangly man, who was said to be the DO official in charge of Iran (the Tower Commission called him "Iran Desk Officer"). Ghorbanifar and I found this difficult to believe, because Patrick had very little knowledge about Iran and spoke no Farsi. I learned a bit later that Patrick was a Latin American operative with no Middle East experience whatsoever. To have expected a man with Patrick's background to evaluate a country as complex and deceptive as Iran was foolish, and unfair to him.

Nonetheless, there he was, and Ghorbanifar spent considerable time with him one evening at our house in Washington. It was difficult for Ghorbanifar, since Patrick had to ask him to spell the names of the top officials of the Iranian government and explain who was who within the country. The bulk of the conversation dealt with terrorism. Late that night, North dropped by to say hello and catch up on the status of the Hawks.

Patrick asked if Ghorbanifar were willing to take a new polygraph, under the most friendly conditions imaginable, with a Farsi-speaking questioner. The questions, Patrick said, would be strictly limited to those areas in past lie-detector tests which Ghorbanifar had "flunked." It should therefore be a brief affair, perhaps a couple of hours. It sounded like an afternoon tea in the country, and Ghorbanifar readily agreed. When I told North about it, he shook his head and said, "there is no way they will let him pass that test. Once the CIA has taken a position on a man, they don't ever admit that they were wrong."

The lie-detector exam was set for the afternoon of January 11th. Ghorbanifar and I met Patrick for lunch at the Four Seasons Hotel in Georgetown, and the atmosphere was calm and friendly. Patrick repeated what he had said before: the exam would be in Farsi, the questions would be limited to the areas previously covered, and Ghorbanifar should be done in a couple of hours.

Not one commitment was honored. The questioner spoke only English. The questions were primarily about recent events (a subject that had been declared off limits, not only by Patrick, but by Casey as well), and the questioning went on for five hours. Afterward, the CIA reported that Ghorbanifar had failed virtually every question, and one wag at the agency told me that the only question Ghorbanifar got right was the pronunciation of his name.

Ghorbanifar was not amused. An extremely volatile man to begin with, and full of suspicion of the CIA, he simply went ballistic when they started in on him on "forbidden" subjects in rapid-fire English. He should have left when it was clear they had lied, but that would have been a loss of face, and he decided to see it through. He arrived at our house in the early evening, exhausted and enraged, and with so many angry black-and-blue marks all over his upper arms where the blood pressure straps had been placed, we called a physician.

There are a lot of good reasons to distrust polygraphs, but an exam given under those circumstances cannot be taken seriously. The indications of "deception" that the machine registers are physiological indications of stress, on the theory that if you are calm, it suggests you are telling the truth. A man like Ghorbanifar is almost never calm, and he was seething throughout the polygraph. North was right; the exam was designed in such a way that it was almost impossible for Ghorbanifar to pass.

The truly worrisome aspect of the affair was not that the people in the Operations Directorate did not want to work with Ghorbanifar; they may have been right. The worrisome aspect was their reliance on such machinery for important decisions. The polygraph has been proven unreliable in so many cases that its continued use—particularly as the primary method for evaluating a person—is scandalous. One of the minor footnotes to the polygraph question comes from the NSC, where McFarlane, enraged at a leak to the *New York Times,* ordered everyone on the staff with access to the leaked information to submit to a polygraph. He failed, not once, but twice. He was so shaken by the results of the test that he called the editor of the *Times,* A. M. Rosenthal, and asked if Rosenthal would tell the president that McFarlane had not been the source of the story. This was done, but Ghorbanifar had no such appeal.

I discussed the polygraph with Casey and pointed out to him that much of what Ghorbanifar had told us had been confirmed in the real world. Casey agreed that Ghorbanifar was potentially useful and ordered Charles Allen to perform an extensive debriefing of Ghorbanifar on the subject of terrorism. Allen concluded that, while it was necessary to carefully evaluate the information Ghorbanifar provided, much of it was accurate and valuable. Clarridge concurred and believed the agency should work with Ghorbanifar on counterterrorism. Later on, the Deputy Director for Operations, Clair George, would tell congressional investigators that Casey had simply ignored the advice of the DO, and had made Allen Ghorbanifar's "case officer." It was not so; Allen had simply done a thorough job of analysis.

Nonetheless, Congress (like the Tower Commission before) adopted the DO view that Ghorbanifar was one of history's great liars and marvelled that Casey, and others of us, thought there was any point in working with the man. Why had the director of Central Intelligence ignored the advice of his Operations Directorate? The answer was simple: Casey had understood the limitations of the DO—and the potential utility of Ghorbanifar—far better than the congressional committees did. Three events will suffice to explain Casey's position:

• In 1981, the DO had hired a young man named Edward Lee Howard and trained him to be a case officer in Moscow for a very important CIA agent named Tolkachev. Tolkachev was an engineer who had provided the agency with sensitive information on Soviet military technology, including up-to-date reports on cruise missile development. Although Howard was known to take drugs (and had a history of petty theft), he went through a full training course, which gave him information on many of the most sensitive operations being run out of the CIA's Moscow station. In the end, Howard's psychological problems were judged too serious to send him to the field, but instead of giving him some other position and keeping him happy and under control, he was simply fired. The FBI, which is supposed to be informed of all serious security risks, was not told about Howard until sometime later, by which time he had established contact with the KGB. In October 1984 Howard eluded the FBI and flew to Austria, where he debriefed KGB officers. Tolkachev was arrested early the following year and later executed. Other American agents in Moscow disappeared, and an American official was expelled from the Soviet Union.

• In June 1985, Senators Hatch and Hecht visited Islamabad, Pakistan, and, along with the local CIA station chief, talked with President Zia. During the conversation, Zia asked if the Afghan *mujehedin*, fighting a war for survival against the Soviet army, could have American

Stinger antiaircraft missiles to use against the awesome helicopter gun-ships the Red Army had deployed against them. It was an official request, and the station chief promised to send it along to Langley. Casey was never informed, and according to John Walcott and Tim Carrington of the *Wall Street Journal,* the request was bottled up by senior CIA officials. Later that year, Stingers were proposed by State and Defense, but the chief of the DO Near East Division told a high-level meeting in the White House that Zia did not want them. Finally, in January 1986, another congressional delegation went to Islamabad, and Congressman Jim Courter asked Zia whether Stingers would be useful for the *mujehedin.* Zia angrily said he had asked for them, but nothing had happened. The matter was then brought to the attention of Don Fortier at the NSC, and he pushed it through. When Fortier asked Casey about it, Casey was enthusiastic and said it was the first he'd heard about the request. In April, the president ordered the CIA to send the Stingers, but CIA officials noted that a Soviet helicopter gunship had just been shot down by Savimbi's forces in Angola, and it had new countermeasures on board that would render the Stingers useless. The Pentagon tested the countermeasures at the White Sands Testing Grounds in May, and found them worthless. The Stingers finally arrived in Afghanistan in late summer, more than a year after Zia's original request.

• In 1984, a senior Cuban intelligence officer, Florentino Aspillaga, defected in Vienna. Aspillaga had been involved in the recruitment of Americans and knew a great deal about Cuban counterintelligence mea-sures aimed against the CIA. He revealed that dozens of Cubans, who the CIA believed to be working for the agency, were in reality double agents. Aspillaga's statements were generally believed at the agency, which concluded that virtually every one of the DO's top agents in Cuba was working for Castro all along. The CIA had been deceived, and it is noteworthy that all of these double agents had passed polygraph tests.

Casey knew all this, and more. The Pollard case revealed that Israel had an agent within the American intelligence community. The dis-covery of the Walker ring—John, his brother and son, and Jerry Whitworth—revealed a Soviet operation that had compromised Amer-ican military codes and satellite communications for nearly twenty years. A National Security Agency employee named Ronald Pelton had given the KGB sensitive information about American intelligence-gathering techniques. Larry Chin, a long-time CIA employee who had passed several polygraph examinations, had passed secret infor-mation to the Chinese.

Finally, just as the CIA was insufficiently attentive to internal security, some agency officers were unduly suspicious of people who were trying very hard to help the United States. This was the case of Arturo Cruz, Jr.—Arturito—who began to help Oliver North deal with Eden Pastora in late 1984. As senior CIA officers came to the conclusion that Pastora was either working for "the other side," or under Cuban and Nicaraguan influence, they became highly suspicious of Arturito, and these suspicions grew stronger as a love affair developed between Arturito and Fawn Hall.

Cruz was investigated, and Hall was given some "dutch uncle" lectures from friends and associates of North, including David Major, the excellent FBI representative on the NSC staff. She was warned about the possible damage to her and North if she continued to see a person under investigation as a possible enemy agent. While the Cruz/Hall romance was destined to end in any event (the cultural differences were too great for a lifetime relationship, and both were mature and intelligent enough to recognize it), the suspicions about Arturito accelerated the process.

So Casey had developed a healthy skepticism about the advice that came to him from men who had found so many reasons to oppose an effective response to Soviet helicopter gunships in Afghanistan, behaved so sloppily in the recruitment of agents, and been proven exceedingly careless in maintaining security. This was particularly so of Clair George, the deputy director for operations, who had been savagely criticized for his handling of the Howard case in a secret report by the president's Foreign Intelligence Advisory Board.

So when the DO lobbied heavily against Ghorbanifar, Casey was not automatically impressed. Casey trusted his own instincts, and he enjoyed people like Ghorbanifar. "He may be a con man's con man," he once remarked to an associate, "but maybe he'll be our con man."

Still, there were limits to how far even Casey was prepared to go when his top Operations people were dead set against Ghorbanifar. So he supported the resurrection of the Iran initiative, but turned thumbs down on any cooperation with Ghorbanifar on terrorism or on the Libya scam.

MISSILES (AND MORE, MUCH MORE) TO IRAN

Throughout January and February, North, Secord, Hakim, Allen, and Nir worked frantically to get the Iran part of the affair moving again. The urgency derived from two sources. First, the realization that funding for the *contras* was running out, and second, the fear

207

that further delay would place the hostages at greater risk. But nothing went smoothly, and anyone who reads the documents for these two months will be astonished at the rapidity with which the plan changed, sometimes during the course of a single day. On January 22nd, North flew to London to meet with Nir, Ghorbanifar, and Secord. The basic plan was to sell four thousand TOWs to Iran for ten thousand dollars per unit (this was five hundred dollars per unit less than the original Israeli selling price in August). In addition, the United States would provide Iran with military intelligence that would help the Iranians in the war with Iraq. As usual, the plan called for a sequential transfer of weapons, prisoners, and information by the Americans and the Israelis, interspersed with hostage releases by the Iranians.

The meeting was secretly taped by North, and we know from the transcript that Ghorbanifar openly discussed helping out with Central America. North subsequently testified that Ghorbanifar had proposed the diversion of profits to the *contras* during a private discussion in the bathroom, but the transcript suggests that it had already become an open secret:

> We do everything. We do hostages free of charge; we do all terrorists free of charge; Central America for you free of charge; American business free of charge.[3]

This basic plan went forward, despite violent objections by John McMahon, Casey's deputy, to providing intelligence to the Iranians, and numerous reservations about the use of Secord as a middleman. In the end, the CIA preferred Secord to Nir as the conduit for funds, since the Near East Division chief didn't want the Israelis to know the details of any CIA bank accounts. The various details were discussed by Ghorbanifar, Nir, Secord, and one of Secord's associates in London on the 7th of February.

This set the stage for a meeting in Frankfurt in February. Present were North, Nir, Ghorbanifar, Secord, Hakim (as translator),[4] the NE Deputy Division chief, and an Iranian group headed by the Australian, by now recovered from his nervous seizure in Geneva the previous November. It was the first meeting between officials of the Iranian and American governments since Reagan's inauguration, and

3. *Report of the Congressional Committees Investigating the Iran-Contra Affair,* p. 216.
4. Ghorbanifar objected violently to Hakim's presence, saying he was considered "an enemy of the state" by the Tehran regime. So Hakim was disguised at the meeting. The NE official also expressed reservations about Hakim, on the grounds that there were too many private persons involved, but North overruled him.

the Iranians were understandably nervous about it. They remembered that the last time a high-level meeting of this sort had occurred was in 1979, when Prime Minister Mehdi Bazarghan had met with National Security Adviser Brzezinski in Algiers. When news of that meeting leaked, Bazarghan was purged, and the Australian wanted to avoid early retirement. Thus, when the Americans arrived for the meeting as scheduled on the nineteenth, there were no Iranians, aside from Ghorbanifar. North returned to Washington to await confirmation that the Iranians were physically present in Frankfurt. That required a few days, and North returned to Germany for a two-day meeting that began on the twenty-fifth.

By then, the first five hundred TOWs had been delivered to Iran, after $10 million had been paid in advance to Secord's Lake Resources account in Geneva (the money, as in August, was advanced by Khashoggi). Secord paid the CIA $3,700,000 for one thousand missiles, the Pentagon provided the TOWs to the CIA, Secord picked them up in Texas and flew them to Iran via Tel Aviv.

There had also been an "intelligence sample," passed by Charles Allen to Ghorbanifar in London in late January. All steps had seemingly been taken, but there was still one caveat. As Secord had communicated to North when the TOWs were delivered (and the hated Hawks had finally been flown out of Bandar Abbas to Tel Aviv), the Iranians expected some good intelligence at the Frankfurt meeting and were prepared to release the hostages "if repeat, if intelligence is good."[5]

As McMahon told Casey, the CIA professionals were violently opposed to sharing useful intelligence with the Iranians, and in the end they only provided some information about a small part of the war front. There may well have been a calculation that the Iranians had such bad intelligence that they would not know the difference. Alternatively, the agency may simply have decided that, even if it scuttled the program, they were not going to give first-rate intelligence to the likes of the Ayatollah Khomeini. Whatever the reason, the intelligence was not particularly useful, and the Iranians were quite capable of seeing that.

But the Iranian unhappiness with the intelligence came later. In the meantime there were significant problems at the meeting. In keeping with his basic methods, Ghorbanifar had raised expectations on both sides in order to get everyone to the table. The Australian clearly

5. *Report of the Congressional Committees,* p. 218.

expected to be able to buy some Phoenix missiles, even though as far back as October 1985 Ghorbanifar had been told repeatedly that this would never happen. And there was some confusion about the hostage question as well, with the NE Deputy Division chief evidently expecting that the hostages would be released as soon as the missiles went in, even though Secord's previous messages to North had stressed that the hostage release would depend on the intelligence provided at the meeting. This was Ghorbanifar's claim as well.

The first day's meeting was devoted to clarifying what each side was prepared to do. It was a replay of the events of the preceding fall and established the model for the tragicomic trip to Tehran in May. First, each side discovers to its surprise that the other has different expectations. But, since they are all there, and have considerable interest in advancing the relationship, they get down to business. Promises are made. And then, on each side, some promises are kept and others are broken. In all the investigations, there was keen interest in finding out why the Americans continued to talk to the Iranians, after so many Iranian promises had been broken. The questioners apparently failed to notice that the situation was even worse from the Iranian point of view. They felt they had been tricked in November (the Hawks), again in February (bad intelligence), and then there would be a massive fraud perpetrated against them in May (spare parts, only a fraction of which corresponded to their request, many of which did not work, and for which an outrageous price was charged). As Ghorbanifar aptly characterized it, the behavior of the United States in Iranian eyes was "an American cheating game."

The conventional American view of Iran is the mirror image of Khomeini's view of America as the Great Satan. We view Khomeini and his men as monstrosities, bloodthirsty fanatics who are determined to unleash havoc on the Western world. All of that is true, yet we tend to forget other elements of the Iranian national character upon which we might capitalize in certain circumstances. First is the great national tradition of Persia, which is treachery. There is perhaps no other country on earth with such a rich literature on the subject, and an Iranian friend of mine once explained to me that his people had decided many centuries ago that while foreign enemies eventually leave, domestic enemies are more durable. Hence, Iranians form a most complex network of alliances, friendships, and working relations (the political equivalent of a Persian carpet), so that they can work against anyone who threatens to accumulate too much power. Sudden shifts in alliance are made with dazzling suddenness, as in the case of Fardoust, the shah's close lifelong friend, who betrayed the shah and became the first chief of Khomeini's secret police. That tradition endures to the present day.

The other Iranian tradition that came into play in America's dealings with the Khomeini regime was the belief that, in all major events, forces more powerful than the Iranians themselves determined the outcome. In some cases, these forces were supernatural, but in others, they were other countries. And the history of Iran taught them that when crisis struck, either the Russians or the West (first Britain, more recently America) would intervene at the appropriate moment. Such a view meant that the Iranians both welcomed and dreaded our return to the Iranian scene, for while they believed—as they always believe—that we had a master plan, they were afraid that our plans might be bad for them.

At first, they were skeptical, knowing that Ghorbanifar's promises did not always remain within the strict limits of objective reportage, but when 100, and then 408 more TOW missiles arrived in late summer 1985, they believed that America had come to save them. The war would be won, the country restored to wealth, and, with America at her side, Iran would flourish once again. Within the circles of power in Tehran, jockeying had already begun to decide who would benefit most from the new alliance, and it was Ghorbanifar's task to ensure that the competing factions all felt they had a stake in a successful outcome. If you asked each faction what was going on, you would undoubtedly have received three similar, but distinctly different versions.

Then came the Hawks, and this happy dream was brutally disrupted. It now appeared that the Americans, in league with the Israelis, were playing some kind of trick. What was the nature of the game? We do not know what dark thoughts passed through the minds of the leading Iranians, but one insight gives us a clue to the way they approached the problem. The Iranians did not believe that Ronald Reagan held ultimate power in the United States. Real power, in their view, was lodged firmly in the hands of Vice President George Bush. Was it not obvious? Bush had been the head of the CIA, in the Iranians' eyes the most powerful of the unseen forces in the world. No one in such a position would ever voluntarily leave it, so Bush's departure from the agency was simply a deception, designed to fool the innocent. But they were not fooled, and they knew that the vice president was the man making the important decisions, as they knew that everything of real significance in the world passed through the tentacles of the CIA.

For many years, they had attempted to decipher American intentions, to find out what Bush and the CIA wanted of them. In order to discover this, they had subjected the unfortunate Buckley to months of torture, believing that he, as a key CIA operative, could provide them the answers. And they must have believed that they had struck a real nerve by taking him, for it was shortly thereafter that the first American contacts were made, and the TOW missiles arrived in Iran.

For the Iranians, then, the "barter" aspect of the affair—the arms for hostages—was a means to an important end. They believed that they might discover America's real intentions through the negotiations for the hostages (it would not have entered their minds that our negotiators would tell them, openly and honestly, what the United States desired in the first hours of discussion).

Finally, there was the question of reward. The Iranians wanted to get the best possible price for the hostages (although we shall probably never have proof, it is highly likely that individual Iranian leaders were making money on the transactions), and that meant they would only part with the hostages very slowly, raising the price as they went along. In this barter, they held a distinct advantage, for human life —particularly the lives of infidels—was of no great consequence to them, while to Americans and Israelis it was priceless. The infidels would pay. The only question was how high the price would be.

It was therefore inevitable, once the Hawk disaster had taken place, that we were in for a long, drawn out process. The Iranians wanted the process to be a slow one, and they would drag out each session as long as possible, in order to plumb the depths of the presumed American cunning as profoundly as they could. But North, Hakim, Nir, and Secord needed results quickly. They needed money for Project Democracy and other covert projects, they cared about the hostages, and they dreamed of being the architects of a new relationship with Iran. If relations improved, North would be famous, and Hakim and Secord would be both famous and rich, for if there were money to be made by simply selling some missiles, think of the fortune that would be theirs if there were a major rapprochement between the two countries! So, in keeping with their objectives and their personalities, they wanted action. Missiles had to be moved, hostages had to be brought out, and the dream of better relations with Iran had to be fulfilled.

This placed the Americans at a terrible disadvantage in the negotiations, for the Iranians were not only not in a hurry, they desperately had to avoid potentially fatal false steps. The Australian had not fainted dead away for nothing—he knew he might have to pay the ultimate price for being tricked by the Americans and the Israelis. Had the

Iran initiative been treated separately, rather than in tandem with the *contra* issue, we might have done what every experienced bazaar shopper does at a certain point in the discussion of price: taken a walk. That would have given us a more reliable indication of how badly the Iranians wanted to pursue the relationship, and, if they really wanted it, bring down our cost. The Americans did not walk away, because they wanted the deal badly, perhaps even more than the Iranians did. This was truly "worse than a crime"; it was a fundamental mistake.

The Americans' resolve to keep the Iran matter moving was also reinforced by the state of mind of Secord and his colleagues in Central America. For while Project Democracy was finally beginning to function (the first effective resupply flights took place in late March and early April), they were discouraged, exhausted, frustrated, and of a mind to drop the entire undertaking. Despite the $6 million profit that would be made from the TOW sales in February, money was short. The CIA, instead of providing timely intelligence, was investigating Secord, Gadd, and Clines. Indeed, Secord went to Casey to complain about CIA meddling, and bemoaned the fact that they could not even get accurate weather forecasts for their flights. And the Southern Front, which would not receive airlifted supplies until the end of the summer, was in its usual state of chaotic ineffectiveness. As Secord testified,

> By this timeframe, I wanted out of this operation in the worst possible way. It had dragged on for too long.
>
> It was becoming very dangerous. We couldn't get support. We were short of money. I wanted out of it.[6]

All of this could and should have been avoided if we had not permitted the hostage question to become the central issue. Iran had to be dealt with on its own terms, just as the Senior Official had told us in the fall. There were two ways in which our relationship with Iran could be improved. The first was to try to change the nature of the regime, but we failed to pursue that avenue. The second was to come to terms with Khomeini, define areas of common purpose (and there were some, from containing the Soviet Union to aiding the *mujehedin* in Afghanistan), and join in common enterprises. If our leaders had addressed the overall question, rather than insisting that the hostages be released before relations could be improved, they would not have been trapped into behaving as they did.

The trap into which they fell was not, as was so often alleged, purely

6. Secord, Published Testimony, p. 187.

of Iranian design. By linking the Iran and *contra* initiatives, the Americans trapped themselves.

These points should have been made, over and over again, by Secretary of State Shultz. He was charged with responsibility for the conduct of American foreign policy, and he hated the Iran initiative from the beginning. Yet Shultz did not get himself involved in this fight, most likely because the president felt so strongly about the hostage matter. But this does not excuse him, for while a president expects, and is entitled to, loyalty from his cabinet, he is also owed consistent, forthright, and even irritating criticism of policies when a cabinet member feels strongly about them. At a minimum, the secretary of state was obliged to keep himself fully informed, so that he could seize on each new failure, and each new potential for disaster, bring it to the president's attention, and urge him to stop and cut his losses.

Shultz did not do that, and, as Poindexter tells us, Shultz seems to have gone out of his way to insure he would not know too much:

> . . . sometime in the—probably the spring of '86. Secretary Shultz and Secretary Weinberger and Director Casey and I periodically had what we called a family group lunch. . . . I used at least one of those occasions to give them an update on the Iranian project and it was either during the lunch or after the lunch . . . that Secretary Shultz said, "Look, you know my feeling on this. I don't think we ought to be doing it. Just don't bother me with details," or something like that, "on stuff I don't need to know."[7]

Indeed, if Shultz did not know the Iran story, he not only had to ignore Poindexter's efforts to inform him, but also those of his own department, for several of his top assistants knew a great deal about the Iran initiative. Ambassador Robert Oakley, the head of the Office to Combat Terrorism, had received a full briefing from North in January 1986 and remained well-informed throughout the year. Several top officials of the Near East Bureau, including Deputy Assistant Secretary Arnold Raphel, were also highly knowledgeable about the status of the initiative. So if Shultz were not well-informed, it could only have been because he did not wish to be.

At the Frankfurt meeting, the Australian promised to have the intelligence evaluated in Tehran. If it was good, another meeting would be held, and he suggested Kish Island—a former resort of the

---

7. Poindexter, Published Testimony, p. 1169.

shah's—as a site. At that time, if all had gone well, some of the hostages would be released as a gesture of good faith. This would hopefully lay the groundwork for subsequent talks in which high-ranking American and Iranian officials would participate, to address the crucial issue of the relationship between the two countries.

With this, the meeting ended. Secord went forward with the delivery of the next five hundred TOWs. Cost to Secord and company: $3.7 million. Payment received from Ghorbanifar: $10 million.

Meanwhile, the Americans were making their first effort to lever Ghorbanifar out of the deal. When the Australian got back to Iran, he found that Hakim had left a message for the Australian to call Washington. The Australian returned the call and heard Hakim urge him to drop Ghorbanifar as the intermediary and deal "directly" through Hakim and Secord. The Australian informed Ghorbanifar of the call, and also told him that the assessment of the intelligence was negative: it was several months old, and worthless for any current campaign. The Iranians felt they had been cheated for a second time. Meanwhile, the military experts had reconsidered their needs. There were enough TOWs for the foreseeable future. The main Iranian problem was not tanks, but airplanes. There were still Hawks in inventory, but they were not operational. Ghorbanifar was provided with a list of spare parts needed for the Hawks, and he passed it on at a meeting with North, the NE Deputy Division chief, Nir, and a new name: George Cave.

With George Cave, the United States government finally had a true expert on Iran in the project. Cave was fluent in Farsi and had developed a taste for Persian poetry. Raised in an orphanage, Cave had demonstrated discipline and tenacity in his agency career. He had served in Tehran, and other middle Eastern locaitons. The consummate professional, well thought of by his colleagues, Cave was an old-timer who had retired in the early eighties but had retained a relationship with the CIA as a consultant. With his clearances in place, he could be brought into the action on short notice. This was done following the Frankfurt meeting. The NE Division chief did not want the Americans to depend upon either Hakim or Ghorbanifar to translate for them. Further, like the top NE people, Cave was concerned about the Israeli role in the operation and wanted to see it reduced. Finally, he had known of Ghorbanifar (he probably knew about the earlier polygraphs at the time they occurred) and was alarmed at *his* role as well. Cave thus brought not only considerable expertise, but also the views of the top NE officials to the group. At the very

215

end of the affair, he would demonstrate a capacity for political courage as well.

With Cave on board, the campaign against Ghorbanifar gathered momentum. In Charles Allen's words,

> . . . there was a general feeling on the part of Colonel North and Mr. Cave that this was not a trustworthy individual, Mr. Ghorbanifar, and we ought to try to set up an alternate means of talking to . . . Tehran and to cut out Mr. Ghorbanifar.
>
> And I recall that I talked to Colonel North and told him that was a mistake. I know Mr. Clarridge, who was aware of this, thought it was a very serious mistake and told Colonel North that Mr. Ghorbanifar, if nothing else, knows too much. If you really want this highly sensitive, highly secret initiative to continue, how can you cut out Mr. Ghorbanifar? Maybe he's inconvenient. Maybe he's difficult. But you're already into this situation in a very deep way.[8]

The logic was solid, and North decided that Hakim's call to the Australian had been a tactical mistake. Ghorbanifar was invited to Washington at the beginning of April, was reassured of the American commitment to him and to the overall project, and was shown samples of new intelligence to be provided to Iran. The agenda had now narrowed to two main points. A meeting was to be arranged in Tehran for a high-level American delegation, led by McFarlane. And, in conjunction with that trip, Hawk spare parts would be sold to Iran, and American hostages would be released from Lebanon.

TOWARD THE TEHRAN RENDEZVOUS

It may seem surprising to find McFarlane back in our story, but in truth he had never left. As Jane Leavy wrote in the *Washington Post,* after McFarlane's resignation

> . . . he regretted the decision almost immediately. He told reporters at a tearful farewell party that he should never have left. And in a way, he never did. He was tied to the White House, to the inexorable momentum of the Iran initiative, by an electronic umbilical cord—his NSC computer.[9]

Although McFarlane did extremely well in his business and lecturing activities after leaving the NSC, he felt he had done the wrong

8. Charles Allen, unpublished deposition to the joint Select committees, p. 559.
9. *Washington Post,* May 7, 1987.

thing. He was uncomfortable in private life, missed the participation in the day-to-day management of foreign policy, and felt that he had "copped out, that I had given up." He hated the thought that he had been driven out of the White House by Regan. The Iran initiative offered him a chance for a comeback.

McFarlane was in electronic contact with Poindexter and North almost daily—one of the best-kept secrets in Washington at the time. No other private person in Washington was wired into the PROFs system, and only a trusted few at the NSC knew that McFarlane was still involved. He was eager to go to Tehran, and compared its potential with Kissinger's secret travels to China.

Unfortunately, he was the wrong man for the mission, as Poindexter was the wrong man to manage it from Washington. To negotiate with the Iranians one needed a person with great patience, at least some experience with Iran, and a sense of humor. McFarlane had business and speaking engagements back in the States, had a visceral dislike of Ghorbanifar, and, especially after his fall from the heights, was not at all whimsical. It was also a mistake to send a delegation in which the three principal figures (McFarlane, North, and Nir) all came from a military background. One needed a chief negotiator who would be willing to challenge the preestablished guidelines when and if the situation in Tehran showed that all the rules were off.

It would also have been well-advised to prepare the trip with great care, and this meant that someone should have met with McFarlane's opposite number before the official meeting. During his April trip to Washington, Ghorbanifar offered to fly North to Iran for preliminary conversations. But Poindexter vetoed the idea, even though North, Secord, Nir, and Cave were all pushing for it.

Poindexter felt one meeting was risky enough, without having to send Americans to Tehran a second time. Furthermore, in his view the McFarlane meeting was not a formal, high-level encounter between government officials. If the McFarlane meeting went well, then an American official could later meet with an Iranian counterpart to formalize the relationship.

The Iranians were also willing to have a preliminary meeting, but were informed by the Americans that none would take place. Instead, Cave and North flew to London in early May to meet Ghorbanifar and Nir. During the talks, Cave spoke twice at length on the telephone with officials in Tehran (once with the Australian, once with another person), to confirm the arrangements. The Americans would arrive with a portion of the Hawk spare parts, then the Iranians would attempt to gain the release of the hostages, at which point the balance of the spare parts and the radars would be flown to Iran. If there were misunderstandings, then, it would be unfair to blame them all on Ghorbanifar (as North did in his testimony).

North and Cave returned to Washington, and Ghorbanifar and Nir, joined by Khashoggi, tried to do an Iranian deal by themselves. They met with Tiny Rowland, a London businessman known for his highly successful investments in East Africa. They proposed that Rowland underwrite a series of arms, spare parts, and grain sales to Iran, promising large profits and low risk. The project, they said, was fully approved by the American government, and Nir told Rowland that the government of Israel would guarantee his investment. Rowland excused himself for a moment, went to another room, and called David Kimche in Jerusalem. Was Nir's promise true? And should Rowland put up the money? Kimche told him that there was no such Israeli guarantee and advised Rowland to steer clear of the project. Further inquiries in Washington produced the same result, and rage on the part of Secretary of State Shultz, who believed that the NSC had organized yet another Iran initiative without telling him anything. Poindexter had to calm him down, telling him "this is not our deal." It was yet another example of Nir's imaginative sales technique at work.

It was also the second time within a month that the Americans believed they had evidence of Ghorbanifar's tendency to free-lance around the fringes of the affair. U.S. Customs had mounted a "sting operation" against a group of American and Israeli businessmen trying to buy military equipment to sell to Iran. The key Iranian middleman was Cyrus Hashemi, a person with whom Ghorbanifar had worked briefly more than a year before, but who had invoked Ghorbanifar's name in his efforts to do business, even though the two had parted company. In mid-April, the "sting" was driven home, and Hashemi was arrested, along with several other men, from the Bahamas to Switzerland. Ghorbanifar was rounded up in the sweep, only to be released twenty-four hours later. Although several people at CIA believed Ghorbanifar had been involved in Hashemi's operation, no evidence ever emerged to support that view.

On the 25th of May 1986, the American delegation (McFarlane, North, Cave, NSC staffer Howard Teicher, and a CIA communicator) plus Nir arrived in Tehran. It was Ramadan, the Islamic holy period when Muslims fast during the day and eat only at sunset. Of all the times to choose for delicate negotiations with Islamic fundamentalists, this was undoubtedly the worst, for the holy period reminded them of the intensity of their religious convictions, and the fasting discouraged political flexibility.

As soon as the delegation left the aircraft, the Iranians carted off the spare parts, which amounted to 5 percent of the total order. When the talks began, McFarlane was dismayed to discover that although Ghorbanifar had earlier promised talks with the president, the prime minister, and Majlis Speaker Rafsanjani, none of these was present. The Australian was again the main interlocutor. Even worse, they insisted that no movement on the hostages could take place until all the Hawk parts had arrived. Enraged, McFarlane withdrew to his room, announcing that he would not participate in discussions until someone of appropriate rank came to talk to him.

McFarlane's anger was easy enough to understand (it's a long trip just to find out that there would be no meeting with the top men), although perhaps if he had known the truth, he would have found the situation amusing. The truth was that the key Iranians did not know who he was. There was no "name recognition" for McFarlane in the Iranian capital, and they did not know what a national security adviser was. It was not until the autumn that it would dawn on the Iranians that a very important American had come to Tehran. As Charles Allen put it in his deposition:

Q: Do you recall Mr. Cave ever telling you that in his meetings with the Iranians in the fall of 1986 they advised him that they had only recently determined who Robert McFarlane and—
ALLEN: Yes, absolutely. That struck me. I was stunned. That was the 19–20 September meeting, 1986, where [   ] he said that they didn't know who Mr. McFarlane was and they later discovered that he really was a very significant figure.
Q: And they also did not know who Colonel North was . . .
ALLEN: That's absolutely the case.[10]

The Iranians did not know who McFarlane was, and Ghorbanifar had been unable to convince them that a man of such stature was coming to Tehran. Moreover, the Australian seems to have misled his own superior, Prime Minister Moussavi, promising that the Americans would arrive with 50 percent of the Hawk spares. Thus, from the point of view of the Iranian leadership, a delegation of relatively unimportant Americans had arrived with only a fraction of what had been promised.

Still, as before, there they all were, and the negotiations got started.

10. Charles Allen, unpublished deposition, p. 665.

On the second evening, a top foreign policy adviser to Rafsanjani (and a member of the Parliament) joined the discussions, and he was judged sufficiently high-ranking for McFarlane to talk to him. In the meantime, the others were talking, and McFarlane was disturbed to hear that Nir had twice gone off for private talks of his own in the corridors. He ordered Nir to stop it.

There were other personal factors that made this a trying experience for the American delegation. As Cave put it, one Iranian official's breath "could curl rhino hide." On the other side, Nir had an angry-looking sun blister on his lip, and when the Australian (after much hugging and kissing) asked one of the Americans what it was, he was told "herpes." None of the Iranians embraced Nir after that.

The first two days of talks confirmed that the Iranians were terribly ambivalent about the prospect of renewed relations with the United States. A good deal of time was spent by Rafsanjani's man (the adviser) denouncing the Americans for their past behavior and warning that it would take a long while for the Iranian people to adjust to a new relationship. If it were going to happen, it would have to take place gradually.

By the third day, the adviser was presenting outrageous demands from the Hezbollah, ranging from Israeli withdrawal from the Golan Heights to American promises that Kuwait would free the Da'wa prisoners. McFarlane said, "No deal." It appeared to McFarlane that the adviser was beginning to have doubts about the reliability of the information he had received from Ghorbanifar and the Australian, and he went off to confer with them and his other colleagues.

Finally, on the evening of the third day, after hours of discussion about the nature of the Iranian Revolution and attitudes toward the United States, the adviser got down to brass tacks: everything else could be resolved, if only the release of the Da'wa prisoners could be managed. McFarlane would not budge: the United States was bound by law, and the Da'wa prisoners had been duly tried and sentenced.

The Da'wa prisoners were never discussed in the five months I had been involved in the Iran initiative the previous year. Why were they suddenly introduced in 1986? The most likely explanation is that the Hezbollahis in Lebanon, who had been compelled to turn over Weir to the Iranians, were insisting that *they* get something for the next American released. And the thing the terrorist chieftain of the Hezbollah—Imad Mugniyeh—wanted above all else was the release of the Da'was, among other reasons because one of them was his wife's brother. Indeed, there was a rumor that Mugniyeh's wife had taken vows of chastity until her brother was freed, which would probably have given the terrorist leader added incentive to work for his brother-in-law's release.

But this only meant that the route of least difficulty for the Iranians ran through Kuwait, not that it was the only route, and both Father Jenco and David Jacobsen were released in 1986, even though none of the terrorists in Kuwaiti jails saw the light of day.

In any event, faced with McFarlane's flat rejection of any American efforts to gain freedom for the Da'wa prisoners, the adviser shifted gears again: "Since the plane is loaded (with the remaining Hawk spares) why not let it come . . . the hostages will be freed very quickly. . . . If the plane arrives before tomorrow morning, the hostages will be free by noon. We do not wish to see our agreement fail at this final stage."

McFarlane and the adviser agreed to let their staffs make an effort to hammer out an agreement that would satisfy both sides, and North, Cave, Teicher, and Nir sat down at 9:30 on the evening of May 27th with the adviser, the Australian, and other officials from Moussavi's office. The meeting lasted two hours, with the Iranians admitting that the hostages could not be delivered as quickly as the adviser had previously promised and pushing for a deal on the Da'wa prisoners. At 11:40 P.M., McFarlane had had enough. He gave orders to pack and prepared to leave Iran. But the Iranians informed him that the American plane was without fuel (despite several previous promises that it would be refueled), and the adviser returned at two in the morning to ask for an extension until six o'clock. By that time, he said, there would be some word on the hostages.

He returned at ten to eight, saying that two could be delivered quickly, but the other two would take a little while longer. McFarlane was not moved: "You are not keeping the agreement. We are leaving." Ten minutes later, the Americans were en route to the airport. The scene on the tarmac was hysterical, as the Australian raced after the Americans, pleading for more time, promising that all four hostages would be delivered, if only the Americans would wait just a little while longer. But it was too late. The plane lifted off at five minutes to nine. The last few words on the runway were exchanged between Cave and the Australian, promising to stay in touch.

In retrospect, it is easy to say that McFarlane should have stayed longer. His rigid interpretation of his instructions to get all the hostages out before sending any further spare parts to Tehran had succeeded in forcing the Iranians to come to terms with the basic questions, and the Iranians seem to have been moving on the hostage issue. Moreover, the crucial question of the U.S.–Iran relationship had finally been discussed, albeit not at the level McFarlane had hoped, and there is every reason to believe that Rafsanjani, Moussavi, and the others (including Khomeini's son) were kept up-to-date on the content of those discussions. In short, there was a lot of evidence suggesting that the Americans might have been on the verge of a breakthrough. North sensed this, and, without consulting with McFarlane, ordered Secord to launch the plane with the remaining Hawk spares from Tel Aviv in the dead of the last night, hoping thereby to give the Iranians material incentive to deliver some hostages. When McFarlane learned of the flight, he ordered the plane to turn around and return to Israel.

The adviser spoke the truth about his own people when he told McFarlane "these things are always resolved at the last minute," but McFarlane did not care to prolong the agony. He was tired, he had been cooped up for nearly four days inside the old Hilton Hotel (now renamed the Independence), and he wanted to go home.

Before leaving the Tehran talks, two points need to be underlined. The first is that at least one of the Americans present—Cave—concluded that the hostages had not been released because the Iranians did not have sufficient control to have it done. We do not know the full basis for this conclusion, but we know from his deposition that he feared the Hezbollahis were not always responsive to Iranian requests, and hence that the effort to get the Americans out of Lebanon by dealing with the Iranian regime was doomed. If Cave was right, it was necessary to deal with Mugniyeh and company as well. My own belief is that, while the Iranians did not fully control the hostages, they had sufficient influence so that if they wanted a release badly enough, they could almost always achieve it. They might have to pay a high price, and they might have to spend a considerable amount of time, but in the end they would always prevail.

The second point is a policy question: why were the Americans so interested in coming to terms with the Khomeini regime? Some weeks before the trip, I learned that it was in the works and visited McFarlane at his Bethesda home. I urged him not to go to Tehran, on the grounds that by doing so he would greatly strengthen the people in power, whereas the goal of American policy ought to be the opposite. We should have been working toward ways to bring about a more civilized regime, not taking steps that would produce an even stronger Khomeini.

THE FINANCIAL CRISIS OF THE SPRING OF 1986

After the May meeting, Cave remained in touch with Tehran, speaking to the Australian by phone and working for a continuation of the dialogue, but doing his best to convince him that Ghorbanifar was an obstacle to a better relationship. Nir and Ghorbanifar were also trying to keep things going, and even though Ghorbanifar was told by the Australian of each of Cave's efforts to arrange for a new channel, Ghorbanifar took the American side in his discussions with top officials in Tehran. He argued that the Americans had essentially lived up to their part of the agreement, even if there had been some confusion as to the quantity of spare parts, and thus Iran should now make a gesture by obtaining the release of at least one further hostage. Nir also weighed in along the same lines, and by late June, Nir informed North that the Iranians would shortly release Father Jenco. North informed Poindexter, and made preparations to fly Jenco out of Beirut, but nothing happened. A few days later, Poindexter directed North to break off all contacts with the Iranians, and to tell Nir the project was over.

This crisis could not have come at a more delicate moment. The $27 million in humanitarian aid for the *contras* had run out, and in May, Secretary of State Shultz had been authorized to approach third countries for additional money. As we have seen, Secord's operation was running short of funds and was not receiving support from the CIA, at the very moment that the resupply airlift was just beginning to get up to speed. On June 2nd, North was informed by Joe Fernandez, the CIA station chief in Costa Rica, that the Southern Front was virtually out of supplies, and that something had to be done at once. Dutton quickly loaded a C-123 aircraft with equipment and sent it south. But the pilot could not find the drop site and attempted a landing on an emergency private landing strip inside Costa Rica. Secord had gone to considerable effort and expense to purchase the land and upgrade the quality of the runway, since he, Gadd, and Quintero had recognized early on that they needed some sort of emergency facility in Costa Rica. However, the strip was in poor condition, and the plane got stuck in the mud. So, not only was the Southern Front still without supplies, but one of the five airplanes used for the airlift was out of operation.

On June 24th, Shultz met with the Sultan of Brunei, and the next day, one of Shultz's aides convinced the Sultan to contribute $10 million to the *contras*. But once again, the fates intervened to frustrate efforts to keep the *contras* in the battlefield. The bank account number given to the Sultan was incorrect, and the $10 million eventually ended up in the account of a Swiss businessman, who, true to his national heritage, immediately invested it in a Certificate of Deposit.

To be sure, the political pendulum was swinging back in favor of the President's Central American policies, and Congress would vote $100 million in aid by August. But the money would not become available before the start of the next fiscal year (October 1), and even the amazingly successful private fund-raising efforts within the United States peaked in the early spring. By June, that cash flow was slowing down as well.

The private network was organized primarily by Carl ("Spitz") Channell, an experienced conservative fund-raiser with an extraordinary talent for raising large sums of money from small numbers of people, and by Richard Miller, a former political appointee at the State Department who had acquired considerable expertise in Central American affairs. Channell and Miller met in the Spring of 1985, and had started working with North that summer. The combination of Channell's fund-raising skills, North's inspirational speeches to donors, and Miller's quietly efficient public relations operation was remarkably effective. Over the course of the next year and half, more than ten million dollars was raised, of which roughly half went either to the *contras'* own accounts, or to Secord's operations. The balance either went to pay for operating expenses, to profit, or to activities related to *contra* support, such as research, accompanying *contra* spokesmen and Nicaraguan defectors around the United States for public affairs and fund-raising appearances, supporting other like-minded public affairs organizations, and the like. It was no mean achievement for a relatively small number of people.

The private network was not limited to conservatives like Channell, and in time it was expanded to include old-fashioned Democrats like Penn Kemble and Roy Godson, as well as moderate Republicans like former Congressman Dan Kuykendahl. These people, sometimes with funding from their own supporters, sometimes with grants from Channell and Miller, organized an extensive lobbying campaign that had considerable effect. And on one occasion in late 1985, Count Alexandre de Marenches, the former head of French Military Intelligence who had briefed President-elect Ronald Reagan at his California ranch in the winter of 1980, was brought to Washington to speak to select members of Congress about the necessity of supporting the *contras*.

In time, the private network ran into grave difficulties, deriving from two political mistakes. The first was an excess of zeal on the part of Channell, who decided to spend some of his money on political campaigns targeting opponents of *contra* aid. He developed his own "enemies list," thereby antagonizing not only those politicians who found themselves threatened, but also many of the pro-*contra* people, who were not interested in such partisan political combat.

The second mistake was to allot some of the money for the purchase of lethal equipment. While there was nothing illegal about raising funds for such purposes in the proper way, it did violate the rules for tax-exempt organizations, and Channell and Miller eventually pled guilty to a charge of violating Internal Revenue Service regulations, even though the money in question was never spent for weapons (it went for radio communications units), and the donor of the money did not claim a tax exemption.

What is central here, however, is the downward trend in fund-raising in the late spring and early summer of 1986. Ironically, the fund-raising effort fell victim to the success of the campaign to restore *contra* aid. Once Congress had voted $100 million in new assistance, donors were understandably less enthusiastic about contributing their own money, even though the $100 million would not become available until late October.

Thus, from late spring until October, the only available source of significant quantities of cash for the *contras* was from the proceeds from the sale of weapons to Iran. There was a positive balance around the time of the Tehran trip, for Ghorbanifar had given Secord $15 million to pay for the Hawk spares. Since the cost of the spare parts was only $6.5 million (to which must be added several hundred thousand dollars in expenses for the shipments), there was a profit of about $8 million. But nothing like this amount was made available to the *contras*. As a matter of fact, when the investigators looked into Hakim's various accounts in early 1987, they found $8 million resting there. Why, if North and Secord were so intensely motivated by a desire to keep the *contras* on the battlefield, should these desperately needed funds be withheld at the moment of the *contras'* maximum financial crisis? Secord had wanted to make money, even if we accept him at his word when he testified that, sometime in the spring of 1986, he informed Hakim that he was no longer interested in profit. And even if Secord had developed an unexpected philanthropic streak, it had not infected Hakim, who had a healthy appetite for personal gain all along, and who did not aspire to high posts in the American government.

But personal greed does not account for the whole story. In particular, it does not explain North's behavior. For the North the world saw on television in the summer of 1987, the North I knew and had occasionally worked alongside for the better part of two years, was not looking for money for his own personal purposes. For him, the mission was all-important, and the mission was to take from the Ayatollah and give to the *contras*. So why was so much money in the bank?

Like so many of North's activities, the explanation lies to a great extent in his own view of his historic role. During the six months since North had taken over both elements of the affair, his ambitions had expanded. He now fancied himself the director of a new covert action service, ready to be put into play at a moment's notice, most anywhere around the world.

North testified to the joint committees that he did what he did at least in part because Bill Casey told him to do it. Indeed, according to North, Casey not only wanted Project Democracy and the Iran initiative, but he wanted an operational capacity, outside the probing eyes and legislative restraints of government. This is the famous "complete, off-the-shelf covert action" capability that could be dusted off and taken into battle when circumstances called for it.

We know that North did other covert things, even though we do not know precisely what they all were. Thus far, at least, his testimony in secret session to the joint committees has remained secret. We do know that at least some of these activities were done in conjunction with Nir, and that Nir was similarly operating outside the normal framework of his government. Indeed, shortly before the Tehran mission, North informed Poindexter that

> Nir is, as you know, operating w/o Mossad back-up and has considerable concern about the CIA becoming more knowledgeable about his activities.

Given Nir's areas of interest, we can presume that some of these activities involved Lebanon. Some others reportedly had to do with Libya (Secord at one point provided a ship to carry out clandestine anti-Qadaffi radio broadcasts into Libya).

Other North activities had to do with the hostages. He raised money for ransom from H. Ross Perot. He also funded activities by two DEA agents to bribe some Lebanese to rescue the hostages. And he wanted to do more. Looking at the number of projects North took on, and reading the massive quantity of written memoranda, PROFs notes, secret communications, notebooks, letters, and speeches that he produced in 1985 and 1986, it is hard to believe that a single person could have done it all. It also explains how mistakes were made, for he never had time to reflect on what he was doing, to review his assumptions, or consider alternative courses of action. If a good idea popped into his head, he tended to pursue it. And most of the time his superiors—whether McFarlane or Poindexter—told him to go ahead.

But the evidence we have does not suggest that these activities were the equivalent of a private CIA, nor does it show that Casey was the guiding spirit of North's frenetic activities. Indeed, we know that on at least some points—most notably the "diversion"—Poindexter instructed North not to tell Casey about it. And there is considerable evidence that Casey did not know about the diversion, from both Casey's deputy, Robert Gates, and from Charles Allen, who is the person who first added up all the evidence, concluded that money was flowing from the proceeds of the Iran weapons sales to the *contras,* and brought it to the attention of the top people at CIA. When Casey was told about it, he seemed to be astonished, and he immediately brought it to Poindexter's attention and urged Poindexter to discuss it at once with the White House counsel. Poindexter testified that he did not believe Casey had been informed of the diversion, and so did Secord.

We also have eloquent testimony from one of New York's most distinguished lawyers to suggest that Casey neither knew nor approved of all of North's projects. Milton Gould was a lifelong friend of Casey, and was preparing to be Casey's counsel for the testimony before the various investigating committees, when Casey had his stroke in late 1986.

I had a number of discussions with Casey about the Iran controversy. . . .

Casey was tortured from the beginning of his job with the fact that he was managing an organization which probably was representative of the only world power that had any concern for morality. It was one of his principles to try to do everything he did with a scrupulous regard for moral principles. In doing that he, as all of us know, had a number of encounters with the Intelligence Committees of Congress. And one of the things that disturbed him most was that there were certain members of the committees whom he could not trust to keep things confidential. . . .

. . . it is tragic that Casey didn't survive to testify before this committee. I can tell you that had he survived to testify . . . he would have told the entire truth. He was prepared to do that and he evinced his readiness to do that. The second thing that I can contribute are the attributions to Casey of total approval of Oliver North's activities. This is false. He did not approve those activities and he never expressed to North or anybody else his approval of those clandestine, illegal, delictual, immoral activities.[11]

Casey expressed great concern after a conversation with Meese, just after the attorney general had learned of the diversion. Shortly after the meeting, Casey told Gould, "there are a lot of things going on that I don't know about."

So far as can be established from the available evidence, Poindexter, and to a lesser extent McFarlane, were the only government officials who might have known about most of North's activities. North alone claimed that Casey was not only witting, but had directed him to do many of those things in the first place.

There is an additional reason to believe that Casey did not know about the diversion, let alone approve of it. This was Casey's concern for the political position of Ronald Reagan. As will be seen, in the autumn of 1986 there was great concern that Ghorbanifar, or others involved in the financing of the Hawk spare parts, would make public the entire Iran initiative. Casey was deeply concerned about this, because he realized that it would be very damaging to the president. This had nothing to do with legalities (it has yet to be demonstrated that the diversion was illegal, after all), but rather with the ability of the president to lead the country. If Casey had known of the diversion—the exposure of which was a far more serious political threat to the president than the revelation of the Iran initiative—he was odds-on to do something about it. And merely sheltering the president from the facts would not have been sufficient for Casey, for he would have recognized that the political damage to Reagan would have been devastating, whether or not the president knew all the details.

Finally, there was Casey's notion of how covert action should be conducted, and who should do it. He was very proud of his accomplishments at CIA, and wanted the agency in the forefront of the policy process. Nothing irritated him more than to have other agencies doing things without CIA input, and he worked hard to make sure the CIA did not get cut out of things. Thus, when the Iran initiative

11. Gould made this statement during the course of a conference of the Federal Bar Association in March 1988. His remarks as quoted here come from an authorized unpublished transcript of the proceedings, and are reproduced here with his permission.

was revived in January 1986, Casey made sure that the NE Division chief, his deputy, Allen, Clarridge, and eventually Cave, all played roles. He did not try to create an air-tight compartment for the initiative, in which North, Secord, and the others operated outside governmental coordination and supervision. That had happened in 1985, at McFarlane's orders, not in 1986, when Casey found out what was going on.

My own conviction, based on several private conversations with Casey in 1985 and 1986, is that Casey thought North was a great talent, that he had a lot of personal affection for North, but that he did not think North had enough experience, or sound enough professional judgment, to run a major operation by himself. I also believe that Casey was concerned about the presence of Secord and Clines, and wanted to be certain that there were enough CIA professionals in the picture to ensure that things would not run out of control.

For me, the clincher is Poindexter's order to North *not* to inform Casey of the diversion. Poindexter knew that the whole thing was an NSC operation, and so Casey had no "need to know." But that wasn't sufficiently romantic for North, who had visions of grandeur. As he learned that money and arms could indeed be obtained, he quickly saw that he could achieve a degree of personal power available to no one else in the American government. He and he alone was capable of mounting a seemingly endless series of initiatives, ranging from raising money to ransom American hostages in the Middle East, to purchasing ships and airplanes for operations from the Caribbean to the Mediterranean, to obtaining arms from third countries (even including Soviet bloc nations). So it came to pass that while North created his own network in response to two specific crises, in the end the "enterprise" became an end in itself: a group of like-minded individuals who obtained the means to strike at America's enemies without the constraints of bureaucracy or oversight. And although they saw themselves as operating within the framework of legality, on occasion it was all too easy to convince themselves that there was a "higher" legality than the measures issuing from the halls of Congress.

I believe this is the explanation for the hoarding of funds that were collected for the support of the Central American Resistance. Why send all that money to the *contras* when tomorrow might bring new opportunities and new challenges? If the "enterprise" lacked funds, it might find itself cut out of future action, and if there was one central theme to North's activities, it was the constant, frenetic search for new challenges and new risks. His demon led North to a quest for danger, excitement, and a constantly expanding sphere of activity. No single project, no matter how important or exciting, could suffice. In the end, the *contras* became secondary; the great game was everything.

The *contras* were kept alive, and that was a worthwhile undertaking. Without North and the others, the *contras* might well have disappeared as a military force. But the Central American operation, surrounded by heroic rhetoric, produced mediocre results. The great resupply network ran with dangerous aircraft landing on muddy airstrips; the prices charged Calero and his men were unnecessarily high. And last of all, there was the one *really* criminal act: the money sat in the bank, it didn't make it to Calero, Matamoros, Robelo, Bermúdez, and César. This was criminal by North's own standards, for if Congress were to be condemned for failure to fund the *contras,* the same should be said about him.

In the end, North and Secord became hostages to their vision of becoming the "real" CIA. But it was their vision, not Bill Casey's. Had Casey really been involved in "running North," he would have made damn sure the money got to the *contras,* instead of drawing interest in a Swiss bank account.

All of which sets the stage for the summer of 1986, when the Iran-Contra affair teetered on its high wire, with success within reach (the *contras* would soon have full funding, and possibilities for a major breakthrough with Iran were seemingly at hand), but disaster just one misstep to either side. As in a Greek tragedy, the Gods were preparing to destroy Oliver North. And they had first made him proud.

8. The Fall

After Tehran, North, Nir, Cave, and Ghorbanifar told the Australian that unless an American hostage was released, the entire project was over. Cave and Allen speculated on the reasons for the Iranian delay, and concluded the most likely explanation was the inability of the Iranians to compel the Hezbollahis to turn over a hostage. But by the latter part of June, the Americans discovered that there was good reason for the Iranian refusal to deliver. The Ayatollah's men had discovered that they had been grossly overcharged for the spare parts delivered in May.

Secord had quoted Ghorbanifar a price of $15 million for the parts, for which Secord had paid the CIA about $6.5 million. The $15 million actually had been put up by Khashoggi, who was charging a 20 percent interest rate for taking the risk. The actual transactions show precisely what the arrangements were: Khashoggi transferred $15 million in two tranches on the 13th and 14th of May, from two of his companies (Trivert and Garnet) to Secord's Lake Resources account in Geneva. At the same time, Ghorbanifar wrote postdated checks for a total of $18 million: $1 million to Garnet, $6 million to another Khashoggi firm (Kremdale), and $11 million directly to Khashoggi.

To cover these costs, and make profit himself, Ghorbanifar had quoted the Iranians a price of approximately $25 million, which, if the $15 million had been the real cost of the parts, would have been within the normal range for such transactions. But the Iranians had obtained a microfiche with the real prices, and they knew that they had been charged nearly five times the actual value of the merchandise. Not surprisingly, they refused to pay.

Ghorbanifar was furious, and spent many hours trying to convince the Iranians that they had been misinformed. One night he called the

Australian from Fouquet's Restaurant in Paris, and ran up a bill of more than Fr 7,000 (over $1,000) arguing about the matter. Nir was also upset, and used some of his own Lebanese channels to the Iranians in order to get at least one more hostage out. When favorable signals came back from Tehran, Ghorbanifar and Nir told North there would be a hostage in time for Independence Day in the United States, but, as we have seen, nothing happened, and Poindexter told North that enough was enough. He was to have no further contact.

While North stopped talking to Nir, he did not shut down all contact with the Israelis and Ghorbanifar; he simply shunted it off to the CIA, in the person of Charles Allen. According to Allen's testimony, Nir was understandably upset to have lost his direct channel to the White House, and he and Ghorbanifar labored mightily throughout July to get an American released. We do not know all the details, but there was apparently a combination of a new deal negotiated by Ghorbanifar with the Australian, the adviser, and other Iranian officials, and some kind of arrangement made by Nir through his own channels to Mehdi Hashemi, a top official of the Revolutionary Guards, and one of the most bloodthirsty figures in the regime. On July 26, 1986, Father Lawrence Jenco, a Catholic priest, was released in Beirut.

The details of the new deal were clarified at a meeting in Frankfurt on the twenty-seventh, involving North, Ghorbanifar, Cave, and Israeli Defense Minister Rabin's top assistant, General Haggai Regev. Ghorbanifar had promised the Iranians that the balance of the Hawk spares would be shipped, along with additional radar systems, and replacements for defective parts from the May delivery. In addition, the United States would provide one thousand free TOWs to make up for the overcharge. The presence of an Israeli official suggests that Nir had made some additional promises to sweeten the pot—something the CIA believed had been going on for some time—but we do not know the details, if any exist. The president approved the shipment of the remaining Hawk spares on the thirtieth, and the delivery was made on August 4th.

The next meeting, and the last time North and Ghorbanifar saw each other, was held at Heathrow Airport Hotel in London on the eighth of August. There were four people present: Nir, North, Cave, and Ghorbanifar. Ghorbanifar reported that the Iranians were unhappy. Not only were the spare parts prices outrageous (and he had provided Nir a microfiche to prove it), but many of the parts were defective. In all, according to the Iranian military experts

- 63 important and expensive units were either defective, or were unsuited to the Iranian Hawk batteries (they came from later generations of the missile);
- 296 units had not been delivered at all;
- there had been a 500 percent price inflation.

North did not challenge the Iranian claim of a huge markup, but said that there were all sorts of reasons for the escalation in the price, from the necessity of having manufacturers making special pieces, to storage costs, special transportation expenses, and the like.

Ghorbanifar proposed a new, staged release, in which the defective parts would be replaced, new radars would be sold to Iran, and one thousand free TOWs would be delivered to compensate for the overcharges. North said he would take it under advisement. Finally, Ghorbanifar gave North a warning: he was aware that Secord and Hakim were attempting to establish a new channel to the regime. This was a mistake, he told North, especially if the Americans intended to leave Ghorbanifar completely out of future deals, with substantial net losses, and discredited in Tehran. These warnings would be repeated throughout the next three months by both Ghorbanifar and Nir, in telephone conversations with Charles Allen. They would go unheeded.

THE PURGE OF GHORBANIFAR

The Hawk spare parts deal had put Ghorbanifar in serious jeopardy. Of the $18 million he owed Khashoggi, only $8.1 million was paid Ghorbanifar by the disgruntled Iranians. The balance due was $10 million. But even worse than that was the fact that the Iranians, having been told at great length by McFarlane and Cave in May that Ghorbanifar was not reliable, suspected that the big markup in the prices of the Hawk spares was exclusively the result of Ghorbanifar's greed, rather than the combination of Ghorbanifar's profit motive plus the desire of North, Nir, and Secord to raise money for other projects. If that impression lasted, his risk might extend beyond his financial liability. His life might be in danger.

But the Americans, understandably frustrated by a year of constantly shifting plans, dislike of Ghorbanifar, and the need to do another deal or two quickly in order to generate some more money for the *contras*, were indeed in search of a new channel. Poindexter had authorized this right after Tehran, and Hakim was the head of the search committee.

Hakim contacted an old friend of his—interestingly enough, a person he had recommended to the CIA in 1983, but who had not been recruited by the agency—an Iranian expatriate living in Europe. This man was flown to New York for discussions, and a friendly polygraph in early July.

Hakim promised that there would be substantial profits, and his friend brought in a second Iranian businessman who had contacts in the Iranian government. By the time the chain of contacts reached inside the government, Hakim had promised payoffs of something like $2 million.

Hakim's efforts bore fruit, and by late August, he and Secord met with Ali Hashemi Bakhramani, an officer in the Revolutionary Guards and a nephew of Majlis Speaker Rafsanjani. Along with the Revolutionary Guards' intelligence officer in the office of the prime minister, Semai'i, they constituted the second channel. I had no knowledge of the second channel while in government. Bob Woodward called them "Bahramani" and "Samaii" in his book *Veil*. The names used here were given to me in early 1988 by a former Iranian official living in Europe.

Bakhramani was a direct channel to Rafsanjani, which the Americans pronounced a distinct advantage over Ghorbanifar, who was dealing with all three factions in the Iranian regime. But in reality, as Bakhramani constantly reminded the Americans in the discussions they held, Rafsanjani was doing precisely the same thing—coordinating each decision with all the factions. In that way, if the efforts succeeded, everyone would share in the benefits, while if the negotiations fell apart, no one would be able to exploit the failure at the expense of others. The fear of treachery—the leitmotif of Persian life—underlay the Iranians' actions.

This carefully balanced maneuvering was undermined by the Americans demand for quick action, and their determination to find a way to achieve it without the hated Ghorbanifar. In part this was sheer coincidence, for they happened upon the Bakhramani channel at a time when Rafsanjani was engaged in a bitter struggle with the Ayatollah Montazeri, Khomeini's designated successor. Montazeri was a complex figure, for while he was intimately involved in the terrorist network that exported the Khomeini revolution to neighboring countries, he was also one of the most conservative leaders in the regime. Montazeri had long argued against centralized governmental control over the economy, and was one of the most outspoken advocates of better relations with the West, and particularly with the United

States. All of this is abundantly documented by Montazeri's public statements during the framing of the Islamic Constitution in the years immediately following the fall of the shah, yet in the over-simplified shorthand in which Iran was often described, Montazeri was generally considered a "radical." But however one classified him, Montazeri was indispensable to any Iranian consensus. If the opening to the United States were attempted without his participation, it would surely fail.

Bakhramani repeatedly told the Americans that Ghorbanifar was a long-time friend of Montazeri, and suggested that the Americans had to find a way to placate Ghorbanifar. It was implicit in what Bakh-ramani said that it would be exceedingly dangerous to the entire un-dertaking if Ghorbanifar were cut out. Further, it was evident that some of Bakhramani's friends were in touch with Ghorbanifar, so he would know whatever was done through the second channel.

Nonetheless, Cave, Secord, and North insisted that Ghorbanifar be cut out. They were encouraged in this decision by a telephone conversation between Cave and the Australian in early September. According to the Majority Report, the Australian told Cave that Mous-savi "approved of the planned meeting between [Bakhramani] and the Americans." In a memo to Poindexter, North reported that Cave believed this call was "confirmation that Rafsanjani may be moving to take control of the entire process of the United States relationship and the hostages."

This was at best wishful thinking, and at worst a serious misreading of Iran. The model of internal conflict among three factions—a de-scription that had been provided by Ghorbanifar more than a year earlier in the "Khashoggi Document"—had been confirmed over and over again, most recently from Bakhramani himself. So Cave, Secord, and North should have realized that any effort to disrupt the internal balance, such as by narrowing contacts and deals to a single faction during an attempt to come to terms with the Ayatollah's regime, was bound to fail. The others would do their best to sabotage everything.

On a more fundamental level, Cave and Secord knew—and Bakh-ramani reiterated it to them during their conversations—that Rafsan-jani was the man in charge of the war with Iraq, and he had become closely allied with the Revolutionary Guards (indeed, both elements of the second channel were officers of the Revolutionary Guards), the most radical organization in the country. The Revolutionary Guards were the mortal enemies of the regular army, and every serious analyst of Iran believed that one route to moderation of Iranian behavior lay in strengthening the regular armed forces. It would seem, then, that the second channel, far from representing a way to moderate Iranian behavior, was in fact the element of the Iranian regime most intensely opposed to moderation.

The pursuit of the second channel and the purge of Ghorbanifar jeopardized the operation (and eventually brought it down), strengthened the most radical elements of the regime (the Revolutionary Guards), and weakened the Iranian institution judged to be a key force for rationality and moderation. It seemed to offer a direct channel to Rafsanjani, and was sold to Poindexter and Casey on that basis. But there was no direct contact with Rafsanjani at any point, and all communications went through the two Revolutionary Guards officials, who claimed to be working with all factions. In fairness, we have to remember that the second channel functioned for less than two months, and it may well be that, over time, a working relationship with Rafsanjani would have developed. There were, however, no grounds to believe that on the basis of what actually transpired.

There were three meetings with Bakhramani: September 19–21 in Washington (the celebrated occasion on which North took Bakhramani on a late night tour of the White House, including the Oval Office), October 6–8 in Frankfurt (negotiating the arms deal that led to the release of David Jacobsen), and October 29–30, in Mainz, Germany. The Washington meetings established the framework for the talks in Germany. North and Cave tried to impress upon Bakhramani the seriousness of the undertaking, and stressed that they were interested in a change in the relationship between the two countries. Still, the hostages remained the major "obstacle" to concrete steps toward a new relationship, and so the discussions inevitably revolved around the hostage question, and around how best to cut Ghorbanifar out of the loop. The hostage issue was discussed in the now-familiar terms of TOW missiles, Hawk spare parts and radars, military intelligence, and other forms of military assistance to Iran (such as repairs to Phoenix missiles and to military aircraft).

There was one brand new subject in the Washington talks: the Iranian desire to see President Saddam Hussein of Iraq removed. And the issue of the Da'wa prisoners in Kuwait remained on the agenda.

North and Cave were sold, and they even managed to stimulate the stolid Poindexter, who arranged to have the president inscribe a Bible for the Ayatollah with a Biblical passage that seemed to suggest the possibility of good relations:

And the Scripture, foreseeing that God would justify the Gentiles by faith, preached the Gospel beforehand to Abraham, saying, "All the nations shall be blessed in you." (Galatians 3:8)

Poindexter sent an upbeat PROFs note to McFarlane, starting "Your trip to Tehran paid off. You did get through to the top. They are playing our line back to us."

But by the time the Frankfurt meetings were held, the curtain was beginning to fall on the Iran-Contra affair. As North left for Germany, a C-123 aircraft, flown by "Buzz" Sawyer and John Cooper, both Vietnam veterans involved in the Secord/Dutton resupply operations, crashed in southern Nicaragua. They were trying to drop a shipment of rifles, ammunition, and grenade launchers to the Southern Front. The only survivor of the crash was Eugene Hasenfus. North learned of the disaster upon his arrival in Frankfurt, and consequently had to turn around after a couple of hours' conversation and fly to Washington to manage the crisis.

He left behind a seven-point proposal, and Albert Hakim. Hakim reached an agreement with the Iranians on a nine-point document that included the sale of five hundred more TOWs (at a 25 percent discount compared to previous shipments), the provision of more military intelligence, a promise to help out with the Da'wa prisoners, and the provision of additional weapons. Poindexter had instructed North and Cave to demand the immediate release of Frank Reed, an American recently taken hostage in Lebanon, and Frank Pattis, an American businessman recently arrested in Iran on charges of espionage. They vanished from the nine-point agreement.

There was a hidden point in the agreement, for the discount on the TOWs was clearly a tactic aimed to discredit Ghorbanifar, and convince the Tehran leadership that Ghorbanifar had been pocketing the difference in earlier shipments. The combination of the new price, and the highly negative attitude of the Americans, eventually produced results in Tehran. Cave reported to the House Select Committee on Intelligence in December 1986 that by early November, Rafsanjani and his allies had concluded that Ghorbanifar was in fact an Israeli agent.

Now on overdrive, North stonewalled questions about American involvement in the Hasenfus flight, helped raise private money to pay for a lawyer to represent Hasenfus in Managua, and sold the nine-point plan to Poindexter and Casey. On October 27th, five hundred TOW missiles for Iran arrived in Israel. But the Israelis took the opportunity to suggest that these be exchanged for five hundred TOWs that they had been sold in May, as replacements for the original shipment to Iran back in the summer of 1985. The Israelis had not been happy with the quality of the replacements, and consequently the unsatisfactory TOWs were sent to Iran, while the newer batch stayed behind in Israel. The inferior five hundred arrived in Iran on the twenty-ninth, just as North, Secord, Hakim, and Cave were meeting with Semai'i and Bakhramani in Mainz.

The tone of the discussion was decidedly gloomy. The Iranians presented complicated analyses of their internal politics, while North, short of patience and desperate to see the plan through, demanded to know why Iran was failing to deliver on the hostage releases. There was some mirthful banter about the possibility Rafsanjani might arrange to have Ghorbanifar invited back to Iran for a long, unpleasant stay there. And there was talk of money. All the Iranians, from Hakim's original contacts to the second channel, were short of funds, and asked the Americans to produce some cash. Secord acknowledged that they were obliged to pay something, but said they were short of cash at the moment.

Finally, there was some discussion of the pursuit of the normalization of relations between the United States and the Islamic Republic of Iran. Back in Washington, both sides had agreed to create joint commissions that would meet to discuss the countries' outstanding differences. The United States had chosen Hakim, Secord, and Cave to sit on the American commission. The Iranians now provided their candidates, which, to the consternation of North, Cave, and Secord, included members of all the factions. Cave testified that the list "really blew our minds."[1] It should have come as no surprise, however. Bakhramani had made no secret of how the process worked in Tehran. But the Americans had not wished to believe him.

As it turned out, there was one group that was unhappy with the process, and that was Montazeri and his followers. While we do not have all the details, it is likely that Montazeri was deeply worried at the Americans' choice of Rafsanjani as their privileged interlocutor. Montazeri would take his revenge. In late October some five million pamphlets were distributed all over Iran, revealing McFarlane's trip in May and demanding that "those responsible" for the trip account for it to the people. But despite the extraordinary print run, this news stayed bottled up inside the Iran cauldron.

1. *Report of the Congressional Committees*, Majority Report, p. 261.

Secord, North, and Cave were terrified that news of the Iranian revelations would reach the United States, as they were deeply concerned that the Hasenfus trial in Managua would reveal their Central American activities. To make matters even worse, there was a threat from yet another front: the Ghorbanifar/Khashoggi connection. One of Khashoggi's American friends (indeed, the person who had introduced Khashoggi and Ghorbanifar), a New York businessman by the name of Roy Furmark, had done some business with Bill Casey in the past, and called Casey in early October to ask for an appointment. When this was granted, Furmark told Casey that Khashoggi was concerned about the $10 million still owed for the Hawk spare parts shipments in May and August. This money, according to Furmark, was not Khashoggi's; he had borrowed it from two Canadian businessmen who were getting quite upset at the delay in being repaid. The two Canadians were said to be friends of Senator Patrick Leahy of the Senate Select Intelligence Committee, a notorious thorn in Casey's side, and were planning to inform Leahy of what had happened if they didn't get paid quickly. This was the second time Casey had heard this tale of woe, for Ghorbanifar had told me the story and I had passed it on to Casey at about the same time. He was worried, but nothing was done about it, aside from asking Furmark to try to calm down the two Canadians.

There are references to the two Canadians in the tape recordings of the meetings with the second channel, showing how keenly North, Secord, and Cave were concerned. In fact, the Canadians did not exist. The story was made up for the occasion by Khashoggi, in a clever attempt to get his money back from the United States government.[2]

Last of all was the unfortunate Ghorbanifar, now worried about his financial condition and increasingly frightened that Rafsanjani would conclude that Ghorbanifar had cheated him. He had no direct channel to North, and ever since August, had communicated exclusively with Nir, who sympathized with the Iranian. Indeed, they were very much in the same boat, for the emergence of the second channel had made Nir largely irrelevant to the proceedings. Bakhramani told North that the Iranians had been angry when they realized that an Israeli had been part of the American delegation to Tehran, and North determined to leave the Israelis out of the second channel. In early October,

2. It may be, by the way, that when the courts finally decide the proper allocation of the $8 million in Hakim's Swiss accounts, they will give at least a part of it to Khashoggi. His claim may well be at least as good as anyone else's.

he dispatched Secord to Tel Aviv to inform him of the new channel, and ask Nir to be patient. Nir had already heard about the Bakhramani connection from Ghorbanifar and had called Charles Allen in early September to see if it were true. Allen, under instructions from North, had lied about it, saying that the Ghorbanifar channel was the only one, and Nir was invited to Washington in September for an elaborate charade. The future of the Ghorbanifar channel was discussed at great length, even though there was no intention to use it. As Allen testified,

> It was an unusual meeting, I thought, bizarre in the sense that Colonel North was there and we were going through trying to supply the remaining HAWK spare missile parts using the first channel . . . as if it was still operational . . .
>
> . . . toward the end of the morning (Nir) raised some questions which implied that he was aware that other contacts were occurring by the United States with Iran, and he was asking probing questions.
> Q: Was he getting answers?
> ALLEN: Not from me.
> Q: How about from Colonel North?
> ALLEN: I don't think Colonel North was all that forthcoming at that stage. I think there was an effort to deflect the questions.

Just before the shipment of the five hundred TOWs in late October, North told Nir to make sure Ghorbanifar kept quiet. At North's instructions, Nir flew to Orly Airport outside Paris to meet with Ghorbanifar. Nir told the Iranian that the Americans were going through with a shipment through the second channel, and that if Ghorbanifar leaked this fact to anyone, the United States would make certain that "his business activities came to an end."

Meanwhile, the five hundred TOWs having arrived in Iran, the second channel promised quick results. North and Secord flew to Beirut, ordered Ambassador Kelly to keep the State Department ignorant of what was happening, and prepared to receive the American hostages. For two days they waited, communicating with Washington to see if anything was happening and despairing of success. North began to wonder if it was all worth it. "This is the damnedest operation I have ever seen," he informed Poindexter in a long-overdue bit of self-examination. "Pls let me go on to other things. . . ." This request was fulfilled with a speed and a violence that he could not have anticipated.

First, success: On Sunday, November 2nd, David Jacobsen was released in Beirut. The event was kept secret in the hopes that other hostages would be released, but Jacobsen was to be the last American saved in the affair. Then, catastrophe: The next morning, the Beirut daily *al-Shiraa* published the McFarlane story.

Fallout and Response

One is tempted to say, "the rest is history," but North, Cave, Secord, and Hakim fought desperately to keep their operations afloat. There was one final meeting with the second channel in Geneva on the 8th of November, with the four Americans and the Revolutionary Guards intelligence officer Semai'i. They discussed the importance of keeping Rafsanjani's name secret, and Semai'i stressed that the major "obstacle" to the release of the remaining hostages was the matter of the Da'wa prisoners. The Americans said they had done all that they could, that they had spoken secretly to the Kuwaitis and urged them to be reasonable, but nothing more could be done. Semai'i was given a secure communications set, with which he could contact Cave in the United States, and was urged to do what he could to get some quick action in Tehran.

There were communications from Tehran for another two months, even after Poindexter and North had left the National Security Council staff. We do not know the contents of these messages, but we can presume that there was sufficient hope for there to be one last effort to achieve a diplomatic breakthrough with Iran. This was a meeting with Semai'i on December 13th in Geneva. The two Americans present were Cave and Charles Dunbar, an Iranian hand (and Farsi speaker) from the State Department.

Secretary of State Shultz had given strict instructions on the parameters for the meeting. He wanted it clear that henceforth there would be no "diplomatic" exchanges with Iran, but only an "intelligence channel." The two countries could trade information, but not discuss substantive issues. Charles Allen realized that this would simply shut down the channel and urged Casey to ask for a change in the Terms of Reference. Casey spoke with Chief of Staff Donald Regan and Acting National Security Adviser Alton Keel and had the Terms of Reference broadened. This enraged Shultz, who now, after months of refusing to learn the details of the Iran initiative, wanted to take over the entire program.

In the event, the meeting with Semai'i, Cave, and Dunbar (Hakim was scheduled to attend, but demanded that his attorney also sit in on the discussions; this was promptly rejected, and Hakim withdrew) was not a great success. Semai'i said that Iran was prepared to go ahead on the basis of previous understandings and immediately demanded that the United States arrange the removal of Saddam Hussein and release military equipment, purchased years ago by the shah, held in America. He further demanded action on the Da'wa prisoners, fifteen hundred more TOWs, one hundred TOW launchers, and implementation of the rest of the nine-point plan.

Dunbar followed his instructions, and informed the Iranian that there would be no further discussion of weapons. Semai'i said that would end the relationship and told Dunbar to go back to Washington to find out what had happened.

Cave stayed behind for one more day of conversation, evidently hoping against hope that there might still be time to convince the Iranians of the importance of a good relationship with the United States. If the American hostages were released, in an act of Iranian good will, it might yet be possible to achieve a diplomatic breakthrough. Cave must have believed that, and, in theory at least, it was probably true. But it was hopeless.

When Shultz learned of the nine-point plan and the Iranian demands, he immediately informed the president. Reagan, in Shultz's words,

> was astonished, and I have never seen him so mad. He is a very genial, pleasant man and doesn't—very easy going. But his jaws set and his eyes flashed, and both of us, I think, felt the same way about it, and I think in that meeting I finally felt that the President understands that something is radically wrong here.[3]

3. *Report of the Congressional Committees*, Majority Report, p. 263.

9. The Investigations and the Hearings

The public hearings were a political bullfight, with the lawyers playing the picadores of the ritual, and the witnesses scheduled as the bulls. The lawyers were supposed to tire the bulls, wound them, drain them of some of their blood and enrage them to the point where they both threatened the matador and were vulnerable to the final sword thrust. As chief counsels, Arthur Liman and John Nields had to tread carefully in the Capitol Hill bullring, for while they had to be sufficiently aggressive to lay bare the significant facts, they also had to take care not to threaten the finely tuned egos of the principals—the committee members themselves. For, just like matadors, the Senators and Congressmen were deathly afraid of being upstaged. They had searched for the best prosecutors they could find, but the picadores are merely the stars of the preliminary skirmishing. The kill belongs to the matador.

The only time there was open dissension within committee ranks came when the members complained that the lawyers were taking too much time with the witnesses. Senator David Boren complained that the members were being transformed into "potted plants," and the lawyers were doing all the talking. But anyone watching the hearings that day knew that Boren's unhappiness was not due to the excessive garrulousness of the counsels, but rather to the fact that the bull of the moment was doing a lot of goring. Boren was particularly irked, since the bull in question was the main event, a toro named Oliver North. If the two picadores, John Nields and Arthur Liman, had been drawing more of North's blood, there would have been no complaint from the Oklahoma Democrat.

LIMAN

Arthur Liman knew what it felt like on both sides of a criminal case. He had supervised the disbarment of Richard Nixon in New York State, was chief counsel to the commission that investigated the Attica prison riots, and was asked by New York City Mayor Ed Koch to investigate charges of misconduct in the New York City medical examiner's office. He had also defended some of the most celebrated "white collar" cases in recent history, from Robert Vesco and Dennis Levine to John Zaccaro. Those who know Liman best stress his single-minded attention to the most minute details of his legal cases (an apparently apocryphal story has him taking a shower with his shoes on during a particularly engrossing case), the breadth of his talents (from advising top corporations—he sits on several boards—to putting together complex mergers and takeovers), and his reputation for fairness. Finally, there was his unabashed participation in Jewish and Zionist activities, which led him to wonder if he should accept Senator Daniel Inouye's invitation to become chief counsel of the Senate committee. He expressed his reservations to the Democratic chairman, but Inouye said, "if that's your problem, don't worry about it. I'm as pro-Israel as you are." Liman took the position, but his concerns proved to be fully justified. After his tough questioning of Gen. Richard Secord, there was a blizzard of anti-Semitic mail.

Liman was not familiar with Washington, although he had a lifelong passion for Constitutional issues. He told the *Washington Post* in early July 1987[1] that "the subject matter is something I haven't looked at since Government 180 at Harvard." For once, Liman was somewhat imprecise. In fact, he had devoted considerable time and energy to the central issue at the hearings during his Harvard senior year. In one of those little tricks that history sometimes reserves for famous people, Liman had written his undergraduate honors thesis on the subject of McCarthy's congressional investigations. It was prophetically entitled "Limited Government and Unlimited Investigation" and concluded that

> congressional investigating committees pose not just a challenge to the relatively few individuals who appear before them but to the whole concept of limited government.

The central argument of the young Liman was that such investigations (with McCarthy's Permanent Subcommittee on Investigations

1. *Washington Post*, Style section, July 7, 1987. Government 180 was a semester survey course in international relations, later taught by Professor Henry A. Kissinger.

as his model) threaten the delicate system of checks and balances created by the Constitution, because the conduct of congressional investigations tilts the balance of power in favor of Congress at the expense of the president. By the time he wrote his thesis (1954), Liman could already speak of a long history of congressional investigations:

> There is a tendency today to think that the use of an investigation to stigmatize somebody or something is a development peculiar to our decade. Investigations have always been utilized to defame or to defend some person or some cause.[2]

So it was with Iran-Contra, and it was ironic indeed that Liman, who had worried so deeply about congressional aggrandizement and the abuse of individual rights during the McCarthy hearings, should become one of the chief instruments of a similar investigation thirty-three years later. While he was a Democratic activist and fund-raiser, Liman was a fair-minded man, but he was the chief counsel for a highly politicized Democratic majority that was determined to advance its political and institutional cause: the power of Congress. The targets of the investigation—many of whom were unfairly damaged in the process—were all those involved in any way with the Iran initiative or the support for the Nicaraguan resistance.

The method used to advance the congressional cause was the "criminalization" of a policy issue by accusing the executive branch of having deliberately and illegally subverted the will of Congress in Central America and Iran. The two issues around which the hearings revolved were therefore those which offered the best chance for criminal indictments: the administration's adherence to the terms of the several Boland amendments, and the handling of money, whether from the Iran initiative or from the private support network for the *contras*. There was very little discussion of foreign policy.

The congressional approach was unfortunate, for it placed the discussion of the affair in the wrong context. The memorable phrase "it is worse than a crime, it is a mistake" could have been made about Iran-Contra. The administration made some terrible mistakes, but there was not much in the way of criminal behavior—at least, not in the sense that ordinary citizens think of it. Among the mistakes were:

• Going behind the backs of Congressmen and Senators to organize secret support for the *contras*, rather than confronting the issues openly.
• Permitting the hostage question to overwhelm the Iran initiative,

2. Arthur Liman, "Limited Government and Unlimited Investigation" (Honors thesis, Harvard University, April 1954), p. 23.

thereby subordinating a question of great strategic importance to concern over individual citizens.

• Failing to admit—and defend—what had been done, after the affair became public, resorting instead to efforts at coverup.

• Mishandling the Ghorbanifar problem in such a way as to guarantee the sabotage of the Iran initiative.

• Failure to supervise North's activities, in order to guarantee that the money would be handled correctly, and that each step in the operation conformed to the instructions of his superiors. This might have avoided the grotesque negotiations concerning the Da'wa prisoners in Kuwait.

These were all serious mistakes (and there were many others), and there is much to be learned from them. But once the context of the investigation and the hearings was defined by the lawyers, such questions were placed on the back burners, and the issues of criminal malfeasance were raised to the boiling point.

One question of considerable importance *was* rightly discussed at great length. This was the issue of deceiving Congress. As usual, the question was handled as a criminal matter (McFarlane ultimately pled guilty to a misdemeanor charge of withholding information from Congress, and Poindexter and North will have to respond to it as well), but it is at least equally political. For the basic reason that the information was not provided to Congress was the fear of disclosure, which would both jeopardize lives and scuttle the policy. Notice that Congress was not singled out: many members of the executive branch, including cabinet secretaries, were likewise kept out of the loop. To be sure, the zeal for secrecy was sometimes so excessive that it became ludicrous, as when Poindexter instructed North to keep Casey ignorant of North's activities. It was all part of a vicious circle: if Casey knew, and were asked during testimony, he would either have to lie or reveal the information.

One can easily sympathize with the position of Poindexter, McFarlane, and North. But it was political folly to withhold all knowledge of the *contra* support program and the Iran initiative from every member of Congress. The White House should have found a way to inform at least a tiny handful of the congressional leaders, no matter how generally. This was particularly true of the Iran initiative, because any dealing with the Ayatollah Khomeini—and particularly anything that looked like an arms-for-hostages deal—was bound to be explosive. Indeed, the administration should have floated some trial balloons in the press, indicating here and there that Reagan might be willing to consider improved relations with Iran under certain circumstances. This would have prepared public opinion for two eventualities: a success of the initiative, or its premature revelation.

There were some thoughtful discussions of this matter (especially by Hyde, Hamilton, and Boland), but for the most part it, like most everything else, was handled in the context of criminality.

It was not a foregone conclusion that the investigations would be conducted in this manner, and indeed in the weeks before the hearings began, the committee members—especially on the Senate side—were deeply divided. One group wanted a criminal prosecutor to take the lead for the committee, while the other felt that it would be better to have someone with considerable foreign policy experience. In the view of the latter group, the criminal investigation should be left to Judge Lawrence Walsh, the independent counsel appointed in December by a panel of three federal judges to investigate the affair, while the Congress should concentrate its energies on the foreign policy questions.

There are many men and women in Washington who have distinguished themselves in both fields of expertise and by the time Chairman Inouye had composed his short list of candidates, it contained the names of some lawyers with foreign policy experience. At least one of these was asked if he were willing to accept the position (he declined). But just as generals prepare to fight the last war, the Congress prepared to replay Watergate, and so the "criminal" view prevailed. Both committees chose men with considerable courtroom experience. After extensive discussions, Senate Committee Chairman Inouye chose Liman. House Committee Chairman Lee Hamilton had no doubt who he wanted and went directly to his friend John Nields, an experienced Washington attorney who had worked with Hamilton on the "Koreagate" investigations during the Carter period, and who attracted attention by his desperate efforts to maintain his long-haired image long after it was materially possible to do so.[3]

The choice of attorneys proved that the committees' primary interest was in criminalizing the process, rather than investigating the many serious policy issues involved in the Iran-Contra affair. Even the ques-

3. Both Nields and Liman presented images of men defiantly reordering their retreating hairlines, rather than gracefully accepting the certain defeat the genetic code had reserved for them. In like manner, they would attempt to show that the people caught up in the Iran-Contra affair were involved in criminal activity, when it quickly became manifest to the viewing public that, whatever one's opinion of the wisdom of their behavior, the intent of the principal figures was certainly not criminal—at least in the commonsense meaning of the word.

tion that dominated much of the hearings—where did the money go?—was treated as a criminal matter, rather than a serious policy error. If the committees' primary interest had been in policy, they would have spent more time asking how so many top government officials had tolerated the interlinking of the Iran initiative with the *contra* support program, to the detriment of both. But very little time was spent on this, and even such talented committee members as Senators Nunn and Mitchell hectored General Secord about where the money should eventually go, rather than on the grave error in judgment that had brought Iran-Contra into being in the first place.

The decision to focus on "criminality" quite obviously suited the president's political opponents, who hoped the investigations would lay the groundwork for the 1988 presidential campaign and permit the Democrats to retake the White House. But this partisan political ingredient, while important, was not the deciding factor. The key element determining the nature of the investigation was that it served the purposes of the advocates of greater congressional power in foreign policy. This group numbered all the Democrats, along with Republicans like Cohen, Trible, and Rudman. Only a few committee members—notably Hyde, Hatch, Courter, Cheney, Broomfield, McCollum, and McClure—fought the efforts to exploit the hearings to advance the ambitions of the Congress at the executive's expense. Congressman Peter Rodino of New Jersey, one of the heroes of the Watergate era, went so far as to speak of "separation of powers principles and Constitutional prerogative [read: executive privilege]" as "completely without merit and . . . legal arguments that have long since been discredited."[4]

This astonishing outburst was provoked by the refusal of White House Counsel Arthur B. Culvahouse to grant the committees' request for an unrestricted fishing expedition through the memory banks of the NSC computer system. Culvahouse's insistence that the White House would not open all its files to the Congress came rather late in the day and represented one of the few occasions on which Congress or the independent counsel were denied anything. For the most part, the White House surrendered virtually all claim to executive privilege.

4. *Report of the Congressional Committees*, p. 640. Rodino, who announced his departure from Congress early in 1988, was attempting to leave a legacy of greatly expanded congressional power, and the efforts to promote a legislative seizure of power were so blatant that one staff member termed the hearings "a failed coup d'etat." It is sometimes forgotten that, while some tapes were voluntarily turned over to the House, congressional attempts to obtain the Nixon tapes were rejected by the courts. The special prosecutor's quest was upheld, but the Supreme Court strongly reaffirmed the doctrine of executive privilege, particularly regarding the need to protect sensitive diplomatic and national security matters, in that case (*United States* v. *Richard M. Nixon*, 1974).

THE WHITE HOUSE SURRENDER

I first became aware of the full extent of the White House's appeasement of Congress when I was subpoenaed by the Senate Select Committee on Intelligence in December 1985. I placed a phone call to the Office of the White House Counsel (at the time Peter Wallison) and asked for guidance. I was in possession of highly sensitive national security information. Some of it involved the names of people who had risked their lives in order to talk to me and other representatives of the United States government, and I was extremely reluctant to provide those names to members of Congress or their staffs. I was prepared to reveal the nature of the contacts I had had, or had arranged for others, but I believed the White House should instruct me to withhold the names.

I am not an expert on constitutional law, and my reasoning was based on a concern about the importance of secrecy in the conduct of foreign affairs. Even within the executive branch itself, access to sensitive intelligence is based on the principle of "need to know." Very few people need to know the precise source of information, even when the information itself, and perhaps a general description of the *kind* of source (a person who has provided good information in the past; a source of unknown reliability; a source who has provided both good and misleading information in the past, and so forth), is widely disseminated. We need to protect our sources, and the risk to our sources increases as the number of persons who know the sources' identity grows.

If the "need to know" principle applies within the executive branch, and even within the intelligence community, it seemed to me that it ought to apply to Congress as well. Why did members of the committees need to know the names of Iranians who had probably risked their lives to meet with American officials?

Furthermore, there was the question of executive privilege—the time-honored principle that Congressman Rodino and a handful of other Democrats termed "discredited." I knew from my own experience that a number of foreign leaders, including some of our closest allies, did not trust the ordinary American bureaucracy with certain kinds of sensitive information. They had come to the conclusion that they could probably trust the White House, and as a result the president had received valuable information through his own channels. This was the reason I had gotten involved in the Iran initiative in the first place. I had functioned as a message carrier for sensitive information between the White House and our European allies. I was afraid that if I now provided that information to Congress, I might jeopardize the precious flow of information between various chiefs of government and the American president. Congress had not had a good record in keeping secrets, but quite aside from the actual performance of our legislators, I felt it was important to maintain the principle that foreign leaders could say things to the president with confidence that they would not be spread around the entire government. After all, if our friends had wanted to use the normal channels to disseminate secret information, they would not have resorted to the back channels to the White House.

So my inclination was to tell the congressional committees fully what had happened, but to withhold the identities of the persons with whom I had met, and whose meetings with other American officials I had helped to arrange. Here and there I found people on the congressional side (and on Judge Walsh's staff) sympathetic to my view of the matter. The first time I was interviewed by FBI investigators attached to Walsh's office, I declined to name the Iranians with whom we had been in contact, on the grounds that this constituted sensitive national security information. The FBI agents agreed with me about the sensitivity, but commented, "we probably have all these names anyway; you are the first person to take this position." Alas, they were quite right. Had the White House taken a principled stand on the president's Constitutional prerogatives, it would have been possible for individuals to withhold some of this material, but it was unrealistic to expect a single individual to risk a contempt citation on his own. But the White House had no stomach for a good fight, even though the national interest would have been better served if the president had brought these issues to a head, even to the point of getting a Supreme Court ruling on these fundamental Constitutional issues.

Wallison's staff offered no support, and I was told that the president had instructed everyone to "cooperate with Congress." The results were predictable. A torrent of secret information poured out of the West Wing and the Old Executive Office Building, and while, late in the day, some committee members (like Rodino, Brooks, Fascell, Aspin, and Stokes) complained when any assertion of executive privilege emerged from 1600 Pennsylvania Avenue, many members were astonished at the massive outpouring of documentation from the NSC files.

The significance of the White House surrender was underlined by North when he was asked about his notes about meetings with various Central American heads of state:

Quite honestly, Counsel, I don't understand why I had to give you those notes. I would have thought, under normal circumstances, that they would have been accorded what we used to call executive privilege. Those were meetings I had with heads of state and representatives of other countries in the conduct of the foreign policy of the United States of America. And I honestly believe to this day, sir, that those ought not to be handed out and bandied about, that they were private communications.[5]

The release of such documentation inevitably affects the ability of American officials to have candid conversations with foreign leaders. In foreign policy, as in daily life, you have a better chance of getting a candid opinion if you have a reputation for discretion. If the United States cannot be relied upon to keep secrets secret, other governments will be less and less candid.

The White House had panicked. The original decision was made by Chief of Staff Donald Regan and was reinforced and supervised by his successor, former Senator Howard Baker, and by Ambassador David Abshire—brought back from his NATO post to manage the president's relations with the Tower Commission and the congressional committees. All three believed that Reagan's very survival was at stake. Both Baker and Abshire had lived through Watergate (Baker was on the Ervin committee, while Abshire was assistant secretary of state for congressional affairs) and, like the committee members, assumed they were involved in a rerun of that trauma. Instead of trying to find out what had happened, and then deciding what Congress was entitled to see, they all tried to get the White House out of the line of fire by giving Congress and the independnt counsel everything they could possibly want. The objective of the White House advisers was to make themselves the allies of the investigators. They hoped thereby to avoid any direct attack upon the president.

One must marvel at the passivity of the president and his men in the face of the crisis. Even given their instincts to avoid any significant conflict with Congress, the advisers in the White House might have insisted that the president instruct North and Poindexter to tell *him* precisely what had happened, so that he could make some rational decisions about how to deal with the crisis. This was even more urgent if one believed, as Baker and Abshire did, that Reagan was in considerable danger of being politically destroyed, and even at some risk of impeachment. Were they not obliged to get the truth? And were

5. Oliver L. North, *Taking the Stand* (New York: Pocket Books, 1987), p. 211.

they not obliged also to protect the institutional and constitutional interests of the presidency?

But if the White House had conducted its own investigation, the Congress would have been enraged, and the media would have ruminated darkly about "cover-up." There was also some concern that if the White House staff started to ask questions, *they* would then be hauled up in front of the Select committees (something that might have been avoided by an assertion of executive privilege, but that claim had already been jettisoned). Hence, the president turned to an "independent commission"—John Tower, Brent Scowcroft, and Edmund Muskie—to look into the matter for the White House. Reagan had surrendered on the matter of executive privilege and now had to await the results of the inquiries.

It was understandable, but it was a grave mistake. By failing to search out the full truth, Reagan guaranteed that the wall of defense around the presidency rested on a claim of presidential ignorance, hardly a sturdy barrier against the congressional onslaught that was sure to come. Once he adopted this strategy he was doomed, regardless of what people concluded about his role in the affair. For if the president really did not know what had happened, he had failed to perform his duties. And if he did know, but was not talking about it, he was stonewalling or covering up. Either way, he was a political loser.

In addition to the president's own political interests, the White House strategy of turning over all its documents and letting others figure out what had happened was an error on much broader grounds. By refusing to assert any claim of executive privilege, the White House acquiesced in a dramatic act of congressional aggrandizement. The consequences of this abdication of executive power were accurately foreseen by the young Arthur Liman in his Harvard thesis:

> If the investigative power of Congress is unlimited, the separation of powers, and the system of checks and balances must break down. . . .
>
> [The Founding Fathers'] solution to this problem was: ambition must be made to counteract ambition. For it was the ambition of the Presidency, and the Congress, brought to fruition in a "court-packing" plan, that liberated the country from the clutches of the Supreme Court in 1936. It will be the ambition of the Presidency alone that will protect the independence of his branch from unwarranted interference by the New Investigation.[6]

6. Liman, "Limited Government and Unlimited Investigation," p. 106.

Liman argued that it was essential for the president to refuse to grant congressional access to certain information on the grounds that "disclosure would be detrimental to public interest." He pointed out that in 1796 President George Washington had refused to provide Congress with documents dealing with the administration's negotiations with the English. Liman then made the crucial point, which is that the struggle between the executive and legislative branches is political. It is a "gray area" in Constitutional law:

> Such refusals are in the shadowland of constitutional law because of the lack of delineation between the powers of Congress and the Presidency. Precisely because the sphere of the legislature is determined by its relative power position in government, and not by constitutional demarcation, the refusals of requests for information must be understood in other than their constitutional aspects.[7]

The Congress found its strategy of aggrandizement unchallenged by the president. But it turned out to be a strangely empty victory, both because of North's tour de force—effectively reversing the roles between hunter and hunted for one week—and because the key question (Did the president know about the diversion?) was answered in the negative.

There was a more serious problem, for while the strategy of the hearings served the narrow political and institutional interests of the majority, it also made it inevitable that the real story of the Iran-Contra affair would not be told.

The committee lawyers, despite their unquestioned intelligence and mastery of the law, were unskilled in the operations of the nationsl security community, and largely ignorant of the way in which foreign policy is designed and conducted. They were prosecutors, not policy analysts, and they looked for signs of criminal activity, not policy blunders. Lacking detailed knowledge of foreign policy, they were unable to judge when actions were usual or unusual, and when the "evidence" in their possession was misleading.

To take just two examples:

- When Liman was questioning North about the trip to Tehran, he asked whether North felt that the Americans should have accepted the Iranian offer of two hostages in exchange for Hawk spare parts. North replied that he did, but that McFarlane had rejected the offer. Liman

7. Liman, "Limited Government and Unlimited Investigation," p. 107.

asked, "Didn't Mr. McFarlane have instructions from the President of the United States on what he could give and what he couldn't?" After a brief exchange, North said, "I was not present when Mr. McFarlane was briefed by the president."[8]

But McFarlane had not been briefed by the president before the Tehran trip. For foreign policy experts, the lack of a presidential briefing was like Sherlock Holmes noting that the dog did not bark in the night. It stood out as a curiosity and told volumes about McFarlane's state of mind at the time. He yearned for a return to action, yet lacked the self-confidence to demand a presidential briefing before leaving on such a dangerous and sensitive mission. In an earlier period, he would certainly have insisted upon talking to the president. Liman missed this point, because he lacked the foreign policy background to notice it.

• In the same session (July 10, 1987), North testified that many of the problems in Tehran were caused by the fact that Ghorbanifar had misled both sides on the nature of the hostages-for-spare parts agreement ("we were misled by Ghorbanifar and so were the Iranians"). Yet it should have been evident to Liman—and to the committee members as well—that the Americans did not trust Ghorbanifar and would never have relied solely upon his word to set up the agenda for the high-level meeting in Tehran. In fact, as we have seen, there had been direct conversations between George Cave and the Australian prior to the trip. And the CIA had given the committees the transcripts of those conversations. If he knew it, Liman did not show any sign of recognizing that North's claim could not have been decisive. Even if Ghorbanifar had lied to both sides, the American government had used its own channel of communication.

More broadly, the lawyers were apparently unaware that much of the documentation produced by governmental officials is written to cover the author's posterior. It is rare, nowadays, for any savvy official to write down the details of sensitive policy questions, let alone delicate operations. The key exchanges on such subjects are oral, not committed to paper or to computer memory.

I was particularly sensitive to the question of documentation, for, as a trained historian, I had worked in governmental archives from Washington to Rome. Knowing the speed with which the American government releases information, I had no confidence that documents dealing with the Iran initiative would remain secret throughout the lifetimes of the Iranians with whom I met. I did not want to become

8. North, *Taking the Stand*, p. 412.

the vehicle of their exposure, at great potential risk to their lives. I therefore made an explicit arrangement with McFarlane that we would not put anything on paper. I took notes at the meetings I attended at McFarlane's instructions, but once I had briefed him, I destroyed the notes. By the time the investigations started, the only records in my possession upon which I could base any sort of reconstruction were my credit card receipts and a couple of memos left behind on a floppy disk. Not only was there no paper trail for the first five months of the Iran initiative, but I had to guess at many dates for crucial meetings.

The best hope for an accurate reconstruction of those events lay in permitting McFarlane and me to sit down together and talk it through. We could probably have arrived at a fairly precise picture, but the "criminalization" of the investigations ruled out this procedure. We couldn't talk, because this would raise suspicions that we were conspiring to cover up something or other. In the end, the committee members (and the Walsh people) had to guess, event by event, which of us remembered things more accurately. In short, the public interest clearly demanded that the most accurate possible story be told, but the committees' methods ensured that this would not happen. The search for malefactors got in the way of the search for the truth.

Second, lawyers tend to measure human behavior against some abstract standard, in order to judge the people involved. But the options available to policymakers are very often *all* unattractive, so that any choice will appear to be poor when measured against a yardstick of absolute goodness. Policy decisions need to be evaluated in context, and a choice of the least of available evils is often the best decision. This was the case in Iran at the time of the shah, when the Carter administration decided that the shah did not live up to our human rights standards and was therefore unworthy of our support. In the context of the Middle East, however, the shah's regime was exceedingly progressive (this was, in fact, the principal reason Khomeini hated him so much), and the alternative to the shah—the Ayatollah—was considerably worse, both from the standpoint of human rights and from that of American interests. Holding the shah up to an abstract human rights standard helped blind the administration and the American public to the real policy options and thereby contributed to the disastrous outcome.

The same considerations applied to Iran in 1985, where, so far as we could ascertain, there were no attractive political forces with which to work. But it might have been possible to achieve working relationships with some relatively more attractive, pro-Western Iranian groups in a position to moderate the international behavior of the regime. This option was discarded, and Poindexter, North, Secord, Hakim, and Cave dealt with representatives of the regime, rather than people who wanted to change it. But even the dialogue with the Australian and Bakhramani—who represented the dread Revolutionary Guards —blocked or delayed terrorist acts against American citizens and targets.

None of the Iranians with whom American representatives were in contact would be candidates for sainthood, but the United States has a definite interest in seeing such people strengthened. The committee could have advanced public understanding by exploring the real policy options, in their proper context:

- Do we wish to work toward a rapprochement with the Khomeini regime?
- Should we be working with the internal opposition within Iran, in an effort to change the regime?
- To what extent are American interests threatened by the success of one side or the other in the Iran/Iraq war?
- Is it important to keep open channels from the West to Iranian leaders, hoping to establish a basis for cooperation once Khomeini is dead?

But such questions were rarely pursued, in part because of the ignorance of the counsels and members of the committees, in part because they insisted on measuring every decision against an abstract standard of good and evil, and in part because there was no political benefit to either side in asking such questions. The Democrats were not eager for a demonstration that the Iran initiative began with an effort to establish contact with pro-Western Iranian leaders, and test the possibility of a better relationship with Iran. The Republicans wanted to avoid any discussion of how we came to sell weapons to the Ayatollah Khomeini, the man most hated in America.

Both Shultz and Weinberger encouraged these unfortunate tendencies. Neither one allowed for the possibility of an Iran policy that might lead to a more attractive regime in Tehran and better relations between the two countries. To listen to them, one would have thought that every influential person in Iran was a murderous fanatic irrevocably committed to the proposition that the United States was Iran's major enemy. This sort of xenophobia plays well with both the Congress and the public, but it rarely helps get us good policy.

There was a somewhat better discussion of Central America, for here was a subject with which the committee members were quite familiar. But the "criminalization" of the hearings again drove the discussion away from the foreign policy questions and toward the minutiae of presumed illegalities. Instead of asking questions about the nature of the Central American crisis, both the lawyers and the members concentrated their attention on the process. Yet, for example, support for the *contras* could not have been carried out without the active participation of other countries in the region. It would have been helpful if someone had asked North or Poindexter or McFarlane to explain the motives for that support, and the broader implications for American foreign policy if the Central American operation failed.

There were some notable exceptions to this general rule. One was Senator Orrin Hatch of Utah, who used almost all his time with North to focus on policy questions. And he also underlined the principal tragedy of the Iran initiative when he said, "finally, if we could have gotten the hostages out, which unfortunately appears, of course in the end to have consumed all of these broader foreign policy goals."[9] Two others were Congressman Jim Courter of New Jersey, who clearly understood the basic issues from the very beginning, and Congressman Henry Hyde of Illinois, who thankfully brought both wisdom and wit to the proceedings.

Third, just as Eisenhower's timorousness in the 1950s encouraged McCarthy and his allies to expand their investigations into a political witch-hunt, so the lack of a principled White House challenge in 1987 encouraged the worst tendencies of the congressional committees and their staffs. The investigations offered members and staffers the opportunity to settle old scores, as well as the chance to explore the validity of some of the wilder conspiracy theories. Once again, Arthur Liman's thesis accurately portrayed this as an inevitable tendency of investigative bodies, and he quoted Walter Lippmann's classic work, *Public Opinion,* to make this point:

> So bad is the contact of the legislators with necessary facts that they are forced to rely on either private tips or that legalized atrocity, the Congressional investigation where Congressmen starved of their legitimate food for thought go on a wild and feverish manhunt, and do not stop at cannibalism.[10]

Liman recognized that a new style of congressional investigation had emerged during the McCarthy period, and he also understood that the trends in mass politics—from the growing importance of

9. North, *Taking the Stand*, p. 561.
10. Walter Lippmann, *Public Opinion* (New York: Macmillan, 1922), p. 289. Quoted in Liman, "Limited Government and Unlimited Investigation," p. 39.

public opinion, to the mounting power of television in the political process—favored the Congress. To be sure, North eventually demonstrated that television could be turned to the advantage of a skilled witness, but such events were rare.

One aspect of the manhunt was the relentless search for evidence of criminal wrongdoing by administration officials. The chief counsel for the House, John Nields, told North quite early in North's week of testimony that the Justice Department had concluded that NSC, Pentagon, and CIA officials had acted illegally in the matter of the November 1985 Hawk shipments to Iran. In fact, the matter was exceedingly ambiguous (nobody was ever indicted for this alleged transgression), but Nields served notice that they were going to brand anything they did not like "criminal."

The real nastiness went on behind the scenes, where the public could not see it. Some of the staffers believed that the Iran-Contra affair was the result of a grand conspiracy, and while there were differing views of the identity of the conspirators, and the organizing force behind the plot, a surprising amount of time was devoted to efforts to prove that there was a vast and sinister plot that could explain all, or most, of the activities under investigation. The two main conspiracy theories were The Israeli Conspiracy and The Secret Government Conspiracy.

The first theory rested on the belief that the Iran initiative had been an Israeli scheme, foisted off on the American government by Israelis and American Jews sympathetic to (or actually working for) Israel. The second held that the Iran-Contra affair was simply one manifestation of a twenty-year covert program conducted by the CIA and some former CIA and military officials. These activities allegedly included drug-running on a world scale, assassinations, the subversion of several countries, all designed and conducted by a small group of immensely powerful people operating outside the control of any elected government. Neither theory had any convincing evidence to support it, yet each had a surprisingly large number of supporters within Washington, even among the members and staffers of the Select committees.

THE "ISRAELI CONSPIRACY"

There are some institutions in the federal government that have a tradition of being relatively inhospitable to Jews. Foremost among these are portions of the intelligence community. The CIA has never had a Jewish DCI, DDCI, or deputy director for either Operations (or Plans, as it used to be known) or Intelligence. So far as I have been able to discover, the highest level to which a Jew has risen in the Directorate of Operations (DO) is executive assistant to the deputy director for operations.

There is also no denying the growing suspicion of Israel, and of American supporters of Israel, within parts of the intelligence community. It was already present before the Pollard affair, and once Pollard was exposed many of Israel's critics came forward to suggest that there were undoubtedly other Pollards at work within the American government. Suspicion immediately fell upon American Jews in high positions within the government, and particularly upon any Jew who had had ongoing contacts with Israel.

This is the immediate background to the behind-the-scenes hunt for presumed Israeli agents involved in the Iran-Contra affair. Those involved in the hunt invariably assumed that Jews were the most likely suspects. This presumption was given some credibility by early efforts by McFarlane, North, and Regan to shift blame to Israel for the entire undertaking. It is a matter that directly concerned me, a Jew, for there were people in the intelligence community, in the Congress, and in the media who alleged that I was a Mossad agent, and that I had acted on behalf of Israel to trick the American government into approving Israeli arms sales to Iran. In fact, during the investigations, a top CIA counterintelligence official (who later became one of the top two men on the National Intelligence Council) remarked to some of his colleagues that "Ledeen is a top Mossad agent of influence, with dual citizenship and an Israeli passport." Every claim was false, and it should have been easy enough to ascertain that there is no dual citizenship, no Israeli passport.

Moreover, when I testified before the Senate Select Committee on Intelligence in December 1986 Senator Thomas Eagleton of Missouri asked a long series of questions, such as: How many times had I been to Israel? How many free trips had I taken there? How many Israeli clients did I have? How many presents had I received from the government of Israel or other Israelis? Had I ever worked for the government of Israel? The implicit point of such questions was to suggest that I had had an intimate relationship with the Israeli government, or its agents. As he heard the answers (no free trips, no Israeli clients, never any relationship with the Israeli government), he became visibly more agitated, and muttered under his breath, "this whole thing was a Mossad sting operation." At the same session, the committee's staff

259

director, Bernard McMahon, twice attempted to get me to say that I had "acted on behalf of Mr. Ghorbanifar," when I had made it clear that my actions throughout had been solely on behalf of my own government. After some animated conversation, he apologized for trying to put words in my mouth.

Nearly a year later, I read the deposition of Clair George, at the time of the affair the CIA's deputy director of operations. George testified that he believed Ghorbanifar was an Israeli agent and implied that I was working in tandem with him. Even though George was soon to leave the CIA under a cloud, I felt compelled to present a detailed rebuttal—on the record—at my final deposition.[11]

The effort to suggest that I had some sort of murky, improper relationship with Israel continued throughout my private testimony before the Select committees, with both staffers and committee members participating. The chief inquisitor was Joel Lisker, an investigator for Senator James McClure, the Republican from Idaho. McClure was particularly exercised about the Israeli role in the scandal, and Lisker, whether on his own initiative or because he had been instructed to do so by McClure, was determined to get to the bottom of an imagined conspiracy. Lisker was well cast in this role, for he had been similarly involved in a lengthy investigation of a close friend of mine, Dr. Stephen Bryen, nearly ten years earlier. Bryen had been a senior staff assistant to Senator Clifford Case on the Senate Foreign Relations Committee, and had become an extremely knowledgeable and effective player in foreign policy debates. In 1978, an official of the National Association of Arab Americans accused Bryen of passing classified documents to Israeli officials during a breakfast in the coffee shop of the Madison Hotel in Washington. Although Bryen's accuser had no evidence and failed a polygraph examination on the question, the FBI opened an investigation. The bureau found no evidence to support the accusation, but Lisker—at the time the head of the Foreign Agents Registration Division at the Justice Department—kept the investigation going for two long years, during which time Bryen was taken off the Foreign Relations Committee staff and forced to scramble for a living.

The campaign against Bryen was one of the nastiest episodes in recent Washington history, and although the investigation into his nonexistent Mossad connections was finally closed, the rumors about

11. The full text of my comments on Clair George's several distortions—from the insinuations about me to the unsupported claim that Ghorbanifar was a Mossad agent to the fanciful allegation that Charles Allen was Ghorbanifar's "control officer"—was made public in the fall of 1987.

him became a staple in the anti-Israeli press and the Washington rumor mill.[12] The rumors continued to circulate despite Bryen's distinguished service in the Pentagon under Weinberger and Carlucci. Between 1981 and 1988, he created and directed a 140-man agency (the Defense Technology Security Administration) devoted to the crucial issue of East-West strategic trade. And he has twice been awarded the highest civilian decoration given by the Pentagon.

Lisker's tenacity on the anti-Bryen campaign was a tribute to his belief that there must be an Israeli conspiracy at work within the American government, and he apparently suspected that I was a member of it. Typically, his questioning of me on this matter was not conducted in the presence of a stenographer, but in one of the "informal interviews" that committee staffers sometimes favored. He began by asking about Jewish friends of mine and of my wife. He then inquired into my brief association with the Jewish Institute for National Security Affairs: Was it not true, he asked, that Steve Bryen and I had been cofounders of JINSA? No, I told him, it was false. It had been founded by Max Kampelman (now chief American negotiator at Geneva for U.S.–Soviet arms talks, and counselor at the Department of State) and Richard Shifter (now assistant secretary of state for human rights). In fact, Lisker even had the goal of the organization wrong. JINSA was created in the mid-seventies to try to muster some support in the Jewish community for a serious American defense budget, as well as to point out themes of common interest to Israel and the United States. JINSA is not part of what is commonly termed "the Israel lobby," but extreme right-wing groups like the Liberty Lobby; extreme left-wing journalists like Claudia Wright; and undefinable extremists like Lyndon Larouche invariably misdescribe it.

This line of questioning was too much even for my normally placid attorney, Jim Woolsey, and it was brought to the attention of Lisker's superiors. We heard no more of it in subsequent questioning. Nonetheless, the rumors had been started, and every so often they made their way into print. The *St. Louis Post-Dispatch,* from Senator Eagleton's home territory, ran a front-page story about me on March 29,

12. The rumors have been kept alive by a succession of conspiracy theorists, both American and foreign. Among the Americans, former Congressman Paul Findley (the author of a particularly conspiratorial book entitled *Dare Call It Treason*) deserves notice, while the most outspoken foreigner is Claudia Wright, at one time a correspondent for the *New Statesman* in Great Britain. She now writes both "scholarly" pieces for publications like *Foreign Affairs* and more explicitly partisan ones for the likes of *Ethnos* (the Greek newspaper with intimate connections to the Soviet KGB) and others of comparable objectivity.

1987, in which an anonymous staff member of one of the investigating committees was quoted as saying that the only reason I was not being investigated more aggressively was that "one Pollard case at a time is enough."

Lisker's boss, Senator McClure, was more difficult to read. He had asked a lot of questions about Israel—more than any other member —and seemed to believe the Israelis had done something he didn't like . . . but couldn't quite figure out what it was. I had been the object of some of these questions, so when it came time for my final deposition, I invited him to attend and ask whatever he had on his mind. His office responded to my attorney, and said that he could not make the date as currently scheduled, that he was certain that if he failed to appear, it would be misunderstood, and that he did not want any misunderstanding. They asked for the deposition to be rescheduled.

This was fair enough, and we rescheduled. McClure came, asked his questions—all quite mild—and pronounced himself satisfied. In the end, although he had threatened to write a dissenting statement on Israel, he did not.

Finally, in the summer of 1987, Noel Koch, my former boss at the Pentagon, joined the circus. For three years we had worked closely on counterterrorism, and he had never found reason to question my credentials or my loyalty. Now, with the investigations under way, he went to the Justice Department and accused me of being an Israeli agent. This was automatically forwarded to the Counterintelligence Division of the FBI for action. The bureau investigated, found the charge groundless, and closed the case.

There had never been any evidence of wrongdoing on my part, not in the hearings, the investigations, the media, or elsewhere. The real basis for the various allegations and innuendos (aside from the usual Washington components of personal malice or political ill-will) seems to have been the deeply rooted suspicion that Jews have divided loyalties to Israel and the United States. The accusation of "dual loyalty" has always been a staple of modern anti-Semitism, and its existence at high levels of the American government is exceedingly disappointing, though hardly surprising. Two of those who pushed the allegations against me—Koch and Lisker—are Jews themselves. Shortly after William Webster became Director of Central Intelligence, I spoke to him about the efforts of some of his officials to spread false stories about my relationship with Israel, and noted that those officials had demonstrated not only ignorance of me, but also a lack of understanding of Israel. It was disconcerting to find supposedly knowledgeable intelligence officers believing such nonsense.

In an ideal world, stories of the sort circulated about me (and about Howard Teicher, the director of political-military affairs on the NSC staff, whose only sin in the story was to have followed orders and accompanied McFarlane on the ill-starred trip to Tehran) would be laid to rest once it becomes clear that there is no evidence. In my case, the lack of evidence was manifest: I had undergone several security checks between 1981 and 1986, and three times was awarded clearances for Special Compartmented Intelligence. Teicher held similar clearances over the same period of time. If there had been any reasonable grounds to suspect that he or I was working for a foreign government, these clearances would not have been granted. But in the frenzy of the investigations, there was little room for reasoned analyses.

THE "SECRET GOVERNMENT"

Despite the abundant evidence that most of human activity is the result of error, chance, and confusion, a surprising number of people believe that events are controlled by some purposeful guiding hand. Whether the Masons, the Jews, the arms merchants, the Wall Street tycoons, the Communists, or the "gnomes of Zurich," small groups are credited with unlimited knowledge and near superhuman abilities to control world events. No matter how often these theories are intellectually discredited, they retain their primal appeal. In the course of the Iran-Contra investigations, a particularly elaborate conspiracy theory gained a considerable measure of support from staffers of the joint committees.

The Secret Government theory was basically a replay of some of the anti-CIA exaggerations of the 1960s, according to which past and present CIA officials were able to manipulate most of mankind to their own sinister purposes.

The prime movers in the spread of the Secret Government theory were Daniel Sheehan and his colleagues at the Christic Institute in Washington, D.C. Sheehan had already developed a reputation for his ability to turn a court process into a variation of advocacy journalism, and to raise astonishingly large sums of money ($40,000 per week by late 1987) for his causes. Sheehan had a knack for wedging his way into cases where it was possible to accuse the federal government of conspiracy. Thus, he had made a reputation in the Karen Silkwood case, and had been involved in the Greensboro, South Carolina, case in which members of a Communist political party were attacked by members of the Ku Klux Klan, as well as the investigations into the Attica prison riots (interestingly, Arthur Liman was on the other side of that investigation). In each instance, Sheehan accused the government of the United States of criminal conspiracy, a pattern that carried over into his most outrageous—and politically and financially most successful—allegation, the Secret Government theory.

According to Sheehan and his supporters there was a deadly conspiracy at work behind many of the most important current events. This conspiracy was said to be masterminded by Theodore Shackley, the former CIA official who was involved briefly at the beginning of the Iran initiative (he once met with Ghorbanifar, some months before any government official established contact with the Iranian middleman and relayed to the State Department Ghorbanifar's belief that William Buckley could be ransomed for money). Sheehan and company claim that Shackley has been in charge of an ultra-secret group of murderers, arms merchants, and drug shippers, that has acted in behalf of a far Right-wing agenda for the past twenty years. Hence people like Shackley, Secord, Dutton, and several others designated by the Christic Institute as members of the group, are said to have been originally involved in the conspiracy at the time of their governmental service, and then continued as private citizens. Sheehan believes that when Carter came to office, the conspiracy "went private" for four years, mounted the *contra* operation, and then turned it back over to the CIA once William Casey was at the helm. But wherever it is located, in government or out, Sheehan believed that this is the *real* government of the United States.

As usual with this sort of theory, in the end its advocates believed that the conspiracy was behind almost everything of significance in the past twenty years or so, including the Iran-Contra affair. Several months before the scandal erupted, Sheehan had publicly accused the Secret Government of organizing a vast arms and drug-smuggling network extending from Southeast Asia to Latin America and the southeastern United States, in part to support the *contras,* and in part to finance their own sinister activities. And, in a fund-raising videocassette produced at the time of the public hearings, Sheehan claimed to have uncovered a plot—masterminded by the Pentagon and the Federal Emergency Management Agency—to distribute weapons to "the Soldiers of Fortune group" under cover of an emergency preparedness training exercise, so that the arms could then be sent on to the *contras*.

In May 1986 the Christic Institute, along with Tony Avirgan and

Martha Honey, brought suit in a Miami federal court against twenty-nine presumed members of the great conspiracy for violations of the Neutrality Act. Honey and Avirgan were two American free-lance journalists who had followed radical Third World revolutionary movements for many years. They had written about the black guerrilla war against the white Rhodesian government, Idi Amin's regime in Uganda, and revolutionary movements in Tanzania and South Africa. In the early eighties, they shifted their headquarters from Africa to Central America and operated out of a luxurious home in San José, Costa Rica. Avirgan attracted some attention when he was slightly injured in late 1984 at the bombing of Eden Pastora's press conference. Subsequently, Honey and Avirgan argued that the CIA had been behind the bombing. When a United States attorney inquired about Honey and Avirgan at the American Embassy in San José in 1986, he was told by the CIA station chief that they were either Sandinista agents, or "very close" to the Sandinistas.[13]

Sheehan went on a nationwide speaking tour to promote his cause and raise money for the suit. And although no major newspaper or magazine was able to confirm any of the central claims in Sheehan's theory, he attracted considerable public support. Like many driven people, he has an animal magnetism of considerable power and can generate an emotional following.

In December 1986 I was on a panel with Sheehan and Avirgan at a meeting of the Media Forum in New York City. When Sheehan had finished his presentation, I asked him a hypothetical question: "You have made Shackley the keystone of your theory. He says he has no involvement whatsoever in the Central America story. If he is telling the truth, would you find it necessary to revise your entire theory?" Sheehan replied that he would not, since at most he would have been proven wrong on the identity of one member of the conspiracy. But he was certain of the accuracy of his theory.

Sheehan was not interested in the facts of the case; he simply wanted to espouse his vision of the Secret Government. Meanwhile, in all the investigations, no one turned up any evidence connecting Shackley to Project Democracy, or any of North's enterprises. But the lack of evidence did not deter Sheehan and his supporters from going forward with their suit, forcing all twenty-nine targets to find the time and money to respond to Christic's legalistic crusade. It was not until the spring of 1988 that the Christic case began to come apart, when the

13. See the deposition of Jeffrey Feldman to the joint Iran-Contra committees, p. 53.

Miami court forced Sheehan to release the deposition of his key witness. It turned out that Sheehan's key source believed, not only that Shackley, Secord, and other former CIA and Pentagon officials were involved, but that Henry Kissinger and James Schlesinger were key figures in the conspiracy as well. With mounting evidence that Sheehan's claims rested on the fantasies of such "sources," Secord and Singlaub brought massive libel suits against Christic and its various "sources."

Given the long history of conspiracy theories, it was not surprising that people like Sheehan or organizations like Christic should convince themselves of the existence of a secret government in the United States. It was, however, rather surprising that some staff members of the joint committees and even members of Congress seemed headed in the same direction.

Some members, such as Senator Kerry of Massachusetts, had long embraced a version of the Christic view of the world. This hard-driving, charismatic former leader of the Vietnam Veterans Against the War was a key member of the anti-*contra* forces in the Senate. But his passionate opposition to the Central American policies of the Reagan administration left him vulnerable to some of the fantasies floating around Washington. A year before the Iran-Contra hearings began, Kerry announced his belief in the existence of a *contra* drug network and launched an investigation to prove it. It was an attractive theory, and there were certainly some individuals in the FDN or ARDE who trafficked in narcotics. But it turned out to be a question of individuals, and not the *contra* organizations, that were involved in narcotics. After two years of investigations, even such an outspoken critic of the *contras* as New York Congressman Charles Rangel concluded that there was no evidence that the *contra* movement as such had been supported by narcotics trafficking. At most, a few individuals had been involved, particularly on the Southern Front.[14] Meanwhile, Kerry showed no interest in the demonstrated connection between Fidel Castro and narcotics trafficking into the United States, even though four members of the Central Committee of the Cuban Communist Party had been indicted for running drugs and arms by a federal grand jury in Dade County, Florida.

14. During the course of the investigation, the Republicans hit on the idea of asking Nields's top investigator—Robert A. Bermingham—to look into the allegations of a *contra* drug network. His report, concluding that there was no such connection, was published as Appendix E to the *Report of the Congressional Committees,* Minority Report. Since it was written by the chief investigator for the majority, it carries considerable weight.

In the search for a broad conspiracy, staffers on the Iran-Contra committees played the lead role. The most important were Spencer Oliver, a long-time aide to Florida's Democratic Congressman Dante Fascell, and Pamela Naughton, a Minnesota lawyer who served as an investigator for the House Select Committee and was brought on board by Representative Peter Rodino. Neither of these bought the full version of the Christic Institute's fantasy (Oliver was rather more inclined to accept it than Naughton), but each suspected that Oliver North sat at or near the center of a vast conspiracy that included drug trafficking, subversion, assassination, and even meddling in the American political process.

Oliver took the lead in the investigations, in which he was an experienced and aggressive player. He was a Democratic party stalwart, and the most powerful staffer on the House committee. His father had spent most of his life as a labor organizer before moving to Washington and getting involved in party affairs. Oliver had started in Maryland Democratic politics, then worked his way up to a fairly high staff position at the Democratic National Committee, just in time to be one of the targets of the bugging of DNC officials during the 1972 presidential campaign. Oliver sued CREEP (Nixon's 1972 Committee to Re-elect the President) for damages, and was awarded several hundred thousand dollars.

Oliver's lawsuit was a watershed experience, both for his own attitudes and for his reputation in Washington. On the one hand, the bugging seems to have had a decisive effect on his personality. Ever since, Oliver has manifested both a passionate dislike of Republicans (and, perhaps even more, Democrats who have left the liberal fold), and a weakness for conspiracy theories. He subsequently held a variety of positions, from staff director of the American Council on Young Political Leaders to a six-year stint as Fascell's man on the Helsinki Commission to chief counsel for the House Foreign Affairs Committee (which Fascell chairs). Secure in a close personal and professional relationship with Fascell, Oliver was (and is) a potent force on the Hill.

Oliver believed that North was simply the tip of a vast iceberg, at the base of which lay Bill Casey and the CIA. Oliver suspected that Casey had placed his operatives throughout the bureaucracy, the better to manipulate both policy and operations to his own liking. Furthermore, Oliver looked at the private fund-raising operation as simply one more string on the conspiratorial bow, as he did the alleged drug-running connection to the *contras*. To try to put flesh on his suspicions,

Oliver wanted to investigate all the groups and individuals who had actively supported the administration's Central American policy. Some of these were private persons or groups, others were government employees. All were distinguished by their outspoken support for the *contras*. Among these were Ambassador Faith Whittlesey, Professor Roy Godson, Ambassador Otto Reich, and Mr. Penn Kemble. Referring to such investigations, the Minority Report observed that during the Committees' investigations

> Committee attorneys questioned witnesses about their political activity, religious affiliations, educational backgrounds, employment history, political lineage, roommate's political contributions, social associations, and more.[15]

Oliver was not always able to get full committee support for his campaign, and on occasion simply acted on his own. At one point he unilaterally had a subpoena sent to Heritage Foundation President Edwin Feulner (the Heritage Foundation awarded a $100,000 grant to one of the Channell/Miller organizations, for the support of a Nicaraguan humanitarian organization). Oliver's action so enraged the Republicans that they threatened to subpoena the heads of the left-wing organizations that supported the Sandinistas and the Salvadoran guerrillas. House Committee Chairman Lee Hamilton quashed all the subpoenas, and neither the Heritage Foundation nor left-wing groups like CISPES and NEST were investigated.

In a dramatic confrontation well out of public view, House staffers—led by Oliver—fought to include their conspiratorial theories in the Majority Report. Had they succeeded, the Majority Report would have contained dozens of unproven allusions to "evidence" of plans for political assassination, the manipulation of the American political process, and a vast conspiracy, with North at the center, to seize control of American foreign policy. To his credit, Arthur Liman would have nothing to do with it and told Nields that if the House committee insisted on putting such nonsense in their report, the Senate committee would issue its own, separate report. This threat was effective, and some of the wilder fantasies were excluded from the final document.

Thwarted in his efforts to get his theories published by the committee, Oliver concentrated his efforts on stigmatizing outspoken *contra* supporters.

15. *Report of the Congressional Committees,* Minority Report, p. 514.

THE CHARGE OF "WHITE PROPAGANDA"

The investigation of Ambassador Otto Reich's Office of Public Diplomacy for Latin America and the Caribbean (S/LPD—a bit of alphabet soup meaning Latin American Public Diplomacy, in the office of the Secretary of State) was a typical example of this technique. S/LPD was a Clark creation, prompted by the lack of effective advocacy by the professional bureaucracy for the administration's policies. So in July 1983 Clark mandated the establishment of an interagency office to coordinate public policy on Latin American affairs. S/LPD was consciously modeled on President Carter's vast lobbying effort on behalf of the Panama Canal Treaties, in which State Department officials were sent the length and breadth of the country to explain and defend the president's policies.

Otto Reich was an ideal choice for the position. The son of Cuban immigrants, fluently bilingual, Reich had served in the Agency for International Development's Latin American section, and was intimately familiar with the sociological, political, and cultural details of the region. Moreover, unlike the Foreign Service officers in the department, Reich was a political appointee, and was thoroughly comfortable with the Reagan policies. He and his colleagues took "a very aggressive posture vis-à-vis a sometimes hostile press."[16]

Reich was not beloved of the State Department, for at least three reasons. First was the usual "turf" problem: the Latin American hands (Motley in particular) felt that Reich was an unnecessary appendage to the department and resented his presence there. It was, as they say, nothing personal, anyone in Reich's position would have encountered the same bureaucratic hostility. This made it hard for Reich to operate, for there were endless delays in getting information, even greater slowdowns in obtaining approval for public presentations, and the usual campaign of rumor and leak directed against his operation.

Second was politics. Clark was right to set up a special office for public diplomacy on Central America, for the professionals were generally not in favor of the general thrust of administration policy in the area. I was in a meeting in the State Department in the fall of 1981, around the time of the first Salvadoran elections, when it was proposed that we send some speakers to college campuses to explain our reasons for supporting the government of José Napoleón Duarte. At the time, although Duarte previously had been overthrown, jailed, and tortured

16. *Report of the Congressional Committees*, p. 34.

269

by his military opponents, he was widely reviled as some sort of right-winger in the leading American newspapers and on network news. There was little enthusiasm among the Foreign Service to debate in Duarte's behalf. One of the top professionals in the Latin American Bureau shook his head and said, "they've got their bastards, and we've got ours. Duarte is our bastard, but he's still a bastard. I don't see the point in going out and defending him."

Reich knew the difference between the antidemocratic forces in Salvador (of both Left and Right) and the beleaguered democrat Duarte, and did not hesitate to say so in every public forum he could reach. As Reich told Iran-Contra committee investigators, "attacking the president was no longer cost-free." This earned him the enmity of those Foreign Service professionals who did not believe Duarte was worthy of their support.

Third was a matter of personal jealousy, as Reich became an increasingly visible and effective spokesman for the administration. Success invariably breeds resentment, in the government as elsewhere.

With *contra* aid restored in 1986, Reich's task had effectively been accomplished (and, with Elliott Abrams as assistant secretary of state, the White House could be confident of an aggressive public campaign in behalf of the president's policies), and he was named ambassador to Venezuela. He could not have imagined that he would be dragged into the Iran-Contra investigation and accused of having run an illegal propaganda operation. But that is precisely what happened.

Congressmen Brooks and Fascell (the latter undoubtedly at Spencer Oliver's behest) asked the General Accounting Office to look into S/LPD's activities, and the comptroller general of the United States (who heads the GAO) wrote a preliminary opinion that concluded S/LPD had engaged in questionable lobbying and "propaganda" activities with "funds for publicity or propaganda purposes not authorized by Congress." The Majority Report accepted the GAO's claim that Reich's office had "sought to place op-ed pieces in major papers by secret consultants to the office." The Majority Report termed this "covert propaganda."

There are no "secret consultants" to the State Department (anyone can obtain a full list of consultants simply by filing a Freedom of Information Act request). The word "secret" was used in an effort to smear Reich's operations. But even without the offensive term, the substance of the GAO preliminary report is misleading. The GAO's conclusion rests in large part upon a single memo written by an S/LPD deputy director named Johnathan Miller to Pat Buchanan at the White House, in which Miller bragged about the achievements of his program. The memo was entitled " 'White Propaganda' Operation," in which Miller claimed credit (on behalf of S/LPD) for several minor achievements, ranging from the briefing of an NBC reporter to informing news organizations of the impending arrival of *contra* leader Alfonso Robelo in Washington, to an op-ed piece in the *Wall Street Journal* written by an office consultant. The comptroller general wrote:

> S/LPD arranged for a university professor, who was also paid as a consultant to S/LPD, to write a newspaper article in support of the Administration's Central America policy without alerting readers or, apparently, the newspaper that the government was involved.

The professor in question was John F. Guilmartin, Jr., a retired Air Force lieutenant colonel and former editor of *Air University Review,* who is an expert on the use of helicopters in antiguerrilla warfare. Guilmartin had done a study on the subject for S/LPD, asked if the office had any objection to his writing an op-ed piece on the subject, was told there was no problem, and submitted the article on his own. There was nothing covert, improper or suspicious about it.[17]

Reich had the last laugh, however, for the committees failed to notice that S/LPD was the source of Ollie North's slide show, which caused the Committee Democrats such consternation during the hearings.

There was another Spencer Oliver effort to smear *contra* supporters, closely related to the White Propaganda affair. This was the investigation of NSC senior staffer Walt Raymond, a long-time CIA officer who had changed careers early in the Reagan administration, and devoted his considerable talents to the fledgling field of public diplomacy. Raymond was a model bureaucrat, not a political appointee, and had worked for years to develop more effective presentations of the government's understanding of Soviet, Afghan, Central American, and arms-control issues, as well as to present the administration's

17. There is an interesting question of journalistic ethics, however. Do part-time consultants have an obligation to inform editors that they are consultants? And, if so, are editors obliged to so inform their readers? It is a close call, for a tag line "so-and-so is a part-time consultant" inevitably suggests that the writer is presenting a proadministration view. But one of the reasons it is a good idea for the government to have part-time consultants is that such people present independent opinions, rather than echoing the views of the bureaucracy. One reasonable approach is to tell the editor of the writer's relationship to the government, and if the editor determines that the article is not official policy presented as if it were an independent opinion, there is no need to identify the author as a consultant.

policies more effectively. Oliver hauled him up for depositions, spent hours exposing every possible detail of Raymond's earlier career, and asked leading questions that implied there was still a working relationship between Raymond and his former employers. Oliver was still trying to demonstrate the existence of a grand conspiracy, and still failing. There was no evidence that Raymond had done anything other than his job.

THE CONGRESSIONAL INQUISITION

In any conflict between an individual and a congressional investigating committee, the individual has very limited rights of self-defense. The committee can—and often does—ask for every conceivable bit of information, from financial documentation to personal history about the individual in question, his family (I was asked for all records of my children's bank accounts, for example), and his friends. Any refusal to provide this information puts the individual at risk of being held in contempt. Meanwhile, the committee members can say anything about the individuals they are investigating, regardless of truth, and are quite free of any legal consequences. For members of Congress are virtually immune from defamation suits (you cannot bring a libel or slander action against a Senator or Congressman for actions taken in the conduct of their official business). And although this may seem to encourage the most demagogic tendencies and irresponsible behavior among our elected representatives, the Supreme Court has repeatedly upheld the principle of congressional immunity.

I learned this to my frustration when Senator William Cohen of Maine asked McFarlane—during his public testimony—if he were aware that I had entered the country "with large amounts of cash." McFarlane looked astonished and replied that he hadn't known that. Cohen then changed the subject. During the next intermission, he was surrounded by journalists asking for details of my alleged trips "carrying large amounts of cash." Cohen said that he had misspoken. But he never corrected the impression he had created, nor did Elizabeth Drew, the commentator on PBS's coverage of the hearings. Ms. Drew got quite excited at Cohen's remarks, commenting that it would be quite something "if it turned out that Ledeen took money."

Nothing of the sort had happened during my six years of working for the government. On two occasions prior to my government employment, my company had been paid in cash for overseas projects, and I had brought the money into the United States.

On each occasion, I had declared the funds at Kennedy Airport, deposited them in American banks, and paid taxes on them. Cohen and the committee investigators were aware of this through routine government forms, yet let the damaging misimpression remain. Ms. Drew knew within minutes of her excited commentary that Cohen had provided no evidence that I had taken money in the course of the Iran initiative, yet she, too, failed to correct the record.

There is yet another weapon in Congress' inventory: in addition to the risk of being indicted for perjury, a simple misstatement of the facts carries considerable liability, for it is a crime to "make false statements to Congress." (McFarlane pled guilty in March 1988 to four misdemeanor counts of "misleading Congress.") I was repeatedly reminded by my lawyers to be extremely careful about what I said, and to stick very narrowly to things I remembered clearly. I could not be indicted for failing to remember something, but I could well get into trouble if, in straining to remember, I misled the committees.[18] The result, perhaps contrary to what Congress might have hoped when it passed the law, was to encourage witnesses to say as little as possible, and thus to deprive the Committees and the public at large of potentially useful information.

Once having obtained the information, Congress can then use it as it wishes. Committee members can leak, distort, or make selective use of documentation, virtually without fear of consequences. The impact of such investigations on witnesses is considerable, for a private citizen caught up in the convulsions of a Congress in full investigative ritual is almost certain to be damaged, regardless of his or her "guilt" or "innocence." Newspaper reports stating that one has been called for a deposition are enough to bring clouds of suspicion over one's head. And the unlucky citizen is virtually obliged to obtain legal counsel, which is a burden few people can imagine.

It is easy—unbelievably easy—to run up legal bills of hundreds of thousands of dollars in such investigations. And while the more celebrated figures—the McFarlanes, the Norths, and so forth—found legal firms willing to take the cases *pro bono* (the publicity is good for the firm, and there are still people in Washington who recognize that public servants rarely have a lot of money, but need good legal advice), the less-celebrated individuals often have to foot their own bills. This

18. Those who derided Admiral Poindexter for "failing to remember" so many things would do well to keep this legal question in mind. Most lawyers advise their clients to testify only about matters on which their memory is clear, and after several months—and wildly differing versions of events appearing in the media—even the clearest memory suffers.

works to the advantage of prosecutors. I have no doubt that Judge Walsh would have had a far more difficult time getting a "guilty" plea out of Richard Miller, for example, if Miller hadn't been faced with a Hobson's choice: defending his name at the cost of financial ruination, or cutting his astronomical legal costs but sacrificing his reputation in the process.

Further, Congress feels free to change or ignore their own rules when it suits their purpose. The rules of both the House and Senate state that no testimony may be taken without the presence of a quorum (defined as at least two members, one from each party). The House Iran-Contra committee got around this by defining a quorum as at least *one* member. And both Select committees arranged for "depositions" to be conducted by staff, with the witness under oath, and an official stenographer present. The only difference between "testimony" and "deposition" is that in the latter case, no member was present. In other words, the committees arranged to have the staff take testimony when it suited members' convenience even though it was a clear violation, both of the committees' rules, and of the rules of the House and the Senate.

This willingness to ignore their own rules could also be seen when it came to giving individuals the opportunity to respond to defamatory statements made about them in public session. There were written rules that seemed to ensure that the committees would guarantee the right to reply, but in practice they were a dead letter. I felt I had been slandered by both witnesses and members (Senator Cohen, for example). I therefore demanded my right to reply. It was denied. Even McCarthy had guaranteed that a person defamed in public session could appear before the committee to clear his name, but Inouye called to say that the committee members had voted unanimously not to call me. Four members later told me they had never attended any such meeting, had not voted on the question, and had not heard of any such vote. Representative Hamilton never replied on this point, either to me or to my attorney.

Third, the chairman of the Senate Committee, Daniel Inouye, showed a discouraging lack of precision. He claimed that the director of the National Security Agency, General William Odom, had written to Inouye to confirm that there had been no leaks of classified information from the committees. Odom denied the statement in writing to Inouye (but, with the exception of the *Washington Times*, no major newspaper mentioned the letter of denial). And, on a talk show the Sunday before Admiral Poindexter's testimony, Inouye claimed that the committee had uncovered a potential "smoking gun" document that suggested the president had been informed about the diversion of money from the Iran weapons sales to the *contras*. Not only was there no such document, but the committees had known for nearly six weeks (thanks to Poindexter's private depositions) that Poindexter had not informed the president.

It is difficult to explain the behavior of Inouye, who, prior to the hearings, was widely regarded as one of the fairest members of the Senate. And many of his actions attest to his concern for the national interest. He insisted, for example, that the hearings be as brief as possible, because of the danger that foreign enemies would attempt to exploit the temporary paralysis of the American government. But once the hearings got going, Inouye behaved like an old-fashioned hanging judge.

The responsibility for the committees' disregard of the rights of individuals to respond to false accusations must be shared among the members, the staff, and the lawyers. For if Arthur Liman and John Nields were really committed to fair hearings and establishing the truth, they had an obligation to fight for fair treatment of all concerned, and not simply act as instruments of the committees.

Much of the committees' behavior can only be explained in show business terms. The start of Fawn Hall's testimony, for example, was delayed until the afternoon, so that she could not finish in a single day. The committee members knew she was a star attraction, and wanted to insure a big audience for at least two days.[19]

Finally, the committees could and did use selective leaks to the press as a method of goring witnesses even before they appeared, and of discrediting others who never appeared in public session. By the time the hearings began, it was virtually impossible for any witness to catch up with the great volume of accusations—some true, some wildly inaccurate—that had been spread through the media.

LEAKS

Members of the committees were understandably sensitive about the accusation that Congress was a major source of leaks of classified information. For the argument that Congress was unreliable was used by North and Poindexter to justify lying to Congress. The committees were on weak ground in protesting their reliability, for the two ranking

19. Barbara Matusow, "Made for TV," in *The Washingtonian*, December 1987, p. 216.

275

members of the previous Senate Select Committee on Intelligence (SSCI)—Senators David Durenberger and Patrick Leahy—were both under investigation by their peers for having revealed secret information. Leahy had provided a draft copy of the committee's report on the Iran-Contra affair to NBC News, and Durenberger had given a speech in Palm Beach, Florida, in which he had disclosed that the United States conducted espionage in Israel.

In the Majority Report, the problem of leaks is acknowledged, but the monkey is placed on the administration's back:

> If the Executive Branch has any basis to suspect that any member of the Intelligence Committees breached security, it has the obligation to bring that breach to the attention of the House and Senate Leaders— not to make blanket accusations.[20]

But even when specific leakers have been identified, Congress has taken no action, as in the Durenberger and Leahy cases. Moreover, even during the hearings themselves, selective leaking went on apace. In late May, the former CIA station chief in Costa Rica, "Tomas Castillo," testified in executive session. When the testimony was over, Senator Rudman pointed out—and Chairman Hamilton concurred— that "it would be inappropriate for any members or staff or anyone else to comment on these proceedings" without Hamilton's permission. Hamilton went one step further, and said that it would require a committee vote for such permission to be obtained. The next day, the papers were full of quotations from committee members about "Castillo's" testimony.

THE GREAT LEAKER: THE EXECUTIVE BRANCH

Yet, for all of Congress's various sins, the executive branch was more sinful by far. In keeping with its surrender of any slight claim of executive privilege, the White House authorized the release of an unprecedented quantity of classified material to the committees and to Judge Walsh. Sometimes, the White House itself released secret documents, as when the Presidential Finding of mid-January 1986 (authorizing the renewal of the Iran initiative) was given to the press. Apparently no one had considered the consequences of releasing the actual copy of a Finding (as opposed to simply handing out its text), but the intelligence community winced. The White House had un-

20. *Report of the Congressional Committees*, Majority Report, p. 14.

wittingly enabled the KGB to forge more authentic-looking "Findings" in the future. Up to that time, Soviet efforts at forged Findings had been caught because the KGB had invariably made some mistake in the format of such documents.

But even this embarrassing decision was nothing compared to the damage done by the release, and subsequent publication, of CIA and NSC documents. The major hemorrhage occurred in the *Report of the Tower Commission*, which was the White House's own creation. It will be recalled that the commission was headed by three "wise men," former Secretary of State Muskie, former National Security Advisor Scowcroft, and former Senator Tower. With the president instructing everyone to cooperate fully with all the investigations, all the available documentation was provided, even though the Tower Commission had no subpoena power.

The wise men were the best chance for a rational investigation, and in some ways they lived up to their billing. They recognized that the errors of the Iran-Contra affair were not due to a flawed structure, but to human mistakes, and they resisted the temptation to recommend an overhaul of the national security system. In the face of the congressional power grab, they stood firm against proposals to make the national security adviser subject to Senate confirmation, and found satisfactory the congressional oversight of the intelligence community. They attributed the errors to human shortcomings, particularly the combination of the president's "management style" and the failure of his top advisers—all of them—to insist that he face the issues and make firm decisions.

It was a superficially attractive critique, but it did not fit the facts, at least in the case of the Iran initiative. Weinberger and Shultz had certainly expressed their opposition to the arms sales to Iran, even if they could and should have been far more vigorous and sustained in fighting the policy. The major error in the Tower Commission analysis lies in the president's role. Far from being a detached observer, or a laid-back overseer of the foreign policy process, the president played a very active role at the beginning of Iran-Contra, and intervened as late as the winter of 1985–86 to insist, over the objections of his secretaries of State and Defense, that the Iran initiative continue. The president wanted the hostages out, and wanted the *contras* on the battlefield, and was prepared to run substantial risks in order to achieve those ends. So it was not a question of "management style" (a euphemism for the view that the president was out of touch on foreign policy matters) at all, but rather the opposite: the president drove the

Iran initiative, and inspired Project Democracy. Later on, to be sure, many of the details of those policies were kept from him, and we can readily believe Secretary Shultz's description of the president's strong reaction of dismay when he heard of the concessions offered the Iranians on the question of the Da'wa terrorists. But these were details of execution, not basic questions of policy. The basic policies were those the president strongly desired, and they were put into effect because of his formal approval.

Further, the Tower Commission was unable to understand the Iran initiative, for the same reasons as the congressional Select committees would misunderstand it later on. First, they totally accepted the CIA analysis of Ghorbanifar. If, as the agency experts maintained, Ghorbanifar were totally unreliable, it was tempting to conclude—or at least suspect—that anyone who supported Ghorbanifar's continued participation in the affair was either crazy or corrupt. Hence the tendency to believe that money was the fuel of the Iran initiative, a tendency reinforced by the stories spread by North and Nir about me and the original Israelis.

Second, there was poor understanding of Iran. The Ayatollah's regime was perceived as monolithic, and the committees did not seem to know what to do with the information that we had established contact with leading Iranian officials who said they wanted to change the policies of the regime. Shultz and Weinberger both reinforced the mistaken impression that all Iranians were bloodthirsty anti-American fanatics. This xenophobic oversimplification carried the day. So far as I can tell, neither the Tower Commission nor the Select committees ever made a serious effort to grapple with the implications of the opening proposed by the Senior Iranian Official.

Third, the commission members were at a loss to establish what had actually happened, and this was the inevitable result of their fondness and respect for McFarlane. McFarlane had worked for both Scowcroft and Tower, and Rhett Dawson, the chief counsel to the commission, had been a colleague of McFarlane's. They were all predisposed to believe McFarlane, but this was made a bit difficult by the fact that he changed his testimony on several points. The wise men ended by accepting McFarlane's final version of events, but there was no more reason to do that than to accept his first account. The fact of the matter—a central element in all the efforts to reconstruct the events of 1985 and 1986—was that McFarlane no longer had a coherent picture of the overall story.

A few months later, in his public testimony, McFarlane responded to a question from Rodino by saying, "I deserve responsibility and I ought to be prosecuted to the full extent of the law and sent away."[21] Plagued by guilt and an exaggerated sense of personal responsibility, his government career in ruin and his own ideals in violent conflict, McFarlane could not be relied upon to present a full picture of what had happened. He had good recollection of some single events, but no overall view of the period. But he was the only major figure in the story who testified to the Tower Commission (North, Poindexter, and Secord all declined the invitation to appear). It was therefore not surprising that the wise men had a hard time arriving at a full picture.

But if they can be excused for the understandable confusions and errors in reconstructing events, there was little justification for their decision to make public virtually all of the information they received, including lengthy excerpts from classified documents. The wise men were asked to evaluate the functioning of the National Security Council system, including the recent events. It did not seem like a blank check for a massive exposé, but, citing the president's admonition to the commission to permit "all the facts to come out," the wise men decided to publish everything they could reasonably include in the *Report*. This included private communications between NSC staff members, highly classified CIA reports, estimates, and memoranda, along with accounts of secret intelligence-gathering operations, in which some sensitive sources were publicly identified for the first time. One of the people named in these documents disappeared in the Middle East a few weeks after his name was published in the *Tower Report*.

The only concern evinced by the wise men about the propriety of publishing all this material was that it be "properly declassified," and the various agencies were urged to race through a pell-mell declassification procedure that virtually guaranteed the release of information that should have remained secret. There was insufficient time available for proper consideration of all the documents, too few substantive experts available for a thorough review, and an excessive burden was placed on some otherwise excellent staff (such as Brenda Reger, senior director for information policy and security review at the NSC, who on one occasion went seventy-two hours without sleep in order to manage the declassification process). The primary burden for protecting secrets fell upon the agencies themselves, and they did not acquit themselves with distinction. The CIA was particularly inattentive to the protection of certain sources and methods involved in the Iran initiative.

If one reads the material released by the CIA, one is immediately

21. McFarlane, published testimony, p. 236.

struck by one aspect of it: everything imaginable about Ghorbanifar, his activities, contacts, friends, and enterprises was included. No such information is provided about the second channel, the one that the agency favored. One does not have to be an expert on intelligence to figure out what happened. The agency officials took care to do the maximum damage to the hated Ghorbanifar, but strained to protect their own sources and friends. By releasing everything they could about Ghorbanifar, they did their best to put him and all his friends in maximum jeopardy. But virtually nothing came out about the second channel, leaving journalists to guess at the identities of the two Revolutionary Guards officials who constituted it. The commission, straining to release everything releasable, and operating under pressure of a tight deadline, had neither the time nor the manpower to sift through the material and make a reasoned judgment on what should be published.

The same process of selective release was used on agency employees. Anyone within the CIA who had argued for working with Ghorbanifar was certain to have damaging information about him appear in print. The case of Charles Allen was the most spectacular, with the Tower Commission and the congressional committees publishing a remarkable quantity of classified memoranda that revealed not only many of Ghorbanifar's secrets, but CIA sources and methods as well. No such release took place from the officials of the Operations Directorate who supported the dumping of Ghorbanifar and the use of the second channel.

The three wise men were uniquely experienced in national security affairs and should have been sensitive to the consequences of excessive disclosure. All three recognized the importance of keeping secrets. All three should have realized that by publishing so much secret information, they would frighten foreign sources from sharing information with the United States, whether these be countries or individuals. Indeed, this is precisely what happened as a result of the investigations and hearings. As the *New York Times* reported on August 9, 1987,

> Revelations in the Iran-contra hearings . . . have shaken the confidence of foreign officials in American secret operations, Government officials say. They add that the disclosures have prompted the intelligence services of some friendly nations to share less information with the United States.

Once the president's own commission had failed to exercise proper restraint, it could hardly be expected that the Congress would. Tower,

Muskie, and Scowcroft are serious people, and are alert to the dangers of releasing secret information. If they failed to restrict the massive outpouring of classified material, it was inevitable that the same would be done by the more than one hundred committee staffers who, in the words of one of their ranks, "were the engine of the investigation."[22] The Majority Report and the hundreds of depositions and appendices published by the joint Select committees contain a gold mine of secret information, from the details of the NSC filing system, to descriptions of Lebanese who helped the United States locate hostages, from secret conversations with foreign allies to transcripts of secret tape recordings of sensitive conversations. These publications compounded the damage done by the *Tower Report*, convincing allies and potential friends around the world that they should think deeply before sharing sensitive information with any American official.

THE COUP THAT FAILED: THE COLLAPSE OF THE HEARINGS

Arthur Liman wrote a strategy memo to his Senate masters in February 1987 in which he proposed that the hearings be staged to build up to North's testimony. At that time, Liman wrote, "North would be immunized—but not against the rigorous cross-examination he would have to undergo by the senators in full view of the American people."

Rarely has an event turned out to be so totally different from expectations as the testimony of Oliver L. North.[23] The committee members and staffers expected a ritual sacrifice, with North the victim. Hours were spent discussing what to do if, as many of them fully expected, North broke down in the witness chair. There had been so much damaging testimony about North that they could not imagine anything other than a few flashy *muletas* from the matadors to paralyze the bull, and then the death thrust.

By the time Charles Cooper of the Justice Department testified that he would not trust North to tell the truth, even under oath, there was only one member of the committees who was still waiting to hear from

22. Dennis Teti, "The Coup That Failed," in *Policy Review*, Fall 1987. Teti was a member of the staff of Congressman James Courter of New Jersey.

23. In one of his more entertaining errors, Inouye had announced, at the end of the previous session, that the next witness would be "Lt. Col. Oliver J. North." I like to think that Inouye was remembering an earlier national hero, one with a certain superficial physical similarity to North: Oliver J. Dragon, of Kukla, Fran, and Ollie.

North before concluding that the lieutenant colonel was a goner. That was Senator Hatch of Utah. During Cooper's testimony Mitchell passed a note down to Hatch: "You're the last passenger on the North Express. There is still time to get off." Hatch read the note, and made a thumbs-up signal back to Mitchell. He would wait until all the evidence was in. But the rest of the committee was by then convinced that North was dead meat.

Instead, North came forward as an unrepentant advocate of the position everyone had assumed Ronald Reagan to have held all along: victory for the *contras*, enthusiastic use of covert actions to advance American interests, and an all-out effort to save American hostages in Lebanon. He vigorously defended the right of the executive branch to conduct foreign policy, and conceded that it was sometimes necessary to lie to the American public in order to keep things secret from America's enemies. By the end of the week, it was clear that the bullfight was likely to produce several mortally wounded matadors, even if the bull would eventually die.

North's testimony showed at least two important things:

• First, North demonstrated the great national political appeal of a forthright declaration of the administration's maximum objectives in Central America. By the time he had finished with his testimony, public opinion had undergone a sea change, at least temporarily, in favor of the *contras*.

• Second, North showed how to behave when one has become the object of a congressional feeding frenzy: the best defense is a direct appeal to public opinion. Televised hearings usually work in favor of the committees, but North (and his feisty lawyer, Brendan Sullivan) showed that this need not always be so. Indeed, a live television appearance where one can confront one's accusers is probably the best chance a citizen has of overcoming a hostile media campaign.

North had stopped a massive political assault on the executive branch. The seemingly preordained scenario—the martyrdom of Oliver North and the end of the Reagan Era—had been shattered, and there might yet be an opportunity for a coherent policy to be forged. But it was not to be. The president was groggy, his own understanding of what he had been fighting for undermined by the welter of contradictory testimony, and the lack of a will to fight on the part of his own generals. Shultz in the State Department, Howard Baker, the president's new chief of staff, Frank Carlucci, the newly sworn-in national security adviser, and White House adviser David Abshire had already accepted the inevitability of defeat, and prematurely surrendered to the congressional forces.

Shultz's testimony was perhaps the low point of the proceedings. For instead of taking the opportunity to demand coherence from Congress, to stress that foreign policy could not be conducted in brief spurts defined by the budgetary cycle of Capitol Hill, and to remind the committees and the nation that America had to have an Iran policy and a strategy for winning the Central American struggle, Shultz adopted a tactic of appeasement. Under cover of the slogans of "accountability" and "working together," he accepted virtually all of the congressional demands for a greater role in policy-making. He sought to protect the position of the State Department at the expense of the authority of the White House. He complained at not having been informed, when it was manifestly clear he had known the main lines of the Iran initiative and had not wanted to know more. He refused to be briefed by me in the summer of 1986, and on other occasions asked Poindexter not to tell him "things he did not need to know." Shultz had expressed his opposition to the Iran initiative, but did not want to know the details. Thus his opposition was episodic, ineffective, and uninformed. Despite his protestations, he knew too much to be innocent, but too little to be secretary of state.

North's victory was short-lived. Less than a year later, Congress voted down aid to the *contras*, who, like a Pavlovian dog submitted to a series of positive and negative stimuli, entered into a state of confusion and paralysis. Unable to depend upon the United States, and barely surviving yet another Sandinista invasion of their remaining Honduran bases, the *contra* commanders secretly decided to come to terms. Without informing the American government, the *contras* signed a cease-fire, and the Nicaraguan Democratic Resistance filed into designated areas to surrender their arms. Back in Washington, yet another national security adviser, Gen. Colin Powell, expressed his amazement. He had told them to hold on just a little while longer. Things had seemed to be going better on Capitol Hill, and there was a chance for some military aid after all. But the back of the democratic resistance had finally been broken.

10. The Aftermath and Some Unanswered Questions

Following the hearings, there was a general purge in the CIA, and the heavy hand of Judge William Webster, Casey's successor as director of Central Intelligence, fell upon some of those who had been directly involved in the affair. Webster had to come to terms with Congress, and the oversight committees were demanding clear evidence that "lessons had been learned." Webster understood political imperatives, having earlier restored the temporarily lost luster of the FBI, but he insisted on an orderly, judicial process.

At the end of 1986, the CIA carried out its own internal investigation of the agency's performance in the Iran-Contra affair, and the inspector general, Carroll Hauver, recommended that stern disciplinary action be taken against two DO officers from the Latin American Division. The basis for his action was that they had not told him the truth during his investigation. He had not concluded that they had acted improperly, but that question was moot, since he had not gotten all the facts.

There were four other officials of the agency who were prime objects of the internal investigation: Alan Fiers, the Central American Task Force chief from 1983 to 1986, Dewey Clarridge, Charles Allen, and Clair George. All were cleared by Hauver, but all remained potential targets for Webster, as for Judge Walsh's ongoing investigation in his lavish offices across the river. Webster decided to have another investigation, and for chief investigator he chose Russell Bruemmer, a young FBI lawyer who had caught Webster's eye at the bureau.

Bruemmer conducted his investigation in the fall of 1987, after all the congressional testimony was completed, and he went about it in

284

a systematic way, reading all the agency documents on the affair, as well as the public testimony and depositions. Oddly, he did not interrogate the men themselves, limiting himself to a brief query: Did they have anything to add to what they had already said? It was a difficult question for the CIA officers to answer, since they did not know what the problems were, and it seemed peculiar to many of them that Bruemmer never gave them the opportunity to respond to what he took to be the case against them.

The "verdict" arrived in time for Christmas 1987. The two Central American officers were to be fired. Alan Fiers, the Chief of the Central American Task Force, was also to be removed. Clarridge was to be reprimanded, demoted, and removed from his post at the head of the counterterrorist unit. Allen was to be reprimanded.

These were serious punishments, for even a simple reprimand at CIA automatically blocks any promotions or raises for two years, and deprives the officer in question of any bonus for outstanding service.

Fiers protested to Webster, and informed the director that if he were asked to leave, half his staff would walk out with him. Fiers maintained he had done nothing wrong and would challenge the decision. Webster reconsidered, told Fiers he could stay at his post for a while longer, but insisted on the reprimand. A few months later, Fiers was offered a position in Europe, found it unattractive, and resigned. He is now in private business.

Clarridge decided not to protest the demotion or the reprimand, although he felt they were grossly unfair. He was charged with having failed to inform his superiors of his activities, particularly in connection with the Hawk missile shipments to Iran in November 1985. A CIA official in Europe had testified that he had informed Clarridge that there were Hawks on the planes to Iran, at a time when Clarridge was maintaining that the planes carried "oil drilling equipment." This was in fact the cover story put out by North, and Clarridge vehemently claimed that he had not known there were Hawks on board the planes until after the event.

The evidence was in fact inconclusive, as the Hauver investigation had revealed. The CIA official in Europe claimed to have sent a cable about the Hawks, but none could be found. While it is conceivable that Clarridge destroyed the cable, it is difficult, since a copy of such cables automatically goes to the office of the Deputy Director for Operations (Clair George, in this case). George could recall no such cable.

The other people in a position to testify about the existence of a cable about the Hawks were the two CIA communicators at either end of the transmission. The communicator in Langley did not remember seeing it. The communicator who had been in Europe had since moved to an African post, and, when first asked about the matter, had no recollection of a cable. He was later asked to come to Washington for further questions, and returned via his former post. By the time he got to Washington, his memory had improved dramatically, and he now not only recalled the cable with graphic clarity, but remembered being quite angry about it, since a relative of his had been a hostage in the American embassy in Tehran in 1979–80. Hauver's investigators found this peculiar, but possible.

Finally, the CIA official in Europe had said he had shown the cable to the deputy chief of mission in Lisbon. But the DCM could remember only hearing about the CIA official's intention to send such a cable, but did not believe he had actually seen a copy of it.

Since there was no convincing evidence against Clarridge, no disciplinary action was recommended by Hauver.

Clarridge had also been accused of keeping secret a trip to one country to discuss, among other things, the possibility of aid to the *contras*. To this, Clarridge responded that by the time he actually travelled there, the instruction to discuss the *contras* had been cancelled, and, furthermore, permission for the discussion had previously been given by both Assistant Secretary of State Motley and Shultz himself.

Clarridge hired a lawyer, protested his treatment, and asked to be kept in his counterterrorist position. Webster relented, but in the spring of 1988 Clarridge was offered an unattractive position at a low level of the agency in Langley. He resigned in mid-May, after thirty-three years in the CIA, and is now in private business.

Allen was accused of being "insufficiently forthcoming" during the internal investigations. The basis for this was the fact that, during the course of Hauver's investigation, Allen discovered four tapes that he had earlier misplaced. The inspector general found no reason to recommend disciplinary action against Allen. Bruemmer did.

The verdict against Allen was particularly perplexing, since he was the only person in the American government who had spotted the diversion of funds from the arms sales to Iran, and who had brought the matter to the attention of his superiors. In October 1986 Allen wrote a detailed memorandum to Casey about the diversion and brought it to Robert Gates. The two of them went to Casey, who immediately called up Poindexter and, as we have seen, urged the national security adviser to raise the matter with White House counsel as soon as possible.

Nonetheless, Bruemmer and Webster judged Allen to have been "insufficiently forthcoming," and issued a reprimand.

Politics are unfair, and Washington is the capital of American politics, so no one was particularly surprised at the CIA purges. It made eminent political sense for Judge Webster to clean house, but it delivered a damaging blow to agency morale. For Fiers, Allen, and Clarridge, while all strong personalities and therefore people who had made their share of enemies, were highly-respected professionals. No one had accused them of criminal activity, and no one could possibly accuse them of incompetence. The lesson was clear: don't be aggressive, don't take chances, go strictly by the book, cover your ass at all times.

Those CIA officers who had opposed the use of Ghorbanifar did much better. The NE Division chief, his deputy, and "Patrick" were all promoted, and currently hold three of the best positions in the agency.

In the winter of 1987–88, Gates, who had survived the storm, wrote a fascinating article for *Foreign Affairs* in which he argued that the CIA was "equidistant" between the executive and legislative branches of the federal government. It was a public confirmation of the successful aggrandizement of congressional power during the investigations. Henceforth, the agency would serve two masters.

There was also a purge at the NSC, but without the legal niceties of Webster's pruning at the agency. The new national security adviser, Frank Carlucci, understood the political climate at least as well as Webster, and in short order, every person associated with the Iran-Contra affair was removed, sometimes with lightning speed. Even the secretaries were not immune. Fawn Hall was demoted and given a job at the Pentagon handling personnel files. The object of a particularly vulgar sexist campaign in the media, she nonetheless demonstrated rare qualities of dignity and common sense, thereby confounding those who insisted on describing her as the sex symbol of the affair. Having been denied the secretarial career she desired, she is preparing for a new career.

UNANSWERED QUESTIONS

The role of Vice President George Bush has been a burning issue ever since the scandal broke.

Bush was a loyal vice president, supporting Reagan's policy. He had reservations about the Iran initiative, of a sort we have grown to

287

associate with many top officials at CIA: he was concerned about Israel's role, fearing the Israelis might gain leverage over the United States. So far as we know, he never expressed concern about any aspect of the Central American affair.

There is a minor mystery concerning Bush. In August 1986 Donald Gregg, the vice president's national security adviser, was briefed on the North/Secord/Dutton resupply operation by an old friend, a Cuban-American named Felix Rodriguez. Rodriguez was a former CIA officer whom Gregg had known for several years, and had gotten involved on the Salvador side of the Central American action. He had proposed an anti-guerrilla program for the Salvadoran government that Gregg found sufficiently interesting to recommend to National Security adviser Clark. Rodriguez had helped Gadd and Secord secure space and landing rights at Illopango Airport in San Salvador, and subsequently worked on the *contra* resupply program. It was he who informed Gregg—at the August meeting—about the roles of Clines and Secord. Rodriguez was very unhappy about his colleagues, and told Gregg that Clines and Secord were overcharging the *contras* for weapons, sometimes as much as three times the fair market value of the merchandise.

Gregg was a long-time CIA professional from the analytical side of the agency and was extremely upset to learn from Rodriguez about the involvement of Clines and Secord. Worried that the taint of Clines's previous involvement with the renegade CIA officer Edwin Wilson would spill over onto the administration, Gregg complained about Clines (and Secord as well) to North. But, according to Gregg's deposition to the joint committees, he never discussed the matter with the vice president.

The minor mystery stems from the fact that when Rodriguez came to brief Gregg in April 1986—that is, four months before the time when Gregg acknowledged being informed of Project Democracy—the appointment schedule indicated that the subject for discussion was "*contra* resupply." Gregg cannot account for that suggestive entry. Rodriguez, Gregg, and Bush aide Sam Watson all deny there was any discussion of the *contras*. And Rodriguez has denied it not only in public, but to many of his closest friends. Bush says he "never, ever" discussed *contras* with Rodriguez. Lacking any evidence to the contrary, such unanimity has to be believed. The mystery, therefore, is a literary one: How did "*contra* resupply" get onto the appointment calendar? It's not the sort of phrase that pops into a secretary's mind out of the blue, after all.

In the Iran initiative, Bush was not a player. I never heard his name mentioned in all my activities and contacts. However, he did play a major role in the minds of the Iranians. They thought he was the most powerful man in the world, hence the man pulling all the strings on the Iran initiative. He actually had a code name among the Iranians: they called him "Battri," because the best-selling automobile battery in Iran is the Busch. So from time to time, someone in the American government would learn of a communication between two Iranians, referring to a powerful American named "Battri." That was always the vice president.

There is a long memorandum, written by Bush's assistant Craig Fuller, summarizing a conversation between Bush and Nir in Jerusalem on the 27th of July, 1986. Nir briefed Bush on the Iran initiative, beginning to end. It is not the sort of briefing one gives to someone who has been "in the loop"; it was designed to give the vice president an overall picture of everything that has happened, complete with the rationale.

Thus, so far as I can tell, and so far as the available documents show, Bush was not a major participant in the Iran-Contra affair, and efforts to drag him into it in some way or other seem to be forced. If Secretary of State Shultz is held to have been largely extraneous, Bush is even more so.

THE SAUDIS

Adnan Khashoggi informed King Fahd of the Iran initiative at its inception, and the king raised no objection. It suited Saudi purposes to have America involved with Iran, for to the extent that the United States could influence Iranian behavior, the Saudis felt more secure. Fahd's tacit approval seems to be the extent of Saudi involvement, but it is a crucial element of the story nevertheless, for when the scandal erupted in November 1986 the administration was widely criticized for having taken actions that would allegedly upset the "moderate Arab countries." Saudi Arabia is the leading such country, yet the Saudis were not upset about our involvement with the Iranians, and can fairly be said to have encouraged the Iran initiative at the beginning. Fahd had only to shake his head to dissuade Khashoggi.[1]

1. There is some suggestive circumstantial evidence hinting at a somewhat larger Saudi role. See John Wallach and Janet Wallach, "The Man Who Knew Too Much," in *Regardie's* (March 1987). John Wallach is the diplomatic correspondent for the Hearst newspapers.

OTHER FRIENDS AND ALLIES

Several other countries knew about the Iran initiative. One country knew because the Iranians told the story to a trade delegation in Tehran in early 1986. At least some members of the British government also knew, probably because they were informed by the White House. The Italian military intelligence service—SISMI—knew something about the arms sales to Iran, but not enough to have anything approaching a full picture.

Other countries were ignorant of American activities, but were doing the same thing themselves. These include both Western and Soviet bloc countries and the People's Republic of China.

Thus, the claims by American politicians and commentators, that our friends and allies around the world would be furious to learn about the American program, were somewhat overstated. There is no doubt that many of them were disappointed, and others—who had refrained from selling arms to Iran at our request—felt cheated (and assumed Operation Staunch had been a subterfuge to corner the Iranian market for American arms). But there was far less moral outrage than has been suggested.

WHO KNEW ABOUT NORTH'S ACTIVITIES?

North testified that he thought several people knew the essentials about Project Democracy: McFarlane, Poindexter, Abrams, Adm. Art Morreau, Casey, and others, like Ambassador Tambs (our man in Costa Rica), Alan Fiers, and Dewey Clarridge. Morreau and Casey are dead. There is no doubt that Casey knew almost everything about North's Central American activities. McFarlane and Abrams say they did not know the details, and that may well be true, for in a certain sense almost everyone in the government—whether the executive or legislative branch—involved in the Central American debate "knew," at least in a general sense, what North was up to. Everybody "knew" that North had found ways to raise money for the *contras*, and most everybody had a sensation that he was doing a lot more.

Everybody "knew" that whatever North was doing was very, very secret, and was likely to be very, very controversial. To know the details of his activities was to risk engaging oneself in the controversy, if it ever erupted. Thus, most people decided that they didn't want to know—concretely and in detail—precisely what North was up to. Poindexter put it nicely in his deposition:

LIMAN: Was there really a point of view that you had that you should not share the information about what the NSC was doing to keep the contras going with the other cabinet officers? That's correct?

POINDEXTER: That's correct.

LIMAN: Did you notice on their part a point of view that they shouldn't ask too many questions?

POINDEXTER: That's exactly right.

LIMAN: Was it ever said in those words, did anyone say "we just don't want to know"?

POINDEXTER: . . . by and large that was the view of the cabinet officers and a lot of other people in Government, but I also think that was the view of many people in Congress.

LIMAN: What do you base that on?

POINDEXTER: . . . in August or sometime in late '86, a resolution was introduced on the floor of the House to require the President to provide documentation on the NSC activities, and it was referred to three of the committees of the House, and the House Armed Services Committee voted it out with a negative report.

By that time, it was relatively common knowledge that there was a lot of speculation that Colonel North was involved, but you know all of that put together told me that people didn't want to know.[2]

So, while everyone "knew" North was running the Central American operation, hardly anyone "knew" (in detail) what he was doing. There were only two questions on everyone's mind:

- Was it authorized?
- Was it legal?

It was evident that McFarlane first, and Poindexter later, had authorized North's activities (and North had created the impression that the president was *au courant*, and approved). That took care of the first question. And on the second matter, many people asked North if all his activities were legal (I once asked him myself). He always said that everything had been checked out "with the lawyers." So that took care of the second question. In keeping with the "need to know" principle, most of North's colleagues felt they "knew" enough.

Nonetheless, it is hard to believe that North's colleagues in the Iran phase of the affair did not know about the diversion of funds. Ghorbanifar talked about it all the time, and all the principal CIA officers

2. Poindexter, Published Deposition, 1167 ff.

(the NE Division chief, his deputy, Cave, and Allen) knew that the Iranians were being charged a fortune for TOWs and Hawk spare parts. The Iranians in the second channel repeatedly asked for money, and it must have been obvious that Hakim had only found the channel by promising payoffs to everyone along the line. Cave testified that he eventually grew suspicious "when he learned that the Iranians were paying significantly more for the U.S. arms than the CIA was receiving, and heard speculation of a diversion to the *contras*."[3] But he didn't report it. Allen did figure it out and reported his suspicions, first to the head of the Intelligence Directorate (Richard Kerr), then to Gates and Casey. So far as we know, neither the CIA's NE Division chief nor his deputy ever expressed concern. Yet both of them were promoted, and Cave continues to work as a consultant to CIA. Only Allen, the sole whistle-blower in the crowd, was punished for his efforts.

Finally, there is the question of the president's knowledge, and approval, of North's activities. North testified that he believed the president knew a lot, and approved of it all, and those who worked with North are unanimous in saying that North certainly appeared to believe it. But all the evidence we have confirms the president's ignorance of the diversion of funds to the *contras*, as well as of details like the nine-point plan, including the promises to help pressure the Kuwaitis to release the Da'wa prisoners.

There is one additional vignette that indicates the president was distinctly unhappy with what he learned about North's activities after the scandal broke. When McFarlane attempted suicide, the president was informed of it, along with the most recent accounts of North's activities, during a meeting in the Oval Office. His reaction was terse and to the point. He shook his head sadly, and said, "the wrong man tried to kill himself."

OLIVER NORTH

Oliver North was a great talent and a great risk. The American government needs people like North, but such people require good management and careful supervision. With proper guidance, they are capable of extraordinary accomplishments, as North's considerable achievements demonstrate. Without it, they can produce equally extraordinary trouble. North did not get much careful supervision during Iran-Contra, and was forced to make decisions for which he lacked

3. *Tower Report*, pp. 158–59.

sufficient experience and understanding. Secord testified that North was treated "like the old army mule," loaded down with heavier and heavier burdens until he finally fell.

It's an effective metaphor, but a bit misleading, for North's work load was in large part his own making. He wanted to carry the heaviest possible burden and fought fiercely to obtain it. Moreover, the lack of supervision was not so much the result of management failures by McFarlane and Poindexter as of the unexpected crises that struck the top people at the NSC: McFarlane's psychological travails in 1985, and the death of Don Fortier in 1986. Had McFarlane been under less strain, or had Poindexter had more time to devote to North's projects, things might have gone better.

North, Poindexter, and McFarlane were driven by noble ambitions (as was Secord, at least in part), yet possessed tragic flaws that led them to make decisive errors for which they paid with their careers. The combination of their personalities and the force of circumstances made their fall inevitable, and the final days of Oliver North provided a dramatic tension and ultimate catharsis as gripping as any classical tragic ending. No fictional drama could offer more.

How Did the Media Miss the Story of the Iran Initiative?

The unsolved mystery about the media is, how did they miss the Iran initiative? Half the world knew about it. Assistant Secretary of State Armitage once told me that he had learned a lot about it from foreign diplomats. One country had sent a trade delegation to Tehran, and the Iranians had told them all about their dealings with the United States. So they raised it with Armitage. But, at least as late as the summer of 1986, no American journalist wrote about it. Why?

One main reason was a failure to understand the nature of terrorism. The Hezbollah had taken several American hostages. From time to time, a hostage was released. Why? The journalists, by and large, were content to tell themselves that the terrorists (a) had a seizure of good will; or, (b) wanted publicity; or, (c) had some devious purpose that could not be discerned. If they had reasoned from first principles, they would have seen that since a hostage had been released, *the terrorists must have gotten something in return*. Once that truth had been acknowledged, the rest was simply a matter of making enough telephone calls around Washington, Tel Aviv, and Jerusalem (or perhaps even Tehran) to get the facts.

WHERE ARE THEY NOW?

EDEN PASTORA is hunting sharks in Costa Rica, returning to the job he held before the Sandinista Revolution.

AL SCHWIMMER is doing what he has always done: helping his friend Shimon Peres on discreet missions throughout the world.

YAKOV NIMRODI has dedicated himself to the discovery of what Amiram Nir really did, and to the expansion of his own financial empire. He recently purchased one of the largest real-estate companies in Israel.

DAVID KIMCHE has founded the Israel Council on Foreign Relations and is involved in private business.

MANUCHER GHORBANIFAR, against all the odds, survived. Once the true story of the deliberate overcharges by the Americans emerged at the congressional hearings during the testimony of Albert Hakim, the Iranian leaders realized that Ghorbanifar had not cheated them. Within a few months, he was restored to his role as privileged emissary from Iran to the West. He played a major role in the release of the French hostages in Lebanon in 1988.

ADNAN KHASHOGGI is fighting for financial survival, beset by numerous lawsuits in the United States and Europe. The yacht is gone, as are some of the sumptuous airplanes, but his life-style seems as vigorous and luxurious as ever.

BUD McFARLANE is writing a book about his experiences and his thoughts about American foreign policy, and is in private business.

DONALD REGAN is now a radio commentator, business consultant, and lecturer. His White House memoirs were published in May 1988.

GEORGE CAVE is a consultant in Washington, D.C.

JOHN McMAHON is a senior vice-president at Lockheed, in southern California.

AMIRAM NIR fell from grace in Jerusalem. On the eve of Ghorbanifar's testimony to the Tower Commission in late 1986, Nir flew to Geneva and met with Ghorbanifar. The trip was not authorized, and when word of it leaked in Israel, Nir was summoned by Prime Minister Yitzhak Shamir for an explanation. Nir offered an unconvincing story: he said that he happened to be passing through Geneva and met Ghorbanifar at the airport. Shamir did not believe it, and Nir was relegated to the bureaucratic equivalent of Siberia. He retained his post as adviser to the prime minister on counterterrorism, but played no policy role. He lost his access to the prime minister and was isolated by the intelligence community. Finally, in March 1988, he was fired and returned to private life. Of the central figures in the Iran-Contra affair, only he has remained totally silent. He has not testified in public, has given no interviews, and has provided no published deposition. Insofar as anyone may have something dramatically new to add to our knowledge of Iran-Contra, it is likely to be Amiram Nir.

Index

Index

Index

Index

Index

Index

Somalia, 12
Somocistas, 31
Somoza, Anastasio, 11, 30, 31, 37, 40, 41,
   44, 46, 48, 51, 53, 54, 57, 58
South Vietnam, 81, 145
Soviet-bloc nations, 36, 88, 229, 290
Soviet Union, 16, 57, 95, 97, 101, 124, 129,
   147, 173, 213, 271
   in Afghanistan, 85, 205–6, 207
   and Central America, 10–12, 21
   deceptions of, 123, 141, 277
   expansion of, 2–7
   and Iran, 92, 96, 133
   and Sandinistas, 20, 42, 48, 50, 59
   structural crisis in, 26
   and torture, 125
   vs. U.S., 4–5, 25
   See also KGB; Russia
Spadolini, Giovanni, 9, 175, 180
Spain, 28, 55, 131
Speakes, Larry, 8, 181
SSCI. *See* Senate Select Committee on
   Intelligence
Star Wars. *See* Strategic Defense Initiative
State Department, 7, 14, 62, 117, 124, 130,
   269, 283
   and *Achille Lauro* affair, 175, 180, 181
   and Central America, 13, 17, 18, 20, 66,
      68–74
   consultants to, 270
   and *contras*, 89
   and Iran, 95, 240, 264
   vs. NSC, 70
   Office of Public Diplomacy, 69
   and Sandinistas, 11n
   and terrorism, 169–70
Stevens, Ted, 66
Stokes, Louis, 39, 250
Stone, Richard, 72
Strategic Defense Initiative (SDI) (Star
   Wars), 7, 149n
Strauss, Robert, 69
Sullivan, Brendan, 282
Supreme Court, 248n, 250, 252, 272
Switzerland, 150–51, 218
Syria, 92, 113, 114, 124, 129, 148

Tambs, Ambassador Lewis A., 73, 290
Tardencillas (Nicaraguan defector), 13–14
Teicher, Howard, 86, 218, 221, 263
Teller, Edward, 149n
Terceristas, 51, 54
Teti, Dennis, 281n
Thailand, 2
Thatcher, Margaret, 29, 177
Timberg, Robert, 76
Tolan, Annie, 37
Tolkachev (CIA agent), 205
Torrijos, Omar, 50, 56
Tower, John, 144, 252, 277, 278, 280–81

Tower Commission, 112n, 126, 164, 203,
   205, 277–81, 294
TOW missiles, Iran's interest in, 112n
TOW shipments, to Iran, 118–20, 123, 124,
   128–34, 140, 151, 152, 161, 164, 183–
   85, 190, 191, 192n, 200, 208, 209, 211–
   13, 215, 232, 233, 237, 238, 240, 242,
   292
Trible, Paul, Jr., 248
Truman Doctrine, 91
Trust affair, 123
Turkey, 94, 104
Turner, Stansfield, 4, 25, 27, 112
TWA skyjacking, 114, 118

United States
   Central American policy of, 10–12
   commitment to *contras*, 81–84
   and Grenada invasion, 60
   and Hawk shipments to Iran, 144, 151–
      63, 209–12, 258, 285–86
   and Hawk spares shipments of, 215–17,
      219, 222, 225, 228, 232, 233, 239, 240,
      253, 292
   and Iran, relations with, 10, 91–96, 112–
      15, 141, 143, 234–35, 238–42, 256
   and Israel, 121, 179–82, 288
   in Nicaragua, symbolic violence of, 61
   and Pastora, 57–59
   and Sandinistas, 19–22, 33–35, 36, 59,
      74, 78
   and Soviet Union, 4–5, 25
   and terrorism, 169–82
   and TOW shipments to Iran, 118–20,
      123, 124, 128–34, 140, 161, 164, 183–
      85, 190, 191, 192n, 200, 208, 209, 211–
      13, 215, 232, 233, 237, 238, 240, 292

Vance, Cyrus, 3, 71
Venezuela, 49, 50, 56
Vesco, Robert, 244
Vietnam, 2, 10, 16, 17, 18, 19, 21, 35, 38,
   39, 40, 78, 81, 89, 90, 125, 145, 146
Villalon, Hector, 95, 96

Walcott, John, 206
Walker, John, 206
Walker ring (of spies), 206
Wallach, E. Robert, 186n
Wallach, John, 289n
Wallison, Peter, 249, 250
Walsh, Lawrence, 188n, 247, 274, 276, 284
   staff of, 250, 255
Walters, Barbara, 145
Walters, Vernon, 112
Washington, George, 253
Watergate, 247, 251
Watson, Sam, 288
Watt, Jim, 74
Webster, William, 262, 284, 285, 286, 287

306